THE WEST THAT WAS

THE WEST THAT WAS

EDITED BY THOMAS W. KNOWLES AND JOE R. LANSDALE

WINGS BOOKS

New York / Avenel, New Jersey

Published by Wings Books, distributed by
Outlet Book Company, Inc., a Random House Company,
40 Engelhard Avenue, Avenel, New Jersey, 07001.

RANDOM HOUSE

New York • Toronto • London • Sydney • Auckland

Printed and bound in the United States of America

Library of Congress Cataloging-in-Publication Data

The West that was / edited by Thomas W. Knowles and Joe R.
Lansdale.
      p. cm.
   Includes bibliographical references.
   ISBN 0-517-08929-7
   1. West (U.S.) – History.   2. West (U.S.) – History – Pictorial
works.   3. West (U.S.) – Literary collections.   4. Folklore – West
(U.S.)   5. Indians of North America – West (U.S.)   I. Knowles,
Thomas W.   II. Lansdale, Joe R.
F591.W459 1993
978–dc20   93-25131
                                                       CIP

ISBN 0-517-08929-7

Consulting Editor: Marc Jaffe

Design Consultant: David Larkin

Designed by Catharyn Tivy

8 7 6 5 4 3 2 1

Dedication

The West That Was is dedicated to the memory of Ray Puechner, who first suggested the idea, and to the men and women who lived the real-life drama of the American frontier.

Acknowledgements

The editors would like to thank all the writers and artists whose contributions made this book possible. Special thanks go to Dale L. Walker and Loren D. Estleman, who infused *The West That Was* with life; to E. L. Reedstrom for his artistic contributions; to Lois Knight and to Troyce Wilson for their timely production assistance; and to Duane and Bobbi Garner. Thanks also to: Joe Fenton, Curator of the Sam Houston Sanders Corps of Cadets Center and the Metzger Collection at Texas A&M University, and his student assistant, Kevin Jimmerson; to Amy Day and Tim Novak of the Texas A&M University Memorial Student Center Forsythe Galleries; to Curator Tom Burkes, assistant Dan Agler, and Archivist Janice Reese of the Texas Ranger Hall of Fame Museum and Moody Library in Waco, Texas; to Photo Archivist Tom Shelton and Librarian Diane Bruce of the Institute of Texan Cultures in San Antonio, Texas; to Nancy Sherbert, Curator of Photographs for the Kansas State Historical Society Center for Historical Research in Topeka, Kansas; to Ellen N. Murry, Director of the Star of the Republic Museum at Washington-on-the-Brazos, Texas; and to Marilyn Peil of the National Cowboy Hall of Fame and Western Heritage Center, Oklahoma City, Oklahoma.

CONTRIBUTORS

BARBARA
BEMAN-PUECHNER

BARBARA BLACKBURN

WIN BLEVINS

DEE BROWN

JEFF CARROLL

LENORE CARROLL

DON COLDSMITH

JAMES L. COLLINS

ROGER N. CONGER

ROBERT J. CONLEY

BILL CRIDER

SCOTT A. CUPP

MARYLOIS DUNN

LOREN D. ESTLEMAN

L. K. FEASTER

ROY L. FISH

VERONICA G. FRIEDLAN

FRANCIS L. FUGATE

HAROLD A. GEER

ABRAHAM HOFFMAN

R. C. HOUSE

W. C. JAMESON

ELMER KELTON

THOMAS W. KNOWLES

MICHAEL MADONNA

YVONNE
CHEEK MARTINEZ

ARDATH MAYHAR

LEON C. METZ

JIM MILLER

BILL O'NEAL

CHAD OLIVER

JAMES M. REASONER

CENA
GOLDER RICHESON

JOYCE GIBSON ROACH

JOE G. ROSA

CAROL J. SCAMMAN

JORY SHERMAN

JAY SMITH

LEE SOMERVILLE

LEE SULLENGER

DALE L. WALKER

MARIANNE WILLMAN

FRANCES M. WOLD

TABLE OF CONTENTS

I. THE PATHFINDERS

From Lewis and Clark to the first shout at Sutter's Mill and the opening of the last frontier in the Klondike; from the Rendezvous to John Colter's Run, from Kit Carson's apocryphal life to Liver-Eating Johnston's revenge.

II. "FROM WHERE THE SUN NOW STANDS"

The meteoric path of the Native American cultures of the Old West, the leaders, the words and the deeds of the People.

III. THE SOLDIER'S STORY

Buffalo Soldiers, frontier scouts, officers and enlisted men, how they rode and fought and died for beans, bacon, and twelve dollars a month. The story of the Little Big Horn, from Custer's last words to the words of Sioux medicine man Black Elk.

IV. ALL ROADS LEAD WEST

The nuts and bolts of moving West; the making of Texas.

GONE TO TEXAS

V. SHE WON THE WEST

The women of the West, from ladies to prostitutes, outlaws to heiresses.

WILDEST WOMEN OF THE WILD WEST

VI. THEY WORE THE BADGE

Tin stars, hangmen, judges, and the law West of the Pecos.

VII. LIFE AND DEATH IN THE WILD WEST

The gunfighter's edge and his end in boot hill, a necrology of shootists, gamblers, outlaws, toughs, and badmen. Tools of the trade, games of chance, and saloons.

OUTLAWS AND BADMEN

VIII. COWBOYS AND CATTLE KINGS

Tom Horn, Charlie Goodnight, Bill Pickett, Shanghai Pierce, chuck wagon recipes, working clothes, and barbed wire.

THE CATTLE BARONS

THE COWBOYS

THE CHUCK WAGON COOKBOOK

PREFACE

HOWDY AND WELCOME TO *THE WEST THAT WAS.* COME ON IN AND sit down by the campfire. Help yourself to the coffee.

You've just entered the storyteller's circle, and as Black Elk of the Oglala would tell you, a circle is a powerful thing. In this circle, the sacred hoop of the Sioux nations is unbroken, Wild Bill Hickok hasn't yet played that fatal hand full of aces and eights, and Jedediah Strong Smith hasn't yet met up with that Comanche arrow. Dodge City is wide open, as are Tombstone and Julesburg and Abilene. Chief Joseph of the Nez Perce is in the Wallowa Valley, peacefully tending to his horses; young John Wesley Hardin is winning races in Texas and living it up. Charlie Goodnight is just starting his herd north on the long trail.

Here, the Old, Wild West is just a breath away. As you read this book, you'll note that we've capitalized all forms of the word "West" except when it describes a simple direction. This is our gentle hint, our way of saying "Remember." So breathe in that word, "West." Let it melt the years away. Look yonder—there's something different to the west of us, waiting just around the next bend of the river or just over the next hill. Listen closely and you'll hear a cowboy on his night ride, singing to calm the nervous herd, or a Kiowa mother singing her child to sleep. There's the faint echo of gunfire from dusty cow-town streets, or from the walls of a crumbling mission chapel far to the south. It's the West. We're here.

The riders who sit around this campfire have come from all over the West (and from east, south and north) to tell you their tales—some of them from farther still. It's been a long ride for all of them, for this book has been seven years in the making. Most of the contributors to this volume are members of the Western Writers of America, and all of them are fine storytellers, the modern inheritors of the spirit of the West. In that sense, the book you hold is their annotated family album, filled with pictures and memorabilia.

We hope it's different from anything you've seen before, an accurate but dramatic guide to the history of the American West. Because we're storytellers at heart, we've concentrated on the anecdotal truths rather than dry dates and dusty facts, on the little-known and the unusual rather than the conventional. Each writer here has translated a part of the history of the West through his or her own unique perspective.

Like a good Texas chili recipe, *The West That Was* contains everything but the kitchen sink, and that's only because we're using the sink as the mixing bowl. It's impossible to detail the West completely in one or even one hundred volumes, but we've gathered together a little bit of almost everything about the West: history and biography, high and low humor, oddities and bits of folklore, songs and chuck-wagon recipes, instructions for scalping and descriptions of tools and weapons. We've liberally seasoned the mixture with quotes and anecdotes we call "Western Spice." We've selected the paintings and photographs and drawings, historical and modern, to put a sharp visual edge on our storytellers' words.

It's a book to be dipped into, to be read and leafed through at your leisure. Or to be devoured whole, depending on your appetite. So feel welcome to dip into the pot, fill your bowl and sit back while we spin our yarns and tell our tales.

Here's *The West That Was.* Enjoy.

"TO THE WEST, TO THE WEST"

BY DALE L. WALKER

WHERE WAS THE OLD WEST? AND WHEN WAS IT?

Those of us who live in the American West must have answers to such questions lest we appear as ignorant as New Yorkers about what occurs west of the Hudson River.

I've bragged to visitors about the wild and woolly history of my hometown—El Paso, Texas—often enough to have developed a pat answer. Illinois kinfolk, back-east writers of "Westerns," and foreign house guests ask me these "when" and "where" questions after they get over their disappointment at seeing no hostile Indians and very few men wearing six-guns, and after they have visited some of the choice local sites: the old Acme Saloon where John Wesley Hardin was murdered in 1895, the town of San Elizario where Billy the Kid was once jailed and where much of the 1877 El Paso Salt War was centered, the remains of nearby ghost towns like White Oaks and Lake Valley, and the ruins of military outposts such as Forts Davis, Shafter, Selden, and Craig.

The truth of the when and where of the Old West is found in that old saw about "a state of mind," but since we Americans are nailers-down of things, we crave more precision than platitudes provide. Let's nail it down.

As for the where: In the nineteenth century, the West was in an almost perpetual state of redefinition. It was the area that lay just beyond the moving frontier, the unknown wilderness into which the settlers from the Atlantic seaboard followed trails blazed by the explorers, the traders, and the mountain men. To Horace Greeley, the West began around Erie, Pennsylvania. To those who came after, the frontier moved to Kentucky, then to the Western Reserve, the Trans-Mississippi region, the Rocky Mountains, Texas, the Southwest, California, and finally to the Northwest—to Oregon and Washington and Alaska.

By the time the general outline of the United States was complete in the mid-nineteenth century, the definitive American West began at the Mississippi River and extended to the Pacific Coast.

To modern Americans it may seem strange to think of New Orleans, Des Moines, and the whole state of Minnesota as parts of the "Old West." We tend to identify the American West with the far West, from the Rockies Westward, rather than with the states that hug the Western banks of the Mississippi. We should remember that it was in Minnesota in 1862 that the Sioux under Little Crow rose against the settlers at Fort Ridgely and New Ulm in one of the bloodiest and most bitter of the Indian Wars. It was in 1876 during an ill-fated raid on the banks of Northfield, Minnesota, only twenty-five miles west of the Big Muddy, that the James-Younger gang nearly bought the farm. Des Moines, Iowa, was founded in 1851 by the Westering homesteaders who were the tag-end of the California-bound migration. New Orleans, the Queen of the Mississippi, was a fabulous port, trade center, and jumping-off point throughout the history of America's Westward expansion.

The Mississippi River makes a highly visible eastern boundary for the West; defining the northern and southern boundaries is a more difficult proposition. On the north there is Alaska to consider, and it doesn't make much sense to exclude that vast territory just because it's not contiguous with the rest of the West. Beginning in 1867, when the U.S. government purchased it for $7.2 million from the Russians, through the frontier settlements and gold strikes at Juneau, Nome, and Fairbanks in the 1880s and '90s, and into the present, Alaska is the wildest example of the Wild West. But if we exclude Alaska for the moment, the northern boundary of the West stretches along the U.S.-Canadian border from Lake Superior to Vancouver.

To the south, another river marks the line. The Rio Grande, close to two thousand miles long from its rising in the San Juan Mountains of southern Colorado to its mouth on the Gulf of Mexico between Brownsville and Matamoras, provides the border between Texas and Mexico. Though the river wasn't officially recognized as the border until 1848, it was always a good place to mark off the American West from Old Mexico. The U.S.-Mexican border from New Mexico west to California completes it.

AND NOW WE TURN TO THE WHEN: SOME HISTORIANS MARK THE beginning of the Old West as Lewis and Clark's 1804 expedition into the Louisiana Purchase territory, and they call it quits with the 1890 Battle of Wounded Knee, the last major instance of Indian resistance to white settlement. But there's a problem in setting the time boundary at this point. The opening of the West began with Thomas Jefferson's bold Louisiana Purchase itself, a year before he sent Lewis and Clark on their epic journey. And even after the end of the Indian Wars, the West remained wild into the turn of the century—consider that the violent death of the Dalton Gang in Coffeyville, Kansas, the heyday of Butch Cassidy and the Wild Bunch, the wild times of the "boomers" of the Cherokee Strip, and the Nome gold rush all took place in the 1890s.

Some like a more circumscribed Old West and limit it to the period between the end of the Civil War and the turn of the century. Some mark the end with the statehood of New Mexico and Arizona in 1912, or even with the death of Buffalo Bill Cody in 1917. Dee Brown, in *Bury My Heart at Wounded Knee*, considers the period between 1860 and 1890 as not only the three decades it took to destroy the American Indian civilizations and cultures, but the period from which came "virtually all the great myths of the American West—tales of fur traders, mountain men, steamboat pilots, goldseekers, gamblers, gunmen, cavalrymen, cowboys, harlots, missionaries, schoolmarms and homesteaders."

But marking the beginning of the West as the 1860s eliminates, except for those tales of them, the entire era of the fur trade and the mountain men, the California gold rush, the Mormon exodus, the Alamo and the Republic of Texas, and the Mexican War—and many more important events from the earlier decades of the nineteenth century.

IT'S BEST TO REMEMBER THE PERIOD OF THE 1860s TO THE 1890s—THE era of the Indian Wars, boomtowns and lawlessness—as the "Wild" part of the Old West. As for the Old West as a whole, it would be best to have a tidy time span, a full century. We can think of the Old West as the one hundred years from 1803 to 1902, from the Louisiana Purchase, which doubled the size of the U.S. and extended her boundaries to the Rocky Mountains, to the publication of Owen Wister's *The Virginian*, the first genuine Western novel.

Though publication of Wister's book seems to pale in comparison to the Louisiana Purchase, the novel was a sensation that established the myth of the Old West in the minds of its readers. People knew instinctively what was meant when the Virginian warned Trampas, "When you call me that, smile!" Here was the real essence of the Old West. *The Virginian* launched the considerable industry of the Western, one that thrives to this day and has been directly responsible for much of what we think we know about the West.

Traditional Westerns typically avoid specific dates. Since Western fiction and its offspring, movies and television, have been the principal sources of information about the American West, there is a compelling timelessness to the myth it has created. Maybe it's no wonder my visitors still half-expect to see men wearing sidearms and riding horses, cowboys and cattle milling in the streets, Indian camps, and saloons with batwing doors. The West lives on, defying the boundaries of time and place.

When all is said and done, the words of Archibald MacLeish best sum up the time and place of the West: "The West is a country of the mind, and so eternal." ■

A Chronology of the Old West Related to World Events

	EVENTS IN THE WEST	EVENTS IN THE EASTERN U.S.	WORLD EVENTS
1803	Acquired from France for $15 million, the Louisiana Purchase doubles the size of the U.S. and extends her western boundary to the Rocky Mountains, adding 828,000 square miles of territory.	Fort Dearborn, later the city of Chicago, is built on the shore of Lake Michigan.	Morphine, a drug named for the Greek god of dreams, is discovered by a German pharmacist.
1804	The Lewis and Clark Expedition to explore the Louisiana Purchase territory begins its ascent of the Missouri River on May 14.	Alexander Hamilton is killed in a duel with Vice President Aaron Burr at Weehawken, N.J., on July 11.	Napoleon becomes emperor of France on May 18.
1805	The Lewis and Clark Expedition reaches the Pacific in November; Lt. Zebulon Montgomery Pike begins his exploration of the headwaters of the Mississippi.	The Michigan Territory is formed with Detroit as its capital; the Louisiana Territory is formed with St. Louis as its capital.	The Battle of Trafalgar is fought on October 21.
1806	The Lewis and Clark Expedition returns to St. Louis on September 3 after 28 months of exploration; Zebulon Pike discovers a mountain "like a small blue cloud," later named Pike's Peak.	Construction of the Natchez Trace begins.	"Twinkle, Twinkle, Little Star" is published in England by poets Ann and Jane Taylor.
1808	John Jacob Astor incorporates the American Fur Co. The *Missouri Gazette*, the first newspaper west of the Mississippi, begins publication in St. Louis.	Importation of slaves into the U.S. is banned.	The Peninsular War begins as British troops under Sir Arthur Wellesley (later duke of Wellington) invade Portugal.
1810		U.S. population reaches 7.2 million; New York City passes Philadelphia as the most populous American city.	
1811	John Jacob Astor establishes a fur trading post at Astoria on the Columbia River; Russians land at Bodega Bay above San Francisco and establish Fort Ross as the center of their sea otter fur trade.	On November 7 at the Battle of Tippecanoe, General William Henry Harrison defeats Chief Tecumseh's Shawnee warriors on the Wabash River.	Iodine is discovered by a French chemist.
1812	Louisiana is admitted to the Union as the 18th state; the Missouri Territory is established.	The War of 1812 begins on June 18 with an American declaration of war against the British.	Napoleon invades Russia; the Battle of Borodino is fought; the French retreat from Moscow.

	EVENTS IN THE WEST	EVENTS IN THE EASTERN U.S.	WORLD EVENTS
1814	General Andrew Jackson takes command of the U.S. forces at New Orleans.	Lawyer Francis Scott Key witnesses the bombardment of Fort McHenry, Baltimore, by British ships. His song, "The Star-Spangled Banner," is published in the *Baltimore American* a week later.	Napoleon abdicates and is exiled to Elba.
1815	On January 8 at the Battle of New Orleans, Andrew Jackson defeats British General Edward Pakenham in one of the most lopsided military engagements in history— American losses were 8 dead, 13 wounded; British losses were 700 dead, 1400 wounded.	Congress reduces the standing army to 10,000 men under two major generals and four brigadiers.	The Battle of Waterloo is fought on June 18.
1818	Fort Snelling, later Minneapolis, Minnesota, is constructed on the Mississippi by Army engineers.	The tin can is introduced.	Mary Wollstonecraft Shelley publishes *Frankenstein, or the Modern Prometheus.*
1819	Major S. H. Long begins a two-year scientific expedition into the far West.	Jethro Wood invents an iron plow with interchangeable parts; John Conat invents the iron cookstove.	A French physician invents the stethoscope.
1820	Moses Austin seeks permission of Spanish authorities in San Antonio to settle 300 American families in Texas.	U.S. population reaches 9.6 million.	Quinine sulfate is used as a specific treatment for malaria. The *Venus de Milo* (circa second century) is discovered on the Aegean island of Melos.
1821	Missouri is admitted to the Union as the 24th state under terms of the slavery compromise, with Thomas Hart Benton as the first senator. William Becknell leads a wagon train of goods from Independence, Missouri, to Santa Fe, New Mexico, to inaugurate the Santa Fe Trail.	Sailors in New Orleans introduce 32-card draw poker, derived from Persian, French, and Italian card games (stud poker evolved much later).	Mexico declares its independence from Spain on May 5 (Cinco de Mayo). Napoleon dies at St. Helena on May 5.
1822	Lt. Governor William H. Ashley and his associate, Andrew Henry, explore the upper Missouri River to find its source; the Rocky Mountain Fur Co. is founded. Expedition members include legendary keel-boatman Mike Fink, 18-year-old James Bridger, Jedediah Strong Smith, William L. Sublette, and Joseph Redford Walker.	The U.S. recognizes Mexico's independence.	French Egyptologist Champollion deciphers the Rosetta Stone, the key to Egyptian hieroglyphics. The first permanent photograph is produced by French physicist J. N. Niepce.

	EVENTS IN THE WEST	EVENTS IN THE EASTERN U.S.	WORLD EVENTS
1823	Stephen F. Austin receives confirmation of his Texas land grant on the Rio Brazos from Emperor Augustin de Iturbide; the grant was originally made to Austin's father, Moses.	The Monroe Doctrine is first publicly stated in the president's message to Congress on December 2.	Rugby football and the mackintosh raincoat are invented.
1824	Jedediah Smith discovers the South Pass through the Rocky Mountains into the Great Basin.	Cherokee scholar Sequoyah devises an 85-character Cherokee language alphabet that enables the Cherokee to become the first literate Indian tribe; they will produce the first Indian-language newspaper, *Phoenix*, in 1828.	Portland cement, Glenlivet Scotch, and Cadbury chocolate are introduced; the first commercial pasta factory is established in Italy.
1825	Omaha begins as a trading post on the Missouri River.	The Erie Canal is completed to connect New York City with the Great Lakes.	Scots explorer Gordon Laing is the first European to visit the fabled African city of Timbuktu.
1826	Jedediah Smith leads the first overland journey to California; the expedition leaves on August 22 from the Great Salt Lake, blazes a trail through the lower Colorado River and the Mojave Desert, and arrives in San Diego on November 27.	Former presidents John Adams and Thomas Jefferson both die during the 50th anniversary year of the Declaration of Independence.	*Burke's Peerage* is first published in England.
1827	Jedediah Smith blazes the first trail from southern California north to Fort Vancouver on the Columbia River.	Joseph Smith, founder of the Latter-Day Saints movement, begins work on the Book of Mormon.	The first friction match, the "Lucifer," is invented by an English chemist.
1829	President Andrew Jackson offers to buy Texas from Mexico but is refused.	Peter Cooper, a New York entrepreneur, produces the *Tom Thumb*, the first U.S.-built locomotive.	Constables, named "bobbies" after Home Secretary Robert Peel, begin patrolling the streets of London.
1830	The first covered wagon train from the Missouri River to the Rockies is led by Jedediah Smith and William Sublette of the Rocky Mountain Fur Co.	U.S. population reaches 12.9 million. Joseph Smith, age 25, founds the Church of Jesus Christ of Latter-Day Saints in Fayette, New York; the Book of Mormon is published at Palmyra.	Stendhal (Marie Henri Beyle) publishes *The Red and the Black*.
1831	Josiah Gregg starts out with a caravan from Santa Fe.	Nat Turner leads a slave rebellion in Virginia.	Louis Philippe creates the French Foreign Legion.
1832	A young Abraham Lincoln serves in the militia in the Black Hawk War in Illinois.	"Rock of Ages" and "America" are composed.	A French chemist isolates codeine from opium.

	EVENTS IN THE WEST	EVENTS IN THE EASTERN U.S.	WORLD EVENTS
1833	Charles Bent and Ceran St. Vrain build Bent's fort on the north bank of the Arkansas River.	The *New York Sun*, the first successful penny newspaper, is published.	The diaphragm contraceptive is invented in Germany.
1834	Congress establishes the Department of Indian Affairs. John Jacob Astor sells his fur interests. (Beaver pelts sold for $6 each in peak times, enabling a trapper to earn $1,000 in a season.)	"Turkey in the Straw" (originally titled "Zip Coon") is published anonymously and becomes the most popular song on the frontier.	French educator Louis Braille devises a system that allows the blind to read.
1836	Marcus Whitman establishes a mission near the junction of the Columbia and Snake Rivers in the Pacific Northwest; his wife, Narcissa, and Elizabeth Spalding accompany him to become the first white women to cross the Rockies.	Samuel Colt patents his repeating revolver. William Holmes McGuffey's First and Second Readers are first published by a Cincinnati publisher; the Readers will be sold until 1927.	
1837	The U.S. recognizes the Republic of Texas; the Texas Rangers are organized.	John Deere of Vermont begins manufacturing steel plows.	Queen Victoria begins her 64-year reign over the British Empire.
1838	In Georgia, Alabama, and Tennessee, 14,000 Cherokee are divested of their tribal lands; they are pushed along the "Trail of Tears" 800 miles along the Tennessee, Ohio, Mississippi, and Arkansas Rivers to Little Rock, thence to Indian Territory west of the Red River. More than 4,000 of them die en route.	Abolitionists organize the Underground Railroad to transport Southern slaves to freedom in Canada.	Charles Dickens publishes *Oliver Twist*.
1839	John A. Sutter establishes Sutter's Fort at a strategic location on the route that crosses the Sierras from Utah and Nevada; the site will later become Sacramento, California.	The Mormons establish a settlement at Nauvoo on the Illinois side of the Mississippi. Abner Doubleday lays down the first rules for baseball.	The British fight in Afghanistan, and in the Opium War in China.
1840	The golden era of the annual trappers' Rendezvous and the Rocky Mountain fur trade ends.	Richard Henry Dana publishes his novel *Two Years Before the Mast*, which eventually leads to reforms in the laws that govern the merchant marine.	The saxophone is invented in Belgium.
1841	The Russians sell Fort Ross, California, to John A. Sutter.	U.S. population passes 17 million, and will be increased by 1.7 million immigrants in the decade of the 1840s.	*Punch* magazine begins its 137-year life in London.

	EVENTS IN THE WEST	EVENTS IN THE EASTERN U.S.	WORLD EVENTS
1842	John Charles Frémont leads a surveying party up the Platte and Sweetwater Rivers, mapping what will become the Oregon Trail.	Dr. Crawford Long of Georgia becomes the first physician to use ether as an anesthetic in a surgical operation.	Nikolai Gogol publishes *Dead Souls*.
1844	Wells-Fargo begins an express service between Buffalo and Detroit.	Samuel F. B. Morse transmits the first telegraph message—"What hath God wrought"—from Washington, D.C., to Baltimore. Mormon Church founders Joseph and Hiram Smith are shot by vigilantes in Carthage, Illinois.	German socialist Karl Marx writes that religion is "the opiate of the masses."
1845	John L. O'Sullivan asserts the U.S. claim to the Oregon Territory "by right of our manifest destiny to overspread and to possess the whole of the continent" in an article in the *United States Magazine and Democratic Review*; the city of Portland is founded in the Oregon Territory and named for the Maine city by a coin toss—the other choice was Boston.	The U.S. Naval Academy is established at Annapolis. The scandal sheet *Police Gazette* begins publication.	The potato famine devastates rural families in England, Ireland, and Russia and prompts mass migrations to the U.S. Alexandre Dumas publishes *The Count of Monte Cristo*.
1846	California settlers in the Sacramento Valley proclaim a republic independent of Mexico and raise a black bear flag.	The Smithsonian Institution is founded.	Dubonnet and the pneumatic tire are introduced.
1847	Jim Bridger leads 15,000 Mormons across the mountains to the shores of the Great Salt Lake. Brigham Young proclaims the "State of Deseret," and says, "This is the place." The Donner party is trapped by snow in a pass through the Sierra Nevadas; 45 of the 89 emigrants survive, some by cannibalism.	Smith Brothers cough drops are introduced to the market.	Karl Marx and Friedrich Engels publish *The Communist Manifesto*. Nitroglycerin is discovered; ether is introduced into British surgical techniques as an anesthetic.
1848	Gold is discovered on January 24 at Sutter's Mill on the American River in California. News of the strike is published on August 19 in James Gordon Bennett's *New York Herald*, and by year's end, 6,000 men are working in the gold fields.	The Associated Press begins as the New York News Agency, using the new telegraph connection between New York and Chicago.	Hungarian physician Ingaz Semmelweis discovers the cause of puerperal (childbed) fever—unsanitary conditions.

	EVENTS IN THE WEST	EVENTS IN THE EASTERN U.S.	WORLD EVENTS
1849	Francis Parkman publishes *The California and Oregon Trail.*	Edgar Allan Poe dies at age 40 in Baltimore; Henry David Thoreau publishes "On the Duty of Civil Disobedience."	French physicist Armand Fizeau establishes the speed of light as 186,300 miles per hour.
1850	California achieves statehood.	Future Union counterintelligence operative Alan Pinkerton opens the Pinkerton Detective Agency in Chicago.	The Taiping Rebellion in China begins a 14-year civil war that will claim more than 30 million lives.
1851	The city of Seattle is founded in the Northwest Territory. The Missouri Pacific begins laying track at St. Louis for the first railroad West of the Mississippi.	*The New York Times* begins publication; *Uncle Tom's Cabin, or Life Among the Lowly* by Harriet Beecher Stowe is published in installments; Herman Melville publishes *Moby Dick,* and Nathaniel Hawthorne publishes *The House of the Seven Gables.*	The first world's fair, the London Great Exhibition, opens.
1853	In the Gadsden Purchase the U.S. acquires the land south of the Gila River in New Mexico and Arizona for $10 million.	U.S. Navy commodore Matthew G. Perry opens bids for formal relations with Japan.	The Turks occupy holy shrines in Palestine, bringing France, England, and Turkey to the brink of war with imperial Russia.
1854	The Kansas-Nebraska Act opens to white settlers Western lands previously reserved by treaty for the Indians.	The Smith & Wesson Revolver Co. opens in Massachusetts.	The Crimean War erupts, with France, England, and Turkey against Russia; at the Battle of Balaclava the Light Brigade makes its famous charge into disaster on October 25.
1855	Pro-slavery "borderers" from Missouri sack abolitionist Lawrence in "bleeding" Kansas.	*Bartlett's Familiar Quotations* is published in Boston.	Cigarettes are introduced in London by Crimean War veterans who bring them back from Russian territory.
1857	At least 135 emigrants bound for California are killed in the Mountain Meadows Massacre in the Utah Territory, September 11.	James Pierpont of Boston composes "Jingle Bells."	The Sepoy Mutiny against the British Empire in India begins on May 10 in Meerut; it will lead to dissolution of the Honorable East India Co.
1858	The city of Denver is founded in Colorado, and Minnesota becomes the 32nd state.	The Mason jar is invented.	Gray's *Anatomy* is published; the controversial "Cancan" is danced in Jacques Offenbach's opera *Orpheus in the Underworld* in Paris.
1859	The Comstock Lode is discovered in Washoe, Nevada, and there is a gold rush to Pike's Peak, Colorado; Oregon becomes the 33rd state.	John Brown launches his fatal raid on the U.S. Army arsenal at Harper's Ferry on October 16.	Charles Darwin publishes *The Origin of Species*; Charles Dickens publishes *A Tale of Two Cities.*

	EVENTS IN THE WEST	EVENTS IN THE EASTERN U.S.	WORLD EVENTS
1860	The first Pony Express riders leave St. Joseph, Missouri, on April 3 to deliver mail to Sacramento, California, in ten days.	Abraham Lincoln is elected president of the U.S.	The internal combustion engine is patented in Paris.
1861	Kansas becomes the 34th state; the Pony Express ceases service in October.	The Civil War breaks out on April 12 as forces of the Confederate States of America shell Union-held Fort Sumter in Charleston harbor; Van Camp's Pork and Beans is developed by an Indianapolis grocer to help sustain Union troops in the field.	Prince Albert, Queen Victoria's consort, dies of typhoid fever.
1862	Congress passes the Homestead Act to give 160 acres of Western land free to any U.S. citizen.	Abraham Lincoln issues the Emancipation Proclamation to abolish slavery on September 22; "Battle Hymn of the Republic" is composed by Julia Ward Howe, and "Taps" by Union general Daniel Butterfield.	English explorer John H. Speke discovers the source of the Nile River—Lake Victoria.
1863	Quantrill's Raiders sack and burn ill-fated Lawrence, Kansas on August 21.	Union and Confederate troops meet in one of the bloodiest battles of the Civil War in July near Gettysburg, Pennsylvania; "When Johnny Comes Marching Home" becomes one of the most popular songs of the era.	Perrier water is introduced commercially in France.
1864	Nevada becomes the 36th state. Chivington's Volunteers massacre a group of peaceful Cheyenne at Sand Creek in the Colorado Territory	Ulysses S. Grant is promoted to the rank of general and is given command of the Union Army; William Tecumseh Sherman begins his "March to the Sea" in November.	Austrian Archduke Ferdinand becomes Emperor Maximilian of Mexico.
1865	Jesse and Frank James form their outlaw gang from disaffected former Confederate guerrillas in Missouri.	The Civil War ends on April 9 ; President Abraham Lincoln is assassinated on April 14; slavery is formally abolished by the 13th Amendment to the Constitution; the Ku Klux Klan is organized in Pulaski, Tennessee.	The Salvation Army is organized in London. Lewis Carroll publishes *Alice in Wonderland.*
1866	The first long cattle drives begin in Texas; the Goodnight-Loving cattle trails are established.	Lynchburg, Virginia, introduces its most famous product, Jack Daniel's Sour Mash Whiskey.	Swedish scientist Alfred B. Nobel (whose fortune will later found the Nobel Prize) invents dynamite.

	EVENTS IN THE WEST	EVENTS IN THE EASTERN U.S.	WORLD EVENTS
1867	The U.S. purchases Alaska from the Russians for $7.2 million; Nebraska becomes the 37th state.	The Pullman Palace Car Co. begins producing railroad coaches.	Emperor Maximilian of Mexico is overthrown in a revolt and executed by a firing squad.
1868	Bret Harte begins publishing *The Overland Monthly* in California.	Ulysses S. Grant is elected president of the U.S.	The Tory Party comes to power in the British Parliament; Tory leader Benjamin Disraeli becomes prime minister.
1869	The Union Pacific and the Central Pacific Railroads link up with the Golden Spike ceremony on May 10 at Promontory Point, Utah.	Rutgers plays Princeton in the first intercollegiate football game—Rutgers wins.	The Suez Canal is completed.
1870	The quote "Go West, young man" is incorrectly attributed to Horace Greeley of the *New York Tribune*.	Standard Oil Co. incorporates in Cleveland, Ohio.	The Franco-Prussian War begins.
1871	Chief Cochise surrenders to General George Crook.	The Great Chicago Fire rages October 8–9, destroying 3.5 square miles of the city.	Upon finding Dr. David Livingstone at Ujiji on Africa's Lake Tanganyika, Henry M. Stanley of the *New York Herald* says, "Dr. Livingstone, I presume."
1872	The James gang robs its first passenger train, the Rock Island's eastbound train, between Council Bluffs and Des Moines, Iowa.	The Montgomery Ward Co. opens for business in Chicago.	The "ghost ship," the *Marie Celeste*, is discovered; her passengers have disappeared without a trace.
1873	Silver is discovered in the Panamint Mountains of Nevada.	Barbed wire is exhibited at the De Kalb, Illinois, county fair; Coors beer is first brewed at Golden, Colorado.	Canada establishes the Northwest Mounted Police.
1874	Levi Strauss adds copper rivets to his denim blue jeans.	The Remington typewriter is introduced.	The works of the French impressionists—Monet, Cézanne, Degas, Manet, Pissarro, Renoir—are featured in a major exhibition in Paris.
1875	Quahadie war chief Quanah Parker, the last Comanche holdout after the Battle of Palo Duro Canyon, ends his resistance and surrenders to life on the reservation.	The orange crate, Hires root beer, the Kentucky Derby, and American Christmas cards are introduced.	The British gain control of the Suez Canal.

	EVENTS IN THE WEST	EVENTS IN THE EASTERN U.S.	WORLD EVENTS
1876	At the Battle of the Little Big Horn on June 25th, 264 men of the U.S. 7th Cavalry and its commander, Colonel George Armstrong Custer, are killed by the Sioux and Cheyenne.	Alexander Graham Bell transmits the first words over his invention, the telephone: "Mr. Watson, come here. I want you." Bradley, Voorhees & Day (B.V.D.) of New York introduces one-piece trapdoor underwear popularly called "Baby's Ventilated Diapers." Heinz introduces tomato ketchup.	General Porfirio Diaz becomes the president of Mexico.
1877	Chief Joseph of the Nez Perce leads his tribe of 750 people on a daring escape attempt through 1,600 miles of Rocky Mountain wilderness toward Canada. When he finally surrenders near the Canadian border of the Montana Territory, he concludes his eloquent speech with "From where the sun now stands, I will fight no more forever."	Thomas Alva Edison invents the phonograph.	Leo Tolstoy publishes *Anna Karenina*; Anna Sewell publishes *Black Beauty*.
1878	The Lincoln County War begins in New Mexico; William Bonney, better known as Billy the Kid, is one of the participants.	Thomas Edison founds the Edison Electric Light Co.	The Russo-Turkish War rages in the Danubian provinces of the Ottoman Empire.
1879	The Lincoln County War ends in New Mexico.	The F. W. Woolworth Co. opens for business in Watertown, New York.	In Russia, Pavlov conducts experiments to prove his theories on conditioned reflexes.
1880	In Leadville, Colorado, Horace "Hod" Tabor and his wife, "Baby Doe," promote their Matchless silver mines.	Lew Wallace, one-time governor of the New Mexico Territory, publishes *Ben Hur*.	Laveran of France discovers the cause of malaria; Ebereth of Germany develops a vaccine against yellow fever, and his countryman, Koch, develops a vaccine against anthrax.
1881	The Earps and Doc Holliday shoot it out with the Clanton gang and the McLowry brothers at the O.K. Corral in Tombstone, Arizona Territory, on October 26.	U.S. population reaches 53 million; President Garfield is assassinated; the American Red Cross is founded by Clara Barton.	Russia's Alexander II is assassinated in St. Petersburg.
1882	Jesse James (age 34) is murdered by Robert Ford on April 3.	The murderous Hatfield-McCoy feud breaks out in West Virginia and southern Kentucky.	British gunboats bombard Alexandria at the opening of the Anglo-Egyptian War.

	EVENTS IN THE WEST	EVENTS IN THE EASTERN U.S.	WORLD EVENTS
1883	The Northern Pacific Railroad is completed at Gold Creek, Montana.	In Omaha, Nebraska, Buffalo Bill's Wild West stages its first performance; Mark Twain publishes his *Life on the Mississippi*; the first issues of *Grit* and *Ladies Home Journal* hit the stands; the Brooklyn Bridge opens.	As a result of the eruption of Krakatoa, a volcano between the islands of Java and Sumatra, 36,000 people are killed. American-born engineer Hiram Maxim invents the Maxim machine gun.
1885	The illegal fencing of public lands in the West is prohibited by an Act of Congress.	The first appendectomy is performed in Davenport, Iowa.	British General Charles George "Chinese" Gordon is killed in Khartoum, Sudan, during the Mahdist Uprising.
1886	Geronimo, leader of the Chiricahua Apache, is captured by troops under General Henry W. Lawton.	Sears, Roebuck & Co. originates its catalog sales business in North Redwood, Minnesota; Coca-Cola goes on sale in Atlanta, Georgia, and Dr. Pepper is introduced in Waco, Texas. The Statue of Liberty is dedicated in New York harbor.	
1887	The worst winter on record continues in the northern Great Plains, killing millions of cattle; families are frozen and ranching syndicates go bankrupt throughout Wyoming, Montana, Kansas, and the Dakotas.	The first of the "Jim Crow" laws is passed in Florida; it segregates blacks from whites on railway cars. Log Cabin Syrup and Wesson Oil are introduced into the market.	The Canadian Pacific Railroad reaches Vancouver to join the east and west coasts of Canada.
1888	"Casey at the Bat" by Ernest Lawrence Thayer is published in the *San Francisco Examiner.*	The Washington Monument is completed; *National Geographic* begins publication.	London is shocked by a gruesome series of murders attributed to the self-named Jack the Ripper.
1889	The Oklahoma Territory is opened for settlement on April 22; those who get an early jump on this land rush, the "sooners," will give the state its nickname. North Dakota, South Dakota, Montana, and Washington become the 39th through the 42nd states.	*The Wall Street Journal* begins publication; John L. Sullivan meets Jake Kilrain in the last of the sanctioned bareknuckled prizefights; it takes place at Richburg, Mississippi, in 106-degree heat, goes 75 rounds, and lasts 2 hours, 16 minutes.	The Orient Express begins operation between Paris and Constantinople; the Eiffel Tower is completed in Paris.
1890	Idaho becomes the 43rd state, Wyoming the 44th.	Peanut butter is invented by George Washington Carver in St. Louis.	Tchaikovsky's ballet *Sleeping Beauty* debuts in St. Petersburg, Russia.

	EVENTS IN THE WEST	EVENTS IN THE EASTERN U.S.	WORLD EVENTS
1891– 1912	The Dalton gang from the Oklahoma Territory is shot down during their foiled raid on the banks of Coffeyville, Kansas, on October 5, 1892. The "boomers" move into the Cherokee Strip in northern Oklahoma, September 1893. Oil is discovered in Corsicana, Texas, in 1894. "World Champion Desperado," Texan John Wesley Hardin is gunned down in El Paso by John Selman in 1895. Utah enters the Union as the 45th state in 1896. Gold is discovered in the Klondike region in 1896, prompting the Alaska gold rush. Butch Cassidy and the Wild Bunch hit their heyday in 1898. The landmark "Spindletop" gusher oil well is struck at Beaumont, Texas, in 1901. Owen Wister publishes *The Virginian* in 1902. Oklahoma enters the Union as the 46th state in 1907. Butch Cassidy and the Sundance Kid are reported killed by troops in San Vicente, Bolivia, in 1911. New Mexico and Arizona enter the Union as the 47th and 48th states in 1912.	"Coxey's Army," a group of disgruntled Civil War veterans, leaves from Massillon, Ohio, and arrives in Washington, D.C., on April 30, 1894.	The 1900 census places the U.S. population at 76.3 million. The Victorian era ends as Queen Victoria Regina of England dies on January 22, 1901. In his speech at the Minnesota State Fair on September 2, 1901, Theodore Roosevelt advises America to "speak softly and carry a big stick." President William McKinley is assassinated on September 6, 1901.
Finis, 1917	Buffalo Bill Cody dies January 10, 1917; the Old Wild West is buried along with him in July in a special steel crypt on Lookout Mountain west of Denver, Colorado.		

I. THE PATHFINDERS

THE TRAIL BLAZERS

LEWIS AND CLARK AND THE CORPS OF DISCOVERY

BY MARIANNE WILLMAN

THE EXPEDITION COMMISSIONED BY PRESIDENT THOMAS JEFFERSON to blaze a trail through the lands he'd acquired for a fledgling United States in the Louisiana Purchase was surely the strangest contingent ever gathered to explore a rugged and untamed land. There was a one-eyed fiddle player, an Irish carpenter, a black "servant" (the Virginia euphemism for slave), a sly French-Canadian guide and his pregnant teenaged Indian wife, guides, hunters, noncoms and enlisted men of the U.S. Army, nine young men from Kentucky, and one frisky Newfoundland dog. The official name of this colorful crew was the Corps of Discovery, but we know it today as the Lewis and Clark Expedition.

It was almost the Lewis and Hook Expedition. Jefferson chose his former secretary, Meriwether Lewis, to lead the scientific journey of discovery up the Missouri River to its source and beyond to the Pacific Ocean. The twenty-eight-year-old Lewis wrote to red-haired William Clark, inviting his old friend and former captain to share command of the expedition, but the letter was inexplicably delayed in transit. Even as Lewis offered the position to Moses Hook, assistant military agent in Pittsburgh, the tardy invitation reached Clark. To Lewis' great pleasure and Hook's equal disappointment, Clark accepted.

When a piqued Congress sandbagged William Clark's appointment as a captain and recommissioned him a second lieutenant, Clark shrugged it off, saying it was "as might be expected." But Lewis was outraged. He wrote to Clark, saying the lower rank would have "no effect upon your compensation, which by G_d, shall be equal to my own." Because there was no time

PREVIOUS PAGE:
Detail from *Out of the Storm*,
painting by Richard Hogue
(courtesy of the artist)

to effect a change, he proposed they quietly bypass the government. Both men would be called Captain, and all command decisions would be made jointly. The other members of the party were not told of the formal discrepancy in rank.

On the bright morning of May 14, 1804, the Corps of Discovery set out from St. Louis, Missouri, to the cheers of spectators. The permanent party

PORTRAITS IN LIGHT AND SHADOW

BY MARIANNE WILLMAN

Meriwether Lewis and William Clark were like night and day. Clark was warm and outgoing, gregarious and at ease in the company of others. Lewis was reserved, an introvert given to periods of deep melancholy. And yet for all their differences, these two men were more than equal to the challenge of sharing command of the Corps of Discovery, better known as the Lewis and Clark Expedition. Under their even-handed leadership, a group of mismatched individuals crossed thousands of miles of uncharted territory and endured more than two years of incredible hardships to accomplish a president's mission.

Though both men were born in Virginia, there is no proof that they'd met previous to Lewis' service under Captain Clark in the U.S. Army. They became fast friends even though Clark was forced to resign his commission early in order to assist his brother, General George Rogers Clark, in untangling the family finances.

When he was asked by President Jefferson to organize the Corps of Discovery, Captain Lewis said he could ask for no better partner than his friend Captain Clark. Upon receiving Lewis' invitation, Clark replied, "My friend, I join you with heart and hand."

Both were expert woodsmen and capable commanders, each man's skills overlapped with and complimented

the other's. Lewis was the astronomer and botanist for the expedition and usually served as its physician, although the Indians preferred his partner's ministrations. Clark was the cartographer, navigator, and weatherman. His maps are still preserved in Yale University's Department of Western Americana.

They shared a firm sense of honor and duty, and a dislike of political intrigue. Though both were respected and honored, Clark was universally loved. He wrote that reason was the most formidable weapon against error, and that "religious duties consist in doing justices, leveing [sic] mercy and endeavoring to make our fellow creatures happy." He practiced his beliefs. Clark paid for the education of Sacajawea's son and daughter, as well as for the daughter of another interpreter. He freed York, the slave who had accompanied him on the expedition, and set him up with wagons and teams for a freight-hauling business. When the former members of the expedition applied to him in need, they found his door always open to them.

Clark went on to prominence in public and private life. He was appointed a brigadier general of the Louisiana Militia, and in 1808 he married his sweetheart, Julia Hancock. When they moved to St. Louis, they were visited by such luminaries as Washington Irving and Henry Schoolcraft. Clark's personal museum, which displayed hundreds of Indian artifacts, was considered in its day to be the finest in existence. As Superintendent of Indian Affairs, Clark interceded for the Indians on many occasions. The Red-Haired Chief was the most influential white man among the Western tribes.

Although he was appointed governor of Louisiana after his return from the West, Meriwether Lewis never achieved the success or happiness his compatriot found. He remained a bachelor, and

found himself displeased with the bargaining and intricacy of political life after the straightforwardness of the expedition. He slipped deeper into his characteristic melancholy. In the fall of 1809, just three years after his triumphant return with the Corps of Discovery, Governor Lewis died violently under suspicious circumstances at a place called Grinder's Stand on the Natchez Trace. He'd reportedly been acting strange prior to his death, possibly from a bout with recurrent malaria. Despite some talk of suicide, his wounds were not consistent with those that might have been self-inflicted. His watch, wallet, and rifle were missing. The coroner's report conveniently disappeared.

Lewis was only thirty-eight when he died; what great accomplishments remained in his future were forever lost to the nation. Upon hearing of his friend's untimely death, Clark was prompted by his experience with Lewis' melancholia to say, "I fear, O! I fear that his mind has overcome him." Later, when he learned the bizarre facts of Lewis' death, he revised his opinion; after that, he could never speak of Lewis without tears filling his eyes, and he believed to the end of his life that his old comrade had been murdered.

Clark became governor of the Missouri Territory in 1813. After his beloved Judy died in 1823, he eventually married her cousin, Harriet Kennerly. Harriet died on Christmas Day ten years later, and Clark didn't remarry. Upon his death at the rather advanced age (at the time) of sixty-eight, he was considered the oldest settler west of the Missouri. William Clark's funeral was the largest St. Louis had ever seen.

Although their paths diverged after their great journey and they were buried far apart, Clark in St. Louis and Lewis in Tennessee, their names are forever linked in friendship and partnership in the history of the West.

consisted of the two Captains, Clark's servant, York, fourteen soldiers, two French boatmen, and a civilian interpreter named George Drouillard. An unofficial addition was Scannon, Lewis' eager Newfoundland.

The Corps members boarded their two pirogues and the fifty-five foot keelboat *Discovery*, which had a cannon at her bow and a cabin at her stern, along with over twenty bales of provisions and Indian trade goods. Soon they were making way up the brown waters of the Missouri, which Clark recorded as holding "half a Common Wine Glass of ooze or mud to every pint." Swift, treacherous currents and undercut riverbanks that caved in without warning made navigation of the river hazardous, as did the snags and "Sawyers," the submerged trees that could suddenly rise to the surface and threaten to capsize the boats. Her square sail and twenty-two oars kept the *Discovery* moving upstream, and the six- and seven-oared pirogues kept pace.

Clouds of hungry "Mesquiters" swarmed them until even poor Scannon howled in misery. Along one three-mile stretch they were puzzled by an enormous quantity of white feathers that covered the riverbanks like fresh snowfall and floated on the waters. Their curiosity was relieved when they came to a sandbar covered with six thousand equally curious pelicans.

There were disciplinary problems even in the early leg of the voyage, and three men faced a court-martial of their peers for infractions of the rules. One deserter was stripped of his standing with the expedition, a stark warning to the rest.

On August 18 Lewis dispensed an extra gill of whiskey in celebration of his thirtieth birthday. The next day, Sergeant Charles Floyd, twenty-one, fell ill. Though Floyd had written in his journal, "I am verry Sick and Has been for Sometime but have Recovered my helth again," his recovery was only temporary. He died on August 20 of a "billious chorlick," most likely a ruptured appendix that had led to peritonitis. His comrades buried him atop a bluff near present-day Sioux City, Iowa, with military honors; they named Floyd's Creek after him. Private Patrick Gass, the Irish carpenter, was promoted to sergeant by vote of the men.

Near what is now Vermillion, South Dakota, the party hiked out to Spirit Mound, a plateau that rises almost one hundred feet above the flat plain to a level area about twelve feet wide by ninety feet long. It was a place of great terror to the local Indians, who believed it to be inhabited by tiny devils with large heads. These devils lived beneath the earth and killed everyone who approached. Lewis and Clark met with no little men, only severe thirst, near heatstroke, and an incredible view of buffalo-filled grasslands that rolled away as far as the eye could see.

By autumn Lewis and Clark had held councils with many Indian tribes: Missouri, Oto, Kickapoo, Yankton and Teton Sioux, Arikara, Assiniboine,

Meriwether Lewis, copy of painting by Charles Wilson Peale (Kansas State Historical Society photograph collection, courtesy of National Park Service)

William Clark, copy of painting by Charles Wilson Peale (Kansas State Historical Society photograph collection, courtesy of National Park Service)

Cheyenne, and Mandan. Clark, an instinctive diplomat who liked and respected the Indians, was in his element. The Indians returned the compliment by calling him the Red-Haired Chief. York also made quite an impression, especially on the Arikara, who at first believed his black skin to be a coat of paint.

Clark faced a tense moment when he was trapped ashore with one pirogue by fifty Teton Sioux warriors with strung bows. Clark drew his sword and held his ground while Lewis ordered the keelboat's cannon and swivel guns aimed to back him up. The Sioux lowered their bows. They returned in force the following day, but this time they were accompanied by their wives and children to proclaim their peaceful intent.

One night the Corps camped on a sandbar in the middle of the river downstream from modern Pierre, South Dakota. During the graveyard watch the sandbar began to break up under the sleeping explorers. The sentry sounded the alarm, sending the men running for their boats. From the safety of the boats they watched the sandbar melt away completely in a matter of moments. After that, the expedition chose more solid ground for its encampments.

It was in October, when the unknown perils of the arduous winter threatened, that a private spoke mutinously to Lewis. The Captain arrested him on the spot. Although the man worked hard for the expedition afterward and Lewis later wrote that he had acquitted him in his own mind, no exception was made in punishment. Despite the hardships they later faced, it was the last disciplinary problem with the members of the Corps, and morale remained high.

NEAR THE SITE OF MODERN BISMARCK, NORTH DAKOTA, LEWIS and Clark held a council with the Mandan Indians. They were a light-skinned tribe believed by some to be the descendants of the Welsh prince Madoc, and by others to be one of the lost tribes of Israel. Clark recorded an incident in which a Mandan mother saved her son from the swift flame of a prairie fire broke by covering him with a green buffalo hide. A similar event in one of James Fenimore Cooper's novels, *The Prairie*, may have been based on Clark's account.

As they moved Westward, Lewis and Clark passed nine deserted Mandan villages; they found the skeletons of the former inhabitants inside the lodges. It was an eerie vision of what the European diseases would do to people who had no natural immunity. At Jefferson's direction Lewis had packed a supply of smallpox vaccine to inoculate the Indians. When the initial supply proved ineffective, Lewis requested another, but it was a futile gesture against an inevitable and cruel tragedy. In the 1700s there were some nine thousand full-blooded Mandans, but by the time Lewis and Clark reached them, there were only twelve hundred. Today there are none.

At Fort Mandan, the expedition's winter quarters, a French-Canadian scalawag entered the scene with his two Shoshone wives in tow. The younger wife of Toussaint Charbonneau was about fifteen and pregnant. Her Indian name translated to Bird Woman, and Captain Clark called her Janey, but we know her as Sacajawea. She was to accompany the expedition as a sign of peaceful intentions, as well as to act as interpreter in dealings with Shoshone-speaking tribes.

Soon the Great Plains winter hit; Clark recorded thermometer readings of 45 degrees Fahrenheit below zero in December. Despite the conditions, the members of the Corps managed to celebrate a merry Christmas. Some of the men also participated in the Mandan fertility rites that were held to lure the buffalo back to their hunting grounds. Clark wrote: "We sent a man to this medicine dance last night, and they gave him four girls." The buffalo appeared right on schedule. So did an outbreak of venereal disease, another dubious gift from the white man to the Indians that was now returned with interest.

On February 11, 1805, Sacajawea went into prolonged labor. Interpreter René Jusseaume suggested a remedy of dried rattlesnake rings in water. Captain Lewis conveniently had these ingredients and prepared the dose. A sturdy boy was born ten minutes later. His parents named him Jean Baptiste, but Clark nicknamed him Pompey, Pomp for short. Years later Clark nicknamed his own son Pomp, perhaps in remembrance of Sacajawea's son.

In spring the boatmen and several others departed for St. Louis aboard the *Discovery*. They carried with them twenty-five boxes of recorded data and specimens collected to that date, as well as cages containing live animals. The boxes and cages contained Indian artifacts, charts, observations, plants, furs, skins, bones, horns and antlers, supposed mammoth bones, magpies, grouse, and a bewildered prairie dog. The permanent party set out in the other direction in the two pirogues and six small canoes. Lewis noted that they were "about to penetrate a country…on which the foot of civilized man had never trod." Like the others, he was in "excellent health and spirits, zealously attached to the enterprise, and anxious to proceed."

Scannon, Lewis' Newfoundland, hunted and retrieved, catching ducks and beavers and on one memorable occasion, a goat. One dark May night a buffalo bull stumbled into the camp and blundered into the white pirogue. The massive beast panicked and ran through the ranks of sleeping men, its lethal hooves missing their heads by inches. When the frightened bull charged Lewis' tent, Scannon jumped out and barked fiercely. The bull veered away and vanished into the night.

In addition to buffalo, elk, and antelope, they now saw large numbers of

"I wish all to know that I do not propose to sell any part of my country, nor will I have the whites cutting our timber along the rivers, more especially the oak. I am particularly fond of the little groves of oak trees. I love to look at them, because they endure the wintry storm and the summer's heat, and — not unlike ourselves — seem to flourish by them."

TATANKA YOTANKA, SITTING BULL OF THE HUNKPAPA SIOUX

bear, deer, beaver, and wolves. Lewis had disparaged reports of the grizzly's ferocity, but he soon learned to respect them. It took Clark and Drouillard five lung shots to bring down a grizzly, and before it died the beast still managed to swim halfway across a river. It measured eight feet, seven and one-half inches in height, and its claws were well over four inches long. The fleece and skin of a grizzly proved to be as much as two strong men could carry. Lewis declared he would rather fight two Indians than one grizzly.

They crossed a river that Clark named the Judith for Judy Hancock of Virginia. Though Clark would later marry her, he'd either forgotten or didn't know at the time that her given name was Julia.

In the high country ahead lay the Continental Divide, the western boundary of the Louisiana Purchase. Lewis and Clark hoped that Sacajawea could help them obtain horses from her people for the mountain crossing. When the expedition met with the Shoshone, she began to dance with excitement.

LEWIS AND CLARK at ST. CHARLES · MAY 21, 1804 ·

Mural by Charles A. Morganthaler depicting preparations for departure from St. Charles, Missouri, on May 21, 1804 (courtesy of St. Charles Savings and Loan Association, St. Charles, Missouri and St. Charles County Historical Society)

EXPEDITIONARY WEAPONS

BY ROGER N. CONGER

The original budget for President Thomas Jefferson's planned twelve-man Corps of Discovery, a sum approved and appropriated by Congress, was a mere $2,500. As the personnel list increased to about forty men, that figure also increased. The longer-than-expected expedition eventually cost approximately $38,000, but there were no complaints about the bigger budget from the members of the expedition. They were jumping off into the unknown; if they were to survive it, they needed the best equipment, in particular the best weapons.

It fell to Captain Meriwether Lewis to select the arms and ammunition for the men under his command. In May 1803 Lewis made a personal visit to the U.S. Armory at Harper's Ferry. He wanted to inspect the prototype of the new Model 1803 Army Rifle, a flintlock with a somewhat shorter barrel than the previous Model 1795. It fired a good, heavy .54 caliber ball, sized about sixteen to the pound. The rifle wasn't yet in production, but after he tried it out on the range, Lewis placed an order for fifteen units.

Lewis had a high priority, for he was acting on the orders of President Jefferson to purchase weapons for the Corps of Discovery. The armory completed the rifles, along with a set of basic spare parts, in good time.

Several of Lewis and Clark's recruits were already provided with the Model 1795 flintlock musket, and some preferred it because, since it was a smoothbore, it could fire either a heavy ball or scatterloads of buckshot or birdshot. The civilian professionals carried the long-barreled "Kentucky" flintlock rifles (actually manufactured in Pennsylvania) of .40 caliber or larger. With these rifles the frontiersmen were legendary and accurate shots.

Lewis took along a new, large-caliber air rifle in which he had found great interest, and which later proved of even greater interest to the Indians. Perhaps as a symbol of authority he also carried his service sword. The armory issued every man a fine belt knife and a tomahawk, and provided the two Captains each with an espontoon, a short, heavy spear or haliberd that was obsolete as a military arm, but perhaps useful in the backwoods.

They mounted a compact, swivel-style cannon on the bow of the keelboat and two smaller swivel blunderbusses on the stern. They also mounted swivel blunderbusses on two of the pirogues. Most likely procured in St. Louis, these swivel guns could be fired in any direction. They could handle loads of balls, buckshot, or scrap iron, and they proved impressive, even decisive in several tense confrontations with some of the less amiable Indians.

The expedition carried lead in heavy bars from which they chopped smaller chunks to mold into bullets. The gunpowder was cleverly sealed up in small, watertight lead casks that, when they were emptied, could themselves be melted down for ammunition. Lewis ordered each man to carry with him at all times a hundred rifle balls or two pounds of buckshot for a musket.

The two Captains kept detailed journals, and so did several others. One of these was Sergeant Patrick Gass, an excellent reporter who kept a fairly close tally of the game delivered daily by the expedition's gunners. A recap of his entries, by varieties, supplies the following remarkable log: 582 deer, 147 buffalo, 35 antelope, and 234 elk. Bighorn sheep and white mountain goats, both previously unknown species, totaled about 25 more. They killed at least 50 black and grizzly-bear.

When the Corps of Discovery completed its incredibly journey and arrived back in St. Louis, Missouri, in September 1806, the Captains paid their men and discharged them with honors. They also held a public auction of all the remaining equipment, which included guns, ammunition, hardware, and canoes. The entire auction realized a total of $408.62. It's intriguing to speculate on just what value modern collectors would place on that assemblage of historic weapons and relics at an auction today.

Editors' Note: a previous version of this article appeared in the October 1978 issue of *The Gun Report.*

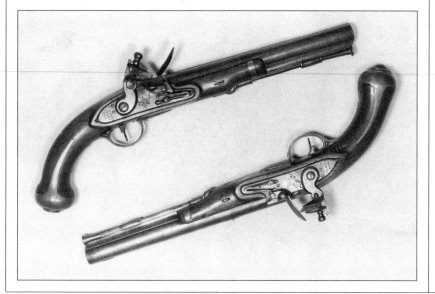

These two Harper's Ferry .54 caliber flintlock pistols with rifled barrels, an 1806 presentation model and an 1807 model, are examples of the first weapon made by the U.S. Armory, similar to those used by Lewis and Clark. (photo by Tom Knowles, courtesy of Metzger Collection, Texas A&M University Sam Houston Sanders Corps of Cadets Center)

She ran to their chief, Cameahwait, threw her blanket onto his shoulders, and wept with joy; Cameahwait was her brother.

Cameahwait provided the party with the needed horses, but he also gave them ominous news. Game and edible plants would be scarce on their planned route. The Rocky Mountains were not a single high ridge, as Lewis and Clark had been told, but range upon range of saw-toothed peaks, a formidable barrier. Cameahwait was right. Their passage through the Bitterroot Range was an ordeal. Near starving and blizzard-driven, they killed their horses for meat and ate candles to survive.

Poor diet and dysentery exacted a toll, and men fell from their mounts and had to be carried to camp on pack horses. Lewis suffered from severe dehydration; Clark injured his hip in a tumble from his horse. For several days the entire Corps lay weak and defenseless. After they survived the crossing, the exhausted party met a kindly group of Nez Perce. The Indians shared their feast of buffalo, dried salmon and roots with the travelers.

In what is now Idaho, the expedition built five dugout canoes and left their remaining horses behind. On a current swifter than a running horse they rode the Snake River into what would become the state of Washington. Then came to the wild Columbia River. They portaged over some of the rougher sections but elected to take on the wicked Dalles, nine miles of churning foam walled by black lava cliffs. Ahead of them through the rain and mist lay the rock-bound harbors of the Pacific where American and British ships frequently dropped anchor. Cold and wet, the members of the expedition reached their goal on a gray November 7, 1805. Clark's journal entry for that day captured their elation. "Ocian [sic] in view! O! the joy!"

Their joy was short-lived. Though the brig *Lydia* was in the area to trade for furs with the Indians, the expedition never met up with her. They met the Flathead, Chinook, and Tillamook Indians, and they found a curious sign of the white man's presence in a woman whose tribal decorations were enhanced by the name "J. Bowman" tattooed on her arm. They made camp and waited in the fog and the rain. No ship appeared, but a weary acceptance of their situation did. There would be no easy shipboard passage home for the Corps of Discovery; they would have to return the same way they had come.

They built Fort Clatsop seven miles inland and lived there four months. It rained continuously, game was hard to find, and there was no whiskey left. Without the hunting skills of Drouillard, who killed seven elk in one day, they would have starved. Christmas dinner 1805 was rancid elk meat, pounded fish, and roots. The men occupied themselves by dancing, fiddling, and visiting the native women, whom they found quite accommodating. Lewis again treated several of the party for venereal disease.

Air gun resembling that used by Meriwether Lewis (courtesy of Eldon G. Wolff and the Milwaukee Public Museum)

Although Lewis observed that English phrases such as "damned scoundrel" and "son of a bitch" had crept into the local patois, proof of previous contact with white men, the Corps made no such contact. When the weather broke, the same tenacity that had carried them through to the Pacific pushed them back across the long overland trail. When they crossed back over the Bitterroots, half their horses were stolen. Private Windsor and Captain Lewis almost fell to their deaths while exploring the Marias River (named for Lewis' cousin Maria Woods). Still, except for one engagement with hostile Blackfoot Indiands in which the party killed two of the attackers, the road home was somewhat easier than their first passage.

Lewis suffered an embarrassing accident. Peter Cruzzat, though an extraordinary fiddle player, was blind in one eye and nearsighted in the other. While hunting with Lewis, Cruzzat mistook his buckskin-clad Captain for an elk and shot him in the buttock. Lewis assumed they were under attack by hostiles and made for the boats, shouting for Cruzzat to follow. Lewis pieced the sequence of events together as soon as he realized there were no Indians following, though poor Cruzzat denied shooting him. With Clark acting as physician, Lewis suffered nothing more than some pain and a severely wounded dignity.

Private John Colter asked Captain Clark to discharge him so he might join some trappers engaged in the beaver trade along the Yellowstone. It was put to a vote, and Colter was sent on his way with a two-year supply of shot and other necessities. Taking back to the water and moving with the current, the remaining members of the expedition made good time down the Missouri. Their hearts lifted, and their weary arms plied the oars with renewed enthusiasm. When they passed a meadow filled with grazing cows, the men broke into cheers. They were almost home.

On September 23, 1806 the Corps of Discovery arrived back in St. Louis to a hearty welcome and the news that they'd long been given up for lost. They had been gone two years, four months, and nine days.

Though Lewis and Clark failed to find an unbroken water route to the Pacific, the expedition was successful in meeting the other goals President Jefferson had set. They established cordial relations with the Indians, except for the fierce Blackfoot and Teton Sioux. They mapped a great, unknown wilderness, discovered and catalogued hundreds of new plant and animal species, and brought back many artifacts of Indian life. The harmony that Lewis and Clark maintained among the forty-five people of varying backgrounds and temperaments who made up the Corps of Discovery through its brief but intense life was exemplary. The Captains were recorded as differing only about the need for salt and the culinary appeal of dog meat—Lewis found it pleasant while Clark did not. Scannon's opinion is not recorded, but it may be assumed that he disagreed with his master. ∎

THE MOUNTAIN MEN

THE GREAT SCOUT, KIT CARSON

BY LEE SULLENGER

KIT CARSON IS ONE OF THE MOST HALLOWED FIGURES OF THE WILD West, and one of the most controversial. His exploits as a mountain man, as a guide and scout for the great explorers and the emigrants, and as an Indian fighter and war hero were the genesis of countless tall tales. His life was a contradiction, for though he loved the Indian way of life, did much to destroy it. His courage, his endurance, and his intelligence were tested time after time in the fires of a new frontier. Add to that the fact that he was a quiet, soft-spoken, unassuming man of no great physical stature, and you have the stuff of legend.

He was born on Christmas Eve, 1809, in Madison County, Kentucky. He was a small baby; his father decided that his name, Christopher Houston Carson, was too heavy a burden for such a tiny person and shortened it to Kit. It was a nickname Carson carried for the rest of his eventful life.

He was the latest addition to a Scots family that had long been on the move to the West, from Scotland to Ireland, then to Pennsylvania and the Carolinas, and to Kentucky. When Kit was only one and a half years old, his family again moved West, this time to Missouri, the frontier jumping-off place, the gateway to the Wild West. It was at this crossroads that the Plains Indians met the increasing flood of white emigrants with growing hostility, the edge of the wild where the trappers and explorers came back to civilization with their tales of the West. In this place the young Kit grew up just as the West was opened, sometimes experiencing the dangers of Indian attack, sometimes listening to the stories the mountain men told of grizzly bears, beavers, the exploits of the wild tribes, the Southwestern deserts, and the fabulous, snowcapped Rocky Mountains.

It's no wonder that when he was apprenticed at age fifteen to a saddlemaker, he found it deadly dull. In 1826 he answered the call of the West and sneaked away to join a trading party headed for Santa Fe. Thus began the adventures that were to make him famous.

Kit joined in with veteran trapper and explorer Ewing Young, who became his tutor in the ways of the mountain man. He worked as a teamster driving freight to El Paso and as an interpreter for a trade caravan to Chihuahua, Mexico, and in 1829 he joined his first trapping party. For the next

Kit Carson

fifteen years Carson wandered all over the West as a hunter and trapper, from Mexico to the Snake River, from the Mississippi to California. During that time he absorbed everything he could about the animals, the Indians, and the best mountain trails. The extensive knowledge and experience he gained during these years were to make him invaluable to a variety of enterprises that settled the West.

At the 1842 Rendezvous Kit fought and won a deadly duel on horseback with another trapper. He met the first of his two Indian wives there, an Arapaho woman who died shortly after their second daughter died. His second Indian wife was a Cheyenne who later left him, probably because she didn't want to be stepmother to his two Arapaho children.

Both tribes soon after became the dreaded enemies of the white settlers, but they always had a deep respect for Carson. In their eyes, Kit was different from other whites. He took the time to learn Indian languages (including Cheyenne and Ute) and grew to understand and appreciate their customs and beliefs. They respected him because he proved himself as a warrior in many battles, sometimes fighting alongside them, sometimes against them. In battle he almost always prevailed, even against overwhelming odds. As they saw it, he was favored by the spirits with strong medicine.

More than once the mere knowledge that Kit Carson was ready to join the other side was enough to prevent conflict. In 1851 Carson was leading a small group of provision-laden wagons from St. Louis to Taos, New Mexico. In southwestern Kansas, near the Colorado border, they met a large group of Cheyenne. The Cheyenne camped peacefully with the teamsters, but Carson overheard them speaking among themselves about their plans to kill the white men and take their goods. Kit, who of course understood their words, confronted them in a rage, brandished his rifle, gave them a tongue-lashing in loud, emphatic Cheyenne, and ordered them out of the camp. When one of the older warriors recognized him and told the rest that this daredevil was Kit Carson, the Cheyenne immediately packed up and rode away without a fight.

Kit served as guide for Lieutenant John C. Frémont, the explorer and surveyor who followed the route of the Louis and Clark Expedition and mapped it for the Army. For four years starting 1842, Carson scouted for Frémont on three expeditions that took them through the wildest lands in the Wild West, the last of which ended in the taking of California for the Union.

Of all the places he'd seen in the West, the one that most touched Kit's heart was Taos, New Mexico. He made it his permanent home and started a ranch with an old comrade of the trap lines, Lucien Maxwell. He also took to the Catholic faith and married into it, choosing as his third wife Josefa Jaramillo, the daughter of a prominent Taos family.

Carson could never settle down for long, and several times he took off on expeditions and trips with Frémont and others. In late 1853 he jumped at the opportunity to become the U.S. Indian Agent for northern New Mexico, a job that again sent him wandering a wide territory and brought him into contact with a variety of tribes. Carson had great respect for the people he'd once fought, and he served successfully until 1861. The Indians liked him, for he was fair and honest and was quick to defend their interests.

WITH THE OUTBREAK OF THE CIVIL WAR IN 1861, CARSON RE-signed to become a colonel in the Union Army and took command of the First New Mexico Volunteer Infantry. He served primarily in New Mexico, with particular distinction in the Battle of Valverde, and was later detached to organize the First New Mexico Cavalry in Albuquerque. He saw most of the action as he fought hostile Indian tribes who exploited the white man's preoccupation with the war in the East. With his Fort Stanton garrison of five mounted troops, Carson fought the Kiowa, Comanche, Arapaho, Apache, and Navajo and rose to the rank of brevet brigadier general. His fame as an Indian fighter stems mostly from his time with the Union Army.

But Carson didn't enjoy his campaigns against the Indians. Military campaigns weren't the same kind of free-for-all fights in which he'd gloried as a young man; they were deadly serious business in which the objective was to destroy the enemy. He sympathized with the Indians, but he was forced by his sense of duty to try to do his job well. And he succeeded. In his summer 1863 campaign against the Navajo, he led his seven hundred troops against a tribe of eight thousand or more and ruthlessly and effectively destroyed them as a free people.

Sickened and weary, Carson resigned his commission shortly after the war and settled in Boggsville, Colorado. Both he and his wife were in ill health, and when he accompanied a group of Ute Indians to Washington to assist them in negotiations, he sought the help of physicians in several Eastern cities—but to no avail. His dear wife, Josefa, died in childbirth in April 1868. Kit wrote out his will and shortly afterward followed Josefa into death. Both were buried in a small graveyard near his favorite place, Taos.

Kit Carson was a physical, practical person, not an intellectual. He was a functional illiterate who could sign his name only with effort. In his heart he longed to live in the wild places; they were his books and his equations. And yet, to those who followed he was the epitome of what a man could become in the Wild West—a man of maturity, wisdom, and spirit, a man made for the frontier. He was the master scholar of the West, of its mountains and its rivers and its people, and he marked its lessons well for those of us who came after. ■

THE MOUNTAIN MEN

Colter's Run

BY WIN BLEVINS

BY EARLY FALL OF 1806, THE LEWIS AND CLARK EXPEDITION HAD CROSSED the wild continent and was within a few weeks of St. Louis. To a weary crew eager for any aspect of civilization, that meant family and friends, hotels and taverns, beds and whiskey and women, and the end of their journey.

To all but one of them, that is. In remote North Dakota, one man turned away from civilization, back into the "Shining Mountains." No one was sure why, though Meriwether Lewis and William Clark thought he wanted to make his fortune trapping beaver. Perhaps he lacked human feeling, as the expedition's first chronicler, Nicholas Biddle, believed. Maybe he had simply fallen in love with the high country, with the smell of sagebrush, the endless prairies, the grandeur of the huge skies, and the mountains on the horizon—with being alone.

His name was John Colter, and he was the first mountain man.

That season, Colter trapped with two partners in Crow country near the Yellowstone and Little Big Horn rivers. The following year, he helped Manuel Lisa build a fort at the mouth of the Big Horn. Before winter set in, he took a thirty-pound sack of gear and set out, alone, on an amazing journey. His assignment was to let the Crow know the fort was open for trade, but wanderlust was his motivation.

After Colter visited Indian villages near the present locations of Cody and Dubois, Wyoming, he set off Westward with no particular destination in mind. Modern scholars cannot accurately reconstruct Colter's route, for though he traced it out later on William Clark's map, his topography was too vague and incomplete. Colter probably walked west over Togwotee Pass along Indian trails that followed the same approximate route as does the modern highway. From the top of the pass he would have had a spectacular view of the "hole" that would later be named for trapper Davey Jackson, and the magnificent Tetons beyond. He found his way north through that jumbled, grand country into the area that would later become Yellowstone National Park.

It would take an act of considerable imagination for the modern tourist who sees the Yellowstone country to reconstruct the impact of that sight on the first white man to sojourn there. To Colter it was a land enchanted, or perhaps haunted, by hot springs, boiling pools, and places where the earth itself bubbled and smoked. He probably bypassed the area in which the geysers were located, but he saw Yellowstone Lake, the splendid river and the magnificent falls, and wildlife in abundance. Colter headed north and east, and by the time he made it back to the fort he'd completed a round-trip excursion of more than five hundred miles through North America's wildest country. His fellow trappers had given him up for lost.

He was soon taking risks again, this time trapping in the country of the Blackfoot, who were bitterly opposed to white incursion into their territory.

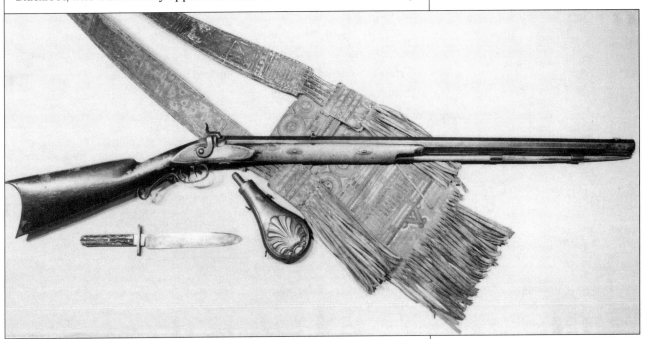

When the Blackfoot caught Colter and killed his companion, they recognized the mountain man as an enemy from a previous fight. In considering his fate, some of his captors argued for immediate torture and death, while others opted for sport. After a lengthy discussion, they asked Colter a question: "Are you a good runner?"

Colter answered noncommittally that some said he was but that he really wasn't. The Blackfoot decided on sport and made Colter what they considered a generous offer—a chance to run for his life, naked and unarmed and pursued by armed warriors. Even though he was hundreds of miles from his fort, he accepted the terms of his captors. The chase began.

Colter first had to reach cover at the Jefferson Fork of the Missouri River, over six miles away across the brush plains. He ran well, ignoring the prickly pear needles that stabbed his bare feet, and was able to outdistance most of the pursuing warriors in the first lap. A vessel burst in his nostril and gushed blood over his chest, but he ignored that as well. What he couldn't

Authentic mountain man gear: classic Hawken St. Louis Plains Rifle in .54 caliber (circa 1840), a hand-tooled and hand-decorated leather hunter's pouch, a shell-decorated brass powder flask, and a Sheffield hunting knife (photo by Tom Knowles, courtesy of Texas Ranger Hall of Fame Museum, Waco, Texas)

ignore was the single fleet warrior who was gaining on him. He stopped and shouted pleas for his life in the Crow tongue. The Blackfoot warrior hurled his spear in reply, but he stumbled as he threw. The point of the spear missed Colter and went into the ground. Colter instantly grabbed the weapon and drove it through the warrior.

On Colter ran, well ahead of the others, toward the Missouri River. As the Indians closed in, he dived into the frigid waters. He swam up under a logjam (perhaps into a beaver lodge) to hide and found an airspace with just enough room for him to breathe. While the Blackfoot searched frantically about for him, Colter waited in his freezing refuge until darkness came to cover his escape.

And what did John Colter do then, alone in the wilderness, naked, shoeless, and without weapons, food, or flint to make a fire? He just turned, started walking, and walked the couple of hundred miles to the fort. After all, he was a mountain man. ■

Sketch of a Mountain Man

By Win Blevins

For most, the mountain man is a caricature painted in the broad, vivid strokes of Western literature. He wears a slouch hat, rides an Indian pony, and leads a string of pack horses laden with beaver hides. His buckskin pants are greasy black, and his knees show through the worn leather. A Green River knife juts through his belt in front, a bowie knife nestles at his back, and a Hawken rifle rides across his saddlehorn. His scraggly beard hangs almost to his waist; it bobs as he calls out to us in the accents of the illiterate Kentucky backwoodsman. "Thyar ye be, coons," he says. "This un's been a-searchin' creation for ye. How's about us'n's set sail for Laramie, afore them tarnation Sioux cut our trail?"

Like most caricatures, this one is false. And true. Mostly false. We label ourselves pork-eaters, the mountain man's word for greenhorns, by giving credence to it. So who was that strange figure of American mythology, the mountain man?

For a representative example, we can consider what ten mountain men might have looked like when they gathered around a Green River campfire in 1830. The time and place are typical—the flood tide of mountain men in the Rockies began in 1822 and crested in 1840, and the valley of Wyoming's Green River was their favorite country. Fort Laramie didn't yet exist.

First, not all of them are Americans. There are three Canadians—Frenchies or *métis* (mixed bloods) in mountain man terms, descendants of a long line of northwoodsmen with a style all their own. Another sounds like a Scot. There's a Spaniard from the Rio Grande country. Another is an American but not a white man—he's a Shawnee or a Delaware Indian.

Only five of our imaginary mountain men are white Americans, probably from the eastern mountains that stretch from the Appalachians to the Ozarks, that great breeding ground of American frontiersmen. Even so, not all of them fit the stereotype. They're not greasy old coots. They're young men, eighteen to thirty. Three are clean-shaven, and the other two wear short, stylish beards like those shown in the mountain man portraits of Alfred Jacob Miller. Compared to the stereotype, these fellows are dandies. Their clothing is more of cotton or wool than of buckskin, and in bright colors. They wear showy blanket coats, and maybe earrings and armbands of brass or German silver. Not a one of them carries a Hawken rifle or a Green River knife; the time for those tools of the mountains lies some years in the future.

They don't talk like backwoods clichés; rather, they speak French and Spanish as well as English. Some of the English is accented with a Scots burr, some with crisp New England syllables. They season it with Native American terms from the languages of the Crow, the Shoshone, and other tribes. Every one of them is something of a linguist, a master of the polyglot Western Tower of Babel.

If the outfit were larger and more typical of the company trappers, they'd be almost military in their precision. There would be a captain, a clerk to keep records, a cook, campsetters, hired trappers who are outfitted by the company and work for wages, and perhaps a few free trappers along for the safety of numbers. But these are free trappers who trap where they like and sell their furs to whatever trader they please.

No matter where they've come from, no matter what they look like or what languages they speak, they are the mountain men.

THE MOUNTAIN MEN

The Wilderness Odyssey of Hugh Glass

BY WIN BLEVINS

THE FIRST TIME HE WOKE UP, MOUNTAIN MAN HUGH GLASS THOUGHT, *I'm thirsty*. The second time, *I hurt*. After many fitful dozings and awakenings, he woke up and thought, *I'm alive, and that's a good start*.

Then he had one more thought—*I'm gonna get even*—and he knew he was going to make it. He would live.

Knowing that, Glass lay there and figured out his next move. He looked over his body to find out in how many places it was torn up and broken. He remembered the big grizzly swatting him here and there, in the ribs, which might be broken, in the neck, where he felt dried blood, and half a dozen other places. He thought he could remember his head being in her mouth, her teeth crunching down and ripping the scalp from his skull. All he could taste was his own blood.

That made him thirsty. He judged that one roll would take him to the edge of the creek, and it did. Then he passed out from the pain. When he woke up, he drank gratefully. It was all coming back to him. After Glass had been mauled by the griz, the Major had bullied two men into remaining behind, had paid them to stay with Glass till he died.

They'd sat around for several days while he'd suffered, half-waking and delirious. The kid, Jamie, had given him water a few times. The older one, Fitzgerald, had gotten after the kid to move out, nettling him off and on about how the Indians would torture him if they caught up with them.

Jamie stuck by his duty, but fear and Fitzgerald's barbs eventually got to him. He agreed to leave, and that's when Fitzgerald told him they'd have to take Glass' gun and knife and other gear to fool the Indians into thinking Glass had died on his own. So not only had they left him to die alone, but they'd taken the equipment that might have given him a chance to survive.

Glass knew he'd have to track them down for that, track them and kill them. In his four decades of life, he'd never felt anything as good as knowing that.

A nineteenth century mounted buffalo head, a reminder of those days when thousands of buffalo roamed much of the American West. (courtesy of Kansas State Historical Society, Topeka, Kansas)

Over the next day he exercised his battered body as much as he could without reopening his terrible wounds. He drank from the stream and managed to pick some buffalo berries to quiet his stomach. And then he started out, crawling toward Fort Kiowa. He was on the Grand River in what would one day be South Dakota. Fort Kiowa was on the Missouri River, a couple of hundred miles away.

No one knows how Hugh Glass managed to crawl, and later hobble, across two hundred miles of incredibly rough country, a land filled with Indians angry from recent skirmishes with the whites. In the 1820s, the country over which he traveled was almost as hostile and unsettled as the dark side of the moon. He had no gun, no knife, no way to make a fire. Legend has it that he found wolves feeding on a buffalo carcass, got to his feet, drove them away, and gorged himself on raw meat.

He got to Fort Kiowa in the second week of October, and his feat amazed the resident traders. They were even more perturbed when Glass insisted on setting out for the fort on the Yellowstone, on the trail of his faithless companions. He caught a ride part way with a boat of fur traders, then set out alone, on foot, for the Yellowstone—at the time the farthest outpost the white men had pushed into the "Shining Mountains."

He reached it in December, but he found it empty. Local Indians told him his outfit had moved to the mouth of the Big Horn River, several hundred miles further west. Glass kept walking.

On New Year's Eve, he burst into the trappers' camp on the Big Horn, revenge in his heart. Their drunken celebration was immediately hushed. When Glass demanded the right to confront the men who had abandoned him, the major told him that Fitzgerald had left the company. Jamie stood before him, hangdog, unable to speak.

Glass found himself unable to carry out his vengeance on the miserable young man. *Never mind the kid*, he decided, *I want Fitzgerald.*

His quest took him back to the settlements—"back to the States," as the mountain men said. It was there he found his betrayer, Fitzgerald, who had enlisted in the Army at Fort Atkinson. When the commanding officer told him that killing a soldier could get him shot, Glass searched his heart and found that his struggle to survive had burned out the fire of revenge. He told Fitzgerald what he thought of him, retrieved his rifle and his gear, and headed back into the mountains. ■

THE MOUNTAIN MEN

Jedediah Strong Smith

BY WIN BLEVINS

USE YOUR DREAMING EYE: SEE THAT CAMPFIRE IN THE TWILIGHT. Pay no attention to the sounds of the annual Rendezvous—the drums, the shouts and groans of gamblers, the slap of cards, and the half-mute cries of the lovers, white men with their rented or borrowed Indian women in the willows.

Instead, notice the men sitting at that campfire. One, old Jim Bridger, is telling a yarn. Illiterate and a blacksmith by trade, he's the best at yarning and most everything else. Next to him is a Frenchy, Antoine, an old hand from Canada. The dudish hoss beside Antoine is Captain William Drummond Stewart, who's on one of his grand hunting tours. Filling out the circle are a Spaniard out of Taos, two Delawares (about the only Indians mountain men accepted as equal partners), and two more Americans from the Appalachian backwoods.

Now, if you can envision it, look for the one who is present in spirit if not in the flesh: Jedediah Smith. Though a Comanche arrow killed him two years before, his shade haunts this Rendezvous. He was a considerable leader of those who hunt these mountains, unique and even strange among these rugged individuals.

Jedediah Strong Smith came out of upper New York and Pennsylvania, an educated man, serious, ambitious. He wanted to explore the West. To make money. To write books about his adventures. And he was determined all the while to remain a Christian. He was powerfully drawn to the wilderness, but he wanted to hold high the light of civilization there. He wore his Bible as hard as he did his boot leather, prayed often, and said solemn words over the dead.

His companions wondered at his inclinations, for they'd as soon the school and the church and the law and white women stayed back east where they belonged. But they admired Captain Smith too much to say so.

Smith came West with the Ashley Company men in 1822, and in the first year he so distinguished himself that General Ashley gave him a command the very next summer. With that outfit he pioneered the land route toward the Yellowstone country. It was the beginning of what would be a long list of explorations.

On that first journey Captain Smith was the one who got hurt—mauled

"LIVER-EATING" JOHNSTON, THE CROW KILLER

BY WIN BLEVINS

"Liver-Eating" John Johnston, alias Jeremiah Johnson, must have been something special even among mountain men. He was sensitively portrayed by Robert Redford in one of our ecologically conscious generation's favorite movies, *Jeremiah Johnson*, and he is the hero of two celebrated books—Vardis Fisher's terrific novel, *Mountain Man*, on which the movie was based, and Thorp and Bunker's more factual biography, *Crow Killer*. Yet in real life, he became famous for his unrelenting one-man war of annihilation against the Crow nation. He's credited with a particularly gruesome (and possibly apocryphal) reputation for signing his Crow kills by eating the warriors' livers—raw.

So who was John Johnston—the terrifying Liver-Eater of legend, or the heroic mountain man of celluloid and prose? Seldom have so many words shed so little light on one man. Though *Mountain Man* and *Jeremiah Johnson* depict him as a man driven to extremes by intense grief, the Johnston of the *Crow Killer* biography is equal parts hero, ogre, madman, and hoax. He is big and strong and violent, an antisocial giant straight out of "Jack and the Beanstalk." He kills human beings as casually as he traps beaver, and even his few cronies don't feel safe around him.

It is difficult to separate the genuine, historical Johnston from the legends, the fictions, and the errors that have crept into his story. But we can piece together a few facts of his life.

He went West as a red-bearded giant in 1843, just at the time the mountain men were leaving the mountains. As a young trapper, Johnston chanced upon a wagon-train family slaughtered by Indians on the Musselshell River. Though the mother, Jane Morgan, had survived the attack, the experience had driven her mad. Johnston buried her family and for years provided her with food. The Indians, traditionally awed by those driven mad by the touch of the Great Spirit, left her in peace.

As did many mountain men, Johnston took a Flathead woman as his bride, but in his case there is some evidence that the relationship was one of genuine affection. While he was out trapping, a Crow raiding party happened onto Johnston's cabin and killed his wife and unborn child. For some years afterward, Johnston devoted himself to a savage, bloody, and oddly personal revenge on the warriors of the Crow nation.

And so Johnston stepped into legend via the stories of the crazy woman of the Musselshell and his own vendetta against the Crow. He stayed out West for twenty years, well through the hardest times for the trappers, and then went back to the States to fight for the Union in the Civil War. After the war, he returned to the West to trap and scout, and at some time he made his peace with the Crow. He served briefly as a law officer in two small Montana towns, became ill, went to California to die, and promptly did. He was buried there in a veteran's cemetery, but in the 1970s he was disinterred and reburied near his old mountain home. Robert Redford served as one of his modern pallbearers.

Those who wish to find out more about the real John Johnston must seek his spirit in his old haunts in the canyons and creeks of Wyoming and Montana. But be careful—it's probably a bilious and wild spirit.

by a grizzly who raked his scalp and nearly tore off one of his ears. He bore the scars for the rest of his life, and he wore his hair long to cover them. It was an odd irony, a man of God who carried the mark of the beast. It symbolized the conflict that was his life.

OVER THE NEXT SIX YEARS HE BLAZED TRAILS THROUGHOUT THE WEST and recorded his wanderings in journals and maps. He made the effective discovery of the South Pass and found the Green River trapping paradise. He led the first white men overland to California, and he led the way across the Sierra Nevadas and the Great Basin.

His relentless, tireless journey wasn't always profitable. At first he brought back hundreds of plews (beaver pelts) for Ashley. Then he and his partners bought out Ashley, and his wanderlust got the better of him. When Smith said he'd go Southwest looking for beaver, the trappers saw California in his eyes and signed on happily—"high-hearted with hunger for the new"—as the poet later put it. Three years he spent on the Pacific Coast— he lost money and he lost men, but he satisfied a part of his hunger. When he finally decided to make one year's hunt for real profit, he chose the most dangerous country in the West, Blackfoot territory, and made it pay.

They were bloody years. The Mojave Indians were friendly to him one year but deceived him the next and killed half his brigade. When his men, against Smith's orders, allowed the Kelawatset into camp, the Indians slaughtered every hand but one. The commander who wanted to save all men's souls led many of them to destruction.

He surely suffered from the guilt. His own conduct was impeccable— he never touched either strong drink or an Indian woman—but men had trusted him and had died for it. There were the Indians he killed in battle (of necessity, of course), and probably those sins of his secret heart which all men commit. But he held himself to higher standards.

At Christmastime 1829, after eight years in the wilderness, he wrote his parents a despairing letter: "I feel the need of the watch and care of a Christian Church—you may well suppose that our society is of the roughest kind...I hope you will remember me before a throne of grace."

When the chance came the next summer, his business good and his fortune made, Smith abruptly quit the mountains and went to St. Louis, Missouri. It was his chance to live in society among people of civilization and refinement, and under the care of that "Christian Church." He even had the capital to start a substantial business.

But the West called to him, and Jedediah couldn't stay away. The next spring found him headed to the wilds again, this time to Santa Fe and Taos and perhaps on to Mexico City, places he'd never been before. The country was barely known, a great opportunity for the able and the daring. One can

"Only to the white man was nature a 'wilderness' and only to him was the land 'infested' with 'wild' animals and 'savage' people. To us it was tame. Earth was bountiful and we were surrounded with the blessings of the Great Mystery. Not until the hairy man from the east came and with brutal frenzy heaped injustices upon us and the families we loved was it 'wild' for us. When the very animals of the forest began fleeing from his approach, then it was for us the 'Wild West' began."

CHIEF LUTHER STANDING BEAR
OGLALA SIOUX

only wonder if Smith knew in his heart that it wasn't money he sought—it was the elusive elsewhere that lay just over the next hill or just around the next bend of the river. It was destiny.

Jedediah Smith was only thirty-two when he returned to the West. He'd never leave it again. His outfit was making the Cimarron crossing when it got hard up for water. Smith rode ahead alone to scout for water and found it. He also found the Comanche waiting for him there. They killed him, took his guns, and left his body for the scavengers, the wind, and the sun—in the wilds, where he belonged. ∎

THE MOUNTAIN MEN

SIR WILLIAM DRUMMOND STEWART, LORD OF THE ROCKIES

BY WIN BLEVINS

IMAGINE THE SOUND OF THE TALK AROUND A ROCKY MOUNTAINS campfire in the 1830s—the uneducated speech of the Kentucky backwoodsman, the soft tones of the Virginia gentleman, the cultivated French of the St. Louisan, and the patois of the half-breed French-Canadian. Now add to those accents the strangest of all, the aristocratic intonations of a Scots laird hobnobbing with the roughest frontiersmen in the world.

He was Captain William Drummond Stewart, late of the King's Hussars. It was during his years in the mountains that he became Sir William, a baronet and the master of Murthly, lord of the very woods of Dunsinane that in legend had marched on the treacherous Macbeth.

Stewart came to America and her mountains a dissatisfied man. The second son of a titled family, he was disenfranchised by the strict custom of heredity. He had served his country well as an officer of the Hussars at Waterloo, but after the war he found himself both bored and short of funds. So he headed for the Rockies, some of the harshest, wildest, most dangerous country in the world—and found there that life was worth living.

Stewart first tasted the life of the mountain man when he traveled along what would later become the Oregon Trail, and he gorged himself on it at the Rendezvous of 1833 on the west side of the Wind River Mountains. The

beaver trade was at its height in the 1830s in the West. The green hands of a decade earlier were now seasoned mountain men. Many were working on their own hook—they called themselves free trappers. The big trading companies, engaged in cutthroat competition, paid top dollar to sign up experienced men.

Washington Irving described this climactic rendezvous of 1833 through the eyes of another soldier in *The Adventures of Captain Bonneville, U.S.A.* It was "a rich treat for the worthy captain to see the 'chivalry' of the various encampments engaged in, contests of skill at running, jumping, wrestling, shooting with the rifle, and running horses. And then their rough hunters' feasting and carousals. They drank together, they sang, they laughed, they whooped, they tried to outbrag and outlie each other, in stories of their adventures and achievements. Here the free trappers were in all their glory; they considered themselves the 'cocks of the walk' and always carried the highest crests. Now and then familiarity was pushed too far and would effervesce into a brawl and a 'rough and tumble' fight but it all ended in cordial reconciliation and maudlin endearment."

This primitive life so attracted the aristocratic Stewart that he made it his own for the next half-dozen years. He was a crack shot, and armed with his expensive Manton rifles he showed even the experienced mountain hunters what shooting was. He explored the country all the way to Fort Vancouver near the Pacific Ocean. Along the way he shared the revels of

SHINING TIMES: THE RENDEZVOUS!

BY WIN BLEVINS

The mountain men lived for the Rendezvous. In fall and spring they roamed the mountain West and waded its icy creeks in search of beaver. In winter when they holed up in their lean-tos and lodges, they told stories of times past and imagined times to come. In the summer they had the Rendezvous.

The first Rendezvous took place in 1825 when the Ashley Company trappers had spread out far beyond the trading posts and army outposts where they could easily resupply and turn in their beaver pelts. The company sent out a supply outfit that set up a central depot and camp at Henry's Fork on the Green River. This worked so well that they kept meeting each summer, usually somewhere on the Green River, until 1840. It became the trappers' one great get-together of the year. They agreed on a certain spot that was easy to reach, had plenty of graze for the horses, good water, and lots of elbow room. Several hundred trappers, and often several thousand Indians, rode in from all over the West, from Fort Vancouver and Taos and St. Louis. Then the fun began.

The official object of the Rendezvous was for the average company trapper to come in, turn over his beaver pelts (or "plews") to his outfit, and get resupplied. The unattached trapper sold his pelts to the highest bidder, then bought DuPont (powder) and Galena (lead), guns, blankets, traps, coffee, and trinkets for the Indian trade. If a trapper made some extra money or had good credit, he might even buy a new pair of cloth pants. Indians and trappers who might have been mortal enemies had they met in the mountains traded with each other for horses and goods.

Unofficially, the Rendezvous was blowout time. There was whiskey to drink, and there were Indian women for the night or for keeps. It was a time to visit with compañeros not seen for a year or two and to find out which ones would never be seen again. It was a time to tell tales of good trapping and bad, of hostiles and friends among the Indians. It was a time to play games of chance like euchre until you had won or lost a fortune, a time to test your horse's speed or your skill with knife, tomahawk, or gun against that of the others.

After 1840, when the trading posts, forts, and other outposts of civilization had found their way into the remote regions of the West and when the price of beaver pelts made it hardly worth setting a trap, the Rendezvous faded into memory.

their shining times with the trappers, fought Indians beside them and courted Indian women with them, and endured without complaint the starvation and hardship that was often their lot.

One summer Stewart brought West an artist, Alfred Jacob Miller, with instructions to capture the romantic life and landscapes in paint on canvas. It was a great service to history, for Miller's paintings and sketches exist today as a priceless record of the mountain man's way of life.

If it had not been for a summons from abroad, Stewart might never have returned to Scotland. A letter came bearing the news of his childless elder brother's death—and a death sentence for Stewart's free life in the West. Captain Stewart was now Lord William. Duty's reluctant servant, he said farewell to his beloved mountains and made his way back to Scotland to assume his ancestral responsibilities.

Back in Murthly Castle, the new laird longed for the Rockies. He often exchanged letters with his old friends of the trail, and he even had antelope, buffalo, and the native flora of the West shipped across the sea at considerable expense. In 1843 he managed one more excursion to the mountains, but it was more a royal procession than a hunting trip. It must have been a sad affair, for in the short time he'd been in Scotland the day of the mountain man and the free trapper had passed into history. The Oregon Trail was filled with thousands of wagons—settlers headed West to tame the wild country of Stewart's memories. He sent word around the mountains that

THE LEGENDARY JIM BECKWOURTH

BY WIN BLEVINS

In legend, Jim Beckwourth is the grandest, toughest, fightingest mountain man and frontier scout there ever was. In life, he was not so much less than that as maybe something sideways of it. The real James P. Beckwourth is now obscured by the myths and tall tales Beckwourth himself took a lusty joy in telling.

Beckwourth was never a slave, but he was born in Virginia to a mulatto mother. His father, Sir Jennings Beckwith, a titled Englishman, is said to have acknowledged his several mixed-blood children and doted on them. When Sir Jennings moved to St. Louis,

Missouri, he took them with him.

Beckwourth set out from St. Louis with an early Ashley Company trading mission, but within a few years he left white life behind and moved in with the Crow Indians. By his accounts, he became a chief and principal warrior of the Crow tribe. Some of the Beckwourth legends tell of one of his Crow wives, Pine Leaf, a warrior woman who led the Crow in battle against their hereditary enemies, the Blackfoot.

After he'd been with the Crow about ten years, Beckwourth tired of Indian life and took to wandering once more. He signed on as an Army scout and fought in the Seminole Wars in Florida. He was a Forty-Niner in the California gold rush. He scouted a good route for wagon trains through the Sierra Nevada mountains and built a road over them. Though a multitude of emigrants used his road and others reaped large profits from it, Beckwourth was done out of his share.

To spread his fame and earn a little money, in the 1850s Beckwourth told

his adventures to a journalist named T.D. Bonner. Bonner's book, *The Life and Adventures of James P. Beckwourth*, earned Beckwourth a reputation as a "gaudy liar" that is not entirely deserved. Many of the stories, though improbable, are the truth—or close to it. Beckwourth expected his listeners to understand that a good story is improved by a little ornamentation. Of course, Bonner cheated Beckwourth out of his share of the profits.

Late in his life Beckwourth was unfortunate enough to find himself scouting for Chivington's volunteers, the irregular force that committed the infamous Sand Creek Massacre. It is hard to imagine what the old mountain man who had lived as a friend and brother with the Indians thought of that unprovoked slaughter of a peaceful band of Cheyenne men, women, and children. In any case, he once again turned his back on the white world and returned to his life with the Crow.

he would sponsor one more Rendezvous. It was the mountain man's last hurrah.

Once more in Scotland, Stewart looked at the huge paintings Miller had made from his Western sketches, all that was left of the American West he had known. He even wrote two autobiographical novels about his adventures there, *Altowan* and *Edward Warren*, books filled with his romantic yearning for past glories. But he never returned to the mountains. ■

THE TREASURE SEEKERS

SUTTER'S MILL OF DREAMS AND THE CALIFORNIA GOLD RUSH

BY LEE SULLENGER

JOHN AUGUSTUS SUTTER WAS LIKE MANY MEN WHO TURNED UP ON the frontier, the kind who always reached for the brass ring but never quite snagged it. He moved West when he became dissatisfied with the life that had been laid out for him in his native country, and his dreams kept him moving toward the sunset. Though he was imaginative and energetic, he frittered away that imagination and energy on get-rich-quick schemes. If he'd been able to develop a little business sense or been a little luckier, he might have achieved success. As it was, the scent of failure clung to him all his life. He is best remembered for his connection with the great California gold rush, which was, for him, a disaster.

Sutter (originally spelled Suter) was a "borderer," born of Swiss parents in a small German town, Kandern, near the Swiss border. His father was the hardworking and moderately prosperous foreman of a paper mill, an inherited position. John Augustus wanted more, so he steered clear of the paper mill and apprenticed at a publishing house in Basil. He soon tired of that and moved to Aarburg, Switzerland, where he clerked in a store.

In Aarburg he met the woman who would become his wife—and his first bankroll. He courted her ardently; the day after the wedding, she presented him with a son. His mother-in-law also gave in to him and set him up in a drygoods store. Sutter preferred high living to hands-on management, and he recklessly borrowed and sold on credit. It took him four years to run the

> **"The reports of my death are greatly exaggerated."**
> MARK TWAIN

business into the ground, and his mother-in-law finally refused to bail him out. Like many others before him and after, he emigrated to America one step ahead of his creditors and debtor's prison. He left his wife and four children behind.

Sutter arrived in New York in 1834, but the East wasn't comfortably far enough from his creditors. He immediately set out for Missouri. He tried farming but gave it up after a year, probably because he couldn't convince anyone to plow, plant, weed, and harvest for him. So he bought a cargo of gaudy trinkets and secondhand clothes and went on a trading expedition to Santa Fe. The expedition was a success, but Sutter spent all his profits when he got back to Missouri. He borrowed money for more merchandise and set out again.

As always, Sutter was going to the well one time too many. The second trip was a disaster. Other expeditions had flooded the Santa Fe market with the kind of merchandise Sutter was peddling. It should have been a bloodbath for Sutter and his partners, but he managed to wiggle out of the bind and leave them holding the bag. The usually talkative Sutter was reluctant to explain how he managed to return to Missouri with enough funds to start a store. Of course, that venture failed within a year. Sutter was able to salvage enough money to get out of Missouri ahead of his partners from the Santa Fe venture, who had straggled back and accused him of selling their jointly owned merchandise and absconding with the money. Sutter had to go farther West to escape them, and understandably he chose the Northwest—he'd worn out his welcome in the Southwest.

But he'd learned the most important lesson about the American frontier. On the frontier, a man could reinvent himself and his past. He traveled West, first with representatives of John Jacob Astor's American Fur Company, then with Astor's chief competitor, the British-owned Hudson's Bay Company. By the time he got to Fort Vancouver, Washington, he was no longer the son of a paper mill foreman but of a Lutheran minister. At various times he claimed to have been a military academy classmate of Louis Napoleon (future emperor of France), and a former captain of the French king's elite Swiss Guards. So accomplished had he become at invention, Sutter could have been Mark Twain's inspiration for the Dauphin, the con man who floated down the Mississippi with Huckleberry Finn.

Sutter's dream was to become a great landowner in California, to produce cattle, wheat, wine, wood, and leather to sell to the growing population of that prosperous land, and to become fabulously wealthy in the process. Unfortunately, there wasn't a ship immediately scheduled to sail down the coast to California, so Sutter took passage on a ship that was headed for Hawaii. California by way of Hawaii might seem a ludicrous detour, but Sutter had his own reasons for a quick departure from Vancouver: He didn't want his past to catch up with him.

In any event, Sutter fared brilliantly. The post commander at Fort Vancouver hated to see him go and gave him glowing letters of introduction. In Hawaii, King Kamehameha III and his court received Sutter with open arms. By the time he left Hawaii he had acquired supplies and tools (on credit) and had recruited thirteen workers to help him build his empire.

Once he was finally in California, Sutter found the perfect place—the Sacramento Valley. All that remained was to persuade the Mexican authorities to grant him the land, and only a Mexican citizen could own land. In short order John Augustus became Juan Agosto, and he named fifty thousand acres of the finest real estate in California as his New Helvetica (New Switzerland).

Loans to construct his house and improve his property he obtained from investors from Mexico, the U.S., and several European countries. Sutter's Fort, the name under which it became famous in California history, was a

Map of the Sacramento Valley area, California, 1886 by Frank A. Gray, published by O.W. Gray and Son, Philadelphia

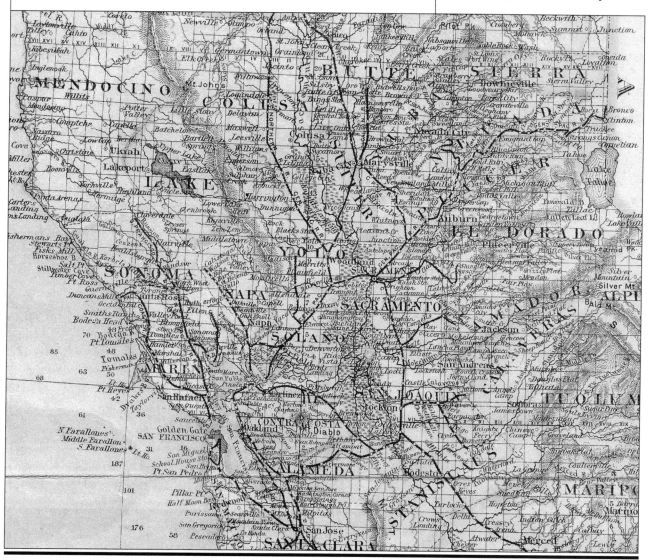

An engraving of John C. Frémont
(courtesy of Kansas University
Libraries)

spacious hacienda surrounded by a stockade fence and defended by brass cannon he'd brought from Hawaii. He staffed the estate with dozens of employees, and his generosity called forth their best efforts. His cattle and horse herds, his vineyards and wheat fields flourished. Sutter's Fort became the way-station for the flood of emigrants that passed through or settled in California. So did Sutter come to the high-water mark of his life. By 1848 he was, though still in debt, within reach of realizing his great dream.

He weathered the storm of the Mexican War, even though for a time his fort was commandeered by John C. Frémont, the explorer who led the Anglos in the Bear Flag Revolt. Sutter remained a Mexican citizen throughout the hostilities, respected if at times distrusted by the Mexican authorities. When the war ended, he recruited skilled laborers from the ranks of U.S. soldiers who had been discharged in California after the victory.

Sutter began construction on two mills, one to grind his wheat into flour and one to cut his timber into boards. Both mills were nearly complete when fate took over and history suddenly lurched into a new direction. It was January of 1848. James Marshall, the foreman of Sutter's sawmill construction crew, while inspecting the recently completed millrace that was to divert water from the American River to the mill wheel, saw something shiny under the surface of the water. He picked it up, along with several similar pieces. Marshall didn't realize it, but he held at that moment the keys to the great California gold rush, the first nuggets of the estimated two hundred million dollars in gold that would be taken from the mountains in the course of the rush.

Marshall and Sutter formed a partnership to keep the find secret. The annexation of California had voided the Mexican land grant, and Sutter hadn't yet reestablished his ownership of the land under the new U.S. government. They promised the other mill workers fifty percent of the gold they found if they swore to secrecy. But gold is an impossible secret to keep. It wasn't long before most of Sutter's employees dropped their tools and left to hunt for gold. Word got out, and by May New Helvetica was swarmed by miners. San Francisco's population decreased drastically as men left for Sutter's Fort. Within a year, the Sacramento Valley was buried under an avalanche of gold seekers who had come from all over the world. It wasn't long before a battlefield of open pits, eroded hillsides, and choked streams was all that was left of Sutter's dream.

Ever the survivor, Sutter managed to find security as the personal ward of his son in Pennsylvania. There he spent the rest of his life trying in vain to regain the estate he'd lost in the gold rush. He even prepared to initiate a lawsuit against the more than fifteen thousand people he'd accused of squatting on his land. But he died in 1880 in Washington, D.C., a continent away from his last, great venture.

THE SECRETS OF THE SUPERSTITION MOUNTAINS AND THE LEGEND OF THE LOST DUTCHMAN MINE

BY W. C. JAMESON

OF ALL THE FABULOUS TALES OF LOST MINES AND BURIED TREASURES in North America, none captures the imagination like the legend of the Lost Dutchman Mine. Located somewhere deep in the rugged and forbidding Superstition Mountains east of Phoenix, Arizona, this elusive source of gold has tantalized researchers and treasure hunters for over a century.

The Superstition Mountains are an appropriate setting for such a tale. Once sacred to the Apache, they are a remote, rattlesnake-infested maze of rocky canyons, sharp ridges, and steep slopes in the most rugged, arid, and forbidding area of the American Southwest.

Long before gold-seeking Spaniards visited the region during the early 1500s, the Apache believed the range was inhabited by special gods who jealously guarded their treasures. The Thunder God who ruled the Superstitions would supposedly roll rocks from the high cliffs onto any who dared to trespass. From these Indian legends sprang the so-called curse of the Superstition Mountains.

The Pima Indians had their own tales. One of their legends reported that the great Aztec ruler Montezuma had gathered his huge fortune and ordered his people to transport it from deep in Mexico into the Superstition Mountains. There, the Aztecs cached the gold and treasure of the dying empire to keep it safe from raiders and conquistadors.

Spanish explorers commanded by Coronado entered the region during the early part of the sixteenth century, and in 1539 an expedition led by Fray Marcos de Niza set forth from Mexico City to find the great quantity of gold the Spanish believed existed in the vast regions to the north. As a result of de Niza's observations, the Spaniards undertook prospecting and mining operations. They discovered gold and silver in many locations and established hundreds of mines. Several of the mines in the Superstition Mountains, both placer and shaft, yielded fortunes in gold. For several generations the Spanish successfully extracted gold from the Superstitions, and every two or three months pack trains loaded with hundreds of ingots plied the hazardous trails from the mines to Mexico City far to the south.

A S THE SPANISH MINING ACTIVITY IN THE SUPERSTITIONS INcreased, so did Apache resentment against the intruders. To the Indians, the Superstitions were homeland and holy ground. And in their quest for food the Spanish hunters slaughtered the deer, buffalo, and antelope to the degree that little was left for the Indians. Eventually and inevitably, the Apache began to retaliate. Initially they attacked and killed small parties of hunters and ambushed pack trains along the narrow trails. As the ranks of the Spaniards grew thin, the Indians began to attack the mining camps themselves. Day-long battles often ensued.

The Spaniards worked the rich mines from 1590 to the mid-1700s, gradually abandoning them as they depleted the ore and as the Indians continued their depredations. Legend has it that the Spaniards covered the entrances to the mines before they left the region.

For decades the Superstition Mountains lay quiet and undisturbed by the ring of pickaxes. Only the Apache passed through the Thunder God's domain, constantly on guard against the return of the invaders. With the Mexican Revolution of 1821, however, came the end of the Spaniards' reign; thus the Iberians would never return to the mountains and their treasures.

In Mexico, a man named Peralta heard tales of the gold mines to the north. For many years the Peralta family had operated several gold mines in Sonora and Arizona, and they were intrigued by the possibility of extending their interests into the Superstition Mountains. During the 1840s Peralta, by that time in his sixties, learned of the impending Treaty of Guadalupe Hidalgo, which would eventually grant the northern part of Mexico to the United States. Peralta hurried to extract what gold he could prior to the effective treaty date of 1848.

Obtaining locational information left behind by the Spaniards, Don Miguel Peralta II organized a party to travel to the isolated range and reopen the rich mines. Not only did Peralta employ miners, geologists, and engineers, he also hired dozens of guards for protection from marauding Indians. When the expedition left Mexico, it numbered over four hundred.

On arriving in the Superstitions the Peralta expedition used the Spaniards' maps to relocate the placer mines, and they reopened several of the shafts. They extracted as much ore as they could. In addition to the impending treaty deadline, they also had to contend with an increasing number of hostile Apache. Miners, hunters, and guards occasionally fell victim to Indian arrows. The curse of the Superstitions became the main topic of conversation among members of the expedition.

As the time to leave approached, Peralta had his men cover all of the mines in the hope that he would someday be able to make the appropriate political arrangements to return to extract more of the rich ore that still lay in the shafts. He had them load tons of gold ingots and ore onto several pack trains to carry most of his new wealth back into Mexico. Because of the time limit and because the pack animals could carry only so much, he had most of the gold cached in secret locations near the mines. The Apache dogged his trail back to Mexico.

EVEN AS THE TREATY OF GUADALUPE HIDALGO TOOK EFFECT IN 1848, the cry of "Gold!" went up in California at Sutter's Mill. The California gold rush eventually linked a German immigrant named Jacob Waltz, also known as the Dutchman, to the legends of the Superstition Mountains.

Waltz came West with considerable mining experience, the most notable from earlier gold strikes in North Carolina and Georgia. Waltz was living in Mississippi when he learned of the Sutter's Mill discovery. Along with thousands of others, he packed his belongings and traveled to the Golden State with the hope of becoming rich. Little is known of the activities of the rather reclusive Waltz until 1860, but it is believed he worked several small placer claims in northern California.

One evening as he enjoyed a beer in a tavern in a small mining town in California, Waltz was distracted by a disturbance. An angry gambler was beating an unarmed, elderly man. Just after the gambler plunged a knife into the defenseless man's stomach, the Dutchman stepped in and subdued the assailant.

Waltz carried the bleeding victim to his room; the wounded man introduced himself as Don Miguel Peralta II. As Waltz nursed Peralta back to health, a friendship formed between the two men. In his gratitude, Peralta gave Waltz his secret, the story of the gold of the Superstition Mountains.

As the Civil War gained momentum in the South, Waltz, using directions provided by Peralta, entered the Superstition Mountains in search of the mines. He had difficulty interpreting Peralta's map, but after several years of searching, Jacob Waltz finally found the gold. In the western end of the range, in the dry bed of an ephemeral stream called Camp Creek, Waltz discovered one of the Peralta placer mines. Nearby he found the ruins of several rock houses and two mine shafts that had been covered over. To the south of these rich deposits stood a sharply pointed peak that many researchers have identified as Weaver's Needle, a prominent landmark; other investigators believe what Waltz saw was Pinnacle Peak. Waltz ex-

NUGGETS

BY W. C. JAMESON

As the Peralta miners evacuated the Superstition Mountains, their several gold-laden pack trains made their way though the canyons toward a trail that would eventually lead them to Mexico City. One of these pack trains consisted of twenty mules, each carrying heavy leather sacks filled with gold ore. As the miners led their mules single-file down the narrow trail that paralleled Camp Creek, the party was suddenly attacked by the Apache.

The few escorts that accompanied the train fled in panic, only to be overtaken and killed by the Indians. After they brought the milling mules under control, the Apache quickly cut the packs away, scattering the gold onto the bed of the dry creek. The Indians cared little for the gold but desired the mules for their meat, a favored delicacy.

Today, hikers along Camp Creek occasionally find gold nuggets in and near the stream, Peralta gold that the Apache carelessly dumped there nearly a century and a half ago.

THE GREAT NAVAJO SILVER MINE CAPER

BY MARYLOIS DUNN

As Navajo silverwork captured the attention of the settlers, traders, and soldiers who came into contact with the Indians, the white men learned of the legends of a gigantic river of silver. It was called Pish-la-ki, the fabled mother lode of the white metal from which the Navajos fashioned their beautiful jewelry. It was said to be somewhere in the Tse-bi-gay, the land "among the rocks" of Utah's Monument Valley, and a good many prospectors set out in search of it.

But the Navajo guardians of the River of Silver weren't about to share their silver with the white men. Their country was their most effective ally. It was a remote and desolate place, surrounded by hundreds of miles of desert in which desiccating winds blew and the relentless sun ruled the bright copper sky. The Navajo kept the locations of the few waterholes a closely guarded secret. Prospectors who ventured into the Tse-bi-gay were seldom seen alive again.

The Navajo weren't as warlike as most of the Southwestern tribes; in fact, their religion considered (and still considers) violence to be a sin of last resort. As late as the time of the Vietnam conflict, Navajo soldiers who went off to fight in the U.S. Army underwent the purifying ceremonies of the Enemy Way to protect them from the spiritual consequences of violence. It was and is the Navajo way to help people when they need help, and never to raise a fist in anger. But when Kit Carson killed or rounded up most of the Navajo nation and sent the survivors away from their beloved land, the small group that escaped to live in the Tse-bi-gay country didn't forget that betrayal.

The deaths of the first few prospectors to disappear into the desert were probably caused by their ignorance of the country. Then Oshkanninee, chief of the Tse-bi-gay Navajo, concocted a scheme that would allow him to secure his revenge on the invaders. He found or traded with other Indians for several pieces of high-grade silver ore; then he and some of his men showed these samples around Fort Defiance, Arizona, and other settlements to excite greed among those hungry for the "money rock." Eager would-be prospectors paid the Navajo a high price in advance for guide service to the fabulous treasure of Pish-la-ki, and the Navajo agreed to meet the prospectors at a rendezvous point on the desert. Of course, the "guides" instructed the prospectors to come fully equipped with pack horses and riding horses, food, tools, weapons, and ammunition.

The prospectors who took the bait never returned. More than twenty parties disappeared into the desert before the Army at Fort Defiance figured that something was going on. They chased Navajo shadows but were never able to trap the wily Oshkanninee.

A couple of prospectors, Mitchell and Merritt, survived their first foray into the Tse-bi-gay, and some say they actually found the mine. If they did, they didn't reveal its location, and they were killed on their second trip. There was no doubt that Oshkanninee was the culprit. Army troopers went pounding into the desert after him, but he outfoxed them. They followed his tracks into the San Juan River near Dandy Crossing and then lost them. Oshkanninee was never heard from again.

A pinnacle in Monument Valley is named Mitchell Butte in commemoration of one of the victims of the Navaho silver mine caper, but only the wind whispers the name of its originator, Oshkanninee.

A Navajo squash blossom necklace (photo by Tom Knowles)

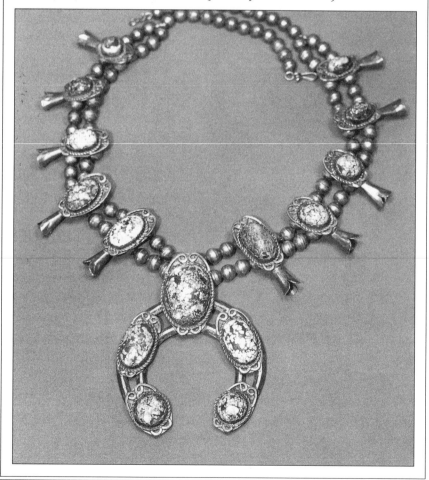

plored the region for several days, and he discovered several caches of the ore and bullion left behind by Peralta.

As for the age-old curse, the Dutchman, who had a practical turn of mind, refused to believe it. Even so, he slept lightly, remained armed at all times, and kept a constant lookout for the Apache.

Waltz bent at once to the task of panning ore from the small stream and excavating the gold from the nearby mine shafts. As he dug out the gold, Waltz allegedly cached large quantities of it in secret locations throughout the area. The only time he left the mountains was to travel to Phoenix to acquire supplies. Waltz paid for his purchases with the purest gold nuggets ever seen by anyone in the region. When townspeople inquired about the source of his gold, Waltz replied that no one would ever find his mine. It was a prophecy destined to prove true.

As more and more people became acquainted with the Dutchman's mining successes, some tried to follow him on his return trips into the Superstitions. The clever Waltz was normally able to elude his trackers, but it is believed that he often waited in ambush to kill those who coveted his gold. Many men entered the mysterious range never to return; this only added to the growing legend of the curse.

Waltz continued to operate his mines for about twenty years, but he eventually grew ill as old age and a hard life took their toll. He shared the secret directions to his mine with only one other person, Julia Thomas. While many researchers believe that the directions he provided to Thomas were accurate, they don't fit with information Waltz revealed over the years to others. People have assembled the bits and pieces of information about trails and landmarks into sets of concise directions, but unfortunately they all contradict one another.

Jacob Waltz finally died in 1891, at the home of Julia Thomas. His death launched one of the longest treasure quests in history. Hundreds of expeditions entered the Superstition Mountains in search of the Lost Dutchman Mine. Dozens of men lost their lives; many were undoubtedly the victims of the Apache, thirst, or snakebite, but there were those who believed they'd fallen prey to the curse.

Despite the thousands of articles, dozens of books, and many movies that have been produced concerning the Lost Dutchman Mine, the immense fortune remains hidden to this day. After Waltz died many claimed to have found the Lost Dutchman, but subsequent investigations proved their claims to be hoaxes. Some contend that Waltz covered up his mines; some believe they were obscured by landslides, and some believe that they never existed at all. But Jacob Waltz undeniably found gold in the Superstitions. The rest of the Dutchman's gold still lies hidden somewhere deep in the secret heart of the Superstition Mountains.

SOAPY SMITH, JACK LONDON AND THE LAST GOLD RUSH

BY BILL CRIDER

THE TIME WAS RIGHT FOR A NEW FRONTIER. IN THE LATE 1800s THE United States was still staggering under the burden of the worst economic depression in its history. There was mass unemployment, monopolies were crushing small businesses, and wheat farmers were being eaten alive by the railroads and the market manipulators. The big-city slums were a national scandal. The gilt had rubbed off the Gilded Age to expose the graft and corruption underneath.

Then came the news: there was gold in the Klondike country, a *lot* of gold. On July 14, 1897, the *Excelsior* steamed into San Francisco and disgorged a disreputable-looking gang of unkempt miners. They carried with them around a million dollars' worth of gold dust and nuggets packed into bottles, cans, bags, and even animal skins. Not far behind came the *Portland*, loaded with more miners and even more gold. Within what seemed like minutes, the rush was on. It was the beginning of a deluge that would eventually take nearly a quarter of a million would-be prospectors to the Canadian Yukon.

Of the 250,000 people who began the trip, perhaps 50,000 arrived at the gold fields. Few of them found gold, and fewer still found even enough to pay their expenses, probably fewer than one thousand. Not to say that no one got rich. Many did, but most of them were already on site in the Klondike when the gold was discovered. It was nearly a year after the first strike that the *Portland* and the *Excelsior* arrived in the States, and by the time the second wave of argonauts outfitted themselves and made the harrowing and savage journey to the Yukon, those who were already there had panned and mined most of the gold.

The first strike was made in August of 1896 by Robert Henderson, a Canadian, on a small, unnamed tributary of the Klondike River. Henderson told a friend, George Carmack, about his luck. Carmack, who was going salmon fishing with two Indian friends, Shookum Jim and Tagish Charlie, camped beside Rabbit Creek—renamed Bonanza—and panned out $700,000 worth of gold before he filed his own claim. The Dawson settlement in the Yukon was already a boomtown by the time Carmack debarked from the *Portland* in San Francisco.

Out-of-work Americans, adventurers, reporters, fortune hunters, con men, and crackpots didn't stop to consider the idea that many Canadians and Alaskans were already draining the Yukon of its treasure. They were determined to get to the gold fields as soon as possible, and by any means. Most went to Alaska by steamer from Seattle or San Francisco, and at least one enterprising soul planned to establish a balloon route to Dawson. Those who couldn't make the trip joined the syndicates and cooperatives which grubstaked one of their number for the expedition. Even a group of Chicago spiritualists sent a representative armed with maps provided by their familiar spirits.

There were two ways to get to Dawson after they reached Alaska. It was far easier and safer to take a steamer up the Yukon River, but it was slow, and most prospectors chose the overland route by way of Skagway or Dyea. From Skagway, they had to traverse the White Pass, which combined treacherous climbing with swamps. From Dyea, they had to cross the heartbreaking Chilcoot Pass. And that was only the beginning.

S KAGWAY WASN'T MUCH OF A TOWN, BUT IT GREW CONSIDERABLY with the invasion of thousands of people infected with Klondikitis. There were those who came there to get rich but weren't interested in the hard and chancy work of prospecting. One such man was Jefferson Randolph Smith, Jr. He arrived in Alaska in 1897 from Georgia via Leadville, Denver, and Creede, Colorado, where he had already earned the nickname Soapy. A consummate con man, Soapy Smith was a master of the shell game and three-card monte, but he was at his best with the soap swindle. He would sell bars of soap, some of which he claimed contained bills of from five to twenty dollars concealed within the wrappers. Sure enough, a man would buy a bar, unwrap it, and discover a twenty. Others would rush to buy, not suspecting that the lucky winner was one of Smith's shills.

This scam was so successful that Smith was able to purchase a number of saloons and gambling halls like Jeff's Place in Skagway, where all the games were crooked and all the drinks were watered. He also ran a telegraph service for miners to wire home when they left Skagway. His customers didn't notice that no wires left the office and all replies were collect. Those who failed to succumb to Soapy's scams and traps were often simply beaten and robbed by members of Smith's gang. Few prospectors made it through Skagway without paying Soapy's toll.

Soapy Smith became the Godfather of Skagway. He performed marriages and divorces, handled court cases, and set himself up as marshal and judge.

After about a year of Smith's rule, the town had had enough and formed a vigilance committee to oppose him. Soapy and his men marched to disperse the assembly and were confronted by the town surveyor, who was armed with a rifle. Smith and the surveyor struggled for the rifle, and both men were fatally wounded. At his funeral, spectators were moved to recall one of Smith's favorite sayings: "The way of the transgressor is hard—to quit."

Dyea had no Soapy Smith, but it was the gateway to the Chilcoot Pass, a portage of legendary difficulty. The experience of a young man named Jack London, later to become the famous author of *White Fang* and *The Call of the Wild*, is typical. He arrived in August of 1897 along with four partners, one of whom was his aging brother-in-law. The brother-in-law took one look at the pass and went home. Between them the four remaining partners had more than 5000 pounds of food and equipment, since each man crossing the Alaska-Yukon frontier was required by the Canadian government to have $500 in cash and one thousand pounds of food—if he didn't, he would be turned back by the Northwest Mounted Police. London had figured he could afford the going rate for Indian porters, which was six cents per pound of baggage at the time he left San Francisco. When he debarked at Dyea, the rate had risen to thirty cents a pound. Before he could catch his breath, the rate jumped to forty cents, then to fifty. Like many others, London and his partners had to carry their own packs.

A strong man could carry perhaps 150 pounds at a time through the mud and shale up four miles of "the worst road this side of Hell" to the head of the pass. It took them days of trip after grueling trip to haul all their food and supplies to the cache point. No one who made the trip even once ever forgot it. The last part of the climb was so steep and terrible that 50 pounds was the maximum load. The next stage of the journey, from the pass to Lake Lindeman, was equally arduous; laden with their 150-pound packs they waded through swamps of icy muck and not-quite-frozen streams. London witnessed sights that burned themselves into his memory. He saw men weary unto death perform incredible feats, and he saw the "Dead Horse Trail," where the worn-out horses abandoned by their owners "rotted in heaps." More than three thousand pack animals died on the trails to the gold fields.

From Lake Lindeman much of the trip was made by boat. Many of the Klondikers built their own vessels, and London and his partners christened their boat the *Yukon Belle*. They set sail just ahead of the winter freeze that trapped hundreds of prospectors, who then had to wait until the following spring. London's descriptions of the ice setting in the boat's wake are doubtless exaggerated, but they convey the urgency of his situation.

Next they faced the rapids and the foaming whirlpool of Lake Marsh. Many miners died as their boats were smashed on the rocks or overturned

... The West That Was

When Wagon Trails Were Dim, Charles M. Russell
(courtesy of National Cowboy Hall of Fame
and Western Heritage Center Oklahoma City)

The Wolfmen, Tom Lovell
(courtesy of National Cowboy Hall of Fame
and Western Heritage Center, Oklahoma City

Hunters Camp In The Big Horn, Frederic Remington
(courtesy of National Cowboy Hall of Fame
and Western Heritage Center, Oklahoma City)

Emigrants Crossing
The Plains,
Albert Bierstadt
(courtesy of National Cowboy Hall of Fame
and Western Heritage Center,
Oklahoma City)

Trouble On The Circle Diamond,
Olaf Seltzer
(courtesy of National Cowboy Hall of Fame
and Western Heritage Center,
Oklahoma City)

In From The Night Herd, Frederic Remington
(courtesy of National Cowboy Hall of Fame
and Western Heritage Center, Oklahoma City)

by the rapids, and many decided to lug their gear and boats overland. A huge traffic jam developed as the Klondikers hesitated, trying to decide which way to take. London believed that if he steered his boat with the current, the rush of water would carry it through. He was right; he managed to avoid the whirlpool and shoot the rapids. He had promised to return for another man and his wife if he was successful, and London steered the second boat through as well.

After London reached Lake Lebarge and fought his way through a terrible storm, he heard of a new strike at the Henderson River. He abandoned his plans to go to Dawson and instead set up camp near the Stewart River in a cabin once used by fur traders. Three days later, London and his partners struck gold—or what they thought was gold. When they traveled the eighty miles to Dawson to register their claims and get their dust assayed, they were told that their strike wasn't gold at all; it was mica. The disheartened group stayed in Dawson for nearly two months, enjoying what it had

WILD YEAST— SOURDOUGH

BY YVONNE CHEEK MARTINEZ

As precious to the prospector as the gold he mined was his sour dough starter. Because yeast is dormant in cold weather, the miner often protected the yeasty concoction from freezing temperatures by wrapping the sourdough crock in his pack. He might even keep it in an earthenware pot in a pouch hung from his neck, tucked under his long johns to keep the brewing mass alive with his body heat. Such measures must have lent a special air to those already aromatic gold prospectors who were little acquainted with soap and water.

Because of their attachment to their pots, Californian and Alaskan gold rushers were dubbed "sourdoughs." Without this valuable bread starter, the leavening ingredient for biscuits, flapjacks, cakes, and breads, the miners would have had only hardtack with their meat and fish dinners.

The first sourdoughs were not miners but the Egyptians of thousands of years ago. People discovered and used the principle of natural fermentation to make wine and beer long before some baker left out his or her dough (perhaps with the accidental addition of an alcoholic beverage) in a warm corner and forgot about it for a while. The yeast in the alcohol, combined with wild yeast spores in the air, bubbled and fermented, "rising" the dough. Cooked, the dough created not the unleavened flat bread of the time but a soft, airy-textured bread.

The sourdough could make his own starter with only a flour and water mixture left to sour in an earthenware pot for three to five days. If the mixture "caught" any wild yeast from the air, or if the miner added yeast-coated berries, bark, potato water, or vinegar, the dough became a bubbling mass with a yeasty or alcoholic aroma.

Prospectors and miners were not the only aficionados of sourdough. The chuck-wagon cook, the westward pioneers, and the frontiersman all depended on starters for that on which man cannot live alone but surely hasn't lived long without. Each time the cook baked she used only part of the starter, then she "freshened" the rest with more flour and water and set it aside to be used the next time. Some families claim that their starters are many years old, handed down from one generation to another. The older the starter, the more delectable the final product.

And what of the famous chuck-wagon biscuits? The cook put flour in a large washbasin-size pan, made a hole in the middle, and poured in the proper amount of bubbly sourdough batter. He worked in shortening, salt, maybe a little baking soda, and kneaded it smooth with flour and water to the desired consistency. Then he pinched off balls of dough and dipped them in melted fat at the bottom of a Dutch oven (or perhaps left the dough in a single disk). He then set the pot in a warm place for a half hour to rise before cooking. Baking bread with Dutch ovens was—and is—tricky. Only a few hot coals were placed on the bottom and several on top, so the biscuit bottoms wouldn't burn before the tops browned.

San Franciscans thought they'd achieved the height of sourdough cookery with the springy texture, thick, crisp crusts, and distinctive flavor of their real sourdough loaves. But the old sourdoughs of the Yukon and California gold fields would have challenged anyone to beat the biscuits and flapjacks they made from their treasured starters. No doubt they would thank the ancient Egyptian discoverer, who ensured that thousands of years later civilization thrived in the godforsaken places where gold was found. Civilization—in the form of real, honest-to-gosh, like-back-home bread.

to offer in the way of saloons and social life before they returned to their cabin.

Dawson was a new city, but its population was already swelling toward 25,000. Streetfront property was selling for $5,000 a foot along the main street, and it was evident that those who sold goods and services to the miners were the ones who were really getting rich. Recent newspapers sold for $3, dancehall girls could earn $100 a night just by pushing drinks and taking an occasional turn around the floor, and seamstresses earned almost as much. Desolate Dawson, built practically in a swamp, was muddy and plagued by pestilent mosquitoes, pariah dogs, and drunken miners, but it was booming.

The cabin to which London and his partners returned after their stay in Dawson was typical of the ones shared by the few miners lucky enough to have them. It was a square box thirteen feet on each side, intolerably cold except for the area around the stove. The inhabitants broke icicles off the ceiling to boil for water, and they kept their axes under the stove so the metal wouldn't become brittle and break.

Housekeeping in the cabin was not a delicate matter, and the miners' diet was mostly flapjacks, bacon, bread, and beans. Sugar was the commodity most missed, fresh fruit the item most needed. Scurvy was common, and London contracted a bad case. Beds were blanket-covered piles of pine boughs that were replaced when the needles fell off. The dirt floor was never swept, and the cook could start the fire by tossing a few handfuls of the wood shavings and pine needles that covered the floor into the stove. There were seldom windows to wash, but some miners made windows of tablet paper rubbed with bacon grease. Two or three inches of ice would form on the inside of these windows in cold weather. It was not a pleasant or comfortable life, and London's partnership, like many others, eventually split up under the pressure of hardship and cabin fever.

The great Klondike gold rush ended nearly as suddenly as it had begun. The streets of Dawson were choked with aimless, drifting miners who, like London, had found no gold at all. When their required half-year's supply of food was gone, they had little left to hold them in the north country. Boats traveling down the Yukon were as full of departing miners as the steamships heading for Dyea and Skagway had been the year before. By midsummer of 1899, the rush was over and the miners had headed for home. Most of them left poorer than when they'd arrived, but they had shared an experience that had changed their lives forever.

Jack London, who later mined his experiences for literary gold, spoke for all the Klondikers when he said, "It was in the Klondike that I found myself. There, nobody talks. Everybody thinks. You get your perspective. I got mine."

II. "FROM WHERE THE SUN NOW STANDS"

INTO THE SUNSET

BY ROBERT J. CONLEY

JUST ABOUT EVERYTHING WE READ ABOUT THE AMERICAN WILD WEST is written from the white man's point of view. The title of Theodore Roosevelt's book, *The Winning of the West*, became a catch phrase for the European settlement of the continent. From the Native American viewpoint, the experience about which Roosevelt wrote was the *losing* of the West. The brave American pilgrimage to the shining West was, for the American Indian, a retreat into the sunset.

The Americas were home to some 1,300 native civilizations. Though their world was no peaceful Garden of Eden, the peoples of these diverse cultures lived comfortably in it according to their own concepts of civilization. They had thousands of years of experience in what was to them not the New World, but their homeland. The Hopi oral tradition describes the destruction of three previous worlds before the world in which we now live. It's interesting to note, as Dr. Geoffrey Goodman points out in his *American Genesis*, that the Hopi tales correspond to the geological history of the area in which Hopi live. If in fact their legends are the result of experiences with actual geological activity, the Hopi have been where they are today for a quarter of a million years.

The Native American experience in the Old West can be characterized generally, but once that generalization is made, it then becomes necessary to take note of tribal and individual reactions to that experience. Though Europeans viewed the Indians as a monolithic and hostile group, the American Indians were actually a rich and diverse patchwork of cultures. The

Indians didn't think in generalities but in terms of tribal identity. This fundamental difference in thought was a crucial factor in the conflict between European and Native American cultures.

If the accidental arrival of Christopher Columbus on the island of San Salvador in 1492 was the first note from the Doomsday trumpet, the Westward expansion of the United States signaled for the American Indians an end to life as they knew it. It triggered their futile, last-ditch effort to save their world. No matter how peaceful or warlike their contacts with whites,

Buffalo Hunt by Indians, a C. F. Wimar painting completed in 1861 (courtesy of Kansas State Historical Society, Topeka, Kansas)

PREVIOUS PAGE:
The Hunting Party 1901, painting by Henry F. Farney (courtesy of Texas A&M Development Foundation, Bill & Irma Runyon Art Collections)

the effects were always devastating to Native American cultures and ways of life. For the Indians, the West was wild only because the white man made it so.

As early as 1805 and as far east as New York, this Indian view was eloquently expressed by Red Jacket of the Seneca in his reply to a missionary's request that they attend his sermon. "We are told," he said, "that you have been preaching to the white people in this place. These people are our neighbors. We are acquainted with them. We will wait a little while, and see what effect your preaching has upon them. If we find it does them good, makes them honest and less disposed to cheat Indians, we will consider again of what you have said."

The more perceptive Indians saw white settlement as a threat to everything they held dear, including their cultural and tribal identities. In 1753 in a letter to Peter Collinson, Benjamin Franklin reported this telling incident from a treaty negotiation between "one of our colonies and the Six Nations." Franklin wrote: "When everything had been settled to the satisfaction of both sides, and nothing remained but a mutual exchange of civilities, the English commissioners told the Indians they had in their Country a College for the instruction of Youth who were there taught various languages, Arts, and Sciences; that there was a particular foundation in favor of the Indians to defray the expense of the education of any of their sons who should desire to take the Benefit of it…The Indians…replied that…some of their Youths had formerly been educated in that College, but…that for a long time after they returned to their Friends, they were absolutely good for nothing."

By the time the Civil War concluded, Indians everywhere were well acquainted with the nature of the white men. The white men fought for no reason the Indians considered civilized. They were seen as an invading force, a strange people with no reverence for anything the Indians held sacred, and who stole what they wanted and destroyed the rest. That view hasn't changed to any great extent in the century that has passed since the end of the Indian Wars. Until recent years there was a certain point in the performance of the Eastern Cherokee ceremonial "booger dance" at which dancers wearing masks representing white men rushed into the arena, attempted to rape all the women, and started fights with all the men. It was a lingering reflection of the fear the time of the Wild West held for the Indians.

And yet stress produces diamonds. The Wild West was also a time of glory in which Indian cultures rose to great heights and experienced their finest hours. Heroes and great leaders emerged to face the challenge, men named Sitting Bull, Crazy Horse, Stone Calf, Red Cloud, Two Moons, Roman Nose, Satanta, Satank, Quanah Parker, Black Elk, Chief Joseph, Washakie, Plenty Coups, Ten Bears, Mangas Coloradas, Cochise, Geronimo, and a host

Cheyenne Indians sitting around a teepee in their village on the Washita river, Indian Territory, 1869 (courtesy of Kansas State Historical Society, Topeka, Kansas)

of others. They fought for their beloved way of life and faced the end of the world as they knew it. In many cases their eloquent words and thoughts on the losing of the West have been recorded for us.

Many Indians died; of those who survived some adapted, but all of them retained memories of what they had lost. In the aftermath of the Minnesota Sioux uprising during the Civil War, while the Minnesota Dakota (also known as the Santee Sioux) were being rounded up and punished for their activities, some small groups escaped into Canada to join Sitting Bull. Among them were the parents of a young man known as Ohiyesa. They decided to provide for their son's safety by sending him to a government Indian school. The boy finished school and went on to college, then to medical school. Ohiyesa, by then known as Dr. Charles Eastman, was the Pine Ridge agency's physician in 1890, where he witnessed the terror of the Wounded Knee massacre of the remnants of the Cheyenne and the Sioux by the 7th Cavalry. Eastman wrote several books that have remained fairly popular and in print over the years, among them *Indian Boyhood* and *From the Deep Woods to Civilization.*

Some Indians adapted to white ways only to reject them later in life. Wassaja, a small Apache boy taken captive following the destruction of his village in a Pima raid incited by white Arizonans, was later sold for thirty dollars to a traveling photographer from Chicago. The photographer renamed him Carlos Montezuma, took him back to Chicago, and subsequently gave the boy to a family in the city. Carlos somehow earned his way through medical school to become a successful Chicago general practitioner. Though wealthy and popular among the local gentry, Montezuma was tormented by something from his past. He abandoned his wealthy patients and practice to work among the city's poor. When his new work damaged his health and he diagnosed his illness as terminal, Dr. Carlos Montezuma returned to Arizona to die in an Apache wickiup, Wassaja once more. ■

THE SPANIARD'S GIFT: HORSES BY THE MILLION

BY DON COLDSMITH

THE SINGLE MOST IMPORTANT FACTOR IN THE DEVELOPMENT OF THE cultures of the American West was the advent of the horse. The entire economy of the Native American of the plains revolved around his use of the horse in the hunt. The term "Indian" conjures up visions of the Plains horseman dashing in pursuit of buffalo or fearlessly charging units of the U.S. cavalry in battle. Without question, the Plains tribes were the finest light cavalry of the nineteenth-century world. And yet, the golden age of the Indian horse cultures lasted only a few generations. Until the Spanish invaded the Americas, there were no horses in the Western Hemisphere.

There were precursors of the horse in the Americas, but they disappeared into extinction thousands of years before the first white men arrived. The great civilizations of the Americas developed with different beasts of burden. In South America, man domesticated the llama and other camel-like relatives, which weren't suited to riding in the hunt or in combat. The natives of North America had even fewer possibilities. Their only domesticated mammal was the dog. Some tribes developed two distinct breeds of dogs, one for meat, the other a more massively built animal for a beast of burden. It wasn't until Christopher Columbus' second voyage, when he established a horse- and cattle-breeding operation on the island of Santo Domingo, that the horse came to the New World.

The horse so impressed the people of the Americas that there were many striking stories of first contact. Some South and Central American tribes at first believed the horse and rider to be one; they were startled when the creature came apart and then reassembled itself. Even after this illusion of the centaur passed, Native Americans believed the horse to be a supernatural creature. To impress a party of visiting natives, Cortez separated a mare from her newborn foal. Her cries terrified the visitors, and Cortez told them the animal was crying out in anger against their disrespect. The ambassadors left and returned with many gifts, including cotton cloth for the "monsters" to lie on and chickens for them to eat. Ironically, the natives later captured Cortez' own black stallion. They deified the horse and took him to the temple where they worshiped him as a god. Garlanded with flowers, he was treated with the greatest reverence as he starved to death on a poultry diet.

Horses were revered by their Spanish masters as well. Diaz, the scribe who accompanied Cortez, wrote: "one (horse) is worth a hundred men." Cortez himself used an entire paragraph to record the death of a favorite mare.

MOST TRIBES OF NORTH AMERICA REMEMBER WHERE, WHEN, and under what circumstances they first saw the horse. It was a turning point, an event that brought about startling changes in their way of life. The Nez Perce changed in a generation from salmon fishermen to buffalo hunters of the plains. The Crow, previously farmers, divided into two groups. One group stayed with the more pastoral pursuits; the other became nomadic hunters who in a short while competed even with the mighty Lakota.

The Plains tribes saw the horse as a magical creature, superior to their traditional beast of burden. It was obviously a kind of dog because it also served man, but a marvelous dog "as big as an elk" wasn't just a dog. It was the "elk-dog," the "wonderful dog," even the "god-dog."

The Crow obtained their first horses from the Shoshoni, the Blackfoot from the Snake and Flathead Indians. The Coeur d'Alene point to an exact spot where they saw their first horse, which was ridden by a Kalispel. The Ponca remember that they were at war with Comanche, who to their great surprise charged them on horseback. After the truce, they traded some of their weapons for their first horses. The Kiowa scout who saw the first horses described them as dogs that were as big as elk and wore a turtle on each of their feet.

Students of the West might wonder where all the horses came from. Many early writers were struck by the huge numbers of wild horses they saw on the plains. In 1580 Don Juan Gauray reported that the plains of Paraguay were "teeming" with wild horses. As early as 1530, John Cabot said he sighted wild horses in the La Plata region of Central America, but his report should be taken with a grain of salt—it also mentioned cities of gold and mines of precious gems, no doubt in an effort to impress his sponsor, the king of Spain.

Members of the Lewis and Clark Expedition wrote at length not only about the great numbers but the quality of the horses they saw, comparing them to "fine English chargers." Other explorers recorded that wild horses were in some areas "more numerous than the buffalo." The Southern buffalo herd alone ran to the millions. That's a lot of horses. In recent years some writers have posed a question: Could the known introductions of the horse have possibly produced these huge herds of wild horses in the West?

Don Pedro de Mondoza released seven horses in Paraguay in 1535, in the area mentioned by Gauray forty-five years later. In 1541, as Coronado crossed the southern plains, a hailstorm caused "nearly all" of his company's twelve hundred horses to break away, and "many" were never recovered. As De Soto explored what is present-day Louisiana in 1543, he released several animals rather than attempt to load them back on ship.

Just how rapidly could these horses—and those released in similar incidents—reproduce? Let's take a theoretical pair, a mare and a stallion of breeding age. At the end of ten years we can expect them to have ten offspring. Half of these are females, and each female over two years old also reproduces. At the end of ten years, we might have as many as twenty-six horses, including the original pair. Let's say six have succumbed to accidents, predators, and age. There are still twenty, of which half are females. Allow each mare ten years of reproductive life, though many mares will double that.

By the end of the next ten years we could have two hundred horses, two thousand by the end of the third decade, twenty thousand by the end of the fourth. After five decades we reach almost a quarter million, easily enough to account for Don Juan Gauray's "teeming" wild horses—all from Mondoza's original seven. By the mid-1600s, a single pair lost by Coronado in the Southern plains in 1541 could have grown to twenty billion horses! Even a more conservative estimate accounts for enough horses to provide every warrior on the plains with an excellent mount, enough for the cowboys and professional wild-horse breakers who followed them.

And so did the chance importation of a foreign species not only form the cultures of the American West but change the course of history. ▪

Rock-a-bye Papoose

BY FRANCIS L. FUGATE

SOMEWHERE IN THE WESTERN HEMISPHERE, WELL BEFORE THE DAWN OF recorded history, an ingenious aborigine invented the cradleboard baby carrier. This marvelously convenient device could be carried on the mother's back, hung on a tree branch, propped against a rock, carried on horseback, or laid on the ground—a portable day-care center and timesaver. It's one of those ironic twists of history that the European invaders discouraged the use of cradleboards among the Indians as part of their campaign to "civilize the savages" and then in the 1960s reinvented the piggyback baby carrier.

It may have taken a period of more than a thousand years for the concept of the baby carrier to spread across the North American continent. As the Indian craftsmen took increasing pride in their skill, and as they shrouded the act of parenthood and childbirth with complex rituals, the basic design of the baby carrier evolved and developed its own elaborate ornamentation. Early archaeological artifacts reveal that the first baby carriers were crude platters woven of flexible sticks and withes, covered with animal skins. Such work has been discovered in the caves of the Basket Makers, a Southwestern culture that ended about A.D. 700.

On the basis of the radical difference in head shape, archaeologists at first thought that the people of the Pueblo culture that followed the Basket Makers were a new breed of broad-headed people who had moved into the area and had merged with the previous culture. Further study of skeletal remains and artifacts revealed that this was not the case. Rather, as they learned to make pottery and to improve their dwellings, the Indians started making their baby carriers out of wood—literally, cradle*boards*. Because there was no padding, the infant's head flattened in back and bulged at the sides to create the broad, deformed head that the researchers had at first taken for a genetic trait.

Though by no means as widespread as the use of baby carriers, the deliberate deformation of heads was a common practice of many tribes, including the use of cradleboards, padding, and bindings designed to produce a particularly desired head shape. Some may consider this a cruel or even uncivilized practice, but how does it differ from using modern elective surgery to alter the shape of one's nose or breast, or to remove one's wrinkles, or allowing a total stranger in a shopping mall to punch holes in one's earlobes? Shortly before the end of the nineteenth century, a Kwakiuti Indian gave a Smithsonian interviewer an answer that could explain the apparent cosmetic foibles of any culture: "So the child will grow up with a round face, *in the way the Indians want to have it.*"

The construction and use of cradles was tied to the often elaborate ceremonies surrounding the birth of a child. These ceremonies differed from tribe to tribe according to the social structure and lifestyle of each, but many tribes attributed magical powers to the umbilical cord. The mother preserved the cord and used it according to tribal customs; evidence indicates that this practice was extant as far back as the early Basket Maker culture. The high infant mortality rate among the Basket Makers provided archaeologists with many specimens. Babies were usually buried in their cradles, which were padded with juniper bark diapers and covered with fur blankets made of the white belly skins of rabbits. Babies were swaddled to the crude stick-and-reed cradles with soft fur cords. Pads of cornhusks, grass,

A Mescalero Apache mother and child, circa 1910, in southern New Mexico (Aultman Collection, courtesy of El Paso Public Library)

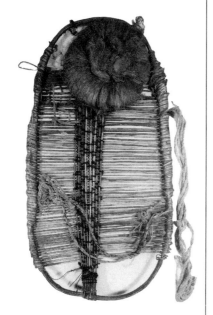

or bark wrapped in prairie dog skins were used to prevent umbilical hernia. The dried umbilical cord was tied to the corner of the outer blanket used in the cradle.

In the 1830s, American artist and ethnologist George Catlin realized that the American Indian cultures were dying out and resolved to record their types and customs against oblivion. From 1832 to 1839 he traveled extensively in North and South America, living among the Indians and making copious notes. He produced hundreds of sketches and paintings.

Catlin documented the Chinook practice of squeezing and flattening an infant's head "by placing its back on a board, or a thick plank, to which it is lashed by thongs, to a position from which it cannot escape, and the back of the head supported by a soft pillow, made of moss or rabbit skins, with an inclined piece (hinged to the top of the cradleboard), resting on the forehead of the child; being every day drawn down a little tighter by means of a cord, until it at length touches the nose; thus forming a straight line from the crown to the head to the end of the nose."

While most white observers viewed this seemingly cruel practice with horror, there was a general agreement that it did not cause much pain and "those who had the head flattened are in no way inferior in intellectual powers to those whose heads are in their natural shape."

Among the Sioux, Catlin found elaborately embroidered cradles that were decorated with porcupine-quill embroidery in the form of men and horses. A broad band of elastic wood passed around in front of the child's face to protect it in case of a fall. Brightly colored bangles, toys, and tinkling shells hung from the hoop to amuse the child. In addition to providing protection from falls and random bumps, the hoop supported a cover during cold or rainy weather, and in the summer it held netting to keep flies and insects away from the baby.

The trinkets dangling from the hoop inevitably included an amulet containing the child's umbilical cord, dried and rolled to the size of a pea. It hung before the child's face as a talisman to bring good luck and long life. When Catlin traded for these trinkets as additions to his collection of Indian artifacts, the mother would invariably cut open the case and retrieve the "sacred medicine" from its protective ball of moss or cotton. The Indian mother firmly believed that parting with the dried umbilicus would endanger the health of her child.

Chippewa mothers stoutly maintained that keeping the umbilical cord insured wisdom for their children, that it would keep them from "becoming foolish." Some said that if the cord was not kept, the child "would always be searching for something." Particularly among the Chippewa, the cradle charms would include one with a spiderweb design. It consisted of a small hoop about three inches in diameter and filled with a web woven from nettle-stalk twine, dyed a dark red with bloodroot juice and the inner bark of the wild plum. It was said that the charm would "catch everything evil as a spider's web catches and holds everything that comes into contact with it." A similar design used by the Pawnee symbolized Spider Woman, a deity who controlled the buffalo.

If a child died in infancy, its mother would carefully preserve the case containing the umbilical cord, treasuring it for years. Catlin observed a custom among the Sioux in which, after the child was buried, the disconsolate mother filled the cradle with black porcupine quills and feathers. She carried this "mourning cradle" with as much care as if the infant were still alive, often for a year or more, chatting to the empty cradle as familiarly and affectionately as if her child still occupied it.

It was usually the father's responsibility to construct or obtain the baby carrier, but he tended to wait until after the birth of the child. This was not procrastination but a practical delay for people accustomed to high infant mortality. A Yakutat Tlingit woman expressed her disapproval of a baby shower given in March for a baby not expected until June: "Too many things might happen."

Among some cultures, cradle materials were selected with great care for their spiritual significance. The Acoma preferred boards made from a tree that had been struck by lightning. Cradle materials were often taken to medicine men who "cured" (i.e., exorcised) them and charged them with spiritual power.

WHEN A BABY WAS OLD ENOUGH TO WALK, THE CRADLE WAS USUALLY abandoned. The Northwestern tribes, such as the Coeur d'Alene, substituted a skin carrier or baby bag as the child grew older. Finally, before the child was completely afoot, mothers would cradle their children on their backs under their robes. An observer described the procedure used by the Omaha: "When a child was old enough to cling to its mother it was thrown over her shoulder, where it hugged her tightly around the neck while she adjusted her robe or blanket. The robe was tied by a girdle around the waist, the upper part was placed over the clinging child, and the ends were crossed in front and tucked into the girdle. Then the mother gave a gentle but decided shrug, and the child loosened its arms and settled into its bag-like bed, from out of which it winked and peered at the world or fell fast asleep as the mother trudged about her business."

Though early white settlers tended to disparage any Indian practice, most had to admit the efficacy of the cradleboard. Catlin noted, "The child in its earliest infancy, has its back lashed to a straight board…by lacing strings, which hold it in a straight and healthy position…which, no doubt, has a tendency to produce straight

OPPOSITE:
Example of padded cradle board, circa A.D. 1–750 (courtesy of National Park Service)
BELOW:
George Catlin's portrait of a Chinook mother and child, her own head flattened and the infant undergoing the process (courtesy of Francis L. Fugate)

limbs, sound lungs, and long life." In 1743 Mark Catesby said of Indian cradles in his *Natural History of Carolina, Florida, and Bahama Islands*, "They cause a singular erectness in the Indians, nor did I ever see a crooked Indian in my life."

The name of one modern baby carrier, the Pak-a-Poose, takes a small step toward acknowledging its debt to its true originators. But of the variety of baby backpacks, sidepacks, and frontpacks on today's market, none is equipped with all the conveniences of the most advanced Indian cradleboards—one of which was a drain for male children which freed mothers from the chore of frequent diaper changes. ■

THE LEADERS OF THE PEOPLE

SITTING BULL, THE VISIONARY WARRIOR

BY BILL CRIDER

SITTING BULL WAS THE GREAT CHIEF AND MEDICINE MAN OF THE Hunkpapa Sioux. A visionary and mystic as well as a warrior, he presided over the defeat of Custer at the Little Big Horn and lived to become a feared symbol of the Indians' resistance to the white man.

Sitting Bull was at first named Slow because of his careful mannerisms, but he was awarded his father's name when, at the age of fourteen, he first counted coup on a Crow warrior. Soon afterward he began to experience dreams and visions that he believed foretold his eventual leadership of the Sioux. His belief was confirmed in the 1860s when be became chief of the Hunkpapa. In the latter part of the decade, when many Sioux chiefs signed an agreement with the government and went to the reservation in South Dakota, Sitting Bull refused to sign. He and his people remained in the Powder River country to the west in an unceded area. Sitting Bull proved to be right in refusing to believe that the agreement meant anything to the government. By 1874, whites were already pushing into both the unceded area and the reservation. In one skirmish with the whites, Sitting Bull walked out between the opposing forces, sat on the ground, and calmly smoked his pipe. Not a single bullet touched him. The incident solidified his fame.

One source of treaty problems was Lieutenant Colonel George Armstrong Custer, who spread rumors of a great gold strike in the Black Hills after he led a scouting expedition there. Miners poured into the region, which forced the government into attempting to purchase it. But the Black Hills contained the last great sacred place still held by the Plains Indians, so the Sioux set an impossibly high price. The government replied by ordering all Sioux out of the unceded lands and onto the reservation; after a certain date all Indians who remained outside the reservation were to be considered "hostiles." Sitting Bull declined the invitation, as did other chiefs. The famous Indian fighter General George Crook led the 1876 campaign against them. Thanks to the Army's actions and the Indians' willingness to defend the Black Hills, Sitting Bull was able to rally all six tribes of the Sioux as well as the Arapaho, Cheyenne, and others into a giant army to do battle with the whites.

Early in June 1876, Sitting Bull performed a sun dance on Rosebud Creek. The participant in this ceremony underwent physical pain and torture (in Sitting Bull's case, fifty cuts in each arm, from wrist to shoulder) and then danced until completely exhausted, going without food and water and staring into the sun until he received his vision. Sitting Bull danced for three days. In the end he was rewarded by the prophecy of a great victory over the white men. He saw the horse soldiers riding through the Sioux nation not as victors but with their heads bowed in defeat. The prophecy was fulfilled on June 25, when the Indians annihilated the troops commanded by Custer at the Little Big Horn river. Sitting Bull didn't participate but apparently watched over the battle, using his medicine to protect the warriors as Crazy Horse and the other war chiefs wiped out Custer's troops.

After the great victory over Custer, the Indians' luck turned. The vengeful U.S. army hunted them down in their small winter camps and destroyed them even as the buffalo hunters destroyed their way of life. One by one the chiefs surrendered—even Crazy Horse. But Sitting Bull continued to resist. In 1877 he left the U.S. altogether, taking his people into Canada so as not to become a reservation Indian. He and his people remained in the land of the Grandmother (Queen Victoria) for four years.

U.S. soldiers couldn't pursue him there, but at the same time he couldn't cross the border to raid and hunt. There was little game, and most of the people missed their homeland. By 1881 fewer than two hundred Sioux remained with Sitting Bull, most of them his relatives. He requested aid from the Canadian government but didn't receive it. Seeing no other choice, he led his few remaining followers back across the border and surrendered.

Now that he was a "tame" Indian, Sitting Bull experienced a strange kind of fame that he had never known before and probably hardly understood. A showman named Alvaren Allen took him out on tour, displaying him to

Sitting Bull, Bismarck, Dakota, 1885

Sitting Bull (courtesy of U.S. Signal Corps, National Archives)

curious crowds who came to see the "Slayer of Custer." He toured as well with Buffalo Bill Cody's famous Wild West; he, Cody, and Cody's main attraction, Annie Oakley (whom he named Little Sure Shot), became good friends. When Sitting Bull decided to retire from show business, Cody presented him with a white hat and a gray horse trained to perform circus tricks.

Cody tried to lure the old chief back in 1887 to perform in London before Queen Victoria, but Sitting Bull refused to go. The government was up to its old tricks, trying to buy Sioux lands at the ridiculously low price of fifty cents an acre. Sitting Bull was defiant again, peaceably this time. Finally, in 1889, the government offered $1.25 an acre, the price at which the Sioux had originally planned to sell the land. The chiefs gave in, except for Sitting Bull.

That same year a new Indian religion developed in the West. A Paiute named Wovoka had a vision in which it was revealed to him that in a very short time the Indian dead would arise. Living Indians would never die, but the whites would disappear. The buffalo would return. Wovoka's doctrine was nonviolent in the extreme, requiring only that his adherents perform the ritual Ghost Dance to bring back the past. The Sioux who followed Wovoka adopted the dance of his vision but not his aversion to violence. They wanted to help God make the whites disappear, and they created "ghost shirts" with magic patterns said to be impervious to the white man's bullets. The obvious Christian overtones of Wovoka's religion notwithstanding, Sitting Bull learned the Ghost Dance and helped spread it among the Hunkpapa Sioux.

None of this activity was calculated to soothe the whites, and Indian agent James McLaughlin decided that it would be best to have Sitting Bull arrested and removed from the reservation. On December 15, 1890, forty-three Indian police, called "metal breasts" because of their badges, went to Sitting Bull's cabin to arrest him. An angry crowd gathered outside, and in the chaos that followed, the Indian police shot Sitting Bull and killed him.

The noise of the firing seemed to bring back memories of Cody's Wild West to Sitting Bull's horse, which began to perform its tricks, bowing and dancing. The fighting stopped as the awed combatants watched the horse perform the Ghost Dance. Then the horse wandered off and the fighting resumed. By the time the battle ended, four of the Indian policemen were dead, along with seven of Sitting Bull's followers. The Army moved to put down the Ghost Dance cult and finished off the last Sioux resistance two weeks later at the resulting massacre at Wounded Knee.

Sitting Bull's body was put in a coffin and buried at Fort Yates. The *Bismarck Daily Tribune*'s cynical obituary read, "He's a Good Indian Now." ■

THE LEADERS OF THE PEOPLE

COCHISE OF THE CHIRICAHUA

BY BILL CRIDER

Cochise, chief of the Chiricahua Apache (courtesy of Western History Collections, University of Oklahoma Library)

COCHISE WAS THE CHARISMATIC CHIEF OF THE CHIRICAHUA APACHE, whose territory included the Dragoon and Chiricahua mountain ranges in Arizona. He became known to a generation of Americans through the movie *Broken Arrow* (1950), in which he was portrayed by Jeff Chandler, and the television series of the same name (1956–60), in which Michael Ansara took the role. Both movie and series were based on the novel by Elliott Arnold and presented Cochise as a sympathetic and even heroic figure, as indeed he was.

For years, in fact, Cochise did little to harass the white man, preferring to devote his attentions to the Mexican states of Sonora and Chiricahua, home of the Apache's traditional enemies for hundreds of years. When the Butterfield Stage Line sought permission to cross Cochise's territory in 1858, he granted it, and even negotiated a contract to supply the stage stations with firewood.

For three years the stagecoaches ran unmolested, and a tentative friendship grew up between the Apache and the whites. Then Second Lieutenant George N. Bascomb came along to change things. At a meeting in his tent, Bascomb accused Cochise of stealing some horses and kidnapping a young boy. Cochise laughed at the charges, explaining that the Chiricahua were at peace and suggesting that some other group was responsible. That seems to have been the case, but the infuriated Bascomb, who had secretly had his soldiers surround the tent, declared that Cochise and the five members of his family who accompanied him were to be held prisoner until the boy was returned. Cochise drew his knife, slit the tent, and escaped, though his family members couldn't follow and remained hostage.

Possibly hoping to work out an exchange, Cochise at once rounded up some hostages of his own, including a Butterfield man, James F. Wallace, and two men who were traveling through Apache Pass with a wagon train. The Apache disposed of the eight Mexican teamsters with the train in an unpleasant way—they tied them to the wagon wheels and burned the wagons. Cochise offered to trade his hostages for Bascomb, making no mention of the dead Mexicans, and Bascomb agreed to the deal but only if the kidnapped boy were included. Eventually Cochise lost his patience and tortured

"We will not have the wagons which make a noise in the hunting grounds of the buffalo. If the palefaces come farther into our land, there will be scalps of your brethren in the wigwams of the Cheyennes. I have spoken."

ROMAN NOSE OF THE CHEYENNE, TO GENERAL PALMER

and killed his hostages, mutilating them beyond recognition. Upon discovering the bodies, Bascomb hanged the three adult males among his own hostages.

This incident reflected in miniature the course of Apache-white relations for the next ten years, during which Cochise and others terrorized the Southwest. Although there is no way of arriving at an accurate accounting, the cost in lives was undoubtedly high as Cochise and his small raiding parties perfected the art of guerrilla warfare. And Cochise's efforts to eradicate the white man only increased in intensity early in 1863 after the treacherous murder of his father-in-law, Mangas Coloradas. Whether or not he was responsible for all the raids, Cochise was the chief whose name was the most well known, so he received the credit—or the blame. By 1871, the commissioner of Indian affairs sent messages asking Cochise to meet with him in Washington. From experience, Cochise didn't trust either the government or its representatives. He carried on as he had been doing.

One white man whom Cochise did trust was Tom Jeffords, known to the Indians as Taglito, the Red Beard. Jeffords was a superintendent of U.S. mails, and he had lost fourteen drivers to the Apache. He decided that the only way to stop the slaughter was to speak to Cochise in person. He went alone into the Apache camp, handed his weapons to a woman, then walked over and sat beside Cochise, asking, after a respectful interval of silence, for safe passage for his drivers. Cochise argued that the drivers carried harmful military messages, but Jeffords explained that such messages were handled by couriers, not the mail service. Believing that a man of such courage could tell only the truth, Cochise agreed not to hamper the mail delivery. He and Jeffords became good friends, and Jeffords paid numerous visits to the Apache camp.

It was Tom Jeffords who eventually brought an end to Cochise's war with the U.S. government. In 1872 President Grant sent General Oliver O. Howard to Arizona. The one-armed Civil War officer's mission was to make peace with the Apache. Howard predictably asked for help from the only white man who had any chance of finding the Apache chief. Jeffords agreed to help only if no soldiers went with him, and Howard agreed. Their party consisted of five men: Jeffords, Howard, Howard's aide, and two Apache.

They located Cochise in a valley in the Dragoon Mountains. For almost two weeks they negotiated. Howard proposed a reservation on the Rio Grande. Cochise insisted on remaining where he belonged, in the mountain ranges where his people had lived since time immemorial. Howard was quite favorably impressed with the chief and his people, though Cochise had some difficulty in understanding why the white general kept dropping down to one knee at crucial moments. When it was finally explained to him that the general was praying, he accepted the action.

Eventually Cochise's arguments swayed Howard. He allowed the Chiricahua to keep their weapons and their traditional territory near Apache Pass, on the condition that Cochise guarantee safety for the whites. There was only one more issue—by law, a white man had to fill the appointment as Indian agent. That was fine with Cochise as long as the agent was Taglito. Jeffords didn't want the job, but he took it at his friend's request. He insisted that he be given sole authority to deal with the Chiricahua as well as the right to bar white intruders from the reservation.

Cochise kept his word, but unfortunately he lived for only two more years. In 1874 he fell ill of a wasting disease (probably cancer) which the doctors could neither diagnose nor cure. At the end, suffering intense pain,

ROMAN NOSE, DOG SOLDIER OF THE CHEYENNE

BY BILL CRIDER

Moquinto, better known as Roman Nose, was a powerful figure both physically (six feet, three inches tall, 230 pounds) and politically among the Dog Soldier Society of the Southern Cheyenne. Though he was not a chief, both whites and Indians recognized him as a great warrior and leader. The young men of the Cheyenne were as likely to follow him as their acknowledged chiefs.

Roman Nose was best known for his powerful protective medicine. During the summer of 1865, White Bull, a medicine man, received a vision of a magical war bonnet. He told Roman Nose to go to a nearby lake and dwell among the water spirits, and for four days the warrior drifted on a raft in the lake, forgoing both food and water, fasting and praying. When Roman Nose returned to camp, White Bull made the bonnet that he had seen in the vision and presented it to the warrior. It contained so many eagle feathers that it nearly reached the ground, as well as a buffalo horn, a kingfisher skin, and a bat. This bonnet would protect Roman Nose from harm as long as he obeyed the taboos set down by White Bull, one of which stipulated that the warrior was not to eat food that had been touched by metal utensils.

In September of that year, Roman Nose, protected by his medicine, performed one of his most remembered feats of bravery. Confronting a group of soldiers in a line in front of their wagons, he rode so close to them that he could easily distinguish their faces. He rode along the length of the line as the soldiers fired at him. When he reached the end of the line, he turned and rode back. He repeated the process several times, and although he had his horse shot out from under him, Roman Nose was untouched. To the Cheyenne, this confrontation became known as Roman Nose's Fight.

Two years later, at Beecher's Island in Colorado, Roman Nose had by accident eaten bread touched by a metal fork, and the time for battle came before he could complete his purification ceremonies. Though he wore his war bonnet, legend has it he rode out knowing that he would die. On his first charge against the soldiers, he was shot in the spine. He survived until nightfall but died before morning.

The death of Roman Nose devastated the young men of the Cheyenne. He had been one of their greatest and most inspiring leaders, and without him they had little hope. The Cheyenne always remembered the Battle of Beecher's Island as the Fight When Roman Nose Was Killed.

Cheyenne torture ceremony (courtesy of Kansas State Historical Society, Topeka, Kansas)

Cochise made one last request of his friend—he asked Jeffords to ride to Fort Bowie for the Army surgeon. Both men knew the chief would be dead before Jeffords could return. And so he was.

The night of Cochise's death, his warriors painted his body with sacred signs, covered him with a red blanket, and took him into the secret heights of the mountains. They lowered his body into a crevice in a location they never revealed to others, not even to Taglito. ∎

THE LEADERS OF THE PEOPLE

GERONIMO, THE LAST APACHE

BY BILL CRIDER

GERONIMO WASN'T A HEREDITARY CHIEF—HE GAINED HIS POSITION through his ferocity and skill in battle. In fact, Geronimo wasn't even his name. He was called Goyathly, One Who Yawns, until he went into battle with the Mexican troops who had treacherously killed his wife and child. For some reason one of the soldiers cried out "Geronimo," the Spanish version of Jerome. No one knows why the soldier cried out the name, or why it stuck, but the mere mention of the name Geronimo was for more than thirty years enough to strike fear into the hearts of Mexican and American alike.

Sometime after this battle Geronimo took a Chiricahua wife—he was previously a member of the Membreno—and lived under the leadership of the great Chiricahua chief Cochise. He didn't accept Cochise's tolerance for certain whites, and even some Apache considered him to be particularly bloodthirsty, but no one ever doubted his courage and determination. For years he rode on raiding parties with various bands, especially when they raided into Mexico, for his hatred for the Mexicans never diminished.

After Cochise died in 1874 his leadership passed to his sons, but they were never able to exert the kind of influence and power held by their father. Cochise and his white friend Tom Jeffords had been able to restrain the Apache, to keep them on the reservation at Apache Pass, but without Cochise to prevent it the raiding broke out again. In 1876 the government relieved Jeffords of his position as agent and removed the Chiricahua to the 2.5-million-acre White Mountain Reservation in eastern Arizona. The new administrator, John Clum, headquartered at the desolate San Carlos agency.

Cochise's son Taza agreed to the move, but not all his people followed him. Many of them escaped into Mexico to hide in the Sierra Madres. Geronimo was among the first to jump the reservation.

For the next few years Geronimo conducted an off-and-on affair with reservation life. When he walked in to see Clum at the agent's request in 1877, Clum had him clapped in irons and taken to San Carlos. It was a high point in Clum's career, but he soon resigned in protest against the Army's move to quarter troops at San Carlos as a "precautionary measure."

San Carlos was a miserable spot—hot, sterile, dry, and apparently useless. The agents cheated the Apache out of their supply allotments or replaced their rations with substandard food. Settlers and miners encroached on the little land that wasn't worthless. After a year of this treatment Geronimo escaped again to Mexico and resumed his raids. He stayed off the reservation until the devastating winter of 1880. In the spring, he led his starving band back to the reservation.

Again he didn't stay put for long. In 1881 a skirmish broke out because of white concern over a new mystical leader, Nakaidoklini. The mystic was killed in the fighting, and Geronimo fled the reservation. For two years he and other renegade leaders raided both Arizona and Mexico, and in March 1883 one band attacked a ranch only ten miles from Tombstone. The same raiders struck a few days later near Lourdsburg, New Mexico. This time they killed a federal judge, H. C. McComas, and his wife, and kidnapped their six-year-old son. The boy died later, a victim of starvation, neglect, or murder at the hands of the band's women.

These events finally forced the Mexican and American authorities into an agreement that allowed the soldiers of both countries to cross the border in pursuit of Apache raiders. The U.S. picked General George Crook, one of the most successful leaders of previous Indian campaigns, to deal with the Apache. He added Apache scouts to his forces, experienced warriors who were glad to join to relieve the boredom of reservation life. His move paid off—the scouts almost at once discovered the mountain hideouts where the renegades had thought themselves safe. Crook's successful surprise attack on the camp of a minor chief called Chato soon brought all the others, including Geronimo, to the negotiation table. Geronimo, now the acknowledged leader of the free Apache, was impressed by Crook's courage. Geronimo surrendered, asking for two months to bring in all of his people. Crook agreed, and Geronimo complied, though it took him nine months instead of two.

Once more Geronimo remained on the reservation for only a short time. In 1885 he and a number of other chiefs defied the government's ban on *tiswin*, the weak beer the Apache brewed from corn, and went on a drunken spree. They expected to be punished, but either Crook wasn't actually

In his later years Geronimo made his living by posing for and selling photographs such as this one. Here he is wearing an inappropriate ceremonial head-dress; he has a Walker Colt (or copy) revolver thrust through an ironically empty ammunition belt. (courtesy of Moody Texas Ranger Library)

notified of the offense or he let it pass. Geronimo grew uneasy and began to fear that the whites were up to some trick. He gathered his followers, cut the telegraph line, and headed for the Sierra Madres. On the way his band attacked a ranch and killed the owner, his wife, and their infant child. The Apache also hanged the rancher's five-year-old daughter from a meat hook. She died soon afterward.

Geronimo's band was little more than thirty warriors and some women and children. Against them Crook mounted three thousand men, one of the largest forces yet assembled for an Indian campaign, but this was mostly for show. Crook relied as before on his Apache scouts to locate Geronimo; they did, early in 1886. Geronimo agreed to speak with Crook, whose orders were to kill the Apache if they offered anything less than complete surrender. The government dictated that those who did surrender would be sent to a reservation in Florida. Geronimo asked that their stay in Florida be limited to two years, after which his people would be returned to Arizona. Crook agreed but was overruled by his superiors in the War Department. Geronimo took twenty warriors, eighteen women and some children and slipped away in the night. Crook resigned his command.

Crook's replacement, General Nelson Miles, pursued the pitiful remnant of Apache greatness with five thousand troops. Despite these incredible odds, even despite the thirty heliograph stations Miles established to flash messages across southeastern Arizona and into Mexico, Geronimo raided almost at will for eight more months, killing cattlemen, settlers, and soldiers while he suffered not a single casualty to his band.

Miles finally sent an emissary, Lieutenant Charles Gatewood, to negotiate with Geronimo much as Tom Jeffords had negotiated with Cochise. Gatewood located the chief by trailing an Apache woman who had gone into a Mexican town to get mescal for Geronimo's men.

Gatewood, accompanied by only one scout, went into the Apache camp, and there he was met by Geronimo himself. Gatewood informed the chief that his family and the other Chiricahua had already been moved to Florida and promised that if he surrendered he would be sent to join them there. This news seemed to stun Geronimo, and he agreed to surrender to General Miles in person. On September 4, 1886, Miles arrived at Skeleton Canyon and accepted the final surrender of the last of the wild Apache. The long and bloody war was over.

For a time after his surrender Geronimo was incarcerated in a tower at Fort Sam Houston in San Antonio, Texas. At last he was transported to Pensacola, Florida, but only a sad remnant of the Chiricahua awaited him there. Many of his people had already died in the cloying humidity so different from the climate of the mountains and deserts of their homeland. Many of their children had died elsewhere, at the Indian school in Carlisle, Pennsylvania, where they were forced to learn English and give up their tribal ways.

In 1894 Geronimo and the remaining Apache were moved to Fort Sill, Oklahoma, where the old chief, by then a broken man, lived the life of a good reservation Indian. He appeared in Theodore Roosevelt's 1901 inaugural parade, where he took part in roping contests. He'd learned the white man's way the hard way, and made a small living by selling cheap bows and arrows and autographing photos.

Looking at those sad photos, one searches in vain for a spark of the fire that kept Geronimo fighting for thirty years to hold on to the land he loved. And indeed, he never returned to Arizona. He died at Fort Sill and was buried in the Apache cemetery in 1909, still a prisoner, last of the Apache chiefs.

The tower that held Geronimo prisoner in 1886 still stands in the Fort Sam Houston compound in San Antonio, only a few minutes from downtown. Tourists now visit the site to walk under the trees and to pet the white-tailed deer—no longer wild—that are kept within the compound, living on the government dole.

"Why should you wish to shorten my life by taking from me my shadow?"

CRAZY HORSE, OGLALA SIOUX, RESPONDING TO A REQUEST THAT HE POSE FOR PHOTOGRAPHS

CHIEF JOSEPH OF THE NEZ PERCE

BY THOMAS W. KNOWLES

HIS TRUE NAME WAS HIN-MAH-TOO-YAH-LAT-KEKHT, THUNDER TRAVELING to Loftier Mountain Heights, but the white men called him Chief Joseph. He was a great orator and a man of peace, but he skillfully led his people, the Nez Perce, through the most incredible running battle in the history of the West.

The Nez Perce "pierced nose" Indians of the Pacific Northwest were generally peaceful and were friendly to whites from their first contact with Lewis and Clark. They'd made an art of horse breeding and so possessed some of the finest stock in the world. They bred those herds and fed them on the rich grass of their ancestral lands, lands the white man coveted. A series of treaties reduced their lands to a reservation that was a fraction of their original range, and still the whites pressed in upon them. Conflict was inevitable.

The treaty of 1863 split the tribe into two factions, one that accepted its terms and one that didn't. Joseph's father, Old Joseph, refused to sign away the Wallowa Valley in what would later become northeastern Oregon. Disillusioned with his former white friends, he renounced his earlier conversion to Christianity. Before he died, he made his son promise to lead his people well and never give up his homeland.

The U.S. didn't recognize the right of the Nez Perce not to sign. Finally, in 1877, General William Tecumseh Sherman ordered troops in to move the "renegades" to the reservation. That thankless task fell to General O. O. Howard. He gave the Nez Perce thirty days to move to the Lapwai Reservation in Idaho or get ready for war.

Some of the Nez Perce wanted to fight, but Chief Joseph used his oratorical skills to persuade the other chiefs to comply with the order; he wished to postpone and possibly avoid violence. Though they had to cross rivers flooded with snowmelt, they made it to the designated meeting place well before the deadline. The chiefs again put forth the argument for war, but Joseph's cool head and wise words prevailed—he knew that war with the Army would lead to the destruction of his people.

It was when Joseph left the camp to lead a party to gather in some straggled cattle that the lid blew off. Frustrated young men struck out on retaliatory raids and killed a number of white settlers. By the time Joseph returned to the camp, it was too late—the Nez Perce had struck the first blow. He knew the Army's retribution would fall upon all of his people, guilty and innocent alike, and he prepared for flight or war.

Joseph and his people faced vastly superior forces who were armed with superior weapons, including artillery, who could transport troops and supplies by rail and could communicate instantly via telegraph. When the first force, approximately 120 cavalry and irregulars commanded by the over-eager Captain Perry, caught up to them at White Bird Creek, the chiefs sent out a small party under a truce flag. Inevitably, someone fired a shot, and the fight was on.

Though the Nez Perce force in place was only about half the strength of Perry's command, and though they were armed mostly with bows, shotguns, and trade rifles, the Indians outshot, outrode, and outflanked him. Only two Nez Perce were wounded as they broke Perry from his position, drove him from the field, and killed more than a fourth of his men.

Thus began a series of battles in which the Nez Perce ran circles around the multiple Army forces, avoiding them when they could but besting them on the field when they couldn't. Their steps were dogged not only by the Army but by journalists. Readers in the East followed their story in the papers, and it became an overnight sensation.

General Howard and the other Army commanders expected traditional Indian fighting, but the Nez Perce did the unexpected—they used non-Indian tactics. Joseph and the other chiefs and leaders, Ollikut, Looking Glass, White Bird, Five Wounds, Rainbow, and Too-hool-hool-zote, joined forces to form a single command. When Howard attacked them at the Clearwater, the Nez Perce took the high ground, formed a skirmish line to halt the Army's advance, dug rifle pits, and laid siege to Howard's defensive position. They effectively surrounded a force that was six times their size and armed with artillery and Gatling guns.

The Nez Perce fled to the east, avoided a fight at the entrance to the Bitterroot Valley, and crossed into Montana. They actually entered the town of Stevensville, where they purchased supplies with hard cash and by trade. Joseph and the other chiefs had decided early on not to raid or to attack noncombatant civilians—if any crimes or atrocities were to be committed in the war, they'd let them be chalked up to the white man.

Colonel John Gibbon and a force of about two hundred men caught the Nez Perce in the Big Hole Valley and staged a surprise attack at dawn. Again, the Nez Perce didn't react in the expected Indian fashion. Though Gibbon's men inflicted severe casualties in the camp, particularly to noncombatants, Joseph and Looking Glass gathered their warriors and counterattacked. They drove the troopers out of the village into a defensive position. The

Chief Joseph of the Nez Perce (courtesy of U.S. Signal Corps, National Archives)

warriors pinned the troopers down with rifle fire while the rest of the Nez Perce gathered their wounded and dead and escaped.

When they failed to secure promises of aid from the Crow in eastern Montana, the chiefs of the Nez Perce decided to try for the Canadian border to the north. They fought running battles with Army units, harassing them and running off their stock, and avoided blockades as they made their way over hundreds of miles of broken, harsh country. They tricked and bypassed a 7th Cavalry unit commanded by Colonel Samuel Sturgis, and they attacked an Army depot at Cow Island on the Missouri River. But they couldn't outrun the telegraph.

Howard sent a message to Fort Keough, far to the northeast of the Nez Perce advance. Colonel Nelson Miles, the officer who would later hunt down Geronimo in Arizona, set out to intercept the Nez Perce with a large force of cavalry, infantry and scouts, about six hundred men.

Though they'd nearly made it to the border, the Nez Perce knew that Howard had fallen days behind them, so they stopped at Snake Creek near the Bear Paw Mountains to rest and resupply. Early in the morning of September 30, Miles attacked the camp.

Again the Nez Perce stood their ground and fired effectively, inflicting terrible casualties that stopped the cavalry charge. Miles had his troops regroup and surround the camp. In the afternoon he ordered another attack. The combat grew fierce, hand-to-hand between the infantry and the Indians in the canyons and gulleys. The battle went on until nightfall. Tool-hool-hool-zote died that day, and so did many others. Joseph knew that his people were finished.

A snowstorm blew in the next day, adding to their misery. As Joseph negotiated with Miles and discussed their situation with his fellow leaders, Howard's force approached. Looking Glass was killed in an exchange of fire when Howard finally arrived on October 4.

On October 5, 1877, heartsick, freezing, and starving, Chief Joseph and his people had little choice but to surrender. His eloquent surrender speech strikes to the heart of the conflict in which the native peoples of the Americas were broken and swept aside: "Tell General Howard I know his heart. What he told me before, I have it in my heart. I am tired of fighting. Our chiefs are killed. Looking Glass is dead...It is the young men who say, 'Yes or No.' He who led the young men is dead. It is cold, and we have no blankets. The little children are freezing to death. My people, some of them, have run away to the hills, and have no blankets, no food. No one knows where they are— perhaps freezing to death. I want to have time to look for my children, and see how many of them I can find. Maybe I shall find them among the dead. Hear me, my chiefs! I am tired. My heart is sick and sad. From where the sun now stands I will fight no more forever."

After all their hardships, the surviving Nez Perce were removed to Fort Leavenworth, Kansas, the Indian territory. The Wallowa was lost to them forever, and few of them were even allowed to return to the Lapwai Reservation. Chief Joseph died in exile on a Washington Territory reservation on September 21, 1904. ■

THE LEADERS OF THE PEOPLE

QUANAH PARKER, LAST WAR CHIEF OF THE QUAHADIE COMANCHE

BY THOMAS W. KNOWLES

Quanah Parker, Comanche chief (courtesy of Institute of Texan Cultures, San Antonio, Texas)

HE WAS A MAN BORN TO GREATNESS AND FORGED IN THE FIRES OF hatred between two warrior races, the Texans and the Comanche. His Comanche name was Quanah, which meant "sweet smelling" or "fragrance," but his white enemies called him Parker out of a certain grudging respect. In his lifetime he lived in two worlds, red and white, and he excelled in both of them.

His mother was Cynthia Ann Parker, a white girl abducted in the 1836 raid on the Parker settlement; the raid was led by his father, Comanche war chief Peta Nacona. Nacona and his sons were hunting when Texas Rangers commanded by Captain Sul Ross raided their camp in 1860, and Cynthia (named Naduah by the Comanche) was recaptured along with her daughter, Topsannah. Although Cynthia and her daughter were returned to their white relatives, both later died. It was not until 1867, when he was attending the Medicine Lodge Treaty ceremonies, that Quanah learned of their deaths.

In his grief over his loss of Naduah in 1860, Peta Nacona had allowed a wound to go untreated and died of blood poisoning. Pecos, Quanah's brother, had also fallen ill and died. The lone survivor of his family, the teenaged Quanah swore vengeance on the whites who had robbed him of his mother. He joined the Quahadie Comanche band, and in their Staked Plains territory he soon grew to be a tall, strong man with bold features. Aside from his height and his blue-gray eyes, little about his appearance suggested his white heritage. He became a splendid rider and learned to handle the traditional Comanche weapons—the lance, the bow, and the shield. By the time he was in his twenties, he was a proven leader. He quickly rose to a position of importance second only to that held by the Quahadie chief, Bull Bear, and he eventually became known as their chief.

At the Medicine Lodge meeting in 1867, Quanah made clear his intention to fight rather than submit to the reservation. In the following years he raided through the Southwest and dueled with the Army, particularly with Colonel Ranald Mackenzie's 4th Cavalry. On one occasion he led a war party on a wild ride right through Mackenzie's camp and made off with the Army's mounts.

But time was running out for the free Comanche as white diseases, soldiers, and hunters took their toll. The Army kept up the pressure and found better success in its efforts against the other bands. By 1874 the Quahadie were the only significant force of Comanche that remained clear of the reservation. Also, the buffalo hunters moved down from Kansas and began to exterminate the great herds, destroying the Indians' livelihood.

Quanah built an alliance between five Plains tribes for the 1874 raid against the hide hunters' settlement at Adobe Walls, but his careful plan of attack failed because the hunters were forewarned. Though Quanah took a bullet in the shoulder, he held his allies together for a siege for three days. Eventually, even he gave up and left.

In the wake of that disastrous assault, Quanah again turned to traditional but deadly guerrilla raids. He blazed a trail of fire and death across the Staked Plains, thus throwing down the gauntlet. Mackenzie, wiser and more seasoned from earlier engagement, was ready to pick it up.

The Kiowa, Comanche, Cheyenne, and Arapaho often wintered in the great Palo Duro Canyon in the Texas Panhandle, a natural fortress that provided them with plentiful water and grazing. They no doubt felt safe and secure there, but on September 28, 1874, Mackenzie caught them napping and attacked. His troopers managed to negotiate a trail down into the canyon before the warriors could get into position. With rifle fire the soldiers drove the warriors back, then destroyed their lodges and their supplies and captured their main horse herd.

After he gave his scouts their choice of horses, Mackenzie ordered his men to destroy the remaining animals, over a thousand of them. An Indian's horse was his prized possession, his means to make war and to hunt. The slaughter must have been a Comanche's version of hell, to stand helplessly by and listen to the thunder of the Army's rifles and the screams of the wounded and dying animals.

Quanah and his Quahadie had enough horses left to hunt and to hold out until spring, but the hard winter and Mackenzie's relentless pursuit left them starving. Quanah knew his people couldn't eat pride, and on June 2, 1875, he led his people into Fort Sill, where Ranald Mackenzie waited for him.

And so Quanah Parker came to walk the white man's road. He went to visit Cynthia Ann's Uncle Silas in East Texas, and the Parker family accepted him. So did the other Texans who had once hated him; they looked upon him as one of their own kind, a fierce and respected warrior. He said of his mother, "If she could learn the ways of the Indian, I can learn the ways of the white man." He obtained a photograph taken of Cynthia Ann and Topsannah after their recapture, and he kept it with him always.

He returned to the Comanche reservation on the Washita, determined to walk the white man's road but not be whipped along it. Quanah had always been a politic negotiator when he was a war chief, so it was natural that he turn his abilities to preserving his people's rights. He managed the reservation grazing rights as a true businessman, and he dealt shrewdly and profitably with the likes of Charles Goodnight. He became an accomplished lobbyist and spoke out against injustices, treaty violations and environmental destruction carried out by the whites, all the while using the white man's law as the basis for his arguments. He even invested in a railroad and served terms as a deputy sheriff, a school district president, and a judge in Oklahoma; he rode on hunts with President Theodore Roosevelt. Most important of all, he won full American citizenship for all of his people.

Quanah Parker on horseback (courtesy of Library of Congress, Prints and Photo Division, Washington, D.C.)

Lieutenant Charles B. Gatewood, 6th Cavalry, with Indian Scouts (courtesy of National Archives)

Quanah Parker, the peaceful Comanche, remained *Comanche*, not a broken reservation Indian, and in doing so he overturned the popular but erroneous stereotypes. He remained a warrior to the end, for even though he was defeated in the venue of armed conflict, he never surrendered his dignity.

Before he died, he brought the bodies of his mother and his sister up from Texas and had them reburied near his home. He was buried beside them under a marker with these words: "Resting here until day breaks and darkness disappears is Quanah Parker, the last Chief of the Comanche. Died Feb. 21, 1911, Age 64 years." ■

APACHE!—THE PEOPLE, THE ENEMY, THE DEAD

BY MARYLOIS DUNN

HE KEPT NO WRITTEN HISTORY, SO WHAT WE KNOW ABOUT THE ORIGINS of the Apache is sketchy. Some say the Apache was in the Southwest when the Spaniards came, others that he was still working his way down from the far north at that time. But by the middle of the 1600s the Apache called a large portion of West Texas, all of New Mexico, a great chunk of southern Arizona, and all of Sonora and Chihuahua in Old Mexico his own.

It was rumored that the Navajo was a cousin of the Apache, but there were so few similarities by the time Anglo settlers met them that it's hard to believe there was ever any connection between them. There are some points of agreement in custom and religion, but less in appearance and absolutely none in temperament.

The Apache was always on the move. His life, his soul, was centered on war. The various bands of Apache—the Chiricahua, Mescalero, Ojos Caliente, Tonto, and others—were often enemies to one another as well as to other tribes. They roamed this vast territory, fighting with the more peaceful Pueblo and desert Indians, raiding, stealing, and killing until they almost destroyed the more passive tribes.

As did all Native American tribes, the Apache called themselves "the People," a name they did not take lightly. Everyone else was not of the

People, and so could be exploited for their use. The first person to write the term "Apache," which meant "enemy" in the language of his Indian guides, was Castaneda, the historian of Coronado's expedition in 1580.

Other Indians agreed with the European invaders that the Apache was the meanest, cruelest, orneriest, freedom-lovingest and foxiest Indian who ever roamed the Southwest. Although he constantly bedeviled the Pueblo tribes, he dropped this enmity to become their ally in the great Pueblo revolt in 1680. Once the revolt was over, the Apache melted back into the wild lands to resume his enemy ways. Despite this the Pueblo welcomed his assistance again in 1745 and 1750 when they tried to toss the Spaniards off the continent.

The Spanish *padres* never reached the Apache with their messages about the European's one true God. After all, the Spaniards were not of the People, so how could they know the true god? The god of the People was everywhere, certainly not contained in the Spaniards' brightly painted dolls. Also, the Apache was no fool—only too often had he seen the Spanish brands burned into the hips or cheeks of the Indians who fallen under the spell of the *padres*. He knew that Indian converts were often herded like animals to the plantations or silver mines, there to work and die as slaves. The Apache was destined to roam the desert and the mountains with the wolf, the mountain lion, the bear, and his mystic brother, the coyote, not to be the prisoner or the slave of any man.

As a child, the Apache was trained to have no pity. Mercy was not a quality he understood. When an Apache sought information, he did not say "please." He hung his captive head down over a slow fire while his women removed, strip by strip, the unfortunate's skin, which they fletched. His favorite method of persuasion, probably because red ants were so plentiful and it was easy, was to stake the naked victim over an anthill and smear his genitals with honey. When he wearied of the screams, the Apache smeared more honey over his victim's ears, eyes, and in his nose and mouth. While the Apache often mutilated his captured enemies without mercy, he rarely took scalps. When he managed to capture a Mexican or pale-eye who had an Apache scalp on his belt, he gleefully experimented with new ways of inflicting a slow, painful death.

Children of a teachable age and disposition who were taken prisoner by the Apache were often incorporated into the tribe. Teenagers might be made slaves, while tots too young to keep up with the tribe might have their brains bashed in. Despite its draconian cruelty, Apache adoption was a system not completely without merit for those who were tough enough to survive. Apache preferred to take Mexican children, and there is historical evidence of more than one kidnapped Mexican child who grew up to be a fearsome and honored Apache warrior.

Naiche, son of Cochise (top), and Haozinne, wife of Naiche

CURANDERA:
an herb doctor or midwife.

JACALE:
a hut of brush or mud used by the Apache and other Southwestern Indians.

HODDENTIN:
the pollen of the tule or the cattail, which the Apache used as a sacrament.

The Apache was a part of the country he occupied. He knew every trail, every water hole, every hideout. He traveled with an economy of equipment that would put a white man to shame. Bow, quiver of arrows, knife, bag of pinole or bundle of jerky, gun and ammunition if he had it—this was all he carried. He wore a breechcloth, an amulet, and moccasins that sometimes laced above the knees. In later years he sometimes wore a cotton shirt, unbuttoned, and trousers with the seat cut out fore and aft. When fighting time came, the warrior abandoned all clothing and went into battle wearing nothing but his paint, his amulet, and his moccasins. He was trained to run from the time he crawled out of his mother's lap; some said he could run fifty miles at a stretch without stopping to take a breather. It is documented that some bands ran as much as one hundred fifty miles in a twenty-four hour period to escape pursuing Army units. The Apache on foot could set a pace that would kill the grain-fed cavalry horses.

STRATEGY SEEMED TO BE BORN IN THE APACHE. HE RARELY CAME over the hill in a wild charge; stealth was his chief weapon. An Apache could become a rock or a bush to the eyes of the untrained, and he could bury himself in sand and lie in wait for his enemy for as much as two days. He almost always attacked using the advantage of surprise. It was a powerful weapon.

The sighting of a single Apache in the vicinity of a ranch or village was enough to send the entire kit and caboodle fleeing to the safety of nearby towns or forts. When an enemy pursuit got too close to a band of Apache, the band would scatter, each individual leading the enemy in a different direction until he lost them and could return to an agreed upon place. It sometimes took months for the members of a band to reassemble, but they generally did.

The Apache was so familiar with the habits of wildlife that he seldom lacked for meat, and he made up the rest of his diet with what the women gathered and the raiders took as plunder. When they had enough peace and time, Apache women might plant a patch of corn, melons, beans or squash. They ground acorns for flour, fermented mescal and made the tiswin beer, and carefully saved certain plant pollens for their religious ceremonies.

After the territory was well settled, the Apache gave over his fondness for game in favor of tame meat. Mules, horses, sheep, goats, and cattle filled out his diet. Most of the bands regarded Mexico as their private warehouse for food.

Unlike the Comanche or the Sioux, the Apache preferred to run rather than to ride; he was a guerrilla fighter, not cavalry. He did use horses and mules when he needed them, and there was a bonus for the warrior who rode into camp—he'd brought his potluck supper with him. Cavalrymen used to say that when they abandoned a worn-out horse, a Mexican could take it and ride it for another fifty miles before again abandoning it in the wilds; then if an Apache found the exhausted animal, he would ride it for another hundred miles until it dropped dead, and then he'd eat it.

Some traditions of Apache family life endure even to this day. An Apache never looked at his mother-in-law or spoke to her; this was how he showed respect. He left the wickiup as soon as she entered it. In the days before he was forced to live by the white man's rules, it was the custom for one Apache man to have two or three wives. It must have been difficult to avoid all those mothers-in-law all the time.

Families were (and in some instances still are) matrilineal—the man entered into the family life of his wife as soon as they were married, leaving his own parents and siblings behind. He might visit with them, but his responsibility was to his wife's family. If she died, as women frequently did in those hard times, he stayed in mourning for a year and then generally married a relative of his former wife.

When a young woman caught his eye, he could not approach her openly. Instead, he would ask a relative to approach her parents on his behalf. The number of horses, blankets, or whatever he gave for presents usually determined his reception.

A family included grandparents, unmarried sons and daughters, married daughters and their husbands, and the married daughters' children. Sometimes an entire band was one family unit including cousins, uncles, and aunts. A clan or band was usually known by some name that described their preferred location. White Mountain Apache are still prominent in New Mexico. Women in the clan found it easier to work together gathering food and preparing it for eating or for storage. Each clan, whether of one family or several, was organized by general consent under a single chief. Clans rarely united with one another; if one clan encroached on another's territory, they would fight each other as they would fight any enemy.

THE APACHE WAS DEEPLY RELIGIOUS. HE BELIEVED IN A SUPREME BEING called Ussen, giver of life. Ussen was without particular place, of no determined sex, and couldn't be reached directly by prayer or supplication. The Apache sought Ussen's power through some totem which had been revealed to him in a dream or vision. This totem became the Apache's guardian and taught him the ways and will of Ussen.

There were special ceremonies for everything. A medicine man was a man of great power and respect, a practical mystic who could sing the sick to health, find lost treasures, and give a warrior protection against natural enemies and man. He could sing arrows and bullets to their targets or protect the clansmen from the weapons of their enemies. He could call the wind,

"Unless every tribe unanimously combines to give a check to the ambition and the avarice of the whites, they will soon conquer us apart and disunited, and we will be driven away from our native country and scattered as autumnal leaves before the wind."

TECUMSEH, SHAWNEE CHIEF

General O. O. Howard (courtesy of Library of Congress)

rain, or sandstorm, and he could make clouds disappear and cause the sun to shine. The Apache's favorite token, next to pollen, was the eagle feather; the downy feather from the eagle's breast was the most prized. He wore it during ceremonies, tied to his pony's mane for good fortune, or carried in his amulet bag.

The wooden wickiup was a rough-appearing dwelling the Apache built from whatever materials were at hand. Tall branches of pine, cedar, mesquite, or juniper were stuck in the ground in a circle and then brought together at the top and tied. The framework was covered with grass, cloth, or skins. It was a short-term dwelling and could be abandoned at quick notice. The wickiup was burned if it became infested with lice or other pests, or if someone died in it.

Apache mothers carried their babies on cradleboards and made cloth slings for older youngsters. In their own way, Apache had a strong sense of humor—indeed, they were mercurial in nature, far from the stoic stereotype of the wooden Indian. They made jokes and laughed often when they were among their own or with friends, but they often gave in to unreasonable and savage fits of temper. Men would sometimes beat their wives for little reason, sometimes to death. And yet, they were tender with their children—it was unheard of for man or woman to strike a child of the clan.

The history of the Apache after the coming of the pale-eyes is long and terrible on both sides. There were many great Apache war chiefs—Magnas Colorado, Cochise, Juh, Victoria Old Nana, Geronimo, Chato, Nachee, and others—and their sagacity and ferocity are legend. Of all the white men in the Apache territory at the time, the ones who dealt honorably with the Apache could be counted on one hand: John P. Clum, Tom Jeffords, General O. O. Howard, General George Crook, and Al Sieber, who was more Apache at heart than white. A few other whites in authority tried to deal fairly with the Apache, but they were so undercut by treachery from Washington and the alien differences between the two cultures that their efforts failed. By the end of the Apache wars, those of the People who had survived the barren hell of the San Carlos Reservation were hauled off to Florida to die in humid squalor.

A later government administration moved the few survivors to Alabama and Oklahoma, where in the white Indian schools the Apache children were stripped of their language, their culture, and their religion. It was only after all the old ones died off that the children of the Apache were allowed to return to the land of the People. Even then, later generations of Apache often referred to themselves not as Apache or as the People, but with the Apache name for the conquered—*Indeh*, the Dead. ∎

THE GHOST DANCE AND THE BATTLE OF WOUNDED KNEE

BY DEE BROWN

DURING THE DECADE FOLLOWING CUSTER'S DEFEAT ON THE LITTLE BIG Horn, the warring tribes of Indians in the American West were gradually shorn of their power and locked within reservations. Many of the great chiefs and mighty warriors were dead. The buffalo and antelope had almost vanished; the old ceremonies of the tribes were becoming rituals without meaning.

For the survivors it was a time without spirit, a time of despair. One might swap a few skins for the trader's crazy-water and dream of the old days, the days of the splendid hunts and fighting. One might make big talk for a little while but that was all.

In such times, defeated peoples search for redeemers, and soon on many reservations there were dreamers and swooning men to tell of approaching redemption. Most of them were great fakers, but some were sincere in their vagaries and their visions.

As early as 1870 the defeated Paiutes of Nevada had found a redeemer in Tavibo, a petty chief, who claimed to have talked with divine spirits in the mountains. All the people of the earth were to be swallowed up, the spirits told him, but at the end of three days the Indians would be resurrected in the flesh to live forever. They would enjoy the earth which was rightfully theirs. Once again there would be plenty of game, fish, and piñion nuts. Best of all, the white invaders would be destroyed forever.

When Tavibo first told his vision to the Paiutes, he attracted very few believers. But gradually he added other features to his story, and he went up into the mountains again for further revelations. It was necessary for the Indians to dance, everywhere; to keep on dancing. This would please the Great Spirit, who would come and destroy the white men and bring back the buffalo.

Tavibo died shortly after he told of these things, but his son, Wovoka, was considered the natural inheritor of his powers by those Paiutes who believed in the new religion of the dance. Wovoka, who was only fourteen

"You may bury my body in Sussex grass, You may bury my tongue at Champmédy. I shall not be there. I shall rise and pass. Bury my heart at Wounded Knee."

STEPHEN VINCENT BENÉT

when his father died, was taken into the family of a white farmer, David Wilson, and was given the name Jack Wilson. In his new home the boy's imagination was fired by Bible stories told to him; he was fascinated by the white man's God.

On New Year's Day of 1889, a vision came to Jack Wilson (Wovoka) while he lay ill with fever; he dreamed that he died and went to heaven. God spoke to him, commanding him to take a message back to earth. Wovoka was to tell the Indians that if they would follow God's commandment and perform a "ghost dance" at regular intervals their old days of happiness and prosperity would be returned to them.

In January 1889 on the Walker Lake Reservation, the first Ghost Dance was performed on a dancing ground selected by Wovoka. The ceremony was simple, the Paiutes forming a large circle, dancing and chanting as they constricted the circle, the circle widening and constricting again and again. The dancing continued for a day and a night, Wovoka sitting in the middle of the circle before a large fire with his head bowed. He wore a white striped coat, a pair of trousers, and moccasins. On the second day he stopped the dancing and described the visions that God had sent to him. Then the dancing commenced again and lasted for three more days.

When a second dance was held soon afterward, several Utes visited the ceremony out of curiosity. Returning to their reservation, the Utes told the neighboring Bannocks about what they had seen. The Bannocks sent emissaries to the next dance, and within a few weeks the Shoshone at the Fort Hall Reservation saw a ritual staged by the Bannocks. They were so impressed that they sent a delegation to Nevada to learn the new religion from Wovoka himself.

PERHAPS MORE THAN ANY OTHER OF THE TRIBES, THE CHEYENNE and Sioux felt the need for a messiah who could lead them back to their days of glory. After the story of Wovoka was carried swiftly to their reservations, several medicine men decided to make pilgrimages. It was a mark of prestige for them to travel by railroad, and as soon as they could raise enough money, they purchased tickets to Nevada. In the autumn of 1889, a Cheyenne named Porcupine made the journey, and a short time later Short Bull, Kicking Bear, and other Sioux leaders traveled all the way from Dakota.

The Sioux accepted the Ghost Dance religion with more fervor than any of the other tribes. On their return to the Dakota reservations, each delegate tried to outdo the others in describing the wonders of the messiah. Wovoka came down from heaven in a cloud, they said. He showed them a vision of all the nations of Indians coming home. The earth would be covered with dust and then a new earth would come upon the old. They must use the

"What treaty that the white man ever made with us have they kept? Not one."

TATANKA YOTANKA, SITTING BULL OF THE HUNKPAPA SIOUX

sacred red and white paint and the sacred grass to make the vanished buffalo return in great herds.

In the spring of 1890 the Sioux began dancing the Ghost Dance at the Pine Ridge Reservation, adding new symbols to Wovoka's original ceremony. By June they were wearing ghost shirts made of cotton cloth painted blue around the necks, with bright-colored thunderbirds, bows and arrows, suns, moons, and stars emblazoned upon them. To accompany the dancing they made ghost songs:

> *The whole world is coming,*
> *A nation is coming, a nation is coming.*
> *The Eagle has brought the message to the tribe.*
> *The father says so, the father says so.*
> *Over the whole earth they are coming,*
> *The buffalo are coming, the buffalo are coming.*

Mainly because they misunderstood the meaning of the Ghost Dance religion, the government policymakers who ran the reservations from Washington decided to stamp it out. If they had taken the trouble to examine its basic tenets, they would have found that in its original form the religion was opposed to all forms of violence, self-mutilation, theft, and falsehood. As one Army officer observed, "Wovoka has given these people a better religion than they ever had before."

The Ghost Dance might have died away under official pressure had not the greatest maker of medicine among the Sioux, Sitting Bull, chosen to come forth from his "retirement" near the Standing Rock agency and join the new religion of the dance. Sitting Bull was the last of the great unreconciled chiefs. Since his return from Canada, where he had gone after the Custer battle, he had been carrying on a feud with the military as well as with civilian reservation agents.

When Kicking Bear, one of the early emissaries to Wovoka, visited Sitting Bull in late 1890 to teach him the Ghost Dance, Agent James McLaughlin ordered Kicking Bear escorted off the reservation. Sitting Bull may or may not have believed in the messiah, but he was always searching for opportunities to bedevil the authorities. Kicking Bear was hardly off the reservation before Sitting Bull set up a dance camp and started instructing his followers in the new religion. In a short time the peaceful ghost songs became warlike chants.

Efforts of authorities to put a stop to ghost dancing now led to resentment and increased belligerency from the Indians. Inevitably the Army was drawn into the controversy, and in the late autumn of 1890 General Nelson Miles ordered more troops into the plains area.

Suspecting that Sitting Bull was the leading troublemaker, Miles arranged

Indian village (courtesy of Kansas State Historical Society, Topeka, Kansas)

informally with Buffalo Bill Cody to act as intermediary. Cody had scouted with Miles in former years and had also employed Sitting Bull as a feature attraction with his Wild West show. "Sitting Bull might listen to you," Miles told Cody, "when under the same conditions he'd take a shot at one of my soldiers."

Buffalo Bill went at once to Fort Yates on the Standing Rock Reservation, but authorities there were dismayed when they read Miles's written instructions to Cody: "Secure the person of Sitting Bull and deliver him to the nearest commanding officer of U.S. troops." James McLaughlin, the reservation agent, and Lieutenant Colonel William Drum, the military commander, both feared that Cody's actions might precipitate a general outbreak throughout the area. The military authorities immediately took it upon themselves to get Buffalo Bill drunk, send a wire to Washington, and have his orders rescinded.

"All the officers were requested to assist in drinking Buffalo Bill under the table," Captain A.R. Chapin later recorded. "But his capacity was such that it took practically all of us in details of two or three at a time to keep him interested and busy throughout the day." Although the rugged Cody managed to keep a clear head through all this maneuvering, he had scarcely started out to Sitting Bull's encampment before a telegram came from Washington canceling his orders.

Meanwhile Agent McLaughlin had decided to take Sitting Bull into custody himself, hoping to prevent a dangerous disturbance which he felt would result if the military authorities forced the issue and tried to make an arrest. McLaughlin gave the necessary orders to his Indian police, instructing them not to permit the chief to escape under any circumstances.

Just before daybreak on December 15, 1890, forty-three Indian police surrounded Sitting Bull's log cabin. Lieutenant Bull Head, the Indian policeman in charge of the party, found Sitting Bull asleep on the floor. When he was awakened, the old war leader stared incredulously at Bull Head. "What do you want here?" he asked.

"You are my prisoner," said Bull Head calmly. "You must go to the agency."

Sitting Bull yawned and sat up. "All right," he said, "let me put on my clothes and I'll go with you." He called one of his wives and sent her to an adjoining cabin for his best clothing, and then asked the policeman to saddle his horse for him.

While these things were being done, his ardent followers, who had been dancing the Ghost Dance every night for weeks, were gathering around the cabin. They outnumbered the police four to one and soon had them pressed against the walls. When Lieutenant Bull Head emerged with Sitting Bull, he must have sensed the explosive nature of the situation.

While they waited for Sitting Bull's horse, a fanatical ghost dancer named Catch-the-Bear appeared out of the mob. "You think you are going to take him," Catch-the-Bear shouted at the policemen. "You shall not do it!"

"Come now," Bull Head said quietly to his prisoner, "do not listen to anyone." But Sitting Bull held back, forcing Bull Head and Sergeant Red Tomahawk to pull him toward his horse.

Without warning, Catch-the-Bear suddenly threw off his blanket and brought up a rifle, firing point-blank at Bull Head, wounding him in the side. As Bull Head fell, he tried to shoot his assailant, but the bullet struck Sitting Bull instead. Almost simultaneously Red Tomahawk shot Sitting Bull through the head. A wild fight developed immediately, and only the timely arrival of a cavalry detachment saved the police from extinction.

News of Sitting Bull's death swept across the reservations, startling the Indians and the watchful military forces in the Dakotas. Most of the frightened followers of the great chief immediately came into the Standing Rock agency and surrendered. Others fled toward the southwest.

Those who were fleeing knew exactly where they were going. They were seeking to join forces with a Ghost Dance believer, an aging chief named Big Foot. For some time Big Foot had been gathering followers at a small village near the mouth of Deep Creek on the Cheyenne River. As the Ghost Dance craze had increased, so had Big Foot's forces, and even before the fatal shooting of Sitting Bull, a small party of cavalrymen under Lieutenant Colonel Edwin V. Sumner, Jr., had been assigned to watch his movements.

As soon as news of Sitting Bull's death reached Big Foot, he began preparations to break camp. Lieutenant Colonel Sumner accepted the chief's explanation that the Indians were preparing to proceed eastward to the Cheyenne River agency, where they would spend the winter. Big Foot was unusually friendly and declared that the only reason he had permitted the fugitives from Sitting Bull's camp to join his people was that he felt sorry for them and wanted them to return to the reservation with him. Sumner was so convinced of Big Foot's sincerity that he permitted the band to keep their arms—a decision that was to precipitate the tragedy of Wounded Knee.

Before dawn the next day, December 23, Big Foot and his ever-increasing band were in rapid flight, moving in the opposite direction from the Cheyenne River agency. The question has never been settled as to whether they were heading for the Pine Ridge agency, as Big Foot's followers later claimed, or for the Sioux recalcitrants' stronghold in the Badlands. But it is a fact that a few days earlier those two leaders, who had once visited the messiah in Nevada, were in the Badlands. And they had with them several hundred fanatical followers, keyed up to a high frenzy as a result of their continual dancing and chanting.

Learning of Big Foot's escape from Sumner's cavalry, General Miles ordered Major Samuel M. Whitside of the 7th Cavalry to intercept the Indians, disarm them, and return them to a reservation. On December 28, Whitside's scouts found the fugitives on Porcupine Creek, and when the major sighted a white flag fluttering from a wagon, he rode out to meet it. He was surprised to find Big Foot lying in the bed of the wagon, swathed in blankets, suffering severely from pneumonia.

Whitside shook hands with the ailing chief and told him that he must bring his people to the cavalry camp on Wounded Knee Creek. In a hoarse voice that was almost a whisper, Big Foot agreed to the order. Whitside, on the advice of one of his scouts, decided to wait until the band was assembled beside the cavalry camp before disarming them.

During the ensuing march, none of the cavalrymen suspected that anything was amiss. The Indians seemed to be in good humor; they talked and laughed with the soldiers and smoked their cigarettes. Not one of the cavalrymen seemed to have been aware that almost all of these Indians were wearing sacred ghost shirts which they believed would protect them from the soldiers' weapons. And the soldiers seemed to be completely ignorant of the fact that their prisoners were obsessed with the belief that the day of the Indians' return to power was close at hand. One of the most fanatical members of the band was a medicine man, Yellow Bird, who all during the march was moving stealthily up and down the line, occasionally blowing on an eagle-bone whistle and muttering Ghost Dance chants.

When the column reached Wounded Knee, the Indians were assigned to an area near the cavalry camp. They were carefully counted; 120 men and 230 women and children were present. Rations were issued, and they set up their shelters for the night. For additional cover Major Whitside gave them several army tents. The troop surgeon, John van R. Hoff, went to attend the ailing Big Foot, and a stove was set up in the chief's tent. Whitside, however, did not entirely trust Big Foot's band. He posted a battery of four Hotchkiss guns, training them directly on the Indians' camp.

It was a cold night. Ice was already an inch thick on the tree-bordered creek, and there was a hint of snow in the air. During the night, Colonel James W. Forsyth of the 7th Cavalry rode in and took command. Significantly, there were now at Wounded Knee five troop commanders—Moylan, Varnum, Wallace, Godfrey, and Edgerly—who had been with Reno and Custer at the Little Big Horn. With Big Foot were warriors who had fought in the same battle. Much would be made of that in days to come.

In Forsyth's command was a young lieutenant, James D. Mann, who was to witness the opening shots of the approaching fight. "The next morning," Mann said afterward, "we started to disarm them, the bucks being formed in a semi-circle in front of the tents. We went through the tents looking for arms, and while this was going on, everyone seemed to be good-natured,

and we had no thought of trouble. The squaws were sitting on bundles concealing guns and other arms. We lifted them as tenderly and treated them as nicely as possible.

"While this was going on, the medicine man (Yellow Bird) who was in the center of the semi-circle of bucks, had been going through the Ghost Dance, and making a speech, the substance of which was, as told me by an interpreter afterwards, 'I have made medicine of the white man's ammunition. It is good medicine, and his bullets can not harm you, as they will not go through your ghost shirts, while your bullets will kill.'

"It was then that I had a peculiar feeling come over me which I can not describe—some presentiment of trouble—and I told the men to 'be ready: there is going to be trouble.' We were only six or eight feet from the Indians and I ordered my men to fall back.

"In front of me were four bucks—three armed with rifles and one with bow and arrows. I drew my revolver and stepped through the line to my place with my detachment. The Indians raised their weapons over their heads to heaven as if in votive offering, then brought them down to bear on us, the one with the bow and arrow aiming directly at me. Then they seemed to wait an instant.

"The medicine man threw a handful of dust in the air, put on his war bonnet, and an instant later a gun was fired. This seemed to be the signal

Members of Big Foot's Band of Hunkpapa Sioux shortly before Wounded Knee (courtesy of U.S. Signal Corps, National Archives)

they had been waiting for, and the firing immediately began. I ordered my men to fire, and the reports were almost simultaneous."

Things happened fast after that first volley. The Hotchkiss guns opened fire and began pouring shells into the Indians at the rate of nearly fifty per minute. What survivors there were began a fierce hand-to-hand struggle, using revolvers, knives and war clubs. The lack of rifles among the Indians made the fight more bloody because it brought the combatants to closer quarters. In a few minutes, 200 Indian men, women, and children and 60 soldiers were lying dead and wounded on the ground, the ripped tents blazing and smoking around them. Some of the surviving Indians fled to a nearby ravine, hiding among the rocks and scrub cedars. Others continued their flight up the slopes to the south.

Yellow Bird, the medicine man, concealed himself in a tent and through a slit in the canvas began shooting at the soldiers. When one of the 7th Cavalry troopers ran forward to slash open the tent, Yellow Bird killed him by pumping bullets into his stomach. Angry cavalrymen responded with heavy fire, then piled hay around the tent and set it to blazing.

Big Foot died early in the fighting from a bullet through his head. Captain Edward Godfrey, who had survived the Little Big Horn (he was with Benteen), was shocked when he discovered he had ordered his men to fire on women and children hidden in a brush thicket. Captain George Wallace, who also had survived the Custer fight (with Reno's battalion), was shouting his first order to fire when a bullet carried away the top of his head.

On the bloody campground Surgeon Hoff did what he could for the wounded. He disarmed a wounded Indian who was still trying to fire his rifle. The warrior staggered to his feet and looked down at the burned body of Yellow Bird. "If I could be taken to you," the wounded Indian muttered to the dead medicine man, "I would kill you again."

Disillusionment over the failure of the ghost shirts had already affected most of the other survivors. With blood flowing from her wounds, one of the squaws tore off her brilliantly colored shirt and stamped upon it.

As it was apparent by the end of the day that a blizzard was approaching, the medical staff hastily gathered the wounded together to carry them to a field hospital at Pine Ridge. In the affair 146 Indians and 25 soldiers had been killed, but the full totals would not be known until several days afterward because of the snowstorm that blanketed the battlefield.

After the blizzard, when a burial party went out to Wounded Knee, they found many of the bodies frozen grotesquely where they had fallen. They buried all the Indians together in a large pit. A few days later, relatives of the slain came and put up a wire fence around the mass grave; then they smeared the posts with sacred red medicine paint.

By this time the nation's press was having a field day with the new "Indian war." Some journalists pictured the Wounded Knee tragedy as a triumph of brave soldiers over treacherous Indians; others declared it was a slaughter of helpless Indians by a regiment searching for revenge since the Little Big Horn. The truth undoubtedly lay somewhere between these opposite points of view. Certainly it was a tragic accident of war.

At Wounded Knee, the vision of the peaceful Paiute dreamer, Wovoka, had come to an end. And so had all the long and bitter years of Indian resistance on the Western plains. ▪

THEY MET AT ADOBE WALLS

BY THOMAS W. KNOWLES

THE WILD WAR CRIES, THE BUGLE CALLS, AND THE THUNDER OF SHARPS rifles no longer trouble the broad, grassy meadow on the Canadian River in the Texas Panhandle. Of the hide hunters' settlement and the old Adobe Walls trading post, only headstones, monuments, and markers remain, but those stones bear the names of the men, red and white, who fought there in two of the fiercest battles of the Indian Wars of the West.

They are the names of the legendary figures of the Old West, the larger-than-life medicine men, scouts, war chiefs, gunfighters, outlaws, hide hunters, and horse soldiers of the Western motion pictures and novels. They are legends now, but they were flesh and blood when they met at Adobe Walls.

Bent's Lost Venture, 1843

Built in 1843 by William Bent of the prosperous Bent, St. Vrain & Company trading family, the earth-brick fortification known as Adobe Walls was probably the first white trading post in the Texas Panhandle. The site Bent picked was just north of the Canadian River in what is present-day Hutchinson County.

Bent believed that a permanent base in the heart of the hunting range would allow him to compete with the Mexican Comancheros for the lucrative Kiowa-Comanche trade in buffalo robes and stolen horses. He didn't count on the wary nature of the plains nomads, who viewed with suspicion any white intrusion into the land they called the Comancheria. Without their

On the Alert, painting by Richard Hogue, depicts a buffalo hunter of the 1870s with his Sharps rifle at the ready. (courtesy of Hutchinson County Historical Museum)

trust, transportation of supplies was dangerous, trade impossible. He was eventually forced to abandon the post to the plains winds that rapidly reduced it to the ruins of its namesake walls.

Kit Carson's Fight: The First Battle of Adobe Walls, 1864

When frontier scout Colonel Christopher "Kit" Carson set out for Adobe Walls in October 1864, his mission was not trade but retaliation. The vital Santa Fe Trail that supplied New Mexico and California, unprotected after the withdrawal of federal troops to the ongoing Civil War, suffered under the deadly attentions of Kiowa and Comanche raiders.

At Fort Bascom, New Mexico, Carson assembled a special expeditionary force of California and New Mexico volunteers drawn from different units, as well as a number of his Ute and Apache friends. Five cavalry companies and two of infantry followed him down the Canadian River into the winter quarters of the Plains Indians.

Carson's advance scouts encountered enemy pickets on the river several miles north of the old Adobe Walls trading post. The ensuing chase led them right into a large village of Kiowa lodges about four miles upstream from Adobe Walls, only one of several Kiowa and Comanche encampments on the river. The advance cavalry units and the Ute-Apache scouts attacked the village.

Kiowa warriors fought a defensive action to cover their retreat, then broke away and fled downriver with the cavalry in pursuit. They turned to fight near the old Adobe Walls post. When Carson arrived with the rest of the troops and the artillery, he found his cavalry dismounted and barely holding their own against the Kiowa counterattack. They were using the remnants of the adobe fortifications as a stable for their mounts and a field hospital for the increasing number of casualties.

A force of about two hundred warriors surrounded the cavalry, but lookouts spotted many more approaching from another huge village to the south. Carson wasted no time in setting up his guns on a knoll near the post; he was just in time. The infantry's brace of twelve-pound mountain howitzers dispersed the Indians before they could group for a charge.

Though the Indians declined to face the artillery head-on, they moved to flank and surround the expedition's position. Kiowa and Comanche reinforcements continued to arrive on the field throughout the afternoon, and Kiowa patrols departed in the direction of the supply train advancing from Mule Springs. Carson soon recognized the desperate nature of his situation. Faced by a vastly superior enemy force, his relief column in danger, he took the only course left open to him—retreat.

He used his artillery to break out of the trap so he could withdraw upstream. Under constant attack, he used a combination of decoying cavalry harassment and howitzer fire to take and destroy a greater part of the first village on the river. Though dogged by angry warriors most of the way, his expedition eventually met up with the supply column and returned safely to Fort Bascom.

Carson's solid tactics spared him the harsh lesson the Sioux would teach George Armstrong Custer twelve years later. Had he been slower to bring up his artillery or had he refused to retreat from his indefensible position, Adobe Walls would have been his Carson's Little Big Horn. Army casualties were recorded as two killed and twenty-one wounded; Indian losses were estimated at thirty to sixty killed and wounded. Unknown to either side was the signing, prior to the battle, of a treaty by which the Kiowa, Comanche and some Apache had agreed to end their raids against the Santa Fe Trail.

The Hide Hunter's War: The Second Battle of Adobe Walls, 1874

The old Adobe Walls trading post remained relatively undisturbed for ten years after Kit Carson's expedition. It was with the invention in 1870 of a new tanning process for buffalo hides, along with the advent of the deadly Sharps rifle, that a new threat arose to the security of the Comancheria.

To the commercial hidehunters, the plains were a vast slaughterhouse. The great herd that was once estimated at thirty million bison was reduced by 1886 to less than a thousand. In the winter of 1872–73 an average of forty thousand hides were shipped east each day from Dodge City, Kansas. It was not long before the Kansas herds were depleted and the hunters began drifting south into the disputed territory of the old Comancheria.

The Indians, most of them by that time living on reservations, considered the hunting rights in the unsettled territories to be reserved for them by the 1867 Medicine Lodge Treaty. Military commanders and Indian agents often overlooked or denied outright the Indians' interpretation of the treaty. They encouraged the removal of the bison as a way to break the Indians' resistance to reservation life. General Philip Sheridan himself commended the hide hunters for their destruction of the "Indians' commissary."

The hunters' incursions into the prime buffalo range and the refusal of the military to honor the treaty enraged hostile and reservation Indians alike. They were not to be satisfied by scattered raids and killings of isolated hunters, and an obvious target for their anger was not long in coming.

In March 1874, two prosperous Dodge City mercantiles that catered to the hide trade followed their customers into the Canadian River country. The site they chose was just one mile north of Bent's old stronghold, but no one at the new post, not even the scouts among the hide hunters, knew the origin of the ruin. They assumed it to be an old Spanish mission or a Comanchero trading fort.

The Myers & Leonard Company constructed a well-stocked emporium, dining hall, and hide-drying facility inside an eight-foot stockade corral. Its principal competitor, Rath & Company, set up shop in less grand style on the south side of what counted for a street. Tom O'Keefe's smithy and James N. Hanrahan's sod-roofed saloon stood between the rival establishments.

Several hide outfits made the new Adobe Walls their base of operations. There were outfits run by honest men like Emanuel Dubbs and brothers John and J. Wright Mooar, and there were also bands of part-time rustlers and horse thieves run by outlaws like Orlando "Brick" Bond and "Dutch" Henry Born. Among the hunters were two young men named William Dixon and William Barclay Masterson. Billy Dixon, an orphan who had left West Virginia to make his fortune on the buffalo range, would find fame as a scout and Indian fighter. Though he would later be renowned as a gunfighter, lawman, and journalist, "Bat" Masterson was at the time a nineteen-year-old Kansas farm boy who had left home to find adventure.

Unknown to the merchants and their customers, the stage for conflict was already set by the visions of Isatai, a young Comanche medicine man. Isatai claimed that the Great Spirit had drawn him into heaven to give him a magic paint that nullified the white man's bullets. With this powerful magic, the tribes would drive their hated enemies from the plains.

The rising star of the Comanche nation was Quanah Parker, the son of Chief Peta Nacona and white captive Cynthia Ann Parker. Although he may have been skeptical of Isatai's magic, Quanah did not doubt the power of the medicine man's words to draw the scattered bands of the People to the warpath. He spent the spring with Isatai making recruitment visits to the different bands of Comanche, Kiowa, Cheyenne and Arapaho. He also attended the annual Kiowa Sun Dance ceremony.

The Comanche held a sun dance of their own in May 1874 on the North Fork of the Red River. They invited their prospective allies to participate and staged a special medicine ritual in which a practice assault was conducted against a model settlement similar to the new Adobe Walls post.

The war council after the ceremony was marred by controversy over the choice of targets for revenge. Some wished to attack the reservations and the Army forts, while others wanted to kill the buffalo hunters who were destroying their way of life. Kicking Bird of the Kiowa opted for peace and withdrew his band from the venture, but Quanah used the influence of Isatai's vision to hammer out an agreement with the remaining leaders. In the end, Stone Calf added the strength of his Cheyenne to that of Lone Wolf's Kiowa and the Comanche bands with Quanah and Big Bow. A small number of Arapaho agreed to go along as observers, not quite ready to join in the war until they were sure of success.

The target selected was the hide hunters' town at Adobe Walls. The objectives were to end the hunters' depredations and to obtain the guns and ammunition with which to fight the Army. On June 26, after a careful reconnaissance of the post and the surrounding countryside, an allied force of from two hundred to seven hundred warriors made camp on a small creek not far from Adobe Walls. They spent the evening relaxing and making medicine for the dawn attack.

Twenty-eight men and one woman occupied the town of Adobe Walls at the time. Most were sound asleep on the morning of the 27th. Many of the hunters were sleeping outdoors to take advantage of the breeze.

At about 2 A.M., those sleeping in Jim Hanrahan's saloon were awakened by a loud crack that sounded like a shot. Hanrahan roused the camp with a warning that the saloon's cottonwood ridgepole was about to give way. He set everyone he could awaken to shoring up the sod roof and gave out free drinks to those who helped. Some of those awakened, Billy Dixon included, noted later that there was no visible crack in the stout ridgepole.

There is evidence that the saloon keeper had received intelligence from Lee and Reynolds, the post traders at Fort Supply in the Indian Territory, of rumors that Adobe Walls would be the target of a raid on the 27th. Rather than become the butt of the hunters' rough humor by predicting an attack that might never happen, Hanrahan had probably fired his pistol and used the ridgepole as an excuse for waking them.

Kit Carson at the First Battle of Adobe Walls, **painting by Richard Hogue (courtesy of the artist)**

"In the old days when we were a strong and happy people, all our power came to us from the sacred hoop of the nation, and as long as the hoop was unbroken the people flourished."

BLACK ELK OF THE OGLALA, AS TOLD TO JOHN G. NEIHARDT

As the hunters began turning back to their bedrolls, Hanrahan played out his last trick. Knowing that Dixon was planning to leave for the hunting grounds that morning, the saloon keeper sent Billy Ogg to hitch up Dixon's wagon team. Dixon stepped outside to load his pack onto his wagon.

It was 4:30 A.M., a half-hour before dawn and precisely the time the Indians chose for their assault. One group ran the hunters' horse herd before them while the main force drove straight for the buildings where they expected to surprise the sleeping whites.

Ogg and Dixon saw the attackers at the same time, Ogg running for his life as Dixon fired the first shot of the battle. They barely made the safety of the saloon as the Indians rushed through the street. They were joined in the saloon by Bat Masterson, Hanrahan, and several others in different stages of readiness.

Blacksmith Tom O'Keefe, followed closely by Sam Smith, ran barefoot from his shop to the Rath & Company store. Inside were store manager James Langston, bookkeeper George Eddy, William Olds, and Andrew Johnson, none of them professional hunters. Hannah Olds, the only woman at the post, was there with her husband.

At the Myers & Leonard store, Fred Leonard broke open a case of brand-new Sharps rifles that had been sent to him for testing and passed them out. Several hunters, including Dutch Henry, had taken refuge in the store, and they eagerly armed themselves with the powerful weapons.

The concerted fire from the men in the saloon covered the settlement for the crucial minutes before those in the other buildings were able to organize their defenses. Handguns proved invaluable in the close combat that followed as the Indians threw their full strength against the sod saloon. They backed their horses against the doors and climbed to the roof, and one warrior even threw a wooden barrel against the door. Quanah proved that he was no behind-the-lines general when he rode in close enough to toss his lance through a slightly open door.

The tide of battle turned against the Indians in those first crucial moments when they lost the element of surprise. As the defenders dug shooting portals in the walls and brought their terrible buffalo guns to bear, the raiders discovered that the magic paint wouldn't turn the bullets of the big rifles.

Quanah had his horse shot from under him and was forced to take cover. A powder horn he wore probably saved his life when it partially deflected a bullet that struck him between the shoulder blade and neck. The attackers were forced to change tactics after Quanah was wounded, and took up firing positions behind the stacks of buffalo hides or dug sniping holes in the stockade. Though some rode through the town and fired from behind their horses, they didn't try another mounted charge into the buildings. Twenty warriors tried to force the door of the Rath & Company store and were repulsed with difficulty.

Billy Tyler, a teamster for Myers & Leonard, made a dash through a hail of bullets to the corral in an attempt to look after the horses. Just as he reentered the store, he delayed a moment to return fire and was hit through both lungs. Tyler and the young Masterson were friends, and the future gunfighter ran from the saloon to the store to be with him. There was nothing Masterson could do; Tyler died shortly afterward.

Brothers Jacob and Isaac Schiedler, teamsters for Brick Bond, were caught sleeping in their wagon at the time of the attack and went unnoticed as the Indians passed around them. When they were discovered, they were killed along with their big Newfoundland dog. The Indians scalped both brothers and the dog as well.

In the first minutes of the fight the Indians charged several times to the calls of their own bugler, possibly a former Army scout. Charley Armitage and Dutch Henry, firing from the Myers & Leonard store, both claimed to have killed him as he stood near the Schiedlers' wagon.

One lone young brave actually charged the Rath & Company store, landed running from his horse, and fired his revolver through a loophole in the sod wall. He inflicted no casualties within but was killed for his daring attempt. Despite covering fire from the warriors in the corral, others were

THE BUFFALO-INDIAN NICKEL

BY LEE SULLENGER

By the second decade of the twentieth century, the United States had been a republic for over 120 years. The buffalo had almost been exterminated, and the Plains tribes had long since been disarmed, unhorsed, and herded onto reservations. Americans who had seen the buffalo in the wild or met the free Indians were themselves aging into oblivion. The time was ripe to bring the buffalo and the Indian out of the dustbin of history, to look upon them with the romantic vision that became a hallmark of the American character.

What better way to use them than on an American coin? The United States had already taken a new direction in the production of its currency by assigning coin design to world-famous artists. The Irish artist Augustus Saint-Gaudens established the trend in 1907 with his designs for the ten-dollar gold piece and the twenty-dollar "Double Eagle"—coins that were immediately hailed for their beauty.

In 1913 one of Saint-Gaudens' students, James Earl Fraser, designed a new five-cent piece. For the face of the coin he used the profile of a Plains Indian. His most prominent model was the Sioux chief Iron Tail, who had fought against Custer's 7th Cavalry at the battle of the Little Big Horn. On the coin's reverse he fashioned a buffalo standing on a Western prairie knoll.

In production until 1938, the coin became one of the most famous American coins. Over one billion were minted. And so were the Indian and the buffalo enshrined in the American mind, as much a part of American history as the Liberty Bell and the Betsy Ross flag.

A 1938 buffalo-Indian nickel. (courtesy of Lee Sullenger)

killed as they rode directly into the hunters' fire in attempts to rescue their wounded and dead. The bold horsemen's deeds even won the admiration of the hardened professional hunters. That the Indians were forced to leave behind the bodies lying close to the buildings attests to the efficiency of the white men's fire.

By afternoon the Indians settled in for a siege they were ill equipped to maintain. Their light trade rifles couldn't match the range, accuracy, and firepower of the heavy modern sporting weapons in the hands of the experienced hunters. The buffalo guns found their targets even when the Indians withdrew to twice the range of their own rifles.

When ammunition ran low at the saloon, Dixon and Hanrahan made a run to the Rath & Company store. The defenders of the store pleaded with Dixon to stay with them to make up for their lack of experienced marksmen

**Possibly Billy Dixon
(courtesy of Kansas State
Historical Society,
Topeka, Kansas)**

and to protect Mrs. Olds. He did so while Hanrahan returned to the saloon with the ammunition.

The Cheyenne were ready to flay Isatai for the failure of his medicine. Isatai had observed the fight from what he thought was a safe distance but had his medicine-painted horse shot from under him anyway. He accused the Cheyenne of violating his medicine by killing a skunk before the battle.

Quanah was sore, tired, and disgusted with Isatai, the Cheyenne, and the whole situation. He had a number of casualties and few scalps to show for them, and while he had captured the horse herd, he hadn't secured the guns and ammunition that were his primary objective. Though he held the siege for about a week, he did so without hope for success. He knew that his dream of a united Indian resistance was dead.

Quanah was correct in his assessment, and on the third day of the siege Billy Dixon added insult to injury. Using one of the new Sharps, he took what he called a "scratch shot" at a group of warriors on a rise to the west of the Rath & Company store. One of the riders fell, struck dead. The distance of Dixon's famed "long shot" was later estimated at fifteen hundred yards. After that, none of the Indians ventured close enough to fire an effective shot.

On the night of July 1, Henry Lease managed to slip past the Indian patrols to carry Fred Leonard's plea for help to Myers in Dodge City. Because they feared that Lease had been intercepted, the hide men sent out another messenger a few days later. Both men arrived safely.

Other hunters, drawn by the gunfire, began to filter in from the plains. Covering fire from the post kept the Indians from following them in. By the sixth day after the attack, there were nearly one hundred refugees at Adobe Walls.

The Indian casualties numbered about thirty killed and wounded, some of whom died later of their wounds. After the Indians withdrew, the hunters decapitated the thirteen bodies they found near the buildings and nailed the heads to the gate of the Myers & Leonard stockade. The last white casualty of the battle was William Olds, killed by an accidental discharge of his own rifle when he fell down a ladder. He was buried not far from the Rath & Company store; Billy Tyler and the Schiedler brothers were buried on the east side of the stockade.

Not knowing how severely they had discouraged the Indians, the hunters and merchants eventually decided to abandon the post and retreat to Dodge. After they left, the Indians returned long enough to burn the buildings to the ground.

Fifty years later, Olive K. Dixon, the widow of the man who had made the long shot, was accompanied to Adobe Walls by veterans Andrew Johnson, Brick Bond, and J. Wright Mooar. Her efforts to memorialize the battle were realized at an anniversary celebration when a red granite monument bearing the names of the white participants was erected at the site. The graves of Olds, Tyler, and the Schiedlers were located and marked with headstones.

In 1929 Mrs. Dixon had her husband's remains removed from the cemetery in Texline and returned to Adobe Walls. On June 27, Billy Dixon was buried with Masonic rites at the site of his "long shot."

It remained for the other side of the conflict to make the last contribution to the memorial. On October 19, 1941, representatives of the Comanche, Cheyenne, and Kiowa tribes met at Adobe Walls to dedicate a monument to the Indian dead. The Comanche delegate was Yellowfish, who as a teenager had participated in the battle. The old warrior stood before the red granite monolith with a Cheyenne chief at one side and a Kiowa at the other as he read the names of the warriors who had faced the thunder of the buffalo guns. ∎

THE LAST SCALPS

BY R. C. HOUSE AND HAROLD A. GEER

EMINENT WESTERN HISTORIAN FREDERICK JACKSON TURNER DECLARED in his much-acclaimed 1893 philosophical treatise, *The Significance of the Frontier in American History*, that for all intents and purposes the American Western frontier had been officially conquered by 1880. Settled and marked off though it may have been, the West was still wild and woolly enough not to see its final recognized incidents of scalping—the brutal and grisly act of taking victory trophies—until much later. One incident, involving only Indians, took place nearly a decade after 1880. The last recorded scalping of whites by Indians happened more than thirty years later, in 1911.

In an in-depth study, the unpublished "Notes on Human Trophies of Frontier North America," Harold A. Geer pinpoints these last acknowledged incidents of scalping.

"No one knows for sure," Geer points out, "when the last scalping took place on the North American frontier. However, the last Indian war party to spill blood in intertribal warfare and the last scalp dance by any of the Plains tribes took place in the summer of 1889.

"A party of Gros Ventres from the United States crossed from Montana into Canada and drove off some horses belonging to the Piegan Blackfoot Indians of Alberta. Six of the Piegans—Young Pine, Crazy Crow, Prairie

Chicken Old Man, Calf Robe, Wolf Sitting Alone, and Hind Gun—went in pursuit of the raiders and overtook them near the foot of the Bear Paw Mountains in Montana. During the firefight that followed, two of the raiders were killed. Young Pine scalped the first one and Hind Gun, the second—the last scalp known to be taken by a member of the Blackfoot Nation.

"The last white men known to be scalped by Indians were some stockmen gathering cattle in northwestern Nevada in January, 1911.

"A party of renegades under Shoshone Mike left their reservation in central Nevada after Mike's tribe told him to get out and stay out. Shoshone Mike was a known troublemaker with a violent temper and hatred for the white man's rules for governing reservation Indians. In leaving, Mike gathered two women, two teenage men, three children, and five adult men like himself. Shoshone Mike had aspirations of leading his small band of 12 renegades to conquest and fame as he would have in the old days when warfare was an honorable profession.

"The weather was very cold, the band was hungry, and became quarrelsome. Suddenly they came upon the ranch hands camped in the shelter of a small canyon. The cowboys were huddled around a campfire eating their evening meal of freshly killed young calf. Shoshone Mike knew he could walk into the camp and ask for food, and that it would be given freely by the unwritten code of the territory. No man would be refused food and shelter when he rode into anyone's camp cold and hungry. But Shoshone Mike did not want hospitality; he wanted scalps.

"After the cowboys were asleep, the Indians crept into their camp, stole the beef carcass and spent most of the night regaining their strength. At dawn the cowboys discovered the meat was missing and reached for their rifles. Shoshone Mike gave his war cry and his party fired two volleys into the men camped in the canyon. As the men fell, the Indians rushed the camp and scalped all four, yanked out their teeth for the gold fillings, stripped them of clothing they needed and dumped the bodies into the ice-covered stream.

"When the ranch hands failed to return to Surprise Valley, a group of ranchers went in search of them and found their bodies in the canyon stream. Ornaments, feathers, and an abandoned tipi were ample evidence of the identity of the attackers. A 22-man posse of sheriff's deputies and state police under a Captain Donnelly, superintendent of the Nevada State Police, was soon on the killers' trail.

"After several days the posse discovered smoke from the Indians' campfire at Rabbit Springs. The posse had crept to within 200 yards of the camp when they were discovered by one of the women going after water. She gave the alarm that opened a firefight with well-aimed volleys from the posse. One of the possemen, Ed Hogle, was killed when he got to his feet to rush

This drawing by Colonel Anburey of General Burgoyne's army was sketched near Ticonderoga, New York, in July 1777. The British war veteran told how General Burgoyne had encouraged his Indian allies to "take the scalps of the dead, when killed by your fire and in fair opposition" but warned (in vain) that "on no account are they to be taken from the wounded or even dying." From *Anburey's Travels*.

the Indian position. When the fight ended, one woman, who surrendered, and three children, were the only survivors of Shoshone Mike's band.

"A search of the bodies and the camp revealed personal effects, clothing and saddles of the slaughtered ranch men. A wave of shame swept the Indian reservation because most of the Indians believed that Shoshone Mike had disgraced all red men by breaking a peace with the white men." ■

THE HANDY DANDY SCALPER'S GUIDE FOR RIGHT- AND LEFT-HANDERS

BY ARDATH MAYHAR

Step 1: Render victim either dead or reliably unconscious.

Step 2: Approach with caution, keeping weapons in position. Many a scalper has been unpleasantly surprised by a "dead" victim. Left-handers should exercise unusual care, since left-handed shots and knife strokes are sometimes unreliable.

Step 3: If victim is face-up, roll over to a face-down position. If right-handed, approach victim from left side and use left foot to precipitate roll. Left-handers, approach from right side and use right foot.

Step 4: Remain alert for any sign of life. To ensure cooperation, bash victim with tomahawk, pistol butt, or rock.

Step 5: Grasp hair in best position for full scalp or scalplock as per your personal preference and pull hair up tight. Right-handers should grasp hair with left hand; left-handers, with right hand.

Step 6: Draw scalping knife with unoccupied hand and hold it with blade facing your body. Knife may be kept very sharp for convenience or rather dull if personal animosity is involved.

Step 7: Visualize cutting circles on scalp in order to choose trophy wisely.

Step 8: Right-handers, set knife against scalp beneath left wrist and cut with brisk clockwise motion. Left-handers, set knife against scalp beneath right wrist and use counterclockwise motion. End cut at beginning to complete circle.

Step 9: Detach scalp with deft, firm jerk.

Step 10: Right-handers usually express appropriate sentiments with triumphant cries. A short celebratory dance is permissible if situation warrants. Some left-handers seem to enjoy waving scalp and emitting Rebel yells, but proponents of good form frown upon excessive use of these expressions. Three waves and two yells, or alternatively two waves and three yells, are the maximum allowed to maintain good manners.

Step 11: Remember to dry well and mount handsomely. Correctly preserved scalp locks and full scalps are tasteful decorations for any wickiup, bunkhouse, lodge, chuck wagon, or longhouse.

Head scalp, complete with ears and cheeks, Sioux, 1836 (courtesy of Paul Dyck Collection, Paul Dyck Foundation, Arizona)

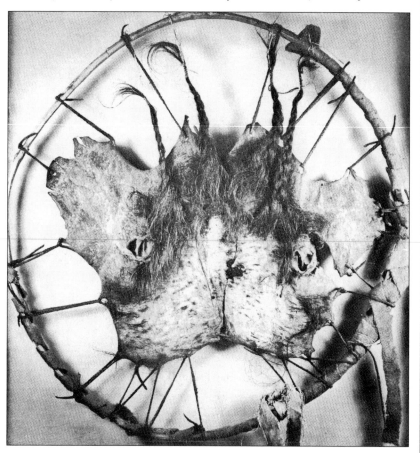

III. THE SOLDIER'S STORY

THE INDIAN-FIGHTING ARMY

BY JAY SMITH

THE NOMADIC LIFESTYLE OF THE PLAINS INDIANS, THEIR ABILITY TO fight from horseback, and the vast area they ranged posed a unique problem for the U.S. Army. All or portions of twenty-five regiments of the U.S. regular army participated in eleven campaigns to solve it.

Army administration separated the U.S. into four divisions. The Division of the Missouri, commanded by Lieutenant General William T. Sherman, was the main site of the Indian Wars; it extended from Canada to the Gulf of Mexico, from the settlements west of the Mississippi River to the Rocky Mountains. This area of more than one million square miles was inhabited by about two hundred thousand Indians. The division had three departments:

1. The Department of the Missouri, commanded by Major General Philip H. Sheridan, covered the area now included in the states of Illinois, Missouri, Kansas, Colorado, New Mexico, and half of Oklahoma.

2. The Department of the Platte, commanded by Colonel Christopher C. Augur, covered the area now included in the states of Iowa, Nebraska, Wyoming, and Utah.

3. The Department of the Dakota, commanded by Brigadier General Alfred H. Terry, covered the area now included in the states of Minnesota, North Dakota, South Dakota, and Montana.

The Department of Texas, added later, included the state of Texas and half of the Oklahoma Territory.

A handful of officers, an exclusive club during Sherman's term as commander, managed the departments. When they transferred, they simply exchanged places. They owed their rank to Civil War service and were comparatively young at the time of their initial assignment. The key members were Sheridan and Augur, Major Generals Winfield S. Hancock and John M.

Schofield, and Brigadier Generals Philip S. Cooke, George Crook, Oliver O. Howard, Edward O. C. Ord, John Pope, and Alfred H. Terry.

Under Sherman, Sheridan was responsible for division operations. Sometimes he gave directions, but most of the time he allowed the department commanders to run their own departments. Some, like Crook, Terry, and Howard, exercised personal command of major expeditions. Others, such as Augur, Pope, and E. O. C. Ord, worked through subordinates.

THE ARMY'S TWO BASIC COMPONENTS WERE "LINE" AND "STAFF." THE line was composed of the branches of the service which did the fighting: cavalry, infantry, and artillery. Combat forces were scattered over the frontier in small two- and three-company posts to provide protection to the entire area. The Army usually thought a battalion (three companies) sufficient force to operate alone on the Plains. Indeed, it was a rare occasion when an entire regiment would serve as a unit, as did the U.S. 7th Cavalry at the Battle of the Little Big Horn. Even rarer was a force of two regiments, like the one Sheridan took into Indian Territory in December 1868.

When forces larger than a battalion were used, they usually consisted of two or more companies from two or more regiments. Often they were mixed arms—that is, both cavalry and infantry. Settlements and railroads had to be protected, so parts of a regiment would be left in garrison and along the rails for patrol duty. The other groups combined to take to the field against hostiles. Half of the forces usually took to the field during the summer months.

The regiment was the Western Army's largest unit. Regiments, or parts of regiments, were often combined under a single commander to operate as a unit. A cavalry regiment consisted of three battalions, each containing four companies—a total of twelve companies. The commanding officer was a colonel, usually on detached service performing higher command duties while a lieutenant colonel held actual field command. Majors commanded the battalions; the company officers were one captain, one first lieutenant, and one second lieutenant. In the infantry, a regiment was ten companies, with one major to a regiment.

The terms "troop" and "squadron" weren't used until 1880. The battalions were numbered first, second, and third, and the companies were lettered *A* through *M*, with *J* omitted to avoid confusion with *I* in handwritten orders.

The nature of frontier service made the company the basic military unit. Soldiers lived in company quarters, ate in company mess halls, participated in company team sports, and were primarily identified with their company. Besides the captain and the two lieutenants, each company had one first sergeant, five line sergeants, four corporals, and a varying number of privates. The first sergeant actually ran the company, and was expected to do so by the officers.

The Declaration of Independence noted that all men were created equal, but when men joined the Army they relinquished their equality. At the top of the caste system the officers had a grade structure of their own, ranging from a second lieutenant to the commanding general. Company-grade officers personally led the troops. Field-grade officers commanded larger units, and senior officers commanded departments, districts, and bureaus.

Officers were responsible for combat readiness in their commands. They had to provide the basic needs—food for both men and animals, clothing and shelter for their men. Continual training and practice drill kept the

SCOUTS AND TRACKERS

BY MARYLOIS DUNN

The scout was a specialist, a man with the extraordinary ability to carry in his mind a map of the terrain he had traveled, to absorb and speak the native languages. If he was a white man, he had probably come west to "see the elephant," to see what lay just around the next bend of the river. When he saw it, it became a part of him.

The scout drew wages far over that of the common laborer because of his abilities, his special knowledge, and his responsible position. Though the Army scout had no formal rank, he usually earned a wage equal to that of a captain, and the wise officer would follow his scout's advice. It was the scout's job to lead a wagon train of westering pilgrims or an Army expedition to the desired destination without benefit of road or map, to see that they had game to eat, and to ensure his charges a sufficient water supply. It didn't matter where he'd come from or if he still used the name with which he'd been born. If he knew the country and could speak Indian tongues, he was in demand.

The scout's work took him out ahead of his party, and he frequently worked in dangerous conditions. If he survived, it was because he was a man of superior common sense and excellent judgment. Some scouts worked alone or with one or two partners. Others, like Kit Carson and Al Sieber, worked with Indians with whom they were fast friends.

Depending on the season, the scout could tell from the condition of the grass who or what had passed over it, how long before, and how many there were. He studied the broken and bent twigs and the displaced rocks for clues. If he hit a long trail, a good tracker could tell which horses were male and which were female, or if there were mules in the party. He could even number the riders and determine their gender. If he was tracking Indians, he could tell which tribe they were. Since he knew the habits of game animals and could identify each species from its sign, he could predict their moves. He seldom lacked for meat.

Even the stones were an open book to the knowledgeable frontiersman. Each stone had its earth side and its weathered side, and it fell or settled heavy side down in hard rains. To a good tracker a displaced stone was a message as clear as a written sign. A stone set on end, leaning against another stone, was a silent SOS, a call for help. An overturned stone signified that an expedition hadn't located its prey. A partly-turned stone meant disaster or bad news ahead. A line of stones set in the natural way, heavy side down, indicated that an expedition had been successful.

Manure, animal and human, was another important source of information. The degree of moisture indicated the time elapsed since it was deposited. The composition of a dropping revealed the animal's food source, since different grasses and foods left special traces. The droppings of a wild horse, for example, weren't likely to contain the corn or other grain fed to cavalry mounts.

Many scouts preferred mules to horses, since on rapid journeys horses required rest and forage at more frequent intervals. A mule could graze as he went, live on food a horse couldn't eat, and go longer without water. The mule couldn't outrun a horse in a flat-out race, but its superior endurance and intelligence made it a more worthy mount for the scout. After all, the purpose of the Army scout was to find Indians, not to outrun or outfight them.

Scouting was a job that, like the West itself, was unforgiving of error. Though there was always the chance of making a fatal mistake, many scouts lived to see old age. Officers or emigrants who failed to heed their scout's advice seldom met with such success. Much to his disgust, George Armstrong Custer's best scouts and trackers refused to accompany him to his fate on that last day at the Little Big Horn. He should have listened to them when they told him of the dust cloud sent up by the immense Indian horse herd. The Donner party's scout warned the members of the party that the mountain pass was too dangerous and unreliable in the winter, then left when they wouldn't abandon their plans to press on.

They should have remembered a Western saying: "When you pay a man to give advice, a smart man will listen."

troops ready to move efficiently in field operations and to fight effectively in battle. At most of the Western posts, contract labor was either limited or not available, and because at least a portion of the officers were West Point graduates trained as engineers, they supervised the enlisted men in post construction.

The promotion system strained the officers' morale. Through the rank of captain, promotion was by seniority within the regiment, and through colonel, in the Army (cavalry, infantry, or artillery). A new second lieutenant could look forward to reaching the grade of major in about twenty-five years.

Officers could marry, and even on the frontier posts, most married officers were assigned some type of quarters. It was a hard life in isolated locations, and field duty caused long separations. Even so, officer families on the frontier seemed reasonably happy. Some officers, by either their own choice or that of their wives, elected to leave their families in the East and were content with periodic visits on leave of absence. A considerable number of officers were bachelors, perhaps because of the shortage of suitable single women in the West. Others were determined on a military career and didn't want to subject a lady to the hardships of the frontier.

Officers were seldom dismissed for minor breaches of discipline, but if

Soldier and horse (courtesy of Kansas State Historical Society, Topeka, Kansas)

convicted they were fined or suspended from service for a period of time. If charges were preferred against an officer and if a court-martial was approved, he was relieved of duty and placed under some type of restriction until the trial. If in garrison, he might be restricted to quarters; in the field, the commander established the restriction.

The number of officers arrested in quarters could be substantial. At critical moments in frontier warfare, a significant number of officers were unavailable for field duty. At the Battle of the Little Big Horn, for example, the U. S. 7th Cavalry went into action with fifteen of its forty-three officers absent, including the colonel, two majors, and four captains.

"Conduct unbecoming an officer and a gentleman" was the single charge in most of the cases in which an officer was dismissed from the service. Drunkenness, stealing, cowardice, and failure to maintain proper moral standards provided the specifics for many court-martials.

Next in order came the noncommissioned officers. They made the Army function by carrying out the orders of the officers. These NCOs directly supervised the enlisted men. They, too, had certain privileges: for example, men in the senior grades were allowed to marry and were furnished quarters when available. They, too, were relieved from mundane tasks, and also were granted substantial legal powers over those of lesser ranks.

The veterans who enlisted in the regular army after volunteer forces mustered out formed the backbone of the noncommissioned ranks for twenty years after the Civil War. The practical experience of these soldiers, many of whom had held commissioned rank in either the Union or the Confederate Army, made them superior noncoms. They were competent professionals.

The lowest order was that of the ordinary soldier, the private. He led a difficult life, often with inadequate food, shelter, and medical care, and at low pay. Constant field duty along with occasional combat made it a hazardous occupation. The military system of justice gave officers significant legal authority over enlisted men. At any time an officer could, and often did, chastise an individual soldier. Court-martial sentences ranged from death during wartime to cruel and unusual punishment for minor offenses in time of peace. It was a normal practice for officers to control enlisted men through fear.

Infantrymen came in all sizes, but the cavalryman was a little man—the horse also had to carry a significant amount of equipment. Top weight was about 165 pounds, optimum between 130 and 150 pounds.

All of the enlisted men were volunteers. Many were recent immigrants—chiefly from Ireland, Germany, and England—and some had seen service in European armies. There were also young farm boys seeking adventure, men looking for a free trip West to get to the gold fields, and those who were

"The only good Indians I ever saw were dead."

GENERAL PHILIP HENRY SHERIDAN

one jump ahead of the law. A soldier had almost no privacy; his assigned living space contained only a bunk and a footlocker in a large room with his comrades. In quarters, on duty, and in the field, virtually every moment he spent in the company of his fellows.

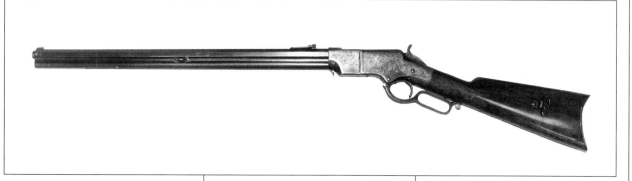

THE HENRY RIFLE

BY JIM MILLER

Some said you could load it on Sunday and fire it all week. Considering that the Henry was the first effective, fifteen-shot repeating rifle at a time when the generally single-shot Hawken, Sharps, and Kentucky Long rifles were still in use, that saying was justified. Like the Spencer rifle, it played an important part in the advancement of firearms and firepower in Western weapons. And, just like the Spencer, it got its baptism of fire on the battlegrounds of the Civil War.

B. Tyler Henry designed the rifle that carried his name. Just as Horace Smith and Samuel B. Wesson had a hand in creating the metallic cartridge and the small-caliber handgun to go with it in 1858, Henry created a large-caliber cartridge for the rifle he patented for use that same year. In 1860 he received a patent for the rifle for which he'd designed the cartridge. Such a venture was a daring feat indeed, for at that time the new metallic cartridge was looked upon as nothing more than a novelty, a passing fad.

It was officially called the Henry Lever-Action Cartridge Magazine Rifle. The shell casing and bullet were a .44

caliber rim-fire. Although it was a lever action rifle, it differed at several points from the Spencer. First, the lever action itself performed the job of ejecting the spent cartridge and loading a fresh one into the chamber. Anyone well versed in the use of the Henry could fire up to thirty cartridges per minute. The standard barrel length was twenty-four inches, and the tubular magazine nested directly under it. At the end of the barrel a collar swiveled out to open the spring-operated magazine for loading.

It weighed in at a hefty nine and a half pounds, but those who got hold of one back in 1860, when the rifle was introduced, learned that it was worth its weight in gold. It was more expensive to produce than the Spencer and might not have gotten much notice had not President Lincoln encouraged its use. The War Department turned the Henry down for use as a Union weapon, saying that it hadn't been sufficently proven. In retrospect this excuse seems difficult to believe, since the Spencer was in reality as brand-spanking new as the Henry. It hadn't been proven either, but it had been test-fired by the president, who approved of it, and was immediately test-fired by the Army and the Navy, who also approved it for use.

The Henry excelled in range, accuracy, and firepower, but it had its shortcomings; dust and dirt could enter the uncovered receiver group and gum up the works. Although the rest of the rifle had a sturdy structure, the cartridge magazine dented easily, a drawback

that significantly decreased firepower since the magazine couldn't be loaded beyond the dented point.

Despite these design flaws, the Henry rifle is worth mentioning as an important weapon, not in only the Civil War but in the Westward movement. It was the forerunner of a series of rifles that still bear the Winchester name today. It was Henry's genius as an inventor, combined with Oliver F. Winchester's knowledge as a businessman, that began an American legend in the field of weaponry, the Winchester Repeating Rifle. Winchester thought so much of Henry for his accomplishments that he decreed that every rim-fire cartridge manufactured by the Winchester Company would bear an "H" stamped on its base.

If you ever wondered what the "H" on the bottom of those .22 cartridges you used as a youngster meant...well, now you know—it stands for B. Tyler Henry.

ABOVE: A .44 caliber Henry repeating rifle with a 24" barrel produced by the New Haven Arms Company under Henry's Patent (1860); this rifle has a brass finish and is presentation engraved with the inscription, "Presented by the U.S. Government To Charles H. Bohmstedt, 1st A.C., Co. A 3rd Regt., United States Veteran Volunteers, For 4 Years Of Faithful Service During the War of Rebellion." (courtesy of Metzger Collection, Texas A&M University Sam Houston Sanders Corps of Cadets Center)

A soldier's rations depended upon what was available. In garrison, it was range beef or occasional game meat, and dried beans either boiled or baked. There was always coffee. When bread wasn't served, there was hardtack. If there was a shortage of meat, bacon or salt pork was issued. Meat was most commonly boiled, even bacon and salt pork. Soldiers also roasted and baked it, or made hash and stew. Condiments included brown sugar, salt, vinegar, and molasses.

A day's field ration was one pound of hardtack, three-quarters of a pound of bacon or salt pork, one ounce of coffee, and a little salt. Much of the hardtack was left over from the Civil War; it was rock hard and often contained weevils. To prepare it, the soldier pounded the biscuit into crumbs and dumped it into soup, fried it in meat fat, or put it into the coffeepot.

Each man was expected to prepare his own rations in the field. His mess kit was a folding-handled frying pan and a shallow plate. He favored a pipe for his after-dinner smoke because it was cheap, better in the wind, and showed less light at night.

Stockpiles of surplus Civil War clothing were used for ten years after the war. The basic issue consisted of the navy blue wool sack coat with a single row of brass eagle buttons, two pairs of light blue kersey trousers, two gray or dark blue flannel shirts, a couple of suits of wrist- and ankle-length two-piece underwear, a caped overcoat of light blue wool, a pair of rough boots, a forage cap, and a leather waist belt with some accouterments. Since they were made of wool, these uniforms were unsuited for warm weather, and they weren't thick enough in really cold weather, but they were issued to soldiers from Texas to Montana. Clothing came in four sizes; the company tailor remade it into well-fitting uniforms.

Soldiers paid little attention to uniform regulations when they were in the field. Supplies were always short, so commanders had to allow the soldiers to wear what was available. An easy next step was to let them wear commercial items; some soldiers bought their own broad-brimmed hats, neckerchiefs, and buckskin trousers.

In the field, everyone slept in tents. Those provided the officers were large and comfortable, and the soldiers erected them. The troops were issued two-man pup tents. In fair weather everyone slept on the ground rather than bother with the tents. Animals were tethered without shelter.

Duty in garrison soon fell into a routine of either training or work. On Saturdays, in place of drill, the men "policed" the parade grounds, quarters, and stables, giving them a thorough cleaning. Sundays were reserved for troop inspections. There were no assigned chaplains except for the six black regiments, who by law were authorized to have them.

Soldiers were always assigned work details. The men on kitchen police chopped the stove wood, carried water for the cooks, waited on tables, and washed the dishes and pots. At many posts, water barrels were filled and hauled around to the mess hall, barracks, and quarters. There were details assigned to obtain wood, hay, and ice, and always there was guard duty.

Barracks conditions varied from post to post. Some were well built and comfortable. Others were just the reverse—leaky, vermin-infested, and crowded.

In the field, soldiers quickly became dusty, dirty, and smelly. Sometimes long supply trains carried everything for a comfortable trip, but there were also "stripped-saddle" marches where the men took only bare essentials. The average march covered about twenty miles in a day. Under normal conditions, a column marched for four or five hours in the morning and halted before noon for about two hours. The horses and mules were fed, watered and rested, then the men fixed their lunch. The soldiers usually went into camp in the afternoon, to allow enough time to set up camp. The O.D. selected camp areas and sites for the picket lines. Horses were cared for, tents pitched, dinner cooked, and guard details posted. Sunday was no exception; it was just another day.

For a march in hostile country, other preparations were necessary. The usual field column marched as follows: far ahead rode the Indian scouts under the command of a young lieutenant; next came the advance guard in front and flankers on the sides; then the commanding officer and his staff led the main body; after them came the chief of scouts, newspaper correspondents, the surgeon, the supply wagons and ambulances or mule trains; last came the rear guard. Once near the enemy, the officers kept the columns closed.

The rate at which cavalry moved across the ground was important, not only on the march but in battle, for thus did the commander plan the timing of his actions. At a walk, cavalry could cover four miles in an hour, or 117 yards in a minute. The maneuvering trot was at a rate of eight miles an hour, or 235 yards a minute, while at the gallop the rate was twelve miles an hour, or 352 yards a minute. The full or extended gallop was at the rate of sixteen miles an hour, or 470 yards a minute. Perhaps the best rapid movement was the alternating gallop and trot. The rate was ten miles per hour, or 293 yards a minute. Obviously, the terrain, weather, and condition of the horses significantly affected the rate.

The slowest or weakest animals determined the pace of the march. When marching together, the cavalry could easily outdistance the infantry for the first three or four days. But by the end of the first week the roles were reversed, and the cavalry would find the infantry already in camp at the end of the day's travel. An officer logged marching records measured by a meter connected to the wheel on an ambulance. The objective was to bring the troops to the right place at the right time, ready to fight.

In order to win battles, soldiers had to be skilled in the art of war and to be disciplined. Training provided the basis for both. In 1863 the Army published a technical manual for cavalry regimental training; it was revised in 1878. These two publications were the bible for the Indian-fighting cavalry.

Similar technical manuals issued for the infantry provided instructions for the individual and units, both dismounted and mounted. The manuals instructed the soldier on how to stand at attention, facings, the way to march, and his manual of arms. Once a soldier developed skill in dismounted techniques, he was ready to learn the same procedures on horseback. There were 70 lessons in the School of the Soldier Dismounted; while mounted, 60 lessons in the School of the Platoon, and 120 lessons in the School of the Troop. Each lesson was one and a half hours long. Once his men mastered those drill lessons, a commander could take his regiment from point A to point B in a disciplined and military manner and maneuver it in combat operations.

The soldiers first learned to shoot without using ammunition. An officer positioned a weapon with sandbags so that the sights lined up on a target. Each soldier looked through the sights at the target to see the correct alignment. Then the officer moved the sights off-target. Each man was required to realign the sights to the officer's satisfaction. After several days of this drill, soldiers knew how to sight their weapons.

Once he learned the techniques of firing, the soldier was ready for the

Government building at Fort Dodge, April 1879 (courtesy of Kansas State Historical Society, Topeka, Kansas)

target range. Recruits supposedly fired at ranges of from 100 to 500 yards as part of their recruit training, and were expected to score fifty percent hits. The regulars, in their scheduled annual target practice, fired ten rounds at each target up to 400 yards and five rounds at each target up to 800 yards. Then in unit training, squads, platoons, and companies fired forty rounds. Marksmanship qualifications, firing ten shots at 400 yards, were: first class, hit the target six or more times; second class, hit the target four or five times; third class, hit the target three times or less.

MR. GATLING'S INFERNAL MACHINE

BY LEE SULLENGER

The idea was as old as Leonardo da Vinci's sixteenth-century doodlings—a multibarreled, self-loading weapon that could fire numerous rounds in rapid succession. Many inventors had tried their hands at it without creating a militarily feasible weapon. Some designs verged on the bizarre, such as the English inventor's gun that fired round bullets for Christian enemies and square slugs for infidels.

Then, in 1862 the American inventor Richard Gatling patented a revolving multibarreled weapon dubbed the Gatling Gun. A hand crank rotated the gun's six barrels around its axis as a clip magazine fed it with .58 caliber cartridges. As each barrel reached the firing position, the striking hammer fell on the cartridge. The earliest model could fire 200 rounds per minute, and though there were some technical problems with the mechanism that ejected spent cartridges and loaded live rounds, the Gatling was nonetheless the first functional machine gun. It changed the face of war forever.

Gatling offered his invention to the Union during the Civil War, which rather foolishly refused to use it until after the war. The Union Army distrusted the infernal machine not only because it was something new and untried but also because of its inventor's supposed Southern sympathies. It was

perhaps an act of providence that the Gatling wasn't accepted for use in the war, for there's no doubt that it would have made that terrible conflict even bloodier.

By the end of the war Gatling had so improved the weapon that it had ten barrels and could fire 400 rounds per minute. These technical innovations made the Gatling a dependable and much-dreaded weapon sought after by armies around the world. Soldiers who could be very brave under fire from single-shot rifles in the hands of individual enemies found it much more difficult to face the Gatling's deadly, impersonal hail of bullets.

The gun went West with troops sent to fight the Plains Indians, but the nature of frontier combat and the Western terrain placed certain limitations

on the gun's effectiveness. For the most part, Indian fighting was a fast-paced cavalry affair in which the troopers found it difficult to keep the heavy Gatling, mounted on its two-wheeled carriage, in the thick of the action. But where it could be used against massed troops, an enemy stronghold, or (unfortunately) an Indian encampment, the Gatling's devastating effect could turn a battle against superior numbers into a rout.

By the early twentieth century the Gatling Gun was obsolete, replaced by more efficient water-cooled and air-cooled single-barrel machine guns that used a reciprocating hammer and belt-fed ammunition. But Richard Gatling had earned his lasting fame as the inventor of the first practical machine gun.

Soldiers spent less time training with pistols since that weapon was intended only for use in hand-to-hand combat. Sometimes they stacked up a pile of hardtack boxes to approximate a man-sized target. The soldiers rode by and fired at a distance of about thirty yards, first at a walk, then a trot, and finally a gallop.

In combat, the officers would direct the fire. For example: (unit) "Company A," (direction) "to the front," (range) "200 yards," (type of fire) "volley."

The model 1873 Springfield became the basic gun for the remainder of the Indian Wars. It was a .45 caliber trapdoor, single-shot, breech-loading weapon, which used a centerfire reloadable cartridge with a 405-grain bullet backed by seventy grains of black powder. The gun was known throughout the West as the .45-70. Total length was forty-one inches with a twenty-two-inch barrel; it weighed seven pounds and fifteen ounces. The Allin action used a rising breechlock that hinged at the front. The hammer had to be pulled back for each shot. The gun was a powerful weapon with a muzzle velocity of 1,150 feet per second and a maximum range of 2,800 yards, and it was accurate at up to 600 yards. Its accuracy was superior to that of all but the best commercial guns.

The Colt .45 caliber pistol issued to the cavalry had a seven-and-a-half-inch barrel and sights fixed-set for fifty yards. The pistol used the 255-grain bullet with forty grains of black powder. It was a powerful weapon with a range in excess of 300 yards, but even an expert shot couldn't rely on accuracy much beyond fifty yards.

There was one weapon that always proved effective against Indians, and its use invariably dispersed and demoralized them—artillery. The Hotchkiss mountain gun was the most popular artillery piece in Western service. A 1.65-inch, two-pounder steel rifle, it could be fired accurately at ranges up to 4,000 yards, and it was lightweight enough to be pulled or mule-packed almost anywhere.

Gatling's rapid-fire weapon fired 350 rounds of rifle ammunition per minute from a bank of ten revolving barrels turned by a crank and fed from a hopper. It was cumbersome, subject to fouling and jamming, and some commanders, like Lieutenant Colonel George A. Custer and Colonel Nelson A. Miles, opposed its use.

The artillery regiments were stationed along the coastal areas and were not available to the armies on the Great Plains. Hence the infantry and cavalry forces who wanted to use artillery against the Indians could requisition the weapons, but had to train their own men to serve as gun crews. They also had to provide the animals, either mules for pack trains or teams of horses to pull the gun carriages. Such teams usually consisted of horses condemned for use by cavalry troops.

The cavalry soldier was armed with a saber. It had a curved blade three feet long, with a triple-branched brass guard, a leather, wire-wrapped grip, and a steel scabbard; it weighed five pounds. After the Civil War, sabers were seldom used in Indian fights; the pistol was more effective at close quarters. In addition, the saber and scabbard made too much noise on the march.

Improved weapons led to significant changes in Army tactics during the Indian Wars. The trained and disciplined soldiers simply outgunned the Indians in any firefight where they could control a field of fire.

The Army purchased good animals for combat. Cavalry horses were from five to eight years of age, from fourteen to sixteen hands high, and weighed from 750 to 1,000 pounds. The ideal was fifteen hands and 1,000 pounds. All troop horses were geldings, though sometimes an officer would have his own privately owned mare. Each man was permanently assigned his horse. Horses were allowed fourteen pounds of hay and twelve pounds of grain per day in garrison. In the field, grain was carried when wagons were used in connection with a march.

When the horses were "colored" in order to make each company uniform, all regimental animals were assembled and separated according to color. The company commanders selected colors for their companies in the order of their rank. Most of the horses were bays (a red color). There were also grays, blacks, and sorrels (orange). A last group called "brindles," which included leftovers and odd colors, was left for the lowest-ranking captain. Then the soldiers within the company chose. Noncommissioned officers selected in order of their rank. In the general distribution, the best soldiers were assigned the best horses.

The condition of the horses was of considerable concern to a good cavalry commander, and his officers and noncoms. A soldier watered, groomed, and fed his horse before he took care of himself. Duty officers and stable sergeants supervised stable activities. Ordinary care required continual checking. For example, horseshoes nailed to the horses' feet needed to be inspected for replacement. A lost shoe meant a lame horse, so the soldier carried extra shoes in his saddlebag.

THE MILITARY STRATEGY FOR FIGHTING THE INDIANS AFTER THE CIVIL War was based on historical experience. Initially, the individual colonies, and then the national government, confronted the Indians over a period of about three hundred years (1609 to 1890). History had shown that the white men would seize the Indians' land if it held mineral or agricultural potential; treaties notwithstanding, the eventual policy of the United States was to put all Indians on reservations.

By 1868, most of the Plains Indians were already located on reservations, but there were still significant numbers roaming the unsettled areas of the plains. The Army's strategy was to destroy the Indians' supplies, property, and livestock by surprise raids on hostile villages. The warriors were driven off while the soldiers burned the tepees and killed the captured horses. Facing almost certain starvation, most of the Indians surrendered themselves to the reservations. Winter campaigns proved to be the most successful tactic. Tribes didn't fight among themselves in such weather, and they considered it unfair for the Army to do so. Indians in the snow, deprived of their food, shelter, and transportation, soon gave up.

In the summer, the strategy was to move converging columns into a battle area. Though less successful, it did keep the hostiles constantly on the move. Although the slaughter of the buffalo was never a stated government policy, it was tolerated, and in the end, the loss of their food supply did more to bring in the hostiles to the reservation than all the other methods combined.

This rare Dance Bros. & Park .44 caliber six-shot percussion revolver with 8" barrel is #177 of the 302 produced at West Columbia, Texas, during the Civil War. (courtesy of Metzger Collection, Texas A&M University Sam Houston Sanders Corps of Cadets Center)

In the Indian Wars, a fundamental mistake on the part of the government was its failure to establish a standard doctrine for the military subjugation of the Indian. Throughout the debates over size, composition, and command of the peacetime army, no one seemed to ask if the traditional organization fitted the needs of the Army's mission in the West.

Three special conditions set that mission apart from the usual military operation. First, the Army was pitted against an enemy hard to distinguish from his kinsmen who were not hostile. Second, the soldier had conflicting emotions about the Indian, often admired him in some ways and loathed him in others. The result was ambivalence, hate mixed with sympathy. Third, the Indian was an unconventional foe in his use of tactics and in defining his war aims — an expert guerrilla fighter on his own turf.

Army tactics were primarily offensive. Soldiers attacked villages, charged Indian formations, and spent a good part of their time chasing hostiles. On the other hand, they were often ambushed and harassed by warriors, and on occasion they were forced into defensive positions.

Cavalry was always supposed to maneuver in column formation. In moving to the attack, it held a slow trot until it came under fire. Then, the soldiers drew sabers or pistols and columns deployed into line, at which point they took to a full gallop. At about seventy-five to fifty yards from the enemy position, the charge sounded and the soldiers closed together knee-to-knee, and the line rushed forward at full speed. Charging in column of fours was a tactic often effective when troops had to attack through a ford in a river. Charging at extended skirmisher intervals was most effective against Indians, especially in charging through their villages.

As a rule, the attacking line was composed of about half the total strength of the force; the support and the reserve made up about a quarter each. In the charge, the dress (alignment) was on the center. At the completion of the charge, the cavalry either defeated and then pursued the enemy, or retreated and then rallied as quickly as possible. The side that produced the final reserve force was usually victorious.

Cavalry troops on the offense had two options for tactics. The first, called a penetration, was the classic European charge. The object was to ride over the enemy line by sheer weight of men and horses. This tactic was generally used in combination with infantry. One's own infantry would consolidate the breakthrough, while the cavalry would continue on and inflict as much damage as possible in the enemy rear.

The penetration tactic didn't work against Indians. They wouldn't meet a charge but would instead retreat, always keeping just beyond effective range. Since the cavalry couldn't catch the swifter Indians, troops would charge only a few hundred yards, stop and regroup, and then, when the Indians stopped, charge again. When the soldiers overextended, they pulled back and the Indians followed. There were few casualties in this kind of fighting. Crook, at the Battle of the Rosebud, with about 1,300 soldiers, fought 1,600 Indians all day long. His men fired several hundred thousand rounds

Unidentified soldiers in a tent (courtesy of Kansas State Historical Society, Topeka, Kansas)

of ammunition but killed only about twenty Indians; the Army losses were half that. At the Battle of the Washita, Captain Robert M. West made his two-company charge against 1,600 Indians, with no recorded casualties.

The more conventional tactic employed in Indian fighting was the envelopment. A holding force engaged the enemy while other parts of the command swung to the right or left and hit him in the rear. This tactic was most effective in capturing villages. Few warriors were killed, since they wouldn't fight on two fronts at the same time.

Whenever possible, the soldiers engaged the Indians in a firefight. The soldiers were deployed as skirmishers, taking advantage of any natural cover available. They then tried to establish control of a field of fire. With open ground and directed volley fire, they were invincible. For example, if 100 soldiers were facing 1,000 Indians, and a commander ordered, "To the front, range 100 yards, volley fire, ready, aim, *fire*! Reload!" he could expect to hit fifty warriors with the first volley. Within one minute, he could expect to fire several volleys. Indians wouldn't sustain such losses and remain to fight.

When Indians did charge volley fire, as at the Battle of the Wagon Boxes in 1866, they were slaughtered. The Indians usually formed at about 1,500 yards distant, advanced to about 600 yards, and stopped. When the Indians won, as in the Fetterman Fight, the terrain didn't allow the soldiers to establish an effective field of fire. The warriors fired arrows from behind ridges, gullies, or other concealment, while the soldiers were left without targets.

Cavalry, designed for offensive operations, had little defensive capability. Therefore, the battle situation had to be desperate before they used defensive tactics. For defense, the regiment consolidated, found a position where they could establish a field of fire in all directions and conceal and protect their horses. Soldiers dug in only when they were resigned to waiting for relief, such as at the Battle of Beecher's Island in 1868 and the Battle of the Little Big Horn in 1876.

The Indian-fighting army was an elite corps of 25,000 men, the result of a selected reduction process from the million-man force at the end of the Civil War. The commanders were young professionals whose leadership had been demonstrated in the Civil War campaigns, and the equipment was new and battle-tested. It was perhaps the finest small army in the world during the latter part of the nineteenth century.

Duty in the field was difficult and dangerous, yet morale was high. Professionals spent most of their military career on the Great Plains, and it was a hard life. When all was said and done, the two things that unmistakably marked a man as a veteran of the Indian Wars were his battered campaign uniform and his thousand-yard stare.

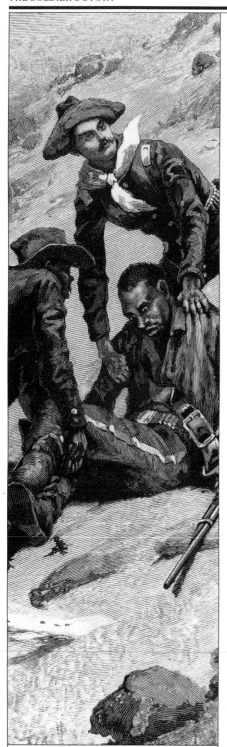

Detail from engraving of the rescue of Corporal Scott, drawn by Frederic Remington, 1886 (courtesy of The Institute of Texan Cultures, San Antonio, Texas)

THE BUFFALO SOLDIERS

BY ELMER KELTON

THE TERM "BUFFALO SOLDIER" COULD EASILY HAVE BEEN INTERPRETED as one of derision rather than admiration, but to the black troopers who manned frontier garrisons through the Indian Wars, it was accepted as complimentary. The term is credited to the Indians, who said the black faces and short, kinky hair of the Negro soldiers reminded them of the buffalo. Fittingly, the emblem of the black 10th Cavalry featured the figure of a buffalo standing triumphant over a field that included a war bonnet and crossed tomahawks.

That the troops served honorably and played an important though sadly ignored part in opening the West is a matter of record, but that role was to some degree an accident of history. The original concept of black regiments grew out of political motives as much as from any genuine intention to elevate the Negro soldier.

In an angry spirit of retaliation just after the Civil War, some of the Union's more vindictive leaders perceived that nothing could be more humiliating to defeated Southerners than to have their former slaves given police authority over them as occupation troops. That this placed the black soldiers in a most uncomfortable and sometimes dangerous position was not accorded much consideration.

In July 1866 Congress authorized the organization of all-black military units. There was a precedent. The First Regiment of South Carolina Volunteers had been organized during 1862–63, again not from the purest motives. The thought, expressed by at least one officer, was that so long as the Rebels were going to kill Union soldiers in any case, white lives could be spared if some of those killed were black. Before the war was over, as the historian William H. Leckie recorded, almost 180,000 black soldiers served in the Union Army; 33,380 of them died.

Against the strong opposition of many prominent Union officers who had just fought a war to free the slaves, four black regiments were formed: two cavalry, the 9th and the 10th, and two infantry, the 24th and the 25th. Circumstances soon altered the role of the black units as they were sent West to wrest from the Indians the freedom that they had so recently won for themselves in four years of bloody warfare.

Where the black soldiers *did* serve as occupation troops—in Texas for example, they often suffered hatred and violence from the civilian population. As the locally visible and accessible symbols of defeat and oppression, they bore the brunt of lingering resistance. One of the first victims of Texas outlaw John Wesley Hardin was a black trooper. Hardin boasted that he commanded the soldier to "surrender in the name of the Southern Confederacy," and when he did not, Hardin shot him.

The unfortunate legacy of civilian animosity toward the black occupation soldiers was handed down for generations, while their genuine contributions to the safety of settlers from Indians were downgraded or simply went unrecorded. More than once, the credit for their gallant deeds and sacrifices was unjustly given to white units. In the view of many at the time, it was not seemly to attach importance to the accomplishments of an "inferior" race. Until very recent years, a casual reader of Western history found few references to indicate that at one time or another during the postwar Indian-

Probably a soldier of the 9th Cavalry, 1880s (courtesy of Kansas State Historical Society, Topeka, Kansas)

fighting years, virtually every Army post of any importance in the West was manned partly or entirely by black troops. The buffalo soldiers for generations remained the invisible men of frontier history.

Despite that neglect, consider the record. Eighteen Congressional Medals of Honor for heroism were awarded to black soldiers during the relatively brief period of the Indian campaigns. It stands to reason that for each heroic act that was recognized and rewarded, many others went unheralded and were forgotten.

Consider also the obstacles. Illiteracy was almost universal among the early black recruits. In their previous condition of servitude most had been discouraged, even expressly forbidden, to learn to read and write. It was recorded that when the 9th Cavalry regiment was organized, only one black trooper in it could read and write well enough to act as sergeant major.

Yet in some respects it was their background of slavery that helped make them good soldiers, as the Army defined the term. They were accustomed to taking orders without question. They were inured to hard work and relatively primitive conditions. If thirteen dollars a month seemed poverty to white recruits, it was a most comfortable sum to men used to being paid much less, if anything at all. Finally, the military uniforms, housing, and food were a step up from anything the average ex-slave, especially the field hand, had ever known. Once the regiments had passed through their shakedown phase, the rate of desertion was only a fraction of that of comparable white units such as George Armstrong Custer's well-publicized 7th Cavalry.

Ironically, the black regiments faced considerable discrimination and doubt from many of the Union officers who had led the fight to free them. Brevet Major General Eugene A. Carr refused a regular lieutenant colonelcy with a black regiment, declaring that blacks were not fit to be soldiers. He revised his opinion under fire in 1869, when the H and I troops of the 10th Cavalry, with whom he was traveling, stood their ground and fought off a fierce attack by several hundred Cheyenne on Beaver Creek in Kansas.

Custer was another who declined to serve with black units, though he was offered a lieutenant colonelcy with the 9th Cavalry. His wife, Elizabeth, later wrote an account of the 7th Cavalry's first Indian fight just outside of Fort Wallace, Kansas, in June 1867. A troop of the 7th charged a large party of Cheyenne and was met by a counter charge. Her story relates that a dozen black soldiers of the 10th happened to be at the fort to obtain supplies for an outpost. When the battle started, they awaited no orders but jumped into the wagon. Whip popping over the heads of four mules, rifles blazing, these soldiers of the 10th charged out on wheels and joined their white comrades in arms, repulsing the Indians.

Black units in those times had black noncoms, but all the officers were white until Lieutenant Henry O. Flipper became the first black West Point

Photo of soldiers in formation with Lt. Frith, Sgt. Smith, and Dr. Butler, October 1899. (courtesy of U.S. Signal Corps, National Archives)

graduate in 1877. Many of the officers, such as Colonel Benjamin Grierson, were kind to their troops and displayed a genuine affection for them. Others, such as Colonel William R. Shafter, were exceedingly tough.

Shafter commanded black troops during most of his years of frontier service, handling them with a curious mixture of ruthlessness and paternalism. He used them hard on many a grueling campaign but stood up firmly in their defense against civilian abuse. In Texas, he led black troops of the 9th into places no white or black man had been before, putting them through incredible hardships, hunger, and thirst, to open up the mysteries of the red man's hidden sanctuaries from the desert sands of the Permian Basin to the deep canyons of the Big Bend.

Despite his reputation as a ruthless disciplinarian, he bristled when anyone else abused his soldiers. At Fort Davis, Texas, his black infantrymen guarded stations along the stagecoach route in Apache country. Elsewhere, white soldiers serving similar duty were allowed to ride a coach back to their permanent posts after their tours of duty, but the line made the black troopers walk and even refused to allow them to eat at the stage stops because it might offend white passengers. Shafter angrily put an end to this discrimination by declaring that a soldier not good enough to enjoy common courtesy would not guard anyone's stagecoach or station. His action made him powerful enemies, but his order prevailed.

His defense of a black trooper in another case led to an incident that haunted his later military career. A sheriff entered the Fort Davis grounds to arrest a soldier for drunkenness. Shafter reasoned that the trooper's color would automatically prevent his receiving fair treatment, so he ordered the lawman off the post. The soldier escaped punishment, but Shafter did not. A complaint was lodged against him, and he was transferred because of the incident. A mark was placed on his record that handicapped him for years.

In the end, however, Shafter prevailed. The blustery old Indian fighter and leader of black troops became commander-in-chief of U.S. expeditionary forces to Cuba in the Spanish-American War.

A similar advancement awaited another frontier commander of black troops, John J. Pershing. He was nicknamed "Nigger Jack" because of his association with Negro units. That name was suitably refined to "Blackjack" before he led black and white troops across the Mexican border in pursuit of Pancho Villa. He later commanded the American forces in France during World War I.

One of the most unusual contributions by black troopers to the subjugation of the Plains Indians was made by the legendary Seminole scouts, who served mainly in Texas with such notable commanders as Colonel Ranald S. Mackenzie. The Seminole scouts were of Negro or mixed Indian

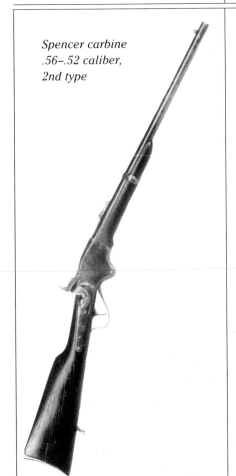

*Spencer carbine
.56–.52 caliber,
2nd type*

THE SPENCER RIFLE

BY JIM MILLER

A lot of the Johnny Rebs referred to the Spencer, the first successful breech-loading magazine rifle, as "that damned Yankee rifle," and rightfully so. Its firepower alone was enough to ensure the newly developed rifle's popularity when it came out at the beginning of the Civil War, but that wasn't what got the Rebs mad about it. It was that President Abraham Lincoln test-fired the Spencers early in the war and armed over 300,000 of his Union soldiers with them.

Christopher M. Spencer was the "damned Yankee" who developed the rifle and its carbine model, patenting it in 1860. Along with the Henry rifle, it was one of the first weapons to utilize the trigger guard as a loading lever. It fired seven shots from a tubular magazine, but the Spencer's magazine and ammunition were loaded from the butt of the rifle rather than fed from under the barrel as with the Henry and Winchester. The ammunition was issued in preloaded tubes that were fitted into the feed port.

Despite its advantages in firepower, the Spencer wasn't without its problems. On more than one instance users reported gas leakages at the breech-chamber joint. Far worse and much more dangerous, the cartridges were prone to explode inside the magazine. This was a special hazard for those cavalrymen who carried the weapon in the old regulation tin-lined boxes that were originally meant for wax-paper cartridges.

Nor did the weapon have the accuracy of range of the old Sharps. Of course, not many battles fought during the Civil War called for strict long-range sharpshooting, so the Spencer still gained a popular following and was even used by Westerners after the war.

It was an effective weapon, but there was one thing you couldn't do with a Spencer—stage a sneak attack. If you carried extra reload tubes on your horse (and who wouldn't?), the shells rattled around so much that they sounded like hail falling on a tin roof! And that, my friend, is not surprise.

and Negro blood, mainly escaped slaves and the descendants of slaves who had fled into the Florida swamps to live with the Seminole Indians. After the Army defeated the Seminole, they were moved to the West, driven into Indian Territory and finally into Mexico, where they could not be pressed back into slavery. Though in appearance they were black, they were Indian in heritage, and as scouts they were famed for their superior ability as hunters, trackers, and fighters.

Captain Frank W. Perry of the 9th Cavalry went into Mexico in 1870 and invited the Seminole-Negroes at Nacimiento to return to the United States and serve the Army as scouts. Land grants and homes for their families were to be their reward. They served initially along the border, dressed more in Indian style than in military uniform, some even sporting buffalo-horn war bonnets.

Under the command of Lieutenant John Lapham Bullis, the Seminole scouts helped take Mackenzie on his famous raid against Lipan and Kickapoo hostiles deep in Mexico in 1873. The following year, twenty-one Seminole scouts did valiant service with Mackenzie on the high-plains expedition that culminated in that officer's decisive victory over the winter-encamped Comanche, Kiowa and Cheyenne in the depths of Palo Duro Canyon. That campaign destroyed most of the Indian horse herd and forced the defeated red men to march afoot to the reservation in Indian Territory. Except for limited outbreaks, they never rose again.

In 1875, during a stiff skirmish at Eagle's Nest Crossing on the Pecos River, Bullis was suddenly left afoot and at the dubious mercies of some twenty-five or thirty Comanche. His three Seminole scouts dashed to his rescue under heavy fire and carried him out through the middle of the Comanche ranks. The three were among the eighteen black recipients of the Congressional Medal of Honor. In the end, however, when their services were no longer needed against hostile Indians, the Army broke Perry's promises of land grants to the scouts and their families.

Again and again, opponents of the frontier black units charged that Negro soldiers would not fight. Again and again, from the Rio Grande to the Big Horns, the buffalo soldiers proved them wrong.

The Western artist Frederick Remington wrote an article in 1889, describing his ride with black troopers in Apache country soon after the Apache campaigns had ended: "I am often asked, 'Will they fight?' That is easily answered. They have fought many, many times. The old sergeant sitting near me, as calm of feature as a bronze statue, once deliberately walked over a Cheyenne rifle-pit and calmly killed his man. One little fellow near him once took charge of stampeded cavalry-horses when Apache bullets were flying loose and no one knew from what point to expect them next. These little episodes prove the sometimes doubted self-reliance of the Negro." ■

Probably a soldier of the 9th Cavalry, 1880s (courtesy of Kansas State Historical Society, Topeka, Kansas)

WILLIAM TECUMSEH SHERMAN: WAR IS HELL

BY CENA GOLDER RICHESON

"It is only those who have neither fired a shot nor heard the shrieks and groans of the wounded who cry aloud for blood, more vengeance, more desolation. War is hell."

GENERAL WILLIAM TECUMSEH SHERMAN

SHERMAN WAS BORN IN LANCASTER, OHIO, IN 1820. HIS FATHER, A state supreme court judge, died of typhoid when Sherman was only nine years old. He was adopted by the lawyer Thomas Ewing; he would eventually marry his foster sister, Ellen.

Ewing secured Sherman an appointment to West Point, and after a checkered career as a cadet, he graduated sixth in a class of forty-two and gained his commission. Disappointed by the nature of his assignments in Florida and during the Mexican War, he resigned in 1853 to practice law. But he found civilian life dull and unprofitable, so he took a position as the superintendent of the military academy in Alexandria, Louisiana.

The South was a second home to Sherman. He witnessed the approach of conflict between North and South with the knowledge that it would force him to make a painful decision. Though the Confederacy offered him a high position in their new military, he chose to fight for the Union as a colonel. When the confusion and inept Union command at Bull Run shook his confidence, he asked the president to replace him. Lincoln instead made him a brigadier general.

Sherman didn't get along with the press, which dubbed him "Crazy" Sherman. They might have ruined his military career had it not been for General Henry W. Halleck, whose command was in St. Louis. According to the historian Bruce Catton, Sherman suffered a nervous breakdown in 1861; General Halleck was instrumental in transferring him to Missouri for a respite.

In a despondent letter to his wife Sherman admitted having contemplated suicide. Mrs. Sherman wrote General Halleck out of concern for her husband. His reply contained an element of humor: "I will willingly take all [that] the newspapers said against General Sherman if he will take all they said about me for I am certain to gain by the exchange."

Later on, Sherman warned Ulysses Grant about the "incense of wanton flattery" of the press. He advised, "Be...yourself and this glittering flattery will be as the passing breeze of the sea on a warm summer day." In many respects Sherman was Grant's alter ego, even to the point of physical resemblance—the same red beard, the same unkempt appearance, and the same determination to win a battle at all costs. But Sherman's verbosity, his love of dancing and his roving eye for pretty women, contrasted sharply with Grant's social reticence.

Sherman's most famous campaign began when Grant ordered him to "move against Johnston's army, break it up. Get into…the enemy's country as far as you can, inflicting all the damage you can against their war resources." Thus, in May 1864 Sherman began his infamous march through Georgia to Atlanta. As his campaign advanced he wrote, "We have devoured the land and our animals eat up the wheat and cornfields…Desolation is behind. To realize what war is one should follow our tracks."

After the Civil War, the Army turned its attention to the West, and to the peoples who stood in the way of U.S. expansion into the continent. Though he spoke in glowing terms of the land itself and the frontiersmen who were tough enough to settle it, Sherman described the Indians as "a class of savages displaced by the irresistible progress of our race. Treachery is inherent in the Indian character."

In 1869 Grant appointed Sherman commanding general of the Army, and so put him in a position to turn his opinion into action. He wrote to Grant: "[Since]…all Indians look alike, to get the rascals we are forced to include all." From his headquarters in St. Louis, Missouri (he hated Washington), he exerted his influence on the Army and the West.

He made it "Sherman's Army." He described George Armstrong Custer as a man possessing "not too much sense," but he agreed with Custer's attempts to eradicate the enemy. He pursued a relentless campaign against the Indians, not content to rest until he'd broken their will to resist and pushed them onto the reservation. He'd learned about hell firsthand in the fires of the Civil War, and he brought it with him to the West.

While en route between Fort Richardson and Fort Sill during an 1871 inspection tour of Southwestern outposts, Sherman and his escort were bypassed by a war party that later ambushed a wagon train on the same route. Sherman's response was the Red River campaign, in which he set out with renewed vigor to smash the last of the Indians who had rejected the reservation. By the time he retired in 1884, he'd nearly achieved his goal. Few Indians remained wild in the Wild West.

The retired general became an active public speaker, but he wanted nothing to do with politics. He declared, "I will not accept if nominated and will not serve if elected." He settled back in the East and wrote a two-volume memoir, a highly acclaimed account of his campaigns. He died of pneumonia in New York in 1891, shortly after turning seventy-one. ■

General William Tecumseh Sherman

Brigadier General George I. Crook, West Point, class of 1852 (courtesy of U.S. Army)

GEORGE CROOK, THE GRAY FOX

BY ARDATH MAYHAR

THE INDIANS DIDN'T NAME GEORGE CROOK "THE GRAY FOX" JUST FOR HIS gray hair and beard. He was one white officer who took the time to understand his opponents and to learn from them. In time, as he served in most of the major Indian campaigns in the West, they came to respect him not only as a canny warrior but as a wise and honorable man.

As did most of the general officers involved in the Indian Wars of the West, Crook began his career in the Union Army. While he served under General McClellan in the Civil War he had the misfortune to be involved in the battle of Antietam, an affair so fraught with blunders it was a wonder any of the Union soldiers got out of it alive. Ordered to cross a creek (which was actually shallow enough to ford), Crook led his brigade toward a bridge that spanned the stream. The area hadn't been scouted, and while the other commanders searched for the bridge or a suitable fording place, Crook forged on. Unfortunately, he completely missed both bridge and ford, and his unsupported troops emerged onto a plateau directly under the Rebel guns.

It was a valuable if costly lesson. In his later campaigns in the West, Crook moved cautiously, always relying on effective intelligence brought to him by knowledgeable scouts.

Crook was born into a family of Ohio farmers in 1829. He and his West Point roommate, Philip Sheridan, graduated from the military academy in the 1850s, and prior to the Civil War, he got his first taste of Indian fighting in the Roue River War and the Yakima War in the Pacific Northwest. Unlike many of his brother officers, he came to respect his opponents, studied their tactics and their way of life.

He started the Civil War with the 36th Ohio Volunteer Infantry. At the battle of Lewisburg he received a serious wound and a brevet promotion to major, and by Antietam he'd reached the rank of brigadier general. He later served in Sheridan's cavalry, and after the war he fought the Paiute in Idaho and commanded another campaign in Oregon.

Crook made himself at home in the West. He was a self-taught naturalist; he studied the plants, wildlife, and geography of the West with the same vigor as he studied the strategies and tactics of its fierce inhabitants. A proficient hunter and fisherman, he often took off on his own to pursue game or wet a line, and he enjoyed providing fresh meat for his soldiers' mess. During the 1876 campaign against the Sioux, he took time out after the Battle of the Rosebud to go fishing. He brought seventy trout back to camp, probably a welcome diversion for his troops after the runaround the Sioux had given them.

Unlike many of his brother officers, Crook preferred simple, practical clothes to fancy uniforms, a mule to a spirited horse. Perhaps because of his unusual ways rather than despite them, his men gave him their loyalty and their best efforts.

Crook was twice charged with mounting full-scale campaigns against the Apache in Arizona. He used a combination of ready negotiation and relentless pursuit to wear the enemy down, but his sharpest weapon was a force of Apache scouts he recruited from bands hostile to those he pursued. Aided by these scouts, he was able to track the hostiles even into the depths of the Mexican Sierra Madres. Crook's use of Indian irregulars served him well. The scouts did much of the hard work of pursuit, allowing Crook to keep his troopers fresh and ready for battle. He knew it was best to set an Apache to catch an Apache, and that by allowing the reservation Indians to fight in his service he was keeping them from joining their former comrades.

Geronimo was, of course, an exception to his success who probably caused much of Crook's trademark gray hair. With a following of usually

Some of Crook's soldiers resting after Slim Buttes (courtesy of U.S. Signal Corps, National Archives)

fewer than twenty warriors, the Apache chief defied Crook, his subordinates, and his successors until 1886. By that time, Crook had been reassigned to duties back East, and so it fell to Nelson Miles to bring in the last of the great Apache chiefs.

Crook, an intelligent and thoughtful man by all accounts, disapproved of some of the government policies that were his duty to carry out. Those policies forced him not only to meet the Apache warriors in battle but to round up old men, women, children and the crippled remnants of that once-proud race so they could be shipped off to the ill-supplied and poorly conceived destiny chosen for them by their conquerors. He knew that transportation to the humid climes of Florida was a death sentence for the desert-dwelling Apache.

He respected Cochise, Geronimo, and their fellows as expert warriors, even though he knew they were the implacable enemies of white settlement in the West. Even his sense of duty couldn't keep him from strongly protesting the War Department's shameful decision to strip his old Apache scouts of their honors and ship them to Florida with the rest of the transportees. The less than honorable way in which politicians half a continent away in Washington dealt with the Indians must have rankled with a man who, at his core, was a true gentleman.

He was, however, a soldier first and foremost. He did his duty, and he did it well. ■

WHISKERS GO WEST

BY LOREN D. ESTLEMAN

As did the ancient Romans in imitation of Alexander, American males inspired by Washington and Jefferson presented bare faces to the world throughout the nation's first ninety-four years. But when Abraham Lincoln took the oath of office and became America's first bearded president, the razor fell into disrepute. During four years of civil war the examples set by Generals Grant, Sherman, and Lee established a hirsute trend that by the time of Appomattox seriously threatened the future of the shaving soap industry.

Out West, mustaches were more common than beards. Popular styles ranged from George Armstrong Custer's inverted horseshoe to the trademark handlebars sported by all five of the Brothers Earp. So close was the family resemblance in this adornment that many Tombstonians were hard put to separate James from Virgil, Wyatt from Warren. When Fred Dodge came to town in similar handlebars, Wyatt and Virgil themselves at first

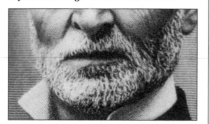

mistook him for their brother Morgan.

President Rutherford B. Hayes's great thatch was embraced by lawyers and politicians and "Hanging" Judge Isaac Parker's chief executioner George Maledon, whose noose-shaped growth grimly advertised his office. Buffalo Bill's characteristic goatee inspired doggerel in the London journals when the Wild West toured abroad, and Plains Indians who had never laid eyes on General George Crook recognized his fierce forked beard from tribal scuttlebutt.

Mining-town elections, having no other criterion to go by in a population of transients, were sometimes decided by measuring the length of the candidates' beards, with the badge of government duly presented to the man with the longest growth.

Toward the close of the nineteenth century, the chiseled profile of Hearst journalist Richard Harding Davis, as popularized by artist Charles Dana Gibson, began to shear away this image. Despite the modest mustaches sported by Theodore Roosevelt and William Howard Taft, facial hair was on its way out. By the time Woodrow Wilson was inaugurated as the first clean-shaven President since James Buchanan, the "soup-strainer" and "mattress" had become quaint relics of a simpler time, and remained so until the 1960s, when they re-emerged as symbols of youthful rebellion.

THE OFFICERS

THE RELENTLESS NELSON MILES

BY BILL O'NEAL

NELSON A. MILES WAS A RELENTLESS INDIAN FIGHTER WHO SUCCESS-
fully employed infantry in wars otherwise dominated by cavalry. Tall and
handsome, an aggressive and well-organized officer, he was also vain, pomp-
ous, and ruthless in pursuing his personal ambitions. He was loath to give
credit to other officers and was deeply jealous of West Point graduates. His
criticism of his brother officers earned him considerable enmity and led him
into feuds that marred his career.

Nelson Appleton Miles was born August 8, 1839, and raised on a Massachusetts farm. The youngest of four children, he was descended from veterans of King Philip's War and the American Revolution. The family farm
offered no outlet for his driving ambition, so he obtained a clerk's position
with an uncle in Boston. The teenaged Miles spent his leisure hours in night
school and in a broad reading program.

By 1860 he concluded that civil war was inevitable and that success in
combat could provide the fame and position he craved. Miles began to study
military volumes and joined a small group that employed a French veteran
to provide instruction in drill. When the War Between the States erupted,
Miles raised $3,500 to organize a volunteer company of infantry, but an
ungrateful governor denied Miles captaincy of his troop. He resentfully
accepted a lieutenant's commission but learned a bitter lesson about the
value of friends in high places.

During the Civil War his courage and a gift for taking advantage of combat
opportunities vaulted him to high rank. He was wounded four times, including a throat wound at Fredericksburg and a stomach wound at Chancellorsville. His exploits at Chancellorsville eventually earned him a Medal of
Honor. At the war's end he was put in charge of a distinguished prisoner,
former Confederate President Jefferson Davis.

He was determined to reach the top ranks of the frontier Army. He found
his friends in high places when he married Mary Sherman, niece of General
of the Army William T. Sherman and of Ohio Senator John Sherman. In 1869
he assumed command of the 5th Infantry, but as the years passed, the
ambitious Miles chafed at his regiment's exclusion from the Indian campaigns. His rivals, Custer, Crook, and Mackenzie were getting all the glory.

**General Nelson A. Miles
(courtesy of U.S. Army)**

At last, in 1874, Sherman assigned Miles to lead a column in the Red River War. Miles brought along a newspaper correspondent to secure his personal publicity. In 1876 Miles joined the general pursuit of the Sioux victors from the Little Big Horn. His command effectively pressured its prey. During winter campaigns Miles bundled in heavy fur clothing; the Indians called him Bear Coat.

In 1877 Miles hurried into the field to intercept Chief Joseph and the fleeing Nez Perce. Without his intervention the Indians would have escaped into Canada. When higher authorities moved Joseph's band to Kansas, Miles protested strongly and worked for years to have them returned to their homeland. In 1878 Miles took time out from a vacation to skirmish with the Bannock Indians, and in 1880 finally received his long-sought star.

In 1886 Geronimo and a few hostile Apache escaped custody after they were corralled by General George Crook, and Miles replaced Crook. He was less than enthusiastic for a conventional campaign with unfamiliar units in Arizona's barren terrain, so he placed guard details at water holes and mountain passes, organized a system of pursuit parties, and established a network of thirty heliograph stations. He hounded Geronimo until the old Apache and his handful of followers finally surrendered.

Miles eagerly accepted total credit for the victory, ignoring Crook's years of effort. When a public subscription for his engraved sword fell far short, Miles discreetly paid the difference, then basked in the presentation ceremonies at Tucson. Major General Crook died in 1890, and Miles lobbied President Benjamin Harrison for his second star. He got it.

In the aftermath of the massacre at Wounded Knee, Miles commanded masterfully, increasing military pressure while working through personal diplomacy to split the Sioux leadership. His efforts helped to avert further bloodshed.

After the Indian Wars ended in the West, Miles led troops to quell the Pullman strike during the 1894 Chicago riot; he then wrote two books about his time in the West. During the Spanish-American War he led reinforcements to Cuba, then invaded Puerto Rico with a force of 3,500 men, conquering the defending troops in a skillful nineteen-day campaign. After the war Miles continued to clash with the War Department and with Presidents McKinley and Roosevelt. He had a public feud with Secretary of War Russell A. Alger; Roosevelt later censured Miles.

In 1901 he was awarded the rank of lieutenant general, but he was denied a combat role during the Philippine conflict. When Roosevelt directed that all officers demonstrate physical fitness by riding ninety miles within three days, Miles raced the distance in nine and a half hours. But less than a month afterward, he reached the mandatory retirement age of sixty-four.

When the United States entered the Great War, the seventy-seven-year-old Miles eagerly volunteered for duty, but his services were declined. On May 15, 1925, Miles took his grandchildren to the Ringling Brothers Circus, and while the National Anthem played, a fatal heart attack struck the old soldier. Miles would no doubt have appreciated his splendid funeral, the pomp and ceremony with which he was buried at Arlington National Cemetery. ■

ON THE LITTLE BIG HORN

THE TROUBLE WITH CUSTER

BY CHAD OLIVER

George Armstrong Custer

THE TROUBLE WITH CUSTER, OF COURSE, IS THAT HE HAS BECOME a symbol. It is hard to say precisely what that symbol stands for, but in the last few decades the image has been essentially a negative one. Custer has taken the heat for everything from the Vietnam War to race relations in South Africa. It is worth remembering that Custer was a human being before he became a symbol for anything.

Custer passed into legend through his death rather than through his life. If there had been no battle at the Little Big Horn River (modern mapmakers prefer to spell it "Little Bighorn," and it's known locally as the "Little Horn") in June 1876, Custer would be, despite a military record that might fairly be called distinguished, just an extended footnote in the story of the Civil War and its aftermath. Instead, we have what is probably the most famous fight in American history. We also have the Custer that everyone has heard of and nobody knows.

If the man himself has been transformed into a symbol by an avalanche of words and paintings and films, what about the battle at the Little Big Horn? It has become Custer's Last Stand, but it is far more than that. Depending on your viewpoint and what you're trying to prove, that struggle has mushroomed into a veritable forest of symbols.

It is perhaps best to start with the standard Custer myth. It goes something like this:

General George Armstrong Custer, the most admired officer in the U.S. Army, concocted a plan to drive the Sioux Indians from the Great Plains. His aim was to force the Indians to flee in terror before his awesome troops, the famed 7th Cavalry, the most experienced regiment on the frontier. The brilliant Custer rode into battle with his long yellow hair flowing in the wind, but he was ambushed by the tricky Sioux, commanded by the crafty Sitting Bull. The 7th Cavalry was wiped out to the last man by roughly 50,000 Indians armed with bows and arrows. When the soldiers' ammunition gave out, they fought on with their gleaming sabers. They were finally overwhelmed after a day-long battle in which the gallant Custer was the last man to fall. The Indians were so impressed by his bravery that when they finally killed the mighty Custer, they left his body intact.

WELL, OKAY, THAT'S JUST *ONE* OF THE STANDARD CUSTER myths, but I am particularly fond of this one because not a single sentence of it is true. Custer's rank at the time of the Battle of the Little Big Horn was lieutenant colonel. Far from being universally admired, Custer was as controversial in life as he has become in death. The joke among troopers of the 7th was that the officers were divided into two groups: Custer relatives and Custer haters. Custer was court-martialed in 1867 and was in so much hot water with President Grant that he almost didn't make it to the Little Big Horn. The plan of attack for the 1876 summer campaign against the Indians was not Custer's; indeed, the force that included the 7th Cavalry was under the command of General Alfred Terry. The 7th was a relatively new outfit, activated in 1866. The very last thing Custer and the other officers wanted was for the Indians to run away; the whole plan was designed to *prevent* the Indians from fleeing.

Custer didn't have long yellow hair at the time of his death at the Little Big Horn. Whatever its exact color—it was usually described as a reddish gold—his famous hair was thinning, so he'd cropped it short. Custer was a rashly brave man with a flair for the dramatic, but even his best friends never called him brilliant. Custer began the fight when he attacked a Sioux village on the Little Big Horn River—an attack against which the Indians were defending themselves.

Nobody "commanded" the Sioux and the Cheyenne, and Sitting Bull probably took no part in the actual fighting. Alas for all the legends, the 7th Cavalry was not wiped out to the last man—in fact, the survivors outnumbered the dead. The classic answer to the question of how many Indian warriors were at the Little Big Horn is: enough. A fair estimate puts the figure at about three thousand fighting men—but nobody called roll, of course. There is even some disagreement about the exact strength of the 7th Cavalry at the Little Big Horn.

The Indians did use bows and arrows, as might be expected, but the evidence is clear that it was their rifle fire that inflicted the heaviest casualties on the 7th. Archaeologists who recently (in 1984 and 1985) studied the battlefield dubbed one Indian position "Henryville" because a profusion of data (cartridge cases) indicated that the Indians had employed Henry repeating rifles. There is reason to believe that the troopers had some difficulty with their Springfields jamming, but they did not run out of ammunition; the Indians recovered plenty—both Colt and Springfield—and used it later. The soldiers did not use sabers in the fight for the excellent reason that they didn't have any. Custer left the sabers behind, along with the Gatling guns, presumably because he didn't want the clanking of the sabers to spoil his surprise attack. He rejected the Gatlings because they would slow him down.

All of the evidence, including the testimony of the Indians who were there, suggests that Custer's portion of the fight was over relatively quickly. It certainly didn't last all day; between thirty minutes and two hours is more like it. And was Custer the last to fall? That is virtually impossible in light of the eyewitness accounts and the nature of the bullet wounds in Custer's body. Custer's corpse was found naked and in a sitting position. He hadn't been scalped, but it is highly probable that the Indians didn't even know who he was.

So much for the myth. What really went on at the Little Big Horn on the 25th of June in the year of 1876?

The genesis of what happened to Custer is, as usual, shrouded in the fog of tangled politics, Indian treaties, and who was supposed to be where. To make this convoluted tale as short as possible, it is the plain truth that the Indians were getting their customary short end of the stick. In December 1875, the U.S. government issued an ultimatum to the Dakota Sioux and the Northern Cheyenne that in effect ordered these people out of their own country, including their sacred Black Hills. It graciously gave them until the end of January 1876 to report to reservation agencies. If they didn't show up, they were to be classified as "hostiles"—in other words, fair game.

Nobody expected the free Indians to come in and meekly surrender. In the middle of winter, with communications ranging from lousy to nonexistent, the Indians probably couldn't have reported even if they had wished to. And they had no such wish. The Sioux, most of them of the Teton Dakota group, were the most powerful tribe on the plains. The Northern Cheyenne, fewer in numbers, had learned about the white man's promises the hard way. They were not dewy-eyed representatives of an antipollution patrol. They were tough, they were desperate, and they were fighters.

It was up to the Army to enforce the edict, and the Army had a Plan. The Plan was simple, in more ways than one. The Army would wait until the early summer of 1876, when the Indians gathered for the Sun Dance and the great communal bison hunts. Then the Army would sock the "hostiles" with a three-pronged offensive that would fence the Indians in and prevent their escape. General George Crook, with some 1,300 men, would attack from the

Curly, the Custer scout who carried the news of the disaster on the Little Big Horn (courtesy of U.S. Signal Corps, National Archives)

Libbie Custer (courtesy of Kansas University Libraries)

southeast. (He started from Fort Laramie in Wyoming.) Colonel John Gibbon, leading a force of more than 400 men, was to strike more or less due east from Fort Ellis, Montana. General Alfred Terry, with the 7th Cavalry ostensibly under his command (about 650 men), would approach westward from Bismarck, North Dakota.

I mention this grand design for one reason only. It's not practical here to follow the Army's maneuvers in detail, but so much has been made of Custer's later division of the regiment that it is worth pointing out that the available Army manpower was *already* split into three parts before Custer was even on the scene. Add up the numbers and you have one of the largest forces assembled by the Indian-fighting Army.

The Custer Expedition in the Black Hills, 1874 (courtesy of National Archives)

On the 17th of June—just eight days before the battle on the Little Big Horn—Crook encountered a large body of Sioux (directed by Crazy Horse) and Cheyenne on the Rosebud River. Crook was a capable officer, but what happened might politely be described as a draw. He did manage to extricate his somewhat battered command while his 260 Crow and Shoshone allies covered his withdrawal in a fierce hand-to-hand engagement with the hostiles, but Crook was knocked out of the fight. Although he was less than a hundred miles from Terry, Crook communicated to him exactly nothing about the force he had encountered. Terry had no idea of what was waiting for him. It may be appropriate that the site of the Rosebud fight is today often deserted, a far cry from the crowds that press in to see the Custer battlefield.

Terry's and Gibbon's commands united all too briefly, and by then Custer had arrived. Terry decided, wisely, to go with Gibbon and leave the 7th to Custer.

Again, there was a Plan. Terry gave both written and verbal orders to Custer. Those orders have been argued about ever since, but the truth is that the orders were not models of clarity. The basic idea was for Terry and Gibbon, who were then on the Yellowstone at its junction with the Powder River, to angle around and approach the supposed location of the Indian camp from the north. Custer was to take the 7th and follow a very large Indian trail that had been discovered. There was a kind of understanding that the two commands would hook up and attack on the 26th of June. Again, the Army's rationale was containment.

Gibbon knew Custer all too well. His last words to him were: "Now, Custer, don't be greedy. You wait for us."

Custer's reply was a masterpiece of ambiguity. "I won't," he said.

It is obvious that Custer had no intention of waiting for anybody. He ran to his tent, grabbed his adjutant, Lieutenant W. W. Cooke, and yelled exultantly: "Cookey, Terry has cut us loose! The Seventh is on its own!"

Custer started off on the 22nd of June, but he really got going on the 23rd. He set a brutal pace; he was not called Iron Butt for nothing. Custer was a man in a hurry. Sitting Bull had a vision of soldiers riding into the Indian camp upside down—that is, dead—but Custer had some visions of his own. We cannot really get inside the man's head with certainty, but it is reasonable to suppose that Custer was out to rebuild his Civil War reputation and to show up the man who had publicly humiliated him—President Grant. There is even some evidence to suggest that Custer figured he had a shot at the presidency if he could pull off the destruction or surrender of the Indian camp.

Custer, the dashing Boy General of the Civil War, was thirty-six years old in 1876. Still famous though reduced in rank after the war, Custer had gone to Washington to testify against the secretary of war on charges including accusations of graft in the allocation of supplies to the Indian reservations. Custer's testimony implicated Orvil Grant, the brother of the president. This hardly endeared him to President Grant, who wanted no more publicity for Custer and even refused to meet with his former fellow officer from the Union Army. Custer had to pull every string he could beg, borrow, or steal to return to the 7th Cavalry for the campaign against the Sioux.

He made it, of course, and he took war correspondent Mark Kellogg with him. Whatever one thinks of Custer, the fact is that he was where he wanted to be. He was no desk officer, and his self-confidence was extraordinary. It was not entirely undeserved, either; "Custer's Luck" was proverbial. It's true that he didn't know exactly what he was up against, but we should consider the nature of the regiment he reclaimed. The 7th was not at full strength.

COMANCHE

BY LENORE CARROLL

It is ironic that Captain Miles Keogh's bay gelding, Comanche, the only surviving member of the five doomed companies of the 7th Cavalry that fought at the Battle of the Little Big Horn, nearly fell victim in the end to a leaky twentieth-century museum roof. The horse earned his name when he made "a Comanche yell" while in action during a scouting expedition, and he carried Keogh on assignments throughout the West, from Kansas in 1868 to the Black Hills of Dakota to the fateful encounter with the Sioux on the Little Big Horn. Comanche received seven wounds during the battle and so was left behind by the Indians. The burial detail found him on the battlefield and walked him down to the mouth of the Little Big Horn, where they bedded him down on the steamer *Far West* along with wounded troopers from Major Reno's companies. From there he was taken to Fort Lincoln and nursed back to health.

General Order No. 7, issued by 7th Cavalry commander Colonel Samuel D. Sturgis, awarded Comanche all the appropriate military honors for his service in the battle. Sturgis declared that the horse would be honored and forev-

er well-treated as a symbol of the 7th's sacrifice. Comanche lived on for many years at Fort Riley, Kansas, where he took part each June 25 in the regimental mourning ceremonies. After his caretaker died at Wounded Knee in 1890, Comanche's own health began to fail. He died on November 6, 1891.

Officers of the 7th commissioned Dr. L. L. Dyche of Kansas University to preserve Comanche's body by taxidermy. Dyche preserved the horse's major bones and his skin, but kept the remains when the men of the regiment failed to collect enough money to pay his $400 fee. The remains ended up at the Natural History Museum on the Kansas University campus in Lawrence

and have for many years been on display there. Each successive Kansas governor has refused petitions by the U.S. Army, the Custer Battle National Monument, and other organizations that have sought to secure the remains.

These last relics of the old warhorse were almost lost to a modern accident. It was discovered in the spring of 1986 that water from a leak in the museum roof had found its way into the display case and had damaged Comanche's skin. The damage was discovered in time, and both the roof and the skin were repaired. Today, both scholars and schoolchildren can view the remains as a tangible connection to history, and can wonder.

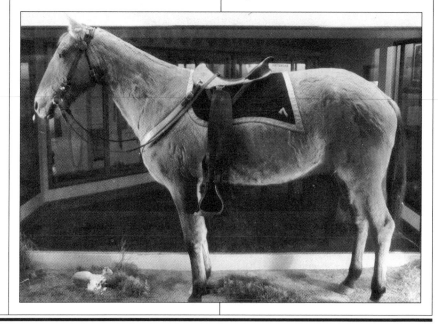

As a lieutenant colonel, Custer was the ranking officer—the nominal commander, Colonel Andrew Smith, had retired, and Smith's successor, Colonel Sturgis, was out of the picture. Custer had a grand total of *one* major—Marcus Reno, of all people. His officers were divided in their loyalties, and hundreds of enlisted men had deserted from the 7th in the decade of its existence. There are estimates that forty percent of the troopers in the 7th were either near-raw recruits or had never fought Indians before. And did any of this worry Custer? As far as we can tell, not in the least!

Sometime around noon on the 25th of June—a day early, and the precise hour is uncertain—Custer had his weary troopers in position to attack a very large Indian village on the far side of the Little Big Horn River (which is, by the way, a decent medium-sized trout stream). He knew only the approximate location of the Indian camp and was personally unfamiliar with the terrain, although he had some good advice—to which he paid little heed—from his Crow scouts. He was badly outgunned and outnumbered, at least three to one and possibly as much as five to one.

Of course, Custer promptly divided his regiment. First he detached Captain Frederick Benteen with Companies D, H, and K. (A company is the same thing as a troop—60 men at full strength, which it never was in the 7th.) Custer rather vaguely ordered Benteen to swing to the left and move from valley to valley while watching for enemy contact—remember, the Army was worried about flight, not fight. The Benteen decision may have been Custer's worst mistake. In effect, he ordered his senior captain and quite possibly his most effective combat officer out of the crucial part of the battle.

Shortly thereafter, when some Indians were actually sighted riding toward the river, Custer again divided his forces. He gave Companies A, G, and M to Major Marcus Reno and issued an astoundingly muddy order: "Charge after them and you will be supported by the whole outfit!"

That left Custer with five companies, C, E, F, I, and L. It is clear at this point that we have encountered another Plan. Custer never bothered to explain it to his officers—a bad habit of his—but his Plan is plain enough in retrospect. Custer's intention was to contain the village with Benteen on the left, Reno in the middle, and himself on the right, but Reno quite naturally assumed from the order that Custer was behind him. Benteen was left wholly in the dark. Custer actually peeled off to the right to hit the village from the other end. Meanwhile, the augmented pack train escorted by Captain Thomas McDougall and B Company struggled along essentially in Benteen's wake.

Major Reno's small force of about 130 soldiers and some Arikara scouts was the only element of the 7th that managed to cross the Little Big Horn to attack the Indian camp. When Reno charged into the village, he found himself in the middle of a hornet's nest. The astonished Indians very quickly recovered from their surprise, tumbled out of their lodges, and opened up a withering fire. Reno's conduct does not induce gasps of admiration today, but as one survivor put it, "If we had not been commanded by a coward, none of us would have gotten out alive." At that point, only Reno's detachment of the 7th had actually engaged the enemy, and he was facing the wrath of the entire Indian camp. Quite simply, Reno took casualties, wavered, and got the hell out of there, hardly a classic military maneuver. It was a headlong retreat back across the river, devil take the hindmost. Reno's command holed up on a high plateau and dug in while its commander wandered among his troops in a daze.

Benteen, occupied with a scouting expedition he regarded as "senseless," encountered no Indians. Eventually and quite reasonably, he turned back to see what was going on. He was not really alarmed until he received what turned out to be the final message from Custer, which was carried by trooper John Martini. Martini, whose English was less than perfect, survived the fight and named his son after Custer. The message, dictated by Custer, written in a scrawl by Adjutant Cooke, and preserved by Benteen, reads: *Benteen. Come on. Big village. Be quick. Bring packs. P.S. Bring pacs.*

THAT WAS THE LAST ANYONE HEARD FROM CUSTER. MARTINI'S horse was slightly wounded, and the spelling error in the final word of the message indicated that Cooke was writing in haste. On the other hand, Martini stated when questioned that the Indians were "skedaddling." The import of the message is no doubt clearer now than when Benteen received it. Benteen was in something of a quandary. All he really knew was that Custer had located the village and wanted more ammunition. Benteen was not in contact with the pack train that carried the reserve ammunition. He didn't know Custer's location.

Nevertheless, Benteen moved. His weary troopers urged their tired mounts into a trot and advanced with their revolvers drawn. Benteen found Reno under siege on his hilltop and joined him there—recall that Custer and Reno were still together when Benteen had last seen them. He discovered that Reno was disoriented and perhaps in shock, certainly in no condition to fight, so he took over effective command. Whatever else may be said of Benteen (and he has his detractors as well as his admirers), he certainly saved the 7th Cavalry from total disaster. With his steadiness and bravery under fire, he rallied the troopers. Under his command, they held their position and managed to get McDougall's pack train safely in.

Could Benteen have rescued Custer once he realized Custer was not with Reno? The answer depends on a murky time factor, some tricky logistics, and whether or not Benteen was actually Superman in a cavalry uniform.

File of Sioux chiefs on the Little Big Horn (courtesy of U.S. Signal Corps, National Archives)

It also depends on your estimation of how formidable the Indian warriors were. There were many more warriors in the area than troopers, and others who had fought them—General Crook, for instance—had found them plenty good enough.

It is fact that Benteen disliked Custer intensely and had no great admiration for Reno, either. As another survivor of the fight phrased it, "Reno was incompetent and Benteen was indifferent." As far as Benteen's *actions* are concerned, whatever his likes or dislikes, he probably did everything he could, short of miracles or suicide.

That brings us to the fate of George Armstrong Custer and his five doomed companies. Two statements can be made with confidence about the battle: one, the Indians were ready for him by the time he tried to ford the Little Big Horn; two, nobody who remained with Custer, approximately 210 officers, enlisted men, scouts, and civilians, lived long enough to talk about it.

The Sioux and their allies were not fools, and they had more than just numbers going for them. Crazy Horse, of whom there remains no authentic photograph, was arguably the best warrior in the world. Sitting Bull, no mean fighter himself in his younger days, was a powerful spiritual force. Gall was the kind of warrior you wanted on *your* side. The Cheyenne Two Moons (or Two Moon) was an able chief. Their experienced warriors went right down

"Know the power that is peace."

BLACK ELK OF THE OGLALA, HIS WORDS INSCRIBED ON THE WALL OF THE VISITOR'S CENTER AT THE LITTLE BIG-HORN BATTLEFIELD NATION-AL MONUMENT

to the level of those who were little more than boys but had been fighting nearly all of their lives. They were well armed, and with numerous repeating rifles they had more firepower than Custer's men. They could see where Custer was going by the dust he kicked up along the ridge. They knew the fords on the river, for they used them all the time. They knew that Reno's attempted advance was blocked by so many Indians that the warriors couldn't all fire at once without hitting each other. What better way to protect their village than to head off Custer before he could reach it?

And that is what they did. Custer never crossed the Little Big Horn. Some four miles distant from Reno and Benteen's besieged position, the Indians greeted Custer with intense fire from at least three different directions. There was a battle, of course, and the Indians' victory was not without cost to themselves, but the five companies of cavalry were cut to pieces, literally annihilated.

Was it a rout? Military men who later looked at that grim field strewn with dead and mutilated bodies tended to think so. Benteen examined the placement of the bodies with care; he said that one could take a handful of corn and scatter it on the floor and come up with a better defensive position. Of course, Benteen was not without bias. There were those, supported to some extent by recent archaeological evidence, who thought they recognized a fairly orderly deployment by companies.

Custer was found with two bullet wounds in his body. The wound in his chest had bled extensively. The other was a bloodless head wound, in the left temple, to be precise. Since Custer was right-handed and there were no powder burns, we can forget suicide. My own opinion, based on the psychology and character of the man, is that Custer was hit in the chest by a rifle bullet quite early in the fight. I believe this reasonable regardless of exactly what time the battle started or where Custer was when he was struck. Custer lived for the attack, and he would have charged the village had he been able to do so. The odds would have made no difference to him.

Terry and Gibbon arrived on the 27th of June. Ironically, in view of Custer's haste, they were a day late. The Indians were gone, the great camp deserted. The bodies of the soldiers lay white and swollen in the sun, but their names echo across the years. Captain Tom Custer, Armstrong's brother and twice winner of the Congressional Medal of Honor. Lieutenant W. W. Cooke, who wrote the last message. Lieutenant James Calhoun, Custer's brother-in-law. Captain George Yates. Captain Miles Keogh, whose wounded horse, Comanche, was the only living thing left on the battlefield. Enlisted men with names like Bucknell, Hathersall, Stungevitz, Boyle, Huber, Brady, Kelley, Riebold...

And all the rest is legend, and will endure. ■

IV. ALL ROADS LEAD WEST

THE TERRAQUEOUS MACHINE AND OTHER WINDWAGONS

BY ROY L. FISH

IN 1853 A FELLOW NAMED THOMAS LITERALLY SAILED HIS WAGON into the town of Westport (now Kansas City), Missouri. It didn't take long, after the dust had settled and the frightened animals were calmed, for Thomas to convince five of the local capitalists to invest in his project— a fleet of sail-propelled freight wagons that could successfully haul goods to and from Santa Fe.

When the first of the proposed freight fleet was ready, "Windwagon" Thomas, as he had been dubbed, climbed aboard. He was joined by four of his partners, but the fifth, a Doctor Parker, decided to observe from his mule. Thomas raised the sail, the wagon moved, and Parker followed at a discrete distance. When the wagon reached high speed, Thomas ignored his passengers' pleas to lower the sail. As the wagon was pushed on to even faster speeds, Thomas tried to alter his course, and a sudden gust whipped the contraption into a reverse circle. Parker and his mule dashed for safer ground, and the passengers took the opportunity to leap overboard. Thomas rode it out to the last, going down with his ship as it finally shattered against a fence. He survived the crash, but not wanting to press his luck with his wrathful backers, he ran to his own windwagon and sailed into oblivion.

Windwagon experiments continued despite the disappointments. One native of Holland rigged a windmill and belt drive to a prairie schooner, only to find that windmills were best left to conventional applications on stable surfaces. One experimental windwagon was teamed onto the plain only to be blown away. Perhaps Windwagon Thomas still pilots it among the stars.

It was in 1860 that Samuel Peppard constructed a light windwagon to carry freight to Colorado. At first the air currents moved the wagon con-

PREVIOUS PAGE:
Detail from *Crossing Water to Escape a Prairie Fire*, n.d., painting by Frederic Remington (courtesy of Texas A&M Development Foundation, Bill & Irma Runyon Art Collections)

taining Peppard and three companions at a fine rate, once taking only three hours to travel fifty miles. They passed the many slower vehicles on the road and jested with their drivers. They had nearly completed their journey and were only a short distance from Denver when a treacherous gust of wind picked up the wagon, hurled it aloft, and smashed it back into the earth. The shipwrecked windwagon sailors were forced to beg a ride with one of the teamsters they'd laughed at.

Not all attempts to cross the prairies by wind-power failed. In the spring of 1860, three men sailed from the Missouri River to Denver in twenty days, a respectable time.

Several years before Windwagon Thomas introduced his vehicle to Missouri, the Texas dairyman Gail Borden built a supposedly amphibious windwagon known as the "Terraqueous Machine." After he treated his closest friends to a late-night meal of his latest experimental food, a compound of slaughterhouse byproducts that were normally discarded, Gail announced that he had another "surprise" in store. He led them to the livery where his "secret invention" waited—the Terraqueous Machine. The revelers piled into the wagon, which was towed to the waterfront on Galveston Island. The horses were unhitched, the sail was hoisted, and very shortly the wagon was moving at an extraordinary clip down the beach. The ladies became terrified, and their hysterical clamor intensified in proportion to the speed. Just before they would have reached the lower end of Galveston Island, Borden braked and lowered the sail.

Borden made his second windwagon run in public and in daylight, and probably without ladies among the passengers. The machine operated so well on land that he decided to test its seaworthiness. He had neglected, however, to tell his passengers about his vehicle's amphibious capabilities. To everyone's surprise and dismay, he steered into the water. Pandemo-

nium ensued. Shrieks of terror drowned the skipper's pleas for order, and the passengers swarmed to the shore side of the craft. Someone dropped the sail and the vehicle capsized, dumping all into the water. Borden climbed atop the inverted hull and tried to explain to his deserting crew that the Terraqueous Machine was unsinkable, that the wheels were designed to function as underwater screws. They paid him no attention, and the Terraqueous Machine became just another idea scorned because it was before its time. Had it been successful, Borden might eventually have used it to distribute his milk and cottage cheese. ■

WHEELS ON THE WIND

ROAD TESTS OF COVERED WAGONS

BY CAROL J. SCAMMAN

IT'S A SHAME THE EARLY SETTLERS DIDN'T HAVE THE CONSUMER'S Union around to rate covered wagons for them. Guidebooks written expressly for Western pioneer emigrants described useful wagon features but didn't compare makes and models. The test of a wagon and team was the trip itself, and sad to say, many flunked. The rate of failure for wagons made of unseasoned wood ran as high as twenty-two out of twenty-six wagons during the time of the Mormon War (1844–46). If Consumer Reports had been in business at the time and had coralled the covered wagons for a road test, here's what the testers might have written:

Our wagon experts tested a whole fleet of prairie schooners on a rugged 2,000-mile journey. The results should be of interest to anyone who feels like yelling, *"CALIFORNY OR BUST!"* A number of different styles and makes of wagons are available to the family moving West. Contrary to popular belief, not all covered wagons are Conestogas; in fact, not many true Conestogas are used out West. Our test fleet included Studebaker, Espenschied, and Murphy wagons. We also tested the generic emigrant or Western wagon and, for old time's sake, the granddaddy of them all, the Conestoga. For the benefit of the economy-minded pilgrim, we included converted farm wagons. We didn't test the Schlutter or Shuttler wagon, as no one wanted to risk a ride in something built by convict labor paid 25 to 50 cents a day.

What makes a covered wagon a covered wagon? The cover, of course.

It can be made out of homespun cloth, canvas, cloth treated with linseed oil, or double Osnaburg duck (a German cousin of the Peking duck). None of the half-dozen or so materials we tried really shed water in a hard rain, not even the duck. We recommend a double cover because they get frequent tears. Flaps or "puckering strings" can be used to foil Peeping Toms, and a clever seamstress can sew pouches to the inside of the cover for extra storage.

Something has to hold the cover in place, and that something is a series of flexible hickory bows or hoops. Other wagon parts include the wooden bed, or box, and the running gear beneath the box. The running gear includes the wheels, the axles, the hounds, and a host of other technical thingies. Hounds, to those in the know, are the wooden, often iron-clad braces that help connect the axle assembly to the wagon tongue and to the reach or coupling pole. To keep all this straight, our engineers sang this ditty to the tune of "Dry Bones":

> *Oh, the front hound's connected to the wagon tongue,*
> *The front hound's connected to the wagon tongue,*
> *Oh, the rear hound's connected to the coupling pole,*
> *The rear hound's connected to the coupling pole…*

A Freeze, *Harper's Monthly Magazine*

—and so on. But we digress. To return to our evaluations, here's what we found:

Although no one of sound mind and body (male or female) wanted to ride in the cramped contraptions, we found the Studebaker wagons to be the best running of the lot. That's because those clever Studebaker boys from South Bend, Indiana, have introduced steel skeins for easier running. The skein is a sort of thimble that fits over the end of the axle. We found the reliability of this wagon much better than average. The Studebaker brothers perfected a process whereby the running gear was soaked and boiled in oil to drive out moisture. This reduces the danger of shrinkage and loose wheels. The axles are made of durable Indiana black hickory, and other hardwoods used in construction are thoroughly seasoned for three to five years.

An aggressive newspaper ad campaign has helped spur wagon sales for the Studebaker brothers, Clem and Henry, who have been in the business together since 1852. They've met the demand by inventing a drying kiln to dry wood quickly. Unlike most wagon makers, they've developed national sales outlets. Thanks to their brother Peter, there is an outlet in St. Joseph, Missouri.

According to their catalog, "slope-shouldered spokes of white oak" add to the overall soundness of construction. (If any of our readers know what a slope-shouldered spoke is, please write to our engineering department.) In appearance, the Studebaker retains the beauty of the Conestoga with upswept ends on the wagon box. However, it is much lighter than the Conestoga. For those concerned about snob appeal, the name "Studebaker" is emblazoned in yellow on the wagon.

Studebakers come as freighters and in many other sizes. Depending on size, they can carry loads up to two tons. For emigrants, a ton and a quarter is the maximum, unless you're carrying feed, so don't go overboard. The smaller vehicles are available for $160–$200, plus cover. The frequency of repair record for Studebakers rivals the well-constructed Murphy wagons.

The J. Murphy or Murphy wagon is the product of Joseph Murphy of St. Louis, Missouri. An Irish immigrant, he started his own firm in 1826. With German workman aiding and abetting him, he has produced one of the largest and most dependable freight wagons available. Despite their reputation as freighters, some twenty thousand Murphy wagons have also been used by emigrants on the Oregon Trail. Trader William L. Sublette purchased a Murphy wagon for $200 in 1830. It was the first wheeled contrivance to arrive in the Rockies after William H. Ashley's cannon in 1827.

In style, the Murphy wagon is a kissin' cousin of the Conestoga. Unlike the Conestoga, Murphy wagons are custom made. They have no standard design. Their wagon boxes do have the curved bottom of the Conestoga,

THE DIRTY DOZEN OF WAGON PACKING, OR DO LEAVE HOME WITHOUT THEM

BY CAROL J. SCAMMAN

1. **Solid oak furniture** (it literally litters the trail).

2. **Sick or lame cow** (Bossy will be sore enough before she gets to the Oregon Territory).

3. **Cast-iron stove** (you will cast it off, potbelly and all).

4. **Your personal library** (unless it consists of two books or less).

5. **Hoop skirts** (just try walking behind an ox team in one).

6. **Unbroken mules** (hee haw).

7. **Year's supply of liquor** (James Reed of the Donner party tried this, and look where it got him).

8. **Grain-fed horses** (picky, picky, picky).

9. **The family's prized pump organ** (see number 1 above—a banjo or fiddle will do).

10. **Cotton clothes** (wool keeps you warm when it's wet).

11. **Wedding dress** (would you want to be the one to discard it?).

12. **A road map of the Hastings Cutoff** (chosen by the ill-fated Donner party; need we say more?).

and this our test drivers found annoying. Those who tried to sleep in one are keeping the chiropractors in business.

On the road, the Murphy wagon's eight-inch-wide wheels allow it to roll smoothly over prairie sod. Because of its size, the freight model we tested required eight oxen to haul it. The wagon box is six feet deep—we could just see the top of a man's head when he stood inside—and sixteen feet in length. The rear wheels are seven feet in diameter, made out of white oak or hickory, and the tires are especially well fitted. The spokes are the size of "young oak saplings," and the tongue measures fifty feet in length.

Why has the Murphy wagon reached such gigantic proportions? It's a tax dodge. In 1839 the Spanish governor of New Mexico slapped a $500 fee onto each wagonload of American goods brought into his province. Murphy responded by creating jumbo wagons that could haul up to two and a half tons worth of goods. Thus has he made his fortune and also rescued the Santa Fe trade.

The Murphy wagon accumulated the fewest sample defects of any wagon we tested. We attribute this to his careful workmanship and an ingenious process—Murphy uses a hot iron to drill bolt holes, and he drills them to

THE BUTTERFIELD OVERLAND MAIL

BY MARYLOIS DUNN

The Butterfield Overland Mail, sometimes called the Southern Overland Mail or John Butterfield's Folly, was operated under an act of Congress which authorized it to convey letter mail, twice weekly, from both directions. The mail was carried in four-horse Concord coaches or spring wagons also suitable for carrying passengers. By law each trip was to be completed within twenty-five days, but the drivers' pride demanded that they try to cut two or three days off the schedule.

The route began in St. Louis, Missouri, ran across northern Texas from the Red River near Preston to Franklin, as El Paso was called then, crossed through southern New Mexico and Arizona, dipped into Mexico, and then headed due north through Los Angeles to San Francisco. It varied slightly from time to time depending on the availability of water and the temper of the local Indians. It was the longest overland mail route in the Americas.

In addition to mail and express carried at 10 cents per half ounce, the coaches had room for five or six passengers, occasionally more. The average one-way fare cross country was $200, not cheap by early 1800 standards, but it was, after all, the scenic route. Passengers were expected to carry firearms and do their part in case of attack by anyone hostile to the mail. If their endurance didn't hold out for the full three weeks, they left the stage at the risk of forfeiting their seats. They sometimes had to lay over a month to six weeks before another stage came by with a vacant space.

Like the Pony Express, the Butterfield Mail was short-lived; it operated from September 1, 1857, to March 1, 1861, covering 2,795 miles of its route faithfully twice each week. It carried the news of the outbreak of the Civil War to California in February 1861, and shortly thereafter it disbanded due to a lack of drivers and horses—they were otherwise engaged in the war.

one size smaller than the bolts. This keeps the wood from cracking and rotting around the bolt holes.

Murphy also produces a smaller, family-type wagon with optional improvised beds or shelves. Iron wasn't available for the tires of his early models but is available on later models.

Bargain hunters, take note. The Espenschied wagon, made by Louis Espenschied of St. Louis and so popular with the Army during the War Between the States, is now available as Army surplus. The ones we bought were still trailworthy. They are also known as "U.S." wagons because of the markings on the side. The "U.S." wagons are high-boxed, and the ends are very erect. This design makes the wagons look much bigger than they actually are. The freight models we tested are wide-tracked and heavy-tired. If you just can't bear to leave everything behind, the Espenschied might be the wagon of choice for you. A freight model will hold up to three and a half tons worth of goods. They are also available new as farm wagons (a more practical choice).

Since 1859, Espenschied has kept some wagons in stock. He might also be persuaded to customize a wagon. He added "a special box on the back to hold fruit trees" for a group of Mormons in 1855. We were unable to confirm reports that he is at work on a self-lubricating axle. If so, it would be a major advance in wagon technology.

The Conestoga wagon is in a class by itself. Its origins are unclear, but it appears to be a cross between the two-wheeled German Palatinate cart and the English road wagon of the 1700s. It derives its name from the Conestoga Creek in southeastern Pennsylvania, that in turn got its name from the Conestoga Indians who used to inhabit the area. This section of the country is part of Lancaster County, famed for its Amish or "Pennsylvania Dutch" people.

The first known reference to a wagon of this type was to a "Conestogoe wagon" in 1717, but a definite style didn't develop until around 1750, and the century from 1750 through 1850 was the Conestoga's heyday. Not many Conestogas have been used out West, since it was designed primarily as a freighter. These wagons were used mostly in Pennsylvania, Ohio, Maryland, and Virginia before the coming of the railroad. When turnpikes were first opened in the East, Conestogas achieved unheard-of speeds of twelve to fifteen miles a day. Conestogas are driven from the left-hand side—hence the American practice of the driver being on the left.

The Conestoga's great appeal lies in its classic lines and beauty, as well as the lore that surrounds it, but in the judgment of our wagon experts the Conestoga is not well suited for prairie travel. Its great bulk wore out teams on unbroken sod faster than we could say "jackalope." Therefore, we judged its usefulness in Indian attacks as much worse than average. The curved,

How to Spot a Conestoga

BY CAROL J. SCAMMAN

1. Curved rather than straight lines.

2. A wagon box that is low in the middle and curved upward on the ends.

3. A body twelve to thirteen feet long on the bottom, sixteen to seventeen feet at the top.

4. Endgates that angle sharply outward.

5. Eight to twelve wooden bows angled to follow the line of the endgates.

6. Bows that are almost flat on top (if the wagon has its original equipment).

7. Wagon cover extends well beyond the endgates in a marked overhang (may reach twenty-four feet end to end).

8. Toolbox (with decorative ironwork) at the center of left side.

9. Three horizontal side rails divided by a number of upright standards, giving it a paneled look.

10. Removable rear endgates for loading.

11. Long brake lever on left side (after 1830).

12. Running gear painted red, body painted blue.

13. Removable feed box on rear.

14. No place for driver to ride other than lazy-board that pulls out from center of left side.

15. Front wheels averaging forty-five inches in diameter, rear wheels sixty inches or greater.

flexible wooden box is difficult and expensive to build or replace. Because the endgates are angled so far outward, there is no seat for the driver. He has to employ "ankle express," ride the left-wheel animal, or perch on the lazy-board. We judge this to be an inconvenience in case of pursuit by Indians or bandits. The overhang of the cover and removable endgates did allow us easy loading and provides cargo protection in bad weather.

The curved bottom does much to prevent load-shifting on uphill and downhill grades. Although it's also aesthetically appealing, the sag is distinctly unappealing to passengers (see our earlier remarks on the Murphy wagon). The quality of workmanship is unsurpassed, and the Conestoga's body integrity is the best we've seen.

Popular opinion has it that the Conestoga is built with a removable boat-shaped box so it can be caulked and floated across streams. Don't try it unless you are prepared to go down with your ship. With its flexible body and removable endgate, it's definitely not seaworthy! In an emergency, other wagons may be floated this way if properly caulked or covered with a raw buffalo hide. We've heard of one desperate fellow who supposedly used snow and ice for caulking.

Late-model Conestogas do have a brake of sorts, which is more than can be said for most wagons, and its high wheels roll easily over rocks and chuckholes. Word from the East is that, with the coming of the railroads, Conestogas are no longer in demand there and a number of used Conestogas are being shipped West by boat.

Trails are more firmly packed now than when the first few emigrant trains struggled through. With that in mind, we consider the Conestoga as well as the Espenschied our picks for Best Buys in Used Wagons.

If you're short on cash, you can "soup up" a farm wagon or even an old farm lumber truck. They are generally sturdy enough for a short haul to the plains or the Rockies. Our drivers don't recommend pushing them any farther. Farm wagons have been in vogue with emigrants since the late 1860s. The cost index is low, and they have good resale value at the mines and to other farmers at trail's end.

The emigrant wagon is quite common on the trail these days. It's smaller and faster than the Conestoga; drawn with mule teams, it has achieved top speeds of twenty to forty miles a day. On a good road and with an ox team to draw, you can expect about twelve to fifteen miles per day. Most of the emigrant wagons lack brakes, so they have been clocked at higher speeds going over cliffs and in stampedes.

The emigrant wagon has a variety of names. It's also known as the Western wagon, prairie schooner, mover's wagon, settler's wagon, schooner wagon, Hoosier wagon, Mormon wagon, and, when stuck in mud, several names that we won't print. Early emigrant wagons looked much like the

Conestoga, but since the Civil War they've sported a number of new features. They shouldn't be confused with the Conestoga. Western wagon makers produce many different models at a single company. Conestogas are a distinct type produced in various sizes by different makers.

The newer emigrant wagons are basically heavy-duty farm wagons with beds that are generally flat and straight or with slightly sloped sides. Our test drivers got a good night's sleep on the floor of one of these. The endgates and end bows aren't angled as sharply as the Conestoga's.

Climate control consists of rolling up the sides of the cover (dust permitting), so it's generally either hot or cold inside. The "drop tongue" which swings up and down for use with oxen is standard equipment. An excellent safety feature is a wagon pole that is jointed to keep it from breaking the hounds as the wagon rolls over chuckholes. If a driver totals his prairie schooner, models equipped with a "shifting or movable" coupling pole can be jury-rigged as temporary carts. Words failed even our most seasoned drivers when we asked them to describe the effects of the springless ride.

The front wheels are smaller than the back wheels to improve maneuverability—that is characteristic of all types of covered wagons. The emigrant wagon has a shorter wheelbase to aid in negotiating tight turns. Some salesmen may try to sell you optional front wheels that swing under the box

Details of the Weber wagon. From *The Picture Gallery of Canadian History*, v.2, by C.W. Jeffreys: Ryerson Press, Toronto, 1945 (courtesy of Carol J. Scamman)

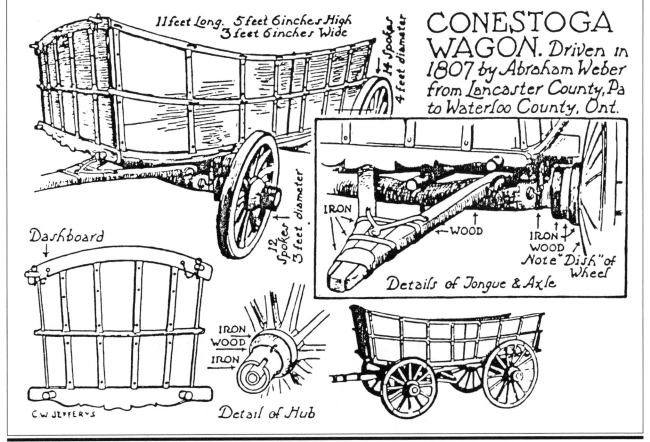

11 feet Long. 5 feet 6 inches High 3 feet 6 inches Wide

14 Spokes 4 feet diameter

CONESTOGA WAGON. Driven in 1807 by Abraham Weber from Lancaster County, Pa to Waterloo County, Ont.

12 Spokes 3 feet diameter

IRON ←WOOD IRON↑ WOOD Note "Dish" of Wheel

Details of Tongue & Axle

Dashboard

IRON WOOD→ IRON

C.W. JEFFERYS

Detail of Hub

and allow ninety-degree turns. We equipped one wagon with them. It lived up to their claims, but the team couldn't keep pace on rough ground and tired rapidly.

We were able to manage some uphill climbs only through the use of double teams or a block and tackle. To go downhill, the wheels could be chained with a "rough-lock" and skidded down the hill. This is risky business as it requires about twelve men to steady a rough-locked wagon. After repeated rough-locking, some of our wagons developed flat wheels. When all else failed, we used the "Mormon brake," a log dragged behind the wagon to slow its descent. One party reported taking a wagon apart and lowering it piece by piece over a cliff.

We loaded our emigrant wagons with about 2,500 pounds of goods, complete outfits such as are available at most jumping-off points. The selection of wagons is usually limited to what is manufactured there, so plan accordingly if you want a particular make or model. We purchased standard emigrant wagons for about $85 each, but for most wagon and teams together you can expect to spend between $300 and $600 dollars. The cover is usually extra, $8 or so; the cover we bought was painted, and it cracked noticeably during the trip. For this reason we have listed painted covers as *not acceptable.*

Mule teams cost the most. We spent $450 for a six-mule team and had to allow for three sets of harness at $8 each. Expect to spend another $600–

LITTLE EMMA

BY ARDATH MAYHAR

Little Emma changed hands in a crap game in Pueblo, Colorado, on July 4, 1882, and entered upon an unusual career. The 0-4-0 type locomotive engine was carried away to haul ore for the Lazensky Company near Clifton, Arizona. Her owner, Henry Arbuckle, took up the profession of engineer and did well. Back and forth he went between the mines and Clifton, negotiating the grades and the cuts with aplomb.

In 1884, with Emma loaded with ore and a full head of steam, Arbuckle started his engine up one of the narrow defiles on his track when he saw that the cut was occupied by a large party of Apache, who seemed to be in full war regalia. They were headed toward Clifton, and Arbuckle assumed that a raid was in the works.

The intrepid engineer tied the throttle wide open—probably in order to free his hands to use weapons, since it's unlikely that he traveled that country unarmed—and roared full ahead into the Apache war party. The cut was deep and steep-sided, and the Indians couldn't climb out in time to avoid the iron juggernaut that was bearing down upon them.

When Little Emma chugged into Clifton, she was decorated with gruesome mementos of her encounter. Along with the human debris, she had quite a collection of warpaint smeared on her cowling.

Iron Horse 1, Indians 0.

$700 for food and other supplies. The pace will be slower if you buy oxen, but they cost less, can be yoked with a milch cow in an emergency, and will also double as dinner if the grub runs low. Horses are out of the question. Most require too much grain and can't survive the harsh conditions and heavy workload. A note of caution: Mules are a favorite target of Indians. We judged the emigrant wagons' resistance to hostile attacks to be better than average when drawn by an ox team and worse than average with mules (and hopeless with horses).

Beware of fancy paint jobs—they may hide unseasoned wood. Most wagon makers have adopted the Conestoga colors of red running gear and blue body. These colors don't show the dirt, and with a white top, you'll be prepared for the Fourth of July tailgate picnic.

Frequency of repair for the typical emigrant wagon is average. Owing to a shortage of seasoned hardwood on the plains, some wagons with parts made of cottonwood and other lighter material have been sold. Predicted reliability is worse than average for such models. The usual length for an emigrant wagon is nine to ten feet, the width of the box about four feet. There's approximately five feet of headroom from the bed to the top of the cover bows. It takes three to four yoke oxen or six mules to pull a loaded wagon.

Custom options include a false bottom for storage, removable pine boxes built the same width as the wagon, carpeting, an extra-wide wagon box (six inches more on each side), and steel axles. We recommend extra storage, as long as you don't exceed 2,500 pounds of cargo. In our judgment, carpeting and wide wagon beds make for better sleeping but add too much weight. Wagons with steel axles are being recalled, as there is no way to fashion a spare when one breaks. Studebaker wagons offer an optional spring seat that retails for $13. Our seat-sore test drivers fought for the chance to use it and endorse it wholeheartedly.

Recommendations: Unless someone makes you an offer you can't refuse on a used Conestoga, we feel you should stick to one of the smaller models produced by one of the "name" wagon makers. The Studebaker wagons are especially durable and widely available. Their latest models display many of the same features as the standard emigrant wagons. The smaller Espenschieds are also a good choice. Murphy wagons are fine if you don't plan to sleep or ride in them. The newer emigrant wagons offer a lot of advantages, if you can find a carefully made one.

We'll cover (no pun intended) New England style wagons and those produced by the Kansas Wagon Manufacturing Company of Leavenworth in future issues, as well as the quality "high-boxed Young wagons" produced by Hiram Young, a free black man of Independence, Missouri. Whatever wagon you choose, keep in mind that it is only as good as its wheels. ■

William Barrett Travis (courtesy of State Archives, Austin, Texas)

WOULD YOU GO?

BY JEFF CARROLL

THE SPRING OF 1836 WAS ONE OF THE WETTEST THAT TEXANS COULD remember. The people of Texas, of Spanish and Anglo extraction alike, were mostly concerned with their own affairs — surviving the end of a cold, wet winter and hoping for a few clear days so they could plant for the future.

In the muddy shantytown called Washington-on-the-Brazos, in a blacksmith's unfinished shop, the elected representatives of the various Texas municipalities argued and fought among themselves. Should they give in to the upstart dictator Santa Anna, or should they declare for independence?

At Goliad, quartered in the old mission of La Bahia, was James Fannin, in command of about 25 Texas volunteers and 425 volunteer mercenaries from Georgia and Alabama who had been promised land and the loot of the town of Matamoras.

At San Antonio de Bexar, quartered in the mission that would become forever known as the Alamo, was William B. Travis. He commanded a mixed bag of Hispanic and Anglo Texans, frontier trappers, doctors, lawyers, and farmers, a total of about 150 men. Here was a true melting pot. There were men from almost every state in the Union plus at least six from the European Continent, and there were representatives of many ethnic groups; there were illiterates and ex-members of the U.S. Congress. None of them had yet received the pay promised for their service.

In between the two fortresses was Santa Anna, the self-styled Napoleon of the West, with an army of over 6,000 men. By now you've heard the story many times, but some parts of it need re-telling.

Fannin was ordered to support Travis. He dithered around for almost a month; because of his indecision, most of his men were later captured and executed.

Santa Anna arrived at San Antonio with at least 4,000 men. Travis was in a bind, and he ordered a general retreat to Gonzales, then to the old mission known as the Alamo. Whether he was a fool or a hero we don't known, for there he choose to hold his position although it meant almost certain death. Above the Alamo he flew the flag of the Mexican Constitution of 1824, which represented the democracy that existed before Santa Anna came to power. The men who fought there never knew that, far to the east, at Washington-on-the Brazos, the council had voted to separate Texas from Mexico. At the Alamo they fought for a Mexican Constitution, but they died for Texas Independence.

Defending a position he was ordered to leave, outnumbered by at least twenty-six to one, Travis sought to buy time for Texas to prepare, and he asked for help. As part of what has been called one of the finest testaments to heroism in history, Travis wrote, "For God's sake and the sake of our country, send us reinforcements."

No one listened—almost no one. Some forty-five miles away was the tiny town of Gonzales. There were no soldiers there, only merchants and farmers with families. They had crops to plant and stock to tend and cabins to keep warm on the cold March nights. They, too, had come from somewhere else to begin new lives in a new land. Some had fought Indians. Some had marched with Old Ben Milam to San Antonio six months before. All of them wanted peace.

And all of them were being asked to choose between their homes and families and certain death—just to support a constitution the Mexican dictator had repudiated.

Thirty-two chose to go. They left their homes. They left their stores. They left their families. They fought their way into the Alamo, and they died there with the rest on March 6.

They didn't die for money, or the promise of land or loot. They didn't even die for independence, because they never knew that it had been de-

Drawing of Texas Rangers preparing for a scout (courtesy of Texas State Library Archives, Austin, Texas)

clared. They died for honor; they died because they weren't afraid to get involved when someone needed help—because, as Travis said, "We consider death preferable to disgrace." In dying they delayed Santa Anna's march to the Louisiana border, thus giving Houston the time he needed. They gave reason to the revolution—it was the "Remember the Alamo!" battle cry that at last united the arguing factions and led to victory at San Jacinto. They didn't die in vain. ∎

GONE TO TEXAS

The Broken Promise

BY JEFF CARROLL

"Poor Mexico, so far from God and so close to the United States."

PORFIRIO DIAZ

THERE ARE A LOT OF "WHAT IFS" IN TEXAS HISTORY. FOR INSTANCE, what if Alvar Nuñez (Cabeza de Vaca) had not been cast ashore on Galveston Island? There might have been no Coronado expedition to seek the fabled seven cities of gold. The turn of a "what if" can change our entire world. Most of the time there is an exceptional individual at the center of a "what if." Take José Urrea...

José Urrea was raised down in the Mexican state of Durango and, when Mexico gained her independence from Spain in 1821, he was already involved as a military professional. Unlike some of his compatriots, he was a very good officer and a good politician to boot. In September 1835, as Stephen F. Austin returned to his Texas colony after spending over a year in a Mexican prison, José Urrea was elected governor of Durango and advanced to the rank of brigadier general. When the Mexican and Anglo colonies in Texas revolted against Antonio López de Santa Anna—he had dissolved the Mexican congress and thrown out the Constitution of 1824—Santa Anna ordered Urrea to Matamoras to take part in the invasion.

Urrea was probably the best officer Santa Anna had. He was of the old school, an officer and a gentleman. Carrying out his part of Santa Anna's plan to perfection, he defeated Texas forces under Johnson at San Patricio and Grant at Agua Dulce. Moving northward along the coast, he rolled up the Texas troops under Amon B. King and then William Ward. He arrived at Goliad just after James Fannin vacated.

Despite Fannin's West Point training, he was an indecisive and reluctant commander. He also had the largest Texas force then under arms. In his retreat from Goliad, he stopped to rest on the prairie between Goliad and Victoria, well short of his objective. There, in the battle of Coleto Creek, Urrea's troops surrounded him and cut him off from water and escape. Ultimately Fannin surrendered.

He surrendered unconditionally; Santa Anna had ordered it that way. But Urrea personally gave Fannin his word, on his honor as an officer and a gentleman, that the surrendered troops would be treated fairly as prisoners of war. Urrea then left Goliad and the prisoners under the control of Lieutenant Colonel José Nicolas de la Portilla, giving him orders to treat the prisoners fairly and use them to rebuild the mission and presidio at Goliad.

Then Portilla received orders from Santa Anna. There were to be no prisoners; they must be killed. On the morning of March 27, 1836, Portilla took Fannin's men out of the fort in small groups and executed them.

General Urrea felt personally dishonored and responsible for the deaths of those he'd promised to protect. He never forgot or forgave Santa Anna for pinning that dishonor, which became known as the Goliad Massacre, on him and his family.

When Sam Houston's rag-tag Texas Army defeated Santa Anna in Peggy McCormic's pasture across from the mouth of the San Jacinto River, Brigadier General José Urrea was less than thirty miles away with the bulk of the Mexican army and most of its supplies. A counterattack the next day could have freed Santa Anna and run the rebels out of the Texas colonies.

Urrea turned around and went home.

In 1837, Urrea was commandante general of Mexican forces in the Mexican states of Sinaloa and Sonora when they, too, rebelled against Santa Anna and the centralist government. His revolt was unsuccessful, but Urrea had already played a role in making Texas free and independent. What if his promise had not been broken by Santa Anna?

There might never have been a Republic of Texas. ∎

THE YELLOW ROSE OF TEXAS

IN PRAISE OF EMILY WEST, THE MULATTO SLAVE GIRL WHO DISTRACTED SANTA ANNA, THUS ALLOWING SAM HOUSTON AND THE TEXAS REVOLUTIONARY ARMY TO TAKE HIM BY SURPRISE AT SAN JACINTO

There's a Yellow Rose in Texas that I am going to see;
No other cowboy knows her, nobody, only me.
She cried so when I left her, it like to broke her heart,
And if we ever meet again we never more shall part.

Chorus:
She's the sweetest rose of colour this cowboy ever knew,
Her eyes are bright as diamonds, they sparkle like the dew.
You may talk about your dearest maids and sing of Rosalie,
But the Yellow Rose of Texas beats the belles of Tennessee.

Where the Rio Grand is flowing, and stars are shining bright,
We walked along together on a quiet summer night.
She said, "If you remember, when we parted long ago,
You promised to come back again and never leave me so."

(repeat chorus)

I'm going back to see her; my heart is full of woe.
We'll sing the songs together we sang so long ago.
We'll pick the banjo gaily, and sing the songs of yore,
And the Yellow Rose of Texas will be mine forever more.

(repeat chorus)

Sam Houston

THE DESPERATE RIDE OF JOSEPH POWELL

BY JEFF CARROLL

HISTORY RECORDS MANY DESPERATE RIDES. SELDOM DID ONE HAVE more impact on a revolution than the ride Joseph Powell made on the night of April 11, 1836.

You've got to look at it in context. On October 3, 1835, the Mexican congress, by order of Antonio López de Santa Anna, declared the Mexican federal Constitution of 1824 null and void. The Texas colonists met in "consultation" on November 6 and voted for a provisional government in accordance with the old constitution and in opposition to Santa Anna.

Santa Anna declared Texas to be "a province in rebellion" and decided to personally lead a force to bring the unruly Texans into line. One thing led to another and on March 2, 1836, a new convention at Washington-on-the-Brazos voted for Texan independence. On March 6, the Alamo fell.

Sam Houston arrived at Gonzales on March 11 as commander in chief of all military forces. He found only 374 men, about two day's worth of supplies, and the news that the Alamo had fallen. That began the "Runaway Scrape" as the military and civilians alike retreated before Santa Anna's advancing army. There was no time to organize or re-equip; no time to stand and fight, and little to fight with.

By the end of March, Houston had reached the Brazos, where he turned north to Groce's plantation near today's Hempstead. At Groce's, Houston organized the army, drilled and rested it, and brought some semblance of order out of chaos. When Santa Anna reached the Brazos at San Felipe, he found the town burned and the crossing defended by Moseley Baker's men. In search of another crossing and in pursuit of the new Texas government, he turned south to the crossing at Fort Bend at today's Rosenberg.

This set the stage for our story.

David G. Burnet, the interim president of the interim government, was at Harrisburg, on the banks of Buffalo Bayou, only thirty miles from the Fort Bend crossing. For the moment Santa Anna forgot about Houston—his scouts told him Houston was many miles away, and the Texas government was within striking distance. Santa Anna could capture the Texas leaders and end the rebellion.

On the banks of the Brazos at Fort Bend stood what I guess we would today call a hotel. Back then it served meals to travelers and provided limited, but usually dry, overnight lodging. The proprietor was Mrs. Elizabeth Powell, a widow, who refused to abandon all that she had to join the evacuation. On the night of April 10 she became the unwilling hostess to Santa Anna and his officers. Her son, Joseph, waited on the tables. Relatively few

A CHICKEN FOR THE GENERAL

BY JEFF CARROLL

Sam Sparks was a boy, but boys became men in a hurry in the 1830s. Sam was seventeen and a student near Nacogdoches when General Cos invaded Texas. According to his recollections, "There being a call for volunteers to meet them, I left school and joined the army." Sam fought at the siege of Bexar and then went back to school.

When Santa Anna invaded Texas, Sam was asked if he would raise a company of volunteers and go to help defend the Alamo. He formed the company, declined the captaincy, and signed his schoolteacher up as the orderly sergeant. Fortunately for them, they didn't make it to the Alamo. They reached Washington-on-the-Brazos about the same time as word of the mission's fall. Things were in a panic. Rumors had Santa Anna's cavalry ten miles from town. Almost everybody who could lit out.

Not Sam. He and four other boys said they "would fight Santa Anna at every creek, river, and thicket to the Sabine River." As it turned out, they were the only fighting men left at Washington-on-the-Brazos. Acting President Burnet commissioned them to make a swing down along the coast to appropriate horses and weapons from those who were fleeing the country. The assignment wasn't to Sam's liking,

but he did it—and he even took one of Burnet's own horses down at Harrisburg.

It wasn't long before General Sam Houston's little army came along, and Sam Sparks and his boys were assigned the job of gathering cattle to feed the men. General Houston had some very strong feelings about property rights. He said that only cattle would be taken—no pigs, no chickens, no corn. Sam and his boys were ordered to take a small herd to a particular farm, where the farmer would butcher beef for the army.

When Sam's boys got there, the farm was deserted. The yard was full of hungry chickens, the smokehouse was full of bacon, and there was plenty of cornmeal in the mill. Sam told his boys to get to work on the cattle and he would fix lunch.

Sam recalled: "I went to work and killed twelve grown chickens, dressed them, and put them in a large wash pot; I also put in some sliced bacon. I then made an oven and a large skillet of cornbread. I took six of the chickens, and put them in a dinner pot, with at least half a gallon of rich gravy, and set it away, together with the oven of bread. By this time the beeves had been butchered and hung up, and I called the men to come to dinner. The yard was covered with feathers, and the men said to me, 'ain't you afraid Houston will punish you if you don't take those feathers away?' I said 'no.' Well, we all did justice to that dinner."

About dark the army came up, and General Houston, along with his officers Rusk, Burleson, and Sydney Sherman, rode up to the yard.

"Gentlemen officers, I wish to see you in the house," said Sam as he led the way through the feathers. Once they were inside Sam said, "General, I

have disobeyed orders; when we arrived here, I found everything deserted and we were hungry — so I killed some chickens and baked some bread, and we had a good dinner."

Houston replied, "Sparks, I will have to punish you. You knew it was against orders."

Sam said, "General, I saved you some," and he took the lids off the pots that contained the chicken and bread and told them to help themselves. Rusk drew his knife first, and all of the others followed suit, except Houston, who had not taken his eyes off Sparks.

Finally he said, "Sparks, I really hate to punish you."

Sam replied, "General, I will submit to whatever you put upon me."

Rusk said, "General, if you don't come on, we'll eat all the dinner. Sparks is a good cook."

Then Houston drew his knife and attacked the chicken. After he had eaten a short time, Rusk said, "General Houston, it is a maxim in law that he who partakes of stolen property, knowing it to be such, is guilty with the thief."

General Houston replied, "No one wants any of your law phrases," and finished the meal. But he made no further mention of punishment for Sparks.

Sam Sparks and his boys went on with the army, led the line at the Battle of San Jacinto, and finally made their way back to Nacogdoches. Sam married in October. In less than a year after he left school, the boy had become a resourceful veteran and the head of a family—and a chicken thief who'd bested a general on a point of law.

Such were the men who built Texas.

Anglos in Texas at that time spoke Spanish. Joseph, however, had learned enough to get along.

While his mother cooked, he listened. He overheard Santa Anna make plans to abandon the search for Houston and the Texas army, leave behind his supplies and the bulk of his army, and, with only 750 men, make a dash to catch the government at Harrisburg. When Santa Anna led his forces out the next day, Joseph also left, riding hard to the north, searching for Houston.

The roads were choked with mud and fleeing refugees. In good weather the ride from Fort Bend to Groce's should take two days. Joseph made it through bad weather in one. On April 12 he reported to Houston that Santa Anna was across the river; for the first time, the Napoleon of the West was separated from his supplies and reinforcements. It was the chance that Houston looked for, the only one he was likely to get. At New Kentucky the road forked and the tiny army turned south, toward Harrisburg and destiny.

By the time Houston reached Buffalo Bayou and the smoldering ruins of Harrisburg, Santa Anna had moved farther east in a vain attempt to capture the government at New Washington.

You know the rest. Houston was between Santa Anna and his supplies and any means of escape; he surprised the Mexican forces during siesta and took the Mexican leader prisoner. The battle of San Jacinto lasted only eighteen minutes and forever changed the history of Texas, Mexico, and the United States. But without Joseph Powell's ride, who knows?

There should be a monument. ■

THE TEXAS RANGER

AN EARLY TEXAS FOLK SONG, THE LYRICS PUT TO THE TUNE OF
A 16TH-CENTURY IRISH BALLAD OR LAMENT

Come all ye Texas Rangers, wherever you may be;
I'll tell you of some troubles that happened unto me;
My name is nothing extra; to you I will not tell;
But here's to all good Rangers, I'm sure I wish you well.

It was at the age of sixteen I joined a Ranger band;
We marched from San Antonio down to the Rio Grande,
And there our Captain told us—perhaps he thought it right—
"Before we reach the River boys, I'm sure we'll have a fight."

And before we reached the River, our Captain gave command,
"To arms, to arms" he shouted, "and by your pony stand!"
I saw the smoke arising, it seemed to reach the sky,
And then, the thought it struck me—my time had come to die.

I saw the Indians coming, I heard them give a yell;
My feelings at that moment, no mortal tongue can tell;
I saw their glittering lances, their arrows 'round me hailed,
My heart it sank within me, my courage almost failed.

I thought of my old mother, who in tears to me did say:
"To you they are all strangers, with me you'd better stay."
I thought her weak and childish, and that she did not know,
For I was bent on roaming, and I was bound to go.

And all of us were wounded, our noble captain slain;
As the sun shone down so sadly across the bloody plain,
Sixteen as brave a Rangers as ever rode the West
Were buried by their comrades with arrows in their chests.

Perhaps you have a mother, likewise a sister too;
Perhaps you have a sweetheart who'll weep and mourn for you—
If this should be your portion and you are bound to roam,
I advise you from experience, you'd better stay at home.

THE FORGOTTEN SAGA OF GREENBURY LOGAN

BY JEFF CARROLL

Portrait of James Bowie, one of the defenders of the Alamo (courtesy of Institute of Texan Cultures, San Antonio, Texas)

THERE OUGHT TO BE A TEXAS COUNTY NAMED FOR GREENBURY LOGAN, or at least a school or two and maybe a few streets. Texas has a habit of recognizing her heroes that way. But as far as I can tell, the powers that be decided to forget all about Greenbury. You see, he was different.

Greenbury was a blacksmith, and a good one. Blacksmiths were in short supply on the Texas frontier. Stephen F. Austin recognized the need and enlisted Greenbury as one of his colonists in 1831. Greenbury was also a fighter and a good leader. That made him three times valuable. With his craft he helped the colonists build the farms and ranches of the Gulf Coast. When called upon to fight, he provided both arms and leadership.

Although he'd intended, like many others, to make his fortune in Texas and return to the United States, he came to love both the land and the people. While the representatives of the colonies debated independence, he put down his hammer and tongs, took up his rifle, and headed for the fight at Gonzales.

On the road from Gonzales to the siege of San Antonio, there were those who wouldn't go until Greenbury agreed to lead them. On October 28, 1835, he fought beside James Bowie at the Battle of Concepción. During the battle of San Antonio on December 5, he was in the lead; he was the third man to fall, his right arm shattered beyond repair. Greenbury Logan was thirty-eight years old, a veteran of the revolution—and a blacksmith who could no longer handle the tools of his trade.

San Jacinto brought Texas independence and freedom. But under the new leadership of Vice President Mirabeau Lamar (Houston's political enemy), the legislature of the Republic passed a law that made Greenbury Logan, the blacksmith who had fought for Texas, *persona non grata*. For you see, Greenbury was black. The self-important Lamar felt that freedmen had no place in Texas society, and he had his way. Without a special act of the legislature, no blacks could live in the Republic of Texas—except as slaves. Ironically, before the coming of the Anglo-American settlers, the Spanish

Two men working at the Will Atcheson's Blacksmith Shop, Greeley, Kansas (courtesy of Kansas State Historical Society, Topeka, Kansas)

census of 1792 recorded that of the 1,600 non-Indian residents of the province, 449 were black, not Mexican or Spanish.

In 1837, twenty-three prominent Texans, including Henry Austin, signed a petition requesting that Greenbury be allowed to stay as a free black. The petition was granted, but his disabilities made it impossible for him to make a living as a blacksmith. Because he was a veteran of the revolution, the government did add to the one-quarter league of land he had by right as an early citizen.

But no sooner was the land granted than he ran into problems caused by his unique status. Document 2582 of the Sixth Congress contained his request. In part, it read:

"…every privilege dear to a freeman is taken away—no chance to collect a debt with out a witness, no vote or say in any way, yet liable for taxes. It is out of power to either settle on my lands or to sell them or to labour for money to pay expenses on them. If my debts was payd I would be willing to leave the land though my blood has nearly all been shed for its rights. I know I have friends. The Congress would not refuse to exempt my lands from tax or otherwise restoure what it has taken from me in the constitution. —yours with respect, G. Logan"

Although many similar petitions for tax exemption were granted to Anglos who had fallen on hard times, Greenbury Logan's request never reached the floor for debate in Lamar's congress. We don't know what happened to him; he dropped from sight.

But there should, at the very least, be a Greenbury Logan Street. ■

v. SHE WON THE WEST

WOMEN OF THE WAGON TRAINS

BY MARIANNE WILLMAN

IT WAS A BACKBREAKING 2,400 MILES FROM THE JUMPING-OFF SPOTS along the Missouri River to the end of the rainbow in Oregon or California, but thousands of women traveled it. Walked it, that is, for that was the way most of them came West, trudging through mud and sand and rocks beside their overburdened wagons. Rich and poor, white and black, free and slave, the women journeyed along the primitive trails, bringing their softening influence and the comfortingly familiar rituals of civilization.

Clara Brown, a black slave who purchased her freedom in 1859, hired on as cook to a group of gold prospectors and worked her way across the plains in a covered wagon. Clara started a laundry in Colorado and after the Civil War went back East to search for the relatives she hadn't seen in over half a century. Having found thirty-four, she brought them to Denver by steamboat and wagon. She later sponsored other trains to bring black families West.

Some women came West in search of adventure or, like Clara Brown, a new and better life. Many came along just to keep their families intact, accompanying husbands, fathers or brothers lured by the promise of free land in California and Oregon. In the period from 1840 to 1870, more than 300,000 pioneers followed the siren call of the West, and their stories were most often preserved in the hundreds of diaries and journals the pioneer women kept along the way.

To give up their homes and their friends for the hardship of crossing the Great Plains was not an easy thing to do, and female physiology made the pioneer woman's role even more difficult. One of five pioneer women was pregnant at some point along the trail, and childbirth was not considered sufficient reason to halt a wagon train in unfriendly country. Babies were born and often buried along the Overland Trail amidst tears and heartache,

PREVIOUS PAGE:
A Prairie Wind Storm,
Harper's Weekly

but the wagon trains went on. And there were serious hazards even for the older children. In the larger trains they could get lost among the wagons and herds of oxen and sheep. They fell out of wagons or off whiffletrees and were occasionally abducted by Indians. They were bitten by snakes, suffered various forms of dysentery and were subject to those terrible ills that have since almost been abolished by modern immunizations: whooping cough, diphtheria, typhoid, and the dreaded cholera.

Some women came West in prairie schooners, the Conestoga wagons so familiar from movies and television, and in the later years a favored few twirled their parasols as they rolled across the plains in well-sprung horse-drawn carriages. Most of them rode in simple wagons much like those used on farms back East, but lighter in weight and built from seasoned hardwood. The flat boards that formed the high sides were planed for more than one purpose, for at journey's end the wagon could be dismantled and the wood used to build a lean-to for a temporary home. Just as often the stout planks were used to shape coffins for those less fortunate emigrants who died along the way. At times during the height of the cholera years, the trail became a graveyard from end to end, marked with newly turned earth or weathered crosses.

Flinty ground, imminent attack by hostile Indians or raiders, and the threat of bad weather often made burials a hasty affair, the graves shallow. When possible the women insisted that the graves be covered or lined with flat stones to keep out hungry wolves and coyotes, as well as grave robbers who might disturb the dead for their rings or jewelry. (When a young woman's burial place, sided and covered with slabs of stone, was recently uncovered by erosion near Emigrant Springs, the remains were reinterred by members of the Oregon-California Trails Association.)

DUTIES ALONG THE TRAIL WERE CLEARLY DEFINED. MEN WERE responsible for maintaining the animals and wagons, and for hunting, fishing, and standing guard. In addition to cooking, sewing, cleaning, and doctoring, women also drove the wagons and often harnessed the teams. There were other, less tangible tasks—the women not only oversaw the raising of the children, they kept the circle of the family intact. They preserved the social order under the most primitive of conditions and set the example for their own basic values.

Indian attack, dreaded by the emigrants of fictional Westerns, was for the actual emigrants a relatively small fear when compared to disease and illness. Natural causes took far more lives than were ever lost to hostile encounters. Except for a few tragic incidents when lives were taken by both sides, most contact with the Indians proved helpful during the many years of emigration. Not every former farmer or tradesman immediately became a proficient hunter or frontiersman. The women of the wagon trains traded calico shirts to the Indians for their assistance in river crossings or for fish and game when their husbands couldn't provide it.

IN ADDITION TO ACTING AS MIDWIVES, WOMEN WERE USUALLY THE unofficial physicians, treating everything from cuts to colic, snakebite to cholera. They were the wardens of the precious stores of medicines, remedies that included willow bark and poke root to bring down fever and reduce pain, sulfur and molasses as the standard "cure" for chills and nausea. They collected spiderwebs and used them to stanch bleeding from wounds and cuts, and they used bread mold for poultices to fight infection a hundred years before the discovery of life-saving penicillin. They used whiskey and laudanum, a derivative of opium, to alleviate moderate to severe pain, opium for more intractable conditions. Malaria, endemic in the pioneer staging areas east of the Missouri, was known as "the ague" or "shaking sickness," and quinine was the standard remedy. Peppermint oil was the standard treatment for an upset stomach, oil of clove or wintergreen for toothache, and chamomile tea for cramps and nervousness. A wise mother also took along a supply of citric acid to ward off scurvy. There was no cure except time for one complaint that struck many at the journey's start, a "seasickness" induced by traveling inside the swaying covered wagon during inclement weather. After a few days or weeks most travelers got their "sea legs."

The Emigrant's Guide to Oregon and California provided a list of necessities for prudent housewives. In addition to powder, lead, and shot for the rifles the guide recommended 200 pounds of flour, 150 pounds of bacon, a meager 10 pounds of coffee, 20 pounds of sugar, 10 pounds of salt, assorted foodstuffs including chipped beef, rice, dried beans and peas, tea, dried fruits, baking soda, vinegar, mustard, and tallow. Food was plain but wholesome, at least in the early weeks of travel.

Fashion wasn't a concern; many women made the crossing in the clothes upon their backs, while those more fortunate had one or two changes of outfit. In the later days they wore bloomers with ankle- or calf-length skirts, a more practical type of garment for the activities involved. One comment illustrates the average sad state of a woman's garment after some time on the trail: Rebecca Ketcham, who traveled with a wagon train, reported that her dress was dirty and torn in twenty places but added that she didn't care as she looked no worse than the other women.

After the hard crossing, those women who survived set out to rebuild their lives in new surroundings and bring the best of civilization to the rough-and-ready West. That they succeeded, and so well, is a tribute to their stamina and courage. ■

ABOUT A PETITE LADY:
"She was no bigger than a bar of soap after a week's wash."

NERVOUS:
"Like a long-tailed cat in a room full of rocking chairs."

Cynthia Ann Parker

BY THOMAS W. KNOWLES

CYNTHIA ANN PARKER'S STRANGE AND TRAGIC DESTINY DIVIDED HER life and left her torn between two hostile worlds. She was born the daughter of hardshell Baptist pioneers from Illinois, but she became the wife of Chief Peta Nacona and lived as a Comanche for almost twenty-five years. Her oldest son, Quanah Parker, became the last great war chief of the free Comanche.

When the Parkers migrated to Texas in 1833, it was still a wild and barely settled province of Mexico. The primary obstacle to that settlement was the ferocity with which the nomadic Comanche defended their plains homeland, the Comanchería. The Parkers eventually erected a log stockade, Parker's Fort, in East Central Texas near the modern site of Groesbeck, and cleared farmland near the Navasota River.

The Parkers probably thought they were safe, since they were a little outside the usual Comanche raiding range, but on May 19, 1836, a war party of more than a hundred Comanche and Kiowa warriors found its way to Parker's Fort. Many of the men from the Parker settlement were working in the outlying fields. Most of the other white settlers in Texas were occupied with the aftermath of Sam Houston's victory against Santa Anna at San Jacinto less than a month before.

It's an obscure point whether the Comanche had come to Parker's Fort with the intent to trade for horses or to raid, but they seized the opportunity to do the latter. They lanced Benjamin Parker and his brother Silas after the two men met them outside the walls for a parley, then killed two more men as they rode screaming in through the gate. Elder John Parker they killed and scalped inside the walls, and his wife, Granny Parker, they stripped, pinned to the ground with a lance, and raped. They took nine-year-old Cynthia Ann captive along with her six-year-old brother, John. They also abducted Elizabeth Kellog, Rachel Plummer, and Rachel's small son, James. The war party rode out just in time to avoid the men who were running in from the fields with their rifles. The short, savage attack had left five white men dead, and two of the women later died of wounds. Granny Parker, who typified the strength of pioneer women, drew the lance from her flesh and survived.

The captives were split up among the bands. The Parker children were taken to eastern Colorado, where they were adopted into Peta Nacona's band. They learned to ride and dress like the Comanche, and they forgot English in favor of the Comanche tongue. The Parkers and their agents made exhaustive efforts to retrieve their lost relatives, and though they eventually recovered John, Elizabeth, Rachel, and James, they were unsuccessful in their attempts to find Cynthia Ann. The Comanche refused all offers of ransom, and in 1840 Cynthia Ann herself informed the Parkers through intermediaries that she had no desire to return. She said that she now called herself Naduah, considered herself a true Comanche, and was happily married. When a U.S. Army officer saw Cynthia Ann at a peace council in 1846, she refused to speak with him.

Her husband was Peta Nacona, the Wanderer. He was a fine warrior and chief of his own band, the Naconi. There is evidence that their relationship went far beyond that of captor and captive. Not only did Cynthia Ann refuse to be parted from him, but Nacona also went very much against Comanche custom by declining to take any other wives. Their first son, Quanah, was

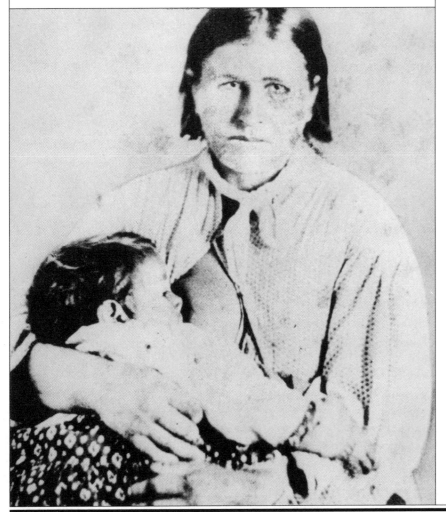

Cynthia Ann Parker

born in 1847, and they had two more children, a son named Pecos and a daughter named Topsannah (Flower).

Cynthia Ann's world was once again turned askew on December 17, 1860. While Nacona was away hunting with his sons and his warriors, Texas Ranger Captain Sul Ross led a mixed force of Rangers, 2nd Cavalry troopers, citizen volunteers, and Tonkawa scouts in a raid against the Naconi camp on the Pease River (near the present site of Quanah, Texas). Though the Indian women and children were permitted targets for the raiders, future cattle baron Charles Goodnight held his fire when he saw dung-greased blond hair and blue eyes under one woman's blanket. The woman and her eighteen-month-old daughter were spared. Though she could speak no English and called herself Naduah, she recognized her own English name—Cynthia Ann.

The Southwestern frontier was electrified by the news: After nearly a quarter of a century as a captive of the Comanche, Cynthia Ann Parker had been rescued. The Parker family welcomed their lost child and her little Flower, and the Texas legislature granted Cynthia Ann a league of land and an annual pension of $100. But Cynthia Ann felt she had not been rescued, only kidnapped once again. Her repeated requests to be allowed to return to her husband and family were denied, and she was put under guard when she tried to escape. When her little Topsannah died in 1864 of a "civilized" disease, she grieved Comanche-style with wailing prayers to the spirits and by self-mutilation. Shortly afterward she starved herself to death.

Peta Nacona never took another wife, and he found his own death from grief by neglecting an infected wound. Pecos fell ill and died as well, but Quanah remained and became strong. And as Cynthia Ann's oldest son grew toward the greatness that would one day make him chief of the Quahadie Comanche, so grew his animosity toward the white civilization that had taken his family from him.

WILD RIPPLING WATER

FROM AN OLD IRISH BALLAD ORIGINALLY CALLED "THE BOLD GRENADIER" OR "THE NIGHTINGALE"

As I was out walking and rambling one day,
I spied a fair couple a'coming my way.
One was a Lady, as fair as could be,
And the other was a Cowboy, and a brave one was he.
He said, "Where are you going my pretty, fair maid?"
"Just down by the River, just down by the shade,
Just down by the River, just down by the spring
To see the Wild Rippling Water and hear the Nightingale sing."

Well they hadn't been there but an hour or so
'Til he drew from his sachel a fiddle and bow.
He tuned his old fiddle all on the high string,
And he played this tune over and over again.
Then saith the Cowboy, "I should be gone."
"No, no," saith the pretty maid, "just play one more song;
I'd rather hear the fiddle just played on one string
Than see the Wild Rippling Water and hear the Nightingale sing."

Cavalry Wives

BY LENORE CARROLL

IN THE DECADES AFTER THE CIVIL WAR, MANY BRIDES FOLLOWED their husbands on assignments to frontier Army outposts. Some, like Frances M. A. Roe, wrote letters home which were later published (see *Army Letters from an Officer's Wife*, 1909). Some kept journals and later published their memoirs, like Martha Summerhayes' 1908 *Vanished Arizona*, Ellen Biddle's 1909 *Reminiscences of a Soldier's Wife*, and Lydia Lane's 1893 *Old Days in the Old Army*. Elizabeth Custer's memoirs, *Boots and Saddles* (1885), *Following the Guidon* (1890), and *Tenting on the Plains* (1887), enhanced the popular myths about her husband, George Armstrong Custer.

Cavalry wives carried West the reminders of their genteel lives—fine crystal and china, woolen riding habits, and civilized manners. It wasn't easy. There were few if any of the amenities to which they'd become accustomed. They traveled for weeks in mule-drawn ambulances only to set up their homes in barren living quarters that were little more than huts; even these living assignments were insecure, for they could be "ranked out" by a superior officer's family and forced to move to lesser quarters.

The frontier Army maintained itself as an ideal of aristocracy. Its code, akin to that of medieval chivalry, had permeated both sides of the military during the Civil War. The officers' wives were required to be the epitome of this ideal and to live by its precepts. They were never to question their presumption of inherent superiority or the divine right of the military hierarchy.

Some of their conceptions of duty and honor were severely put to the test. The Army cut back its ranks in the post-Civil War era, and some West Pointers spent ten to twenty years as lieutenants before moving up in rank. A wife might be of "dual mental states" (Frances Carrington, *My Army Life*, 1910) when she first went West, but she kept her doubts secret and publicly voiced her devotion to "serious duty."

The cavalry wife adapted to and even tolerated moral conduct and conditions that were unthinkable in the East—as Martha Summerhayes said, "everything that I had been taught to think wicked or immoral." But when Summerhayes considered the dreary years men spent on the frontier without families, she was "willing to reserve...judgment." She eventually learned

Martha Summerhayes
(courtesy of Lenore Carroll)

to take siestas and to smoke cigarettes, and she even longed to wear the cool *camisa* of the local women instead of Eastern clothes. She expressed her mixed feelings during a difficult trip through Arizona's Mogollon Basin: "Surely I have never seen anything to compare with this—but oh! would any sane human being voluntarily go through with what I have endured on this journey, in order to look upon this wonderful scene?"

Even the simplest of housekeeping tasks were made difficult by the privation and isolation of the frontier. Servants and nurses were almost nonexistent, and many women relied on enlisted men, "strikers," to build fires and help with other chores. Summerhayes put aside her civilized prejudices to accept the presence of a nearly naked Indian who was "tall and well-made, with clean-cut limbs and features, fine smooth copper-colored skin, handsome face, heavy black hair done up in a pompadour fashion and plastered with Colorado [River] mud, which was baked white by the sun, a small feather at the crown of his head, wide turquoise bead bracelets upon his upper arm and a knife at his waist…this was my butler." He also watched the baby.

The diet at a frontier post was limited to Army rations—hardtack, bacon, flour, beans, canned beef, and coffee—unless one could afford to buy canned goods at the sutler's store, or fresh milk, eggs, butter, and vegetables from people living near the posts. Enlisted men were encouraged to grow gardens, but still many soldiers and their families suffered from scurvy and other diseases caused by nutritional deficits and the general hardships of their lives.

Enlisted men were allowed to marry only with the permission of

Frances M. A. Roe and her dog, Hal (courtesy of Lenore Carroll)

their commanding officer. Their wives were usually post laundresses. The laundresses were official employees of the Army, hired at the rate of one to every nineteen and one-half soldiers and paid first when funds were disbursed.

Pleasures were few even for officers' wives. Their opportunities were often severely restricted; they couldn't travel unescorted for fear of hostile Indians and bandits. Even so, Libby Custer found respite in riding over the Kansas prairie. Some wives hunted with their husbands, and others, like Frances Roe, became accomplished and enthusiastic anglers. Her delight in the mountain streams of Montana is apparent in her letters. She lived in tents for months on end, trained her Chinese cooks, and, after several years didn't want to go back to Omaha to live cooped up indoors.

Cavalry wives also organized singing groups, amateur theatricals, cotillions, and masked balls. The Friday night "hops" were a regular feature of garrison life. Every lady, no matter her age or social standing, could count on filling her dance card. The women sewed together, nursed one another through sickness and childbirth, and comforted one another as the men marched off to the tune of "The Girl I Left Behind Me."

They shared many hardships, the high infant mortality rate chief among them. One wife died in childbirth en route to her husband's post. Another reportedly went blind from the glare of the sun on the white canvas of the Army tent in which she was secluded for her labor. Children and mothers who survived childbirth faced even greater odds for continued survival against cholera, smallpox, typhus, and undiagnosed illnesses; many women buried their young children at obscure outposts throughout the West. And yet Mrs. Orsemus Boyd declared the fresh air beneficial for children; considering the condition of many Eastern cities, she may have had reason to believe this.

Only Libby Custer wrote of a life during which the sun always shined. The other cavalry wives conveyed the negative as well as the positive aspects of their experiences, but they infused their writings with a sense of cheerful martyrdom. There is a notable lack of self-pity in their accounts of their hardships on the frontier.

Summerhayes ended her memoirs with the following passage: "Sometimes I hear the still voices of the Desert; they seem to be calling me through the echoes of the Past. I hear, in fancy, the wheels of the ambulance crunching the small broken stones of the *malapais* [badlands], or grating swiftly over the gravel of the smooth white roads of the river bottoms. I hear the rattle of the ivory rings on the harness of the six-mule team; I see the soldiers marching on ahead; I see my white tent, so inviting after a long day's journey…The army life of those years is past and gone and…has vanished from the face of the earth." ■

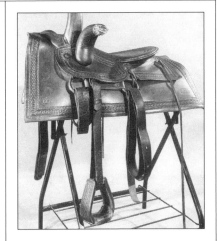

SIDESADDLE

BY MARYLOIS DUNN

Mollie Goodnight, wife of cattle baron Charlie Goodnight, often accompanied her husband when he rode out to the cow camps. She usually brought along one of her famous berry cobblers or one of her huge golden pound cakes to give to the cowboys. She loved to hitch up her calico skirt and petticoats, hook one knee over the saddle horn, and accompany the men when they rode the pastures or checked the fences. Charlie knew that her leg sometimes went to sleep on the ride, so he had a saddle made with a second horn lower on the fork. This supported her left knee to make the ride safer and more comfortable. Charlie's partner, an English lord named J. G. Adair, had a similar saddle made for his wife, and the unusual design quickly became popular both in the United States and England.

ABOVE:
The actual Goodnight sidesaddle. (courtesy of *Texas Highways* magazine and the Panhandle Plains Museum)

Lay That Pistol Down, Babe: Defending the Home Front

By Joyce Gibson Roach

THE CODE OF THE WEST WAS AN UNWRITTEN EXPRESSION OF THE philosophy of Westering folk, notably people of the cattle kingdom. One legendary subheading of the code addressed the unwritten rules governing the use of firearms. Eugene Manlove Rhodes put the gun code into words in a piece of fiction, "Beyond the Desert": "It was not the custom to war without fresh offense, openly given. You must not smile and shoot. You must not shoot an unarmed man, and you must not shoot an unwarned man…"

Women, too, observed a gun code in the West. While the code had little in common with the ideas of fair play expressed by Rhodes, its standards were honest. From diaries, reminiscences, books, letters, and newspapers, it's possible to piece together the rules of feminine gun play and illustrate it with examples.

Women's gun rules ran along the following lines:

1. Strange men will do for you to shoot; or you can scare them to death.
2. Shoot first, ask questions later.
3. If you shoot a man in the back, he rarely has a chance to return fire.
4. Shoot from ambush if possible.
5. If a man needs killing, go ahead and do it, especially if there is no one you can consult about it.

The gun code for Western women may have been less romantic and chivalrous than the men's code, but it was effective. At the turn of the century, Mrs. Frank Adams, a Texas woman who rode, drank, and shot expertly, was thought to have plugged a man in the back. An unnamed South Texas woman who ramrodded her own ranch and broke her own horses blew the top off a cowboy's head with a .45 when he got fresh and pinched her ankle—in fun. Evidently these men needed killing.

The mother of Bob Crabb threatened to let her trigger finger do the talking when two strangers stole some oxen from the family ranch in the Texas Panhandle and then offered to sell them back to her for $35 dollars.

Mrs. Crabb told them she didn't have that much money. They came back the next day with the oxen and said they would take $5. When she wouldn't pay, they started to leave. Mrs. Crabb reached for her .45 and said, "Go ahead, but I will kill both of you before you get away." They men didn't call her bluff—lucky for them. Bob testified his mother could "kill a bird on wing—she hardly ever missed."

A New Mexico woman known as Lady Castile fired just past her herder's ear—he'd gotten smart with her and had refused to leave when she told him to. She said, "I didn't try to hit you that time, but I just wanted to show that I mean what I say." He left.

Mrs. Cassie Redwine of the Texas Panhandle practiced the code on outlaws. She didn't necessarily shoot men in the back, but she did ambush a few. Black Pedro's robbers were terrorizing the upper Red and Canadian rivers. When five hundred head of her own stock disappeared, Cassie decided to hunt down the culprits. It took three days for Cassie and her posse to find the rustlers' secret camp, capture the men there, and change into their clothes. Black Pedro was not among them. When he rode in later, Cassie, dressed in rustler's clothes, picked him off. The rest of the outlaws were either killed or captured. When Cassie's men prepared to hang or shoot the prisoners, Cassie would take no part in it.

Another woman, unidentified except that she was dangerous, made use of disguise to pass as a cowboy on the cattle trails. She went from one herd to another until she located her false lover. Part of her costume was a revolver, and when she found her former paramour, she used it. She never told what she'd done to him, but she did remark, "I'll bet he won't trifle with another girl's affections."

One gun wasn't enough for some ladies. A Mrs. Wheeler of Mobeetie, Texas, figured that two guns were better than one when she set out to get back her daughter, who had been "stolen away." Armed with a six-shooter and a Winchester rifle, the good mother prowled the streets of the town, looking not for her daughter but for the person responsible. Bystanders (including the marshal) watched from behind a fence until Sheriff Cap Arrington arrived. The lawmen drew their weapons and threw down on Mrs. Wheeler, ordering her to drop her guns. Before they could get her to jail, she tripped them and drew a pistol from her bosom. After more scuffling, the law finally prevailed.

Guns could equalize a situation, and sometimes armed women would wade in to see that justice was served. When three strangers from Texas shot a ranch hand at the Bassetts' Colorado ranch in the back, Mrs. Bassett took Winchester in hand and got the drop on them. She disarmed them, marched them back to the dying man, and demanded an explanation. The one who had done the shooting claimed that Rollas, the Bassett man, had

Pearl Hart

shot and killed his brother in Abilene, Kansas. He was just settling the score. Mrs. Bassett explained that shooting a man in the back was *not* the way they settled a score in Colorado. The lady lined the three up against the bunkhouse wall and invited Rollas to shoot one, two or all three if it suited him. By that time, however, Rollas was too weak to hold the gun.

GUNS PROVIDED SOME WOMEN WITH COURAGE THEY MIGHT not have had otherwise. Ellen Casey of Lincoln County, New Mexico, became excited when a party of Apache stole some cattle and horses from the Casey ranch. Declaring that she was not afraid, Ellen grabbed a shotgun and hastily loaded it. Her husband, who watched her preparations, tried to advise her against going, but she brushed him aside. When she returned with the horses, he pointed out that she'd loaded her shotgun with both charges of buckshot in one barrel, put all the powder in the other barrel, and had set only one percussion cap (which was on the barrel filled with buckshot).

And then there's the rule that allows a woman to scare strange men to death. When a party of Apache accosted Mrs. Mary Nugent near her Tombstone, Arizona, ranch, she knew she couldn't get to her gun quickly enough. She let them know she saw them and she wasn't afraid—and she invited them to breakfast! After they'd feasted, she told them she needed some help and put them to work hauling supplies into a storeroom with a heavy door. When the Apache were off guard, Mary slammed the door and bolted it. Then she ran for her rifle and fired into the door to warn them not to come out. They didn't try. When they were later released, nobody thought to ask them why they'd come to the Nugent ranch in the first place.

No female was better known for a readiness to use her weapons—pistols, a rifle, a shotgun, a whip, and a vocabulary in both English and Spanish that would have scalded the hide off a dog—than Sally Skull. Few were her equal in the use of firearms. Sally rode in daylight and dark across the Mexican border to trade horses, went through at least three husbands, reputedly played poker with John Wesley Hardin, won at least one gunfight with a man, and drove a freight wagon during the Civil War. Sally was without mercy when she got angry, and some said it didn't take much to make her mad. She once called out a man who'd made unfavorable remarks about her and fired at his boots until he danced.

Ranch women sometimes dealt justice with weapons other than guns. Mrs. Victor Daniels ran a ranch jointly with her husband in the upper Gila Valley of Arizona. Ordinarily she was on the range with her husband, but a sick baby kept her home one day. Looking up from her work, Mrs. Daniels noticed two strange men driving off part of the herd. She sprang into the saddle, raced after them, built a loop and caught one of them by the neck, jerking him out of the saddle. As he fell, she drew her pistol and invited the other thief to drive her cattle back to the ranch. When that was done, she told him to clear out. The first rustler lay in the chaparral with his neck broken. There was no official inquiry.

Alice Stillwell Henderson guarded the perimeters of the Big Bend country with her husband and brothers, often living in a tent on the open range. She was a crack shot. During one incident, Alice made an all night ride alone to get help to recover stolen cattle, and five bandits rode into her camp just as she set up. She disarmed them and entertained them at gunpoint all day long until her own riders returned with the stolen herd.

On one occasion Alice's husband had some difficulty with the Mexican Rurales. Nobody said exactly what the trouble was, but he had to leave the country in a hurry. He told Alice before he fled that the Mexicans had his rifle and some cattle; he asked her to recover both. She wasted no time in getting back the rifle. Ed Lindsay met up with Alice right after she had galloped into Rancho Conejo in Coahuila, Mexico, entered a building, had taken the rifle from under the nose of a Captain Rivera and some fifty men under his command. Her horse was tired, and she'd surely have been caught except that Lindsay led a wagon train across her path. Alice asked Lindsay for his horse, and since she was holding a gun on him, Ed didn't mind in the least. Alice got away. It took her longer to recover her husband's cattle, but she took back some two thousand head over the next two years.

Dime novels and newspapers featured tales of female gunslingers, outlaws and cattle thieves—like Calamity Jane, Belle Starr, Cattle Annie, Little Britches, and Rose of Cimarron—right along with stories of completely fictional characters. Most of what was written was fiction, whether it was about real or imaginary characters. But even the most imaginative dime-novel plot couldn't hold a candle to reality.

Take the case of Mrs. Stevens, who lived in Lonesome Valley, Arizona. She kept a gun handy at all times, especially when her husband, Lewis, left to travel the thirty miles to town. When Mrs. Stevens, left alone with her children, looked out the window, she saw what looked like a rag hanging on a bush outside. She didn't remember hanging anything out there, so she grabbed her gun, drew a bead on the rag, and plugged an Apache right between the eyes. He wasn't alone; his fellows had the ranch house surrounded. She reloaded and kept firing, holding off the Indians until some cowboys who were in the vicinity heard her shots and came to the rescue. When things settled down, the cowboys prepared to ride away. They asked Mrs. Stevens if she wanted to send a message to her husband. She wrote:

Dear Lewis,

The Apaches came. I'm mighty nigh out of buckshot. Please send more.

Your loving wife.

Dodge City working girl, Squirrel Tooth Alice, and her pet prairie dog (courtesy of Kansas State Historical Society, Topeka, Kansas)

MADAMS AND PROSTITUTES

BY LENORE CARROLL

AS SOON AS STOREKEEPERS AND SALOON OWNERS OPENED FOR BUSINESS in a frontier town, prostitutes were there to welcome the miners and soldiers and cowboys who were their best customers. These prairie nymphs arrived in their own wagons, ready to pitch their tents and start working. Others built shacks or worked out of a covered vehicle known as a "cat wagon."

Prostitutes were so numerous on the frontiers that they may well have made up twenty percent of the female population of California in 1850. They usually outnumbered "respectable" women in mining towns twenty-five to one. As the Western population grew, most towns got big enough to support a regular brothel staffed by four or five women.

The Cyprian sisters were as varied as their clientele. Some were indeed beautiful and obviously cultured, as well as tastefully dressed in the latest styles. Others looked like bad illustrations from an anti-vice tract. One of the most often reproduced photographs depicts cow-town tart Squirrel Tooth Alice (she wasn't) with her pet prairie dog in her lap. In the Kansas cow towns of the 1800s, painted ladies tended to be between fourteen and thirty; the average age was twenty-three. Though most *filles du joie* were white, many brothel photos include black, Asian, and Hispanic women. Julie Bulette, a famed Virginia City courtesan, was black. Most prostitutes were single, but some were married to their pimps or managers.

There were all levels to the profession. Expensive and intelligent courtesans often married well or retired with enough money for a comfortable and respectable lifestyle. Others used their profits to open their own "sporting houses." Those who came to the attention of the law were usually of the lowest caste.

Brothel owners, operators, and employees were the cream of the profession. They scorned the women who rented rooms over saloons and the "crib" girls who peddled themselves from the front windows of their tiny establishments. Streetwalkers were the dregs of the prostitute's world, and were often treated cruelly by customers and police alike.

Prostitution as a career was no doubt objectionable to nineteenth century society in general and to moralists and reformers in particular, but for many women it represented an otherwise unobtainable economic freedom. With a few notable exceptions, white slavery was a myth. Most women who entered "the life" did it with a full and practical knowledge of their actions— which indicates not that a prostitute's life was truly appealing or romantic, but rather that opportunities available to the women of those times were otherwise limited to sewing, washing, cooking, or making pastry.

Most female factory workers in the big cities weren't paid anywhere near living wage for even a single woman. Women in dressmaking and millinery were subject to seasonal layoffs. Prostitution was an alternative to poor wages, job insecurity, and starvation. As one Denver woman said, "I went into the sporting life for business reasons and no other. It was a way for women in those days to make money, and I made it."

Kansas City madam Annie Chambers willingly entered a bagnio as a prostitute with a vow to live, "a short life, but a fast and merry one." She lived to be ninety-two.

Another madam described her early career: "I've laid it in all of 'em [oil towns]. I threw my fannie twenty-one times a night, five bucks a throw, and 'time old red-eye [the sun] come up I was eatin' breakfast drunker'n an Indian."

At the turn of the century the Everleigh sisters in Chicago could demand from their clients fifty dollars and a formal recommendation. On the frontier prices ranged from five dollars at posh establishments to a dollar or less for run-of-the-mill service for the less than fastidious customer.

Of course, the myths of the Wild West and its modern cliches obscure the truth about the frontier working girl. While the calico queen wasn't exactly the white slave forced against her will to a fate worse than death, neither was she a spangled tart with her heart of gold hidden beneath a strategic minimum of satin ruffles. She was an accepted part of the fabric of life in Western towns, and she answered to colorful names like Timberline, Rose of Cimarron, Irish Molly, or Cotton Tail. Big Nose Kate Elder, once a Magdalene, was Doc Holliday's mistress.

A soiled dove might split fifty-fifty with the madam of her parlor house, or she might pay a flat fee per night or week. Other expenses included fines levied by local law enforcement, often used by frontier towns to raise money for civic development. Public officials not only tolerated the trade but often profited from it, and fines fell heaviest on freelancers. Some women paid fines outright in cash, while others paid a portion and worked out the balance in prison. One Texas court released women to earn the rest of their fines at the same occupation that got them arrested in the first place.

The frail with a heart of gold was probably the product of wishful thinking by horny cowboys. Prostitutes were often generous to one another, chipping in to support a sick colleague or to make the monthly payment to the "baby

UNDERNEATH IT ALL

BY LENORE CARROLL

What the passionate lady had to take off before she could be indiscreet with the hero:

Reticule, hat, and gloves.

Cloak, basque, shawl, or jacket.

Stockings, garters, and shoes, probably buttoned.

Waist: could be shirting material or the same fabric as skirts, but would probably be a separate piece of clothing, fastened with frogs, ties, buttons, or hooks and eyes.

Skirt: a farm housewife might have a simple dress or skirt, but a town lady dressed to go out would have an underskirt with a protective dust ruffle sewed inside the hem, and an overskirt draped over the underskirt. Sometimes she would wear a bustle of stiffened canvas held in place with ties.

Petticoats: up to four, including a flannel one in the winter.

Corset and corset cover: *steel* stays, not whalebone

OR

Camisole with no corset: is this where the expression "loose woman" originated?

Drawers: knee-length, tied or buttoned at the waist, could be "open" or stitched closed.

After all this, the modern romantic reader might wonder if they had any energy left. Or was this a kind of foreplay practiced by our forefathers and foremothers?

This Cresswell photo captures the luxury of Madam Eva Prince's parlor circa 1900. (courtesy of University of Kansas Libraries)

farm" that cared for a friend's child. But in the mining and cow towns, the women tended to be as tough as the men they served—hard-drinking and hard-living. Some of them "found" items like wallets and got themselves into trouble with their customers, and they sometimes got mixed up in murders and robberies committed by their clients—in 1885 Maggie Moss, a seventeen-year-old Denver hooker, assisted her lover in an armed robbery. Others were not above using violence to defend themselves—in 1878 Frankie Lester fired her gun to quell two soldiers who caused a disturbance in her Cheyenne, Wyoming, saloon. Some were jailed, some were injured or killed by their customers, and some succumbed to tuberculosis or other diseases.

The official reason for the presence of laundresses at every military post in the West was a regulation that required the soldiers to have regular changes of clean clothes. Enlisted men were usually not allowed to marry, and so the authorities tended to look the other way when some of the laundresses supplemented their income with a second profession. Low class bordellos known as "hog ranches" also sprang up near army installations.

Because women were scarce on the frontier, even soiled doves were treated with some consideration and respect, and they were romanticized by the men who came into contact with them and sometimes wrote about them. But as the frontier disappeared, towns grew respectable and banned the bawdy houses and nightwalkers. The local madam and her girls, once an accepted part of frontier culture, were gradually excluded until there was no place for them except in the imaginations of men and the legends of the Wild West. ■

"Calamity" Jane Cannary

By Bill O'Neal

"CALAMITY" JANE DIDN'T LOOK LIKE DORIS DAY, JANE RUSSELL, YVONNE de Carlo, or any of the other Hollywood actresses who portrayed her on the silver screen. Her figure could most charitably be described as sturdy. Photographs reveal that she liked to wear buckskins or leather chaps, and she wore her slouch hat even when she sported a dress. She had light eyes and prominent cheekbones, but the shape of her broad nose suggested that it may once have been flattened by a fist. She drank to excess and habitually cursed and chewed tobacco. She occasionally worked as a "sporting lady." And she is the most readily identifiable wild woman of the Wild West, even though none of the tales told about her reliably report the circumstances under which she acquired her famous sobriquet.

Martha Jane Cannary was born probably in Mercer County, Missouri. According to the census of 1860, she entered the world in 1844, but with traditional feminine vanity about her age, Calamity claimed to have been born on May 1, 1852, in Princeton, Missouri.

In 1865 her family moved to Virginia City, Montana, but by the early 1870s Martha Jane left the gold-mining center and drifted into Wyoming. In 1874, she was working at a hog ranch five miles west of Fort Laramie. In 1875 and 1876 she signed on as a teamster with military expeditions. To get these jobs she masqueraded as a man, but both times her sex was discovered and she was fired. In 1876 she ended up behind bars in Cheyenne; several times she served jail terms for disturbing the peace.

Calamity gravitated to Deadwood in 1876, not long before Wild Bill Hickok was slain there. She claimed a long and intimate association with the famous gunfighter, and in her spurious autobiography she stated that they had married, then divorced so he'd be free to wed Agnes Lake.

During her time in Deadwood, Calamity displayed a classic heart of gold by taking the unlikely role of nurse. Sometimes working for no pay, she cared for a smallpox patient, a stabbing victim, a dying girl, and a premature baby. Her other job, as a bullwhacker driving a team of oxen in the Black Hills, was a little more in line with her legendary image.

After 1880 she left Deadwood and spent most of the rest of her life drifting. She married a man named Clinton Burke in El Paso in 1885; two years later she bore him a daughter. Back in Deadwood in 1896, Burke fled town and his family after embezzling money. Their daughter was taken away and sent to a convent, and Calamity went back to drifting.

Later in her life she made a few stage appearances as a Western scout and cowgirl, but by that time she was deep into alcoholic addiction. She was found ill and drunk in a Negro house of prostitution in Horr, Montana, in 1901, and two years later she collapsed in Terry, a mining town near Deadwood. She became ill and delirious. On August 1, 1903, she spoke her last

Calamity Jane

words—they were about her daughter—and died.

Calamity's friends claimed that her dying wish was to be buried next to Wild Bill. They arranged to have her interred within twenty feet of Hickok's grave, and they even changed the date of her demise to August 3, the twenty-seventh anniversary of Wild Bill's murder. ■

WILDEST WOMEN OF THE WILD WEST

CHARLEY PARKHURST: THE GREAT MASQUERADE

BY CENA GOLDER RICHESON

A widely published illustration of Charley Darkey Parkhurst, 1812–1879.

OF ALL THE STAGECOACH DRIVERS WHO HELPED MAKE THE WEST truly wild, Charley Parkhurst was the most bizarre and fascinating. A rugged individual who stood about five feet seven inches, Charley had a weathered face and one blue-gray eye. The other, lost while he was shoeing an intractable horse, was covered by a black patch. His tobacco-stained chin and lips were atypically beardless, and he spoke in a whiskey tenor voice. He was not himself boisterous or given to lengthy storytelling, but his legend grew as his passengers and acquaintances told and retold hair-raising yarns about the exploits of "One-Eyed Charley."

Charley's stage run took him to a rickety bridge over the Tuolumne River, and once during a heavy rainstorm he found the bridge swaying in the swirling torrent of the rain-swollen river. Other drivers would have turned back at the sight, but Charley cracked his whip and urged his six horses forward. He was halfway across when the rotting timbers creaked, popped, and collapsed. Charley laid the lash to his team, and they lunged full speed ahead. They barely reached the other side before the bridge tore loose from its moorings and was swept away by the raging floodwaters. His passengers were unharmed, though some of them had fainted from fright.

Road agents soon learned they couldn't count on robbing any stage Parkhurst drove, not if they valued their lives. Shortly after Charley began driving the Sierra stage routes he was held up by a highwayman nicknamed Sugarfoot—so called because he wore gunnysacks over his huge bare feet. Having a sawed-off shotgun poked at him made Charley hopping mad, and

SOILED DOVES

BY LOREN D. ESTLEMAN

Calamity Jane
Belle Starr
Squirrel Tooth Alice
Chicago Joe
Big Nose Kate
Cattle Kate
Annie Chambers
Julie Bullette
Rose of Cimarron

when he swore, "Next time I'll be ready for you!" he meant business. From then on he carried a six-shooter. On his next run-in with Sugarfoot a year later, Charley stampeded the coach horses toward the thieves, drew his pistol, killed Sugarfoot, and gave two other gang members bullet wounds as souvenirs of the fiasco.

Details of Charley's early years are sketchy. Eastern-born, he ran away from a Massachusetts orphanage when still a youngster and wound up in Worcester. There he found work as a stable boy for Ebenezer Balch, who trained him to drive the horse teams for buggies and coaches. When Balch moved his operation to a hotel and livery stable in Providence, Rhode Island, young Charley went along. There he met Frank Stevens and Jim Burch, the enterprising Yankee teamsters who established the California Stage Line. From San Francisco they wired Charley an invitation to come West for a paying job and plenty of action. And go West Charley did.

J. Ross Browne, one of Charley's passengers, wrote of his stage travels in the West in *Adventures in Apache Country* (1869). His stated purpose in mentioning Charley was to "rescue" him from oblivion, and he related several of the coachman's deeds. In one accident, Charley's stage capsized and left him with "my sides busted in." Even so, Charley took great pride in the fact that not one passenger on that trip or on any of his runs was injured. Though Charley was known to gamble, to chew 'backer, and to take a drink in a saloon with his comrades, he was very critical of drivers who imbibed on duty. He told Browne that smashups were generally due to "whiskey or bad driving." Also, the knight of the lash referred to his horses as his "beauties" and loved them obsessively. Nobody dared mistreat an equine critter in his presence, for Charley was known to more than hold his own in a fight.

But despite the tales of Charley's derring-do as a driver—and he ranked with the likes of Hank Monk and Al Grinell—despite his flamboyant attire, his repertoire of curses, and his surface friendliness, away from the coach Charley was a loner. He had certain eccentricities. He confided in no one, and he preferred to bed down in the stable with his horses when he was on the road. He loved children, and for those at each stop he carried gifts of candy and playpretties. Charley never bathed in the public bath house, only privately or in a creek out of sight. He never displayed a sexual interest in women, though he was known to take charitable actions on their behalf. He once bought a widow's house when the sheriff foreclosed on it, then handed it back to her. Whenever any marriage-minded spinster brazenly pursued Charley, he'd solve the problem by switching routes.

He eventually drove all the main Sierra routes from Placerville to Virginia City as well as the Rough and Ready to Sacramento and Stockton to Mariposa and all points in between. He later took the runs from Oakland and San

Francisco to San Jose and on down to Monterey. When rheumatism forced him to stop driving, he settled near Santa Cruz and opened a stage stop on the route to Watsonville. In 1867 he became a bona fide citizen by registering to vote; the record for November 3, 1868, listed him as: Parkhurst, Charles D. / Age: 55 / Occupation: Farmer / Native of New Hampshire / Residence: Soquel.

Charley's rheumatism worsened with his advancing age, and then he developed cancer of the tongue. He spent his final years in a cabin near Watsonville and refused medical help by threatening to blow the head off any doctor who came near.

When death came to Charley on December 28, 1879, it revealed the truth behind his masquerade. A doctor who examined the body stuttered out the news that Charley was a fully developed woman. The

Belle Starr and Blue Duck

disclosure sent a shock wave through California that rivaled its famed earthquakes. Newspapers picked up the story and embellished it with often outlandish editorial speculation. The reactions of Charley's friends and acquaintances varied from stupefaction to anger to puzzlement to just ordering another shot of redeye. Despite the wild stories that flourished, there was no evidence to suggest that Charley was a transvestite or a lesbian. It appears that *Charlotte*, a young woman left on her own in a male-dominated society, started her masquerade as a way to earn a decent living and then became either accustomed to it or trapped in it. Although the doctor who examined her at her death affirmed that Charley had at one time given birth to a child, there is no other record of it. Charley's legacy was a mystery and remains so to this day.

Charley's fellow lodge members so greatly respected "him" that they insisted burial take place in the Odd Fellows Cemetery in Watsonville. Fresh flowers are often left on the gravesite by those who revere the memory of the West's most unusual history maker, the first registered woman voter in the United States. ■

LITTLE CASINO, HEARTS AND DEUCES

BY FRANCES M. WOLD

AN EPITAPH:
Here lies Charlotte,
She was a harlot.
For fifteen years she pre-
served her virginity
A damn good record for
this vicinity.

SHE RECEIVED MAIL UNDER TWO NAMES—IDA LEWIS AND ELIZABETH McClellan—but the famed madam of the toniest bawdy house in the Dakotas of the 1870s was best known as Little Casino.

In the card game called casino, the "little casino" is the deuce of spades. The deuce of spades emblazoned on a large sign identified the house in Bismarck, Dakota Territory, where the notorious madam entertained her customers. It was her calling card, and it became a guarantee of instant credit when she presented it to local merchants.

It was 1873 when Little Casino stepped down from one of the first passenger trains to arrive in the frontier settlement that was then called Edwinton. Local businessmen later changed the name to Bismarck in an attempt to influence Germany's Iron Chancellor to invest in the town and the railroad, but the name of the place wasn't important to the town's newest businesswoman. Her own origins were obscure—she had come to the Dakotas from Brainerd, Minnesota, where, rumor had it, she had worn out her welcome with the local authorities.

Bismarck was a perfect location for Little Casino's business. It was the terminus of the Northern Pacific Railroad, a steamboat stop, and the jumping-off place for miners and prospectors headed for the Black Hills in the 1874–77 gold rush. Most important, the U.S. 7th Cavalry was stationed at Fort Abraham Lincoln, just across the Missouri River.

A newspaper reporter of the time wrote: "After the arrival of the Seventh Cavalry the character of the town changed materially for the worse. New dance halls were opened on Fourth Street, and demi-monde congregated there in large numbers, and there was no cessation in the daily and nightly routine of revelry and wickedness." That same reporter declared, "Bismarck at this time became notorious as one of the wickedest cities in the world."

In 1874, even though the actual Bismarck population was only 1200, 18 saloons stood open around the clock to serve the troops and passers-through. Most of the saloons were located on Fourth Street, familiarly known as Murderer's Gulch or Bloody Fourth because of the frequent shootings, knifings, and bar fights.

Casino's located her establishment at 701 Front Avenue, just across the railroad tracks. It was the premier emporium of its type in town, its reputation no doubt enhanced by Casino's acquisition of one of the first pianos to reach the territory. Muleskinners and bullwhackers who drove the freight lines in and out of the busy settlement often took the tassels from the window curtains of Little Casino's bordello and used them to adorn the lead animals of their pack trains. Casino replaced the curtains many times.

A tiny, demure woman who loved elegant but conservative clothing, Little Casino did nothing to attract unusual attention to herself during her frequent trips around town. She preferred to avoid publicity but was sometimes forced to appear in court to bail out her girls when they got into trouble. The *Bismarck Tribune* duly reported her appearances. Casino acquitted herself well in the Bismarck courts—she'd once been hauled into the tough Chicago courts for her questionable recruiting methods.

As for her "working girls"—her regulars had names like Canada Nell, Big Rose, Gentle Annie, and Be Jesus Lil. The more prosaically named Nell Watson died of inflammatory rheumatism while in Casino's employ, her illness complicated by addiction to alcohol and morphine. Casino had supported Nell and her drug habit.

LITTLE CASINO MADE MONEY—A GREAT DEAL OF IT, BY SEVERAL accounts—but she also spent it. During the successful campaign to make Bismarck the capital of the Dakota Territory, she gave $1,200 to the cause, even though her name never appeared on the list of donors. She was always generous to those down on their luck, and she had her own expensive tastes. She chartered a private rail car to travel to the St. Louis World's Fair and had it side-tracked so she could use it as her own luxurious living quarters during her stay. Rumors abounded as to a lover or lovers, but all that was known for sure is that she didn't always travel alone.

In those days of her prosperity, Casino invested in commercial lots in Bismarck, as well as some rural property about twenty miles north of town in an area that had proved to be rich in coal deposits.

Predictably, her prosperity didn't continue. As Bismarck changed from a roaring frontier village to a respectable family town and state capital, public opinion forced the red-light houses to close. A mortgage foreclosure in 1893 cost Little Casino her Bismarck real estate. Aware of the increasingly hostile climate, and with her own health failing, she decided to move to her rural property. There she operated a small coal mine, known to most as the Little Casino Mine.

The mine never made much money, partly because Casino's generous nature made her an easy mark for bums and loafers. Many of them holed up at the mine for the winter, supposedly digging enough coal for their keep, but really just making the touch for free room and board.

People who had known the dainty, fashionable madam of Bismarck would have had trouble recognizing the haggard crone Casino became in her later days. A woman who recalled seeing her come into the small town of Wilton for her weekly shopping described her: "She reminded me of a little bedraggled bird. She was always dressed in rusty black clothes of yesteryears—skirts full and touching the ground. She was old and looked weak, and had a rattling cough, and I would guess she didn't weigh more than 80 pounds. She looked dirty and unkempt. She would smear white liquid face paint over her wizened features, which showed up the dirty furrows in her scraggly neck. Her tiny, brownish hands, with uneven, dirty nails made me think of a bird's claws."

Casino drove to town in a topless spring buggy pulled by a bony black horse, followed by a procession of mangy hounds. She bought large orders of groceries and other supplies, paying for them with cash she secreted in an inner pocket of her voluminous skirt. As if conscious of her marked status, she never wasted time on small talk but conducted her business as quickly as possible. Her voice was so raspy and hoarse that little children were afraid of her. Small boys hooted and jeered at her as she passed, calling her "Dirty Casino," but they kept their distance out of a healthy respect for the long buggy whip she kept near to hand.

BUT EVEN THOUGH HER LIFE BECAME A MOCKERY OF ITS FORMER elegance, Casino's compassionate nature survived. When she stopped one cold winter day at the Wilton railroad depot to pick up some machine parts she'd ordered, she noticed in the freight room a crate that contained several drooping, miserable-looking turkeys. In answer to her inquiry, the freight agent offhandedly replied, "I wish whoever they belong to would come and get them before they freeze or starve to death."

Early the next morning, sitting high on her old buggy in the frigid wind, Casino drove the six miles back to the station. Half-frozen, she handed the amazed freight agent a burlap sack of grain and a jug of water. She explained, "I couldn't get those poor turkeys off my mind."

Casino's house near the mine shaft was small and low—a hovel, the neighbors called it—surrounded by piles of coal and ashes. Empty tin cans, broken mining machinery, and discarded clothing and boots littered the yard. The hangers-on she cared for occupied the main level. Casino had to climb ladderlike steps to an attic hole where she slept on a bed of rags.

And so Little Casino lived until September 16, 1916, when she suffered "a stroke of paralysis," according to her obituary in the *Wilton News*. The report, which gave her age as seventy-six, stated: "Although she had been in ill health for some months, her condition was not regarded as serious, and she was able to come to town and go about her daily work up 'till the day she died." The column, headed "Pioneer Passes," identified her as Mrs. Elizabeth McClellan and made no reference to Little Casino's colorful past. The *Bismarck Tribune*, which years earlier had carried many accounts of her days in court, took no notice of her death. Perhaps the editor didn't notice that a pioneer citizen had passed on, or maybe he decided to ignore the death of that particular pioneer.

When the Wilton undertaker and his helper climbed into the low loft to remove Casino's remains, they were confused by the conditions they found. The undertaker declared that never had he prepared for burial so dirty and neglected a body as that of the former madam. It was as he set about this

**Little Casino's headstone
(photo by Francis M. Wold)**

task that Little Casino's final secret came to light. Suspended on a grimy ribbon and lying between her withered breasts was a ring set with a beautiful two-carat diamond. Was it a memento of a former lover, an insurance policy against a destitute old age, or a reminder of vanished elegance? Only Little Casino knew, and the answer died with her.

The minister of the local Presbyterian church arranged for Casino a Christian burial, and nine persons, including the local businessmen who served as the pallbearers, attended. There were no women among her mourners.

One of the small boys who had kept his distance from the frightening harridan with the raspy voice watched that day from the yard of his home, across the street from the church. Years later, as an old man, he recalled the funeral: "What I remember best is that her hound dogs were trotting along behind the buggy. They waited outside during the service, and then when the men started for the cemetery with the body, the dogs trotted right along behind. It looked so pitiful that I never forgot it."

In the capital city of North Dakota, the offices of the *Bismarck Tribune* now stand at 701 Front Avenue, where the deuce of spades once advertised Little Casino's famous bordello. Her grave in Riverview Cemetery, just outside of Wilton, overlooking the Missouri River, lay unmarked until 1989. During the North Dakota centennial celebrations, donations and funds raised from a play based on Little Casino's life went to Wilton's community centennial project—a headstone inscribed with her trademark deuce of spades, the "little casino" from which she'd taken her name, followed by the words, "Gone but not forgotten—ye without sin cast the first stone." ■

Editors' Note: An earlier version of this article appeared in Day In, Day Out: Women's Lives in North Dakota, *edited by Elizabeth Hampsten, published by the University of North Dakota for the state's 1989 centennial celebration.*

WILDEST WOMEN OF THE WILD WEST

POKER ALICE, QUEEN OF THE WESTERN GAMBLERS

BY MARIANNE WILLMAN

POKER ALICE, THE CIGAR-SMOKING, GUN-TOTING QUEEN OF THE WESTern Gamblers, started life far away from the shadows of the Rocky Mountains in the quiet town of Sudbury, England. Born Alice Ivers in 1851, the only daughter of a British schoolmaster, she was reared in an exclusive girls' school where poker, faro, and shooting from the hip were definitely not included in the school curriculum. Slight, fair-haired, and blue-eyed, she might have become a schoolteacher herself and faded into anonymity had the Ivers family not immigrated to Virginia shortly before the Civil War. After the fall of Richmond her father packed up his family and moved once more, this time to Colorado, where the silver boom had just begun. So was the foundation laid for a Western legend.

Alice was nineteen when she met and married mining engineer Frank Duffield and moved to Lake City, Colorado. "It was love at first sight," she recalled later. Duffield's untimely death in a mine cave-in less than a year after their marriage changed her life forever.

Some storytellers said Alice perfected her fast deal and her poker face while Frank was still alive, but others believed it was the desperation of being a woman alone in the West that led her to the lifestyle that made her famous. No one could deny that Alice had an unmatched love for a challenge.

Alice gathered her nerve and asked the manager of the local saloon if she could play a few hands at one of his tables. He humored her and was amazed by the young widow's skill—she was a born card counter. He hired her on the spot to deal cards for a cut of the winnings. Cheered by her success, Alice left for Silver City, New Mexico, where new mines were opening and the miners were free with their money. There she found a hot game of faro, joined in, and played until her skill and luck frightened the dealer. He closed the bank. Alice shot him a contemptuous glance and immediately opened her own bank with her winnings. "Gentlemen," she said, "the game is open and the sky's the limit." Over $100,000 dollars changed hands during the course of the game. When a triumphant Alice rose from the table in the wee hours of the morning, she took away a $10,000 profit.

In town after town Alice repeated her success. When she broke out the cards she became all business, never smiled and spoke only in monosyllables. She had two inviolable rules that surprised some people but earned their respect: She never ran a crooked game, and she never gambled on Sunday. And to ensure that she had the respect of those who didn't appreciate her skill or her morals, she always packed a gun, either a .38 or .45. Alice worked hard for her money and wanted to make sure she kept it.

A Colt's 1869–72 Model Police revolver, the Thuer conversion to .38 caliber "long Colt" center fire ammunition, with 5½" barrel, creep-style loading lever and safety. (photo by Tom Knowles, courtesy of Metzger Collection, Texas A&M University Sam Houston Sanders Corps of Cadets Center)

She celebrated her victories in grand fashion. Alice cleared the table of her winnings and lit out for New York City on the first available stage east. Her visits lasted as long as her money, and she spent it with open hands on sumptuous dinners in elegant restaurants, shopping sprees through all the most fashionable stores, and nights at the theater. Then, when her purse got thin, Poker Alice would pack her bags and her .45—and head West once more.

ALICE NEVER STAYED IN ONE PLACE FOR LONG, AND WHEREVER SHE went, her adventures were legend. For a time she even worked for Bob Ford, the man who shot Jesse James in the back. Since James was living under the alias "Thomas Howard," Ford became notorious in song as "the dirty little coward who shot Mr. Howard, and put Jesse James in his grave." Poker Alice was sitting in on a game with Bob Ford in his saloon in Creede, Colorado, when Edward O. Kelley walked in and killed Ford with a blast from a double-barreled shotgun.

With her .38 or .45 always strapped to her side, Alice had no fears for herself. Faced with a dishonest dealer in Pecos, Texas, she pulled her .45 and said that she wouldn't complain if he'd done it cleverly but that she had no use for a clumsy crook. It was in Deadwood that Alice first adopted the small black cigars that became her trademark, and it was there that she met W. G. Tubbs, a handsome gambler. At first they were rivals and there was no love lost between them. Then one night a drunken miner pulled a knife on Tubbs and went for his jugular. A shot rang out: the miner staggered back, drilled through the arm by Alice. It seemed that in the West Cupid had traded his bow for a .38, for shortly afterward Alice became Mrs. Tubbs.

The two lovebirds soon retired from gambling and started a homestead, where they raised chickens and vegetables and—almost—lived happily ever after. In the winter of 1910 Tubbs contracted pneumonia; he died in

A deadly array of small arms that might be found in an outlaw's boot, a lady's handbag, or a gambler's vest pocket. (*Clockwise from the top*) E.R. Remington and Sons .22 caliber "Zig-Zag" 6-shot revolver, Elliott's Patent (1860) with 3⅛" barrel. Colt's First Model Derringer (1870–90), all-metal .41 caliber rimfire, the first single-shot pistol Colt made. Sharps Breech Loading 4-shot .32 caliber derringer, engraved: "Presented to W.C Watson by his Reese River Friends on Nov. 20, 1863." Smith & Wesson .22 caliber short 7-shot pocket revolver, Springfield, Missouri (1856). E.R. Remington and Sons .22 caliber revolving 5-shot Vest Pocket Model, Elliott's Patent (1861) with 3" barrel. E.R. Remington and Sons over-and-under .41 caliber derringer, Elliott's Patent 1865 (second model issue), 3" barrel. E.R. Remington and Sons .41 caliber single-shot derringer, Elliott's Patent (1867) with 2⅜" barrel. Colt's 3rd Model derringer 1875–1910, high-hammer, .41 caliber rimfire single-shot Thuer conversion, 2½" barrel. (photo by Tom Knowles, courtesy of Metzger Collection, Texas A&M University Sam Houston Sanders Corps of Cadets Center)

Alice's arms, thus ending what she later called "the happiest years of my life." Determined to do right by her late husband, Alice didn't let a terrible blizzard prevent her from setting out for the nearest town. She arrived in Sturgis, forty-eight miles from her home, with Tubbs's frozen body in the back of her sled. She stopped only once along the way, and that was to pawn her wedding ring for the grand sum of $25. At the undertaker's she made arrangements for Tubbs's burial, which took the entire amount. But Alice was one widow who knew how to take care of herself. She marched into the local saloon and gambled until she made back the money she'd spent. By nightfall her wedding ring was back on her finger. Thereafter she always went by the name of Alice Tubbs.

She knew that without Tubbs to share it, the quiet life would quickly pall, so Poker Alice returned to the cards again. It was probably loneliness that eventually compelled her to try marriage a third time, this time to George Huckert of Sturgis, whom she'd previously hired to run her sheep ranch for her. Huckert, undeterred by Alice's unfortunate track record with marriage, had proposed to her many times over the years. Upon totaling up his back wages Alice discovered she owed him over $1000; she had less than $50 on hand. She accepted, claiming, "It would be cheaper to marry him than to pay him off."

THE SHEEP RANCH FAILED, AS DID THE MARRIAGE. THEY SEPARATED, and eventually Alice found herself widowed again. She never married again, convinced that at least in her case, the adage "Lucky at cards, unlucky in love" was true. She continued in her own establishment with honest cards and friendly girls, but in 1912 even her gambling luck began to run out. When a group of rowdy and drunken troopers from Fort Meade tried to force their way into her gaming parlor, Alice fired through the door, killing a trooper from Company K, 4th Cavalry. She was arrested and taken to the jail in Deadwood.

Eventually acquitted of murder, she was later arrested for running a "disorderly house." This time she was convicted. The people of Sturgis petitioned the governor for clemency based on her age and reputation, and the sixty-one-year-old Alice was pardoned. She closed her gambling house and settled down again with her memories. Poker Alice estimated that during her career over half a million dollars had passed through her fingers, but observed in her wry fashion that "very little stuck."

In 1930 she fell ill. The doctors told Alice she needed immediate surgery but warned that her chances of surviving such surgery at the age of seventy-nine were slim. "Go ahead," she said. "I was never one to buck the odds." It was her last, best game and she staked everything she had.

This time, Poker Alice lost.

OKLAHOMA'S GIRL BANDITS: CATTLE ANNIE AND LITTLE BRITCHES

BY VERONICA G. FRIEDLAN

JENNIE METCALF WAS SIXTEEN AND ANNIE McDOULETT WAS SEVEN-teen in 1893 when fate took the two innocent country girls to a hoedown in Ingalls, Oklahoma, a small town just over the Payne County line south of Pawnee. As they watched several handsome strangers twirl their partners to the scrape of a fiddle, they overheard someone say, "That's the Doolin gang!"

The Doolin gang. The girls had heard of the outlaws who hid out in a cave on the Cimarron not far from Guthrie. Like many a modern-day teenager, they were not immune to the glamour of renegades.

Red Buck (George Weightman) drew the girls into the dance and intro-duced them to the other members of the gang—the dashing Bitter Creek (George Newcomb, a.k.a. the Slaughter Kid), Little Dick West, Tulsa Jack Blake, Dan Clifton (alias Dynamite Dick), Charley Pierce, Arkansas Tom, Little Bill Raidler, Bill Dalton (brother to the late Bob Dalton), and the group's leader, Bill Doolin.

History doesn't record just which of these outlaws stole Annie McDoul-ett's heart that night, but after one dance Annie knew that the simple life of a sodbuster's daughter wasn't for her. Immediately upon returning to the family farm, she stole the hired man's clothes to make up her outlaw trous-seau and rode out. The horse threw her, forcing her to walk almost ten miles to a nearby farm to catch a ride home. Undeterred, she again donned the hired hand's pants and found a more suitable horse to take her to Ingalls and into the arms of her new beau.

When Annie introduced Jennie Metcalf to another member of the gang, Jennie joined them. Both country girls took to the outlaw life as if they'd been born to it. They kept camp, tended the horses, and rode with the gang across Oklahoma, Texas, Kansas, and Missouri, stealing livestock, robbing trains, and "drawing" on banks. Life was fast but good for the first few months, and the outlaws often returned to their favorite hideout near Ingalls. The two girls who traveled with this fast, hard crowd won outlaw fame and outlaw names—Cattle Annie and Little Britches.

In September 1893 the law attempted to rout the gang from their stronghold. When the smoke cleared after the Battle of Ingalls, the Doolins retired with a slightly wounded Bitter Creek and left three dead marshals behind them. The word went out among the irate lawmen: "Run the gang to death or arrest."

Armed with a special fund, Marshals William Tilghman, Chris Madsen, Heck Thomas, and others set out on the Doolin gang's trail. At first the chase was filled with dead ends and wild geese, owing to the many friends the outlaws had made in the wild Cimarron country. Though 1894 was the gang's most profitable year, with their Texas raids netting them large sums while Bill Doolin suffered only a slight head wound, the law pressed hard, and in June the marshals cornered part of the gang in the Chickasaw nation. In a

Annie McDoulett and Jennie Metcalf, a.k.a. Cattle Annie and Little Britches (courtesy of Oklahoma Historical Society)

THE HIT PARADE

BY LOREN D. ESTLEMAN

The top ten tunes to which Wild Western ladies danced and sang were:

1. "Sweet Betsy from Pike"
2. "Darling Clementine"
3. "Oh! Susannah"
4. "Buffalo Gals"
5. "Shenandoah"
6. "Dixie"
7. "Whispering Hope"
8. "The Ballad of Jesse James"
9. "She Wore a Yellow Ribbon"
10. "John Brown's Body"

Of course, if you were in Texas at the time of the revolution, you might want to include "Come to the Bower" and the *De Guella*.

blazing gun battle Marshal Dave Booker of Ardmore killed Bill Dalton.

The beginning of the end for the Doolins came in 1895. Their luck ran out when Tulsa Jack, Bitter Creek, Red Buck, and Charley Pierce rode out in July to rob the Rock Island Railroad at Dover, Oklahoma. Chris Madsen was waiting for them. When his posse picked up the robbers' trail, he called in all available deputies to converge for a showdown. The lawmen surprised four Doolins who had holed up in a canyon, and soon Tulsa Jack Blake lay dead.

The three survivors fled to the remote ranch of a friend named Dal Dunn. They were looking for safety and rest, but it proved to be an eternal rest for Bitter Creek and Charley Pierce. Dunn turned greedy informant and shot them while they slept. He received $1,500 for Bitter Creek from the Santa Fe Company, $1,000 for Pierce from the Rock Island Railroad.

In October Tilghman pursued Little Bill Raidler to a ranch on Mission Creek in eastern Osage country and stopped the outlaw's run with a shotgun. The marshal bandaged the outlaw's wounds and rode with him to Elgin, Kansas. Tilghman carefully saw Raidler through a critical fever, ensuring his recovery to stand trial.

Then Tilghman got word that Bill Doolin had been seen in Eureka Springs, Arkansas, taking the hot mineral baths for his rheumatism. Disguising himself as a preacher, Tilghman pursued the outlaw leader into the baths and got the drop on him. The public gathered 5,000 strong to welcome the train that brought Tilghman and Doolin to Guthrie. The marshal signed autographs while Doolin waved his unshackled hands at the crowd. For the first time in his life, Doolin found himself in a jail cell. His compatriot, Dick West, was there to greet him. Doolin and West escaped in 1896, but Marshal Heck Thomas caught up with Doolin and killed him not long after.

With the rest of the gang dead, jailed, or scattered, Marshals Tilghman and Steve Burke turned their attention to the capture of Cattle Annie and Little Britches. Word came that they were traveling with a whiskey trader named Wilson. Armed with warrants for rustling, selling whiskey to Indians, and accessory to robbery, the two lawmen caught up with the girl bandits in a farmhouse near Pawnee, Oklahoma.

Little Britches tumbled out a rear window and mounted her horse. She fled across the prairie, all the while throwing shots at the pursuing Tilghman. The marshal was a crack shot and avoided wounding the outlaw, instead shooting her horse out from under her. Jennie tried to leap clear but caught her boot in the stirrup and was pinned beneath the dead horse. Her revolver lay close at hand; she was struggling to reach it as Tilghman approached. He managed to get the gun first, even though the girl flung dirt in his eyes. When the marshal removed the cartridges from the gun and pulled Jennie free of the horse, he found that he'd grabbed hold of a wildcat. Though she raked his face with her nails and pulled his hair, the stocky, imperturbable Tilghman simply turned her over his knee and severely dusted the seat of her namesake britches.

Steve Burke was by no means having an easy time convincing the cornered Cattle Annie to give up, so he decided to play a waiting game. He stood patiently against the house and waited until Annie peered out the window to size up the situation. When Burke grabbed her and dragged her out over the window sill, he found himself holding not a wildcat but a tiger. Annie clawed, punched, and bit. When Tilghman rode up with Jennie in tow, he found Burke standing there, exhausted, gripping Annie in a bear hug, holding on for dear life.

In Perry, Oklahoma, the marshals had the girls washed and dressed in "proper" feminine clothing. When they appeared in this manner before Judge A. G. C. Brierer, the ferocious female bandits seemed to be no more than frightened teenagers. Influenced by pleas from the surprisingly forgiving Tilghman, the judge sentenced Jennie Metcalf and Annie McDoulett to short terms at the women's facility in Framingham, Massachusetts. Marshal Everet Nix escorted them to the penitentiary and they were greeted in Boston by a large crowd eager to get a look at the famous female outlaws. ■

SPANISH IS THE LOVING TONGUE

A POEM OF BORDER ROMANCE ADAPTED TO SONG BY AN ARIZONA COWBOY

Spanish is the loving tongue,
Soft as Springtime, light as spray.
There was a girl I learned it from,
Living down Sonora way.
Now I don't look much like a lover,
Yet I say her love words over
Late at night when I'm all alone:
"Mi amor, mi corazon."

On the nights when I would ride
She would listen for my spurs,
Fling those big doors open wide
And raise them laughing eyes of hers.
And how those hours would get to flying;
All too soon I'd hear her crying:
"Please don't leave me all alone,
Mi amor, mi corazon."

Then trouble came, I had to fly;
I got into a foolish gambling fight.
I had to say a swift goodbye
In that black, unlucky night.
As I rode North her words kept ringing,
And in the distance, I could hear her singing:
"Please don't leave me all alone,
Mi amor, mi corazon."

I ain't seen her since that night;
I can't cross the line, you know.
She was Mexican and I was white;
Like as not, it's better so.
And yet I've always sort of missed her
since that very last time I kissed her;
I left her heart but I lost my own.
"Adios, mi corazon."

Sarah Winchester's Forever Mansion

BY CENA GOLDER RICHESON

THE DAINTY CONNECTICUT DEBUTANTE SARAH L. PARDEE (SHE STOOD two inches under five feet and weighed less than one hundred pounds) was the darling of New Haven society. William Wirth Winchester, son of Oliver Winchester, the man who invented and manufactured the famous repeating rifle, found her irresistible. They married on September 30, 1862.

Four years later their only child, Annie Pardee Winchester, died in infancy of an undiagnosed wasting disease colloquially known as marasmus. It was a tragedy from which Sarah would never recover. While she was still grieving for her daughter, Sarah was dealt another blow; William succumbed to pulmonary tuberculosis. Her inherited fortune—$20 million plus an income of $1,000 a day from the Winchester Repeating Arms Company—was overshadowed by her grief.

Sarah turned to psychics in her search for answers, and one soothsayer counseled her to go West. The psychic explained that the Winchester fortune was the cause of Sarah's misery; it was blood money, and Sarah was being haunted by the ghosts of all those people, innocent and guilty alike, who had been killed with Winchester firearms.

The psychic outlined a course of action Sarah could take to break the curse: She must move far away and purchase a new house, one she could continually expand under the guidance of friendly spirits. As long as the carpenters continued to work round the clock, 365 days a year, Sarah would have eternal life and peace.

Sarah followed the psychic's advice. She bought an unfinished eighteen-room house on a farm near San Jose, California, and then oversaw a continuous construction project that lasted thirty-eight years until her death. During this period "Winchester House" grew into a 160-room castle that was at once beautiful and bizarre. Its lavish features included Tiffany art glass doors, stained-glass windows, elegant wallpaper, fifty exquisite fireplaces (no two of which were alike), parqueted floors laid in patterns that created optical illusions, and gold and silver chandeliers. The meticulously land-scaped grounds and the greenhouse with its thirteen glass cupolas con-

Seen from the air, the Winchester Mystery House sprawls over six acres in San Jose, California. Among the world's oddest dwellings, the $5.5 million, 160-room mansion was built by Sarah L. Winchester, widow of the Winchester rifle manufacturer's son. (courtesy of Winchester Mystery House)

tained expensive roses, feather and fan date palms, imported trees, shrubs, herbs, and flowering plants of every description and color. The gardens were filled with fountains and statuary.

The house was served by six kitchens and three elevators. Out-of-the-ordinary features included two thousand doors and ten thousand windows (some of which opened onto blank walls), fifty-two skylights (many enclosed within the house), fifty staircases (which occasionally ended at the ceiling and went nowhere), and trapdoors that might plunge the unsuspecting visitor into fifty feet of empty space. Floor windows and secret peepholes allowed Sarah to spy on the servants, and she had special upside-down posts installed to confound the wicked spirits.

As with any self-respecting haunted house, the nights at Winchester House were filled with inexplicable and eerie goings-on. The lady of the manor kept unfriendly ghosts from guessing her whereabouts by playing a game of musical bedrooms—she had forty from which to choose. Before she retired in the wee hours of the morning, she performed a peculiar ritual. When the midnight bells (designed to summon friendly spirits) sounded in the tower, Sarah flitted through the Victorian labyrinth of winding staircases and twisting passageways as if she were herself a spirit. She pushed a button to open a secret panel, descended a flight of stairs that joined yet another staircase that ascended to another room. At last she came to the Blue

Séance Room, to which she alone held the key. Only when she was satisfied that she had ditched any possible fiendish followers did Sarah turn the key and enter her sanctum.

Each morning Sarah made rounds with her foreman, John Hanson; together they relayed the new building orders and checked on the progress of the ever-toiling carpenters. Hanson, unconcerned with the reasoning behind the orders, devoted himself to following them to the letter.

As the years passed Sarah grew increasingly reclusive. Frances Merriman, her niece, acted as her live-in secretary and only companion. Sarah took to wearing heavy veils even around the house except in the presence of her Chinese butler. When she went shopping, the merchants brought their wares out to the curb so that she could make her selections from the concealment of her lavender Pierce-Arrow.

Sarah eventually ceased to receive visitors. In 1903 she even turned away President Theodore Roosevelt with a curt "The house is not open to strangers." When two workmen inadvertently caught a glimpse of the widow's bare face in 1912, they were discharged with one year's salary.

All building stopped when the grim reaper came for Sarah Pardee Winchester on September 5, 1922. She must have expected him despite the psychic's prediction, for she had drawn up a will that left the bulk of her estate (which had dwindled to a mere $4 million) to her niece. She also provided for a tuberculosis foundation named in honor of her husband.

The house remained unfinished, and the enormous stockpile of ornaments and furnishings were auctioned off. It took workmen six weeks to haul it all away, not only because of the quantity of items but because of the disorienting maze of rooms from which it had to be removed—workmen and appraisers often lost their way.

Some critics may have branded Sarah Winchester a hopeless eccentric or worse, but those who knew her personally came to her defense. Her personal physician, Dr. Clyde Wayland, and her attorney, Roy F. Lieb, swore that she was clear-minded and sane to the very end of her life. All of her employees concurred. She was a closet philanthropist who anonymously donated generous sums to orphanages, medical research, and other worthy causes.

Whatever else was said about her, it is clear that Sarah Winchester was one of a kind. Her home continues to awe sightseers and historians. The Winchester Mystery House was designated a California Registered Historical Landmark in 1974 and was later listed in the National Register of Historic Places by the U.S. Department of the Interior. It survives as a reflection of Sarah's personality and a monument to her grief; even to this day, employees, sightseers, and séance attendees report sighting a diminutive apparition dressed in period costume that walks the maze of Winchester House. ■

VI. THEY WORE THE BADGE

MASSACRE AT THE O.K. CORRAL

BY LOREN D. ESTLEMAN

AT 1:30 P.M. ON WEDNESDAY, OCTOBER 26, 1881, NINE MEN CAME together in a fifteen-foot-wide lot ninety feet west of the O.K. Corral in Tombstone, Arizona. Seven of the nine were armed. Thirty seconds later, three were dead, three were wounded, and two more were on the run. That brief, violent encounter became the most famous gunfight in the wild history of the Wild West, the gunfight at the O.K. Corral.

But strictly speaking, there was no gunfight *at* the O.K. Corral. The fracas started three doors down from the corral's rear entrance, in a narrow passage between Camilius Fly's boarding house and the private home of W. A. Harwood. It spilled out into Fremont Street, where the gunsmoke got so thick the combatants had difficulty distinguishing friend from enemy. The transcripts of the inquest into the deaths contain numerous references to the corral, through which the Clantons and the McLaurys took a shortcut to their destiny a few minutes later. The popular confusion about the setting of the gunfight was inevitable.

The fight was the climax of troubles dating back to the arrival of the Brothers Earp and their deadly friend Doc Holliday in Tombstone in 1879. At that time, the silver boomtown and much of the surrounding country were controlled by a gang of rustlers and bandits commanded by Newman Haynes Clanton (the Old Man) and his sons, Ike, Phin, and Billy. The gang included Curly Bill Brocius, Pete Spence, Frank Stilwell, Frank and Tom McLaury, and the enigmatic Johnny Ringo. They drove stolen cattle north from Mexico and knocked off an occasional stagecoach hauling silver bullion or mine payrolls. They once ambushed a party of Mexican muleskinners in nearby Skeleton Canyon, slaughtered nineteen Mexicans, and made off with thousands of dollars in smuggled bullion.

Their only opposition came from a few *vaqueros* and Geronimo's Apache. The nearest law of any consequence was fifty miles away in Tucson; local

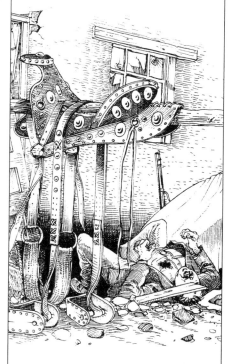

authorities were concerned only with maintaining order in Tombstone. The first sheriff of Cochise County, a political hack named Johnny Behan, was firmly in their pocket.

The Earps changed things. There were five of them: James, Virgil, Wyatt, Morgan, and Warren. They were all tall and rawboned, fair-haired and mustachioed. They had checkered backgrounds in gambling, saloonkeeping, pimping, and law enforcement, and they were determined to make themselves rich. On their heels came John Henry Holliday, a tubercular dentist from Georgia. He was a man with no future but with a talent for cardplaying, drinking, and killing, and he'd left a string of violent episodes stretching behind him from Fort Griffin to Dodge City. He was intensely loyal to his one true friend, Wyatt Earp.

THEY ESTABLISHED THEMSELVES QUICKLY. VIRGIL EARP WRANgled appointments for himself as deputy U.S. marshal and Tombstone chief of police, and he deputized his brothers so they could carry weapons legally to protect their interests. Those interests included mineral, water, and timber rights in the Dragoon Mountains to the northeast, a piece of the gambling concessions in the Oriental, Alhambra, and Eagle Brewery saloons, and ownership of the Sampling Room saloon on the south side of wide-open Allen Street. Wyatt became Pima County deputy sheriff for a time but withdrew his application for Cochise County sheriff when Behan, the favorite, promised to make him under-sheriff following his own appointment. Behan later reneged and named the *Tombstone Nugget* editor Harry Woods in Wyatt's place, which drove deeper the wedge between the two factions.

The wedge had been introduced by Josephine Sarah Marcus, a nineteen-year-old actress from San Francisco with the Pauline Markham theatrical troupe. She'd lived with Behan for a time as his common-law wife, only to desert him for Wyatt. The sheriff never forgot or forgave the humiliation, and from that point on he sided with the Clanton cowboy faction in all its efforts against the Earps and Holliday.

On March 15, 1881, a band of cowboys led by Bill Leonard, Harry Head, and Jim Crane attempted to waylay a stagecoach bound for Benson carrying eight passengers and a load of silver bullion. The stage didn't stop, and in the bandits fired, killing the driver, Bud Philpot, and a passenger, Peter Rocrig.

Johnny Behan, preparing to square off against Wyatt in the upcoming election, tried to pin the failed robbery and killings on Doc Holliday. Wyatt made Ike Clanton a counteroffer: Ike could have the reward for the arrests of Leonard, Head, and Crane if he'd deliver them to Wyatt. Wyatt would take credit for their capture.

Ike conferred with Frank McLaury and the pair agreed on condition that the reward would hold dead or alive. They feared retribution from their fellow cowboys if word of their duplicity got out. Wyatt accepted the condition and made plans to lure the three into a trap.

Fate took a hand before Wyatt could spring his trap. In July, Jim Crane was killed along with Old Man Clanton and others when friends of the Mexican muleskinners killed in the Skeleton Canyon raid ambushed them in the Guadalupe Mountains. Billy Leonard and Harry Head were shot down when they attempted to rob a store in Huachita, southwest of Tombstone. Meanwhile, Behan got Holliday's mistress, Big Nose Kate Fisher, drunk and persuaded her to sign a statement implicating Holliday in the attack on the Benson stage. Holliday was arrested.

Although the Earps sobered Kate up and browbeat her into withdrawing the statement in court, Ike Clanton started causing trouble, loudly accusing Wyatt of talking publicly about their deal. Early on the morning of October 26, Holliday braced Ike in the Alhambra and taunted him to go for his gun. Ike refused—a wise decision. Morgan, Virgil, and Wyatt presently joined Holliday in the saloon, and Ike took his leave, muttering some threats of his own.

LATER THAT MORNING, VIRGIL AND MORGAN SURPRISED IKE FROM behind, disarmed him, pistol-whipped him, and took him before the justice of the peace to be fined for carrying a revolver and a rifle on the street. Wyatt joined his brothers at the courthouse to rag a shaken and bleeding Ike.

"You cattle-thieving son of a bitch," Wyatt said. "If you are so anxious to make a fight, I will go anywhere to make one with you."

"All I want is four feet of ground," Ike responded.

Wyatt had two more run-ins with the cowboys that morning. He pistol-whipped Frank McLaury's brother Tom in the street across from the courthouse, and he exchanged threats with Tom and Frank, Ike's brother Billy, and a freshly released Ike in a Fourth Street gunshop where Frank and Billy were seen loading up their cartridge belts. When Virgil and Morgan showed up, the Clantons and the McLaurys left.

Doc Holliday joined the Earps on the corner of Fourth and Allen. The dentist leaned on a cane, obviously suffering the effects of a bad night. Sheriff Johnny Behan came up and spoke with Virgil, who said that the Clantons and the McLaurys must be disarmed. Behan announced that he'd disarm them and started toward Fremont Street. The Earps waited a few minutes, then struck off in that direction. When Holliday followed, Wyatt stopped and faced him.

"This isn't your fight, Doc," Wyatt told him.

Holliday, hurt, replied, "That's a hell of a thing for you to say to me."

Morgan Earp (top) and Wyatt Earp

Edward L. Schieffelin, the man who named Tombstone, Arizona.

Wyatt relented. Virgil traded Holliday his Wells Fargo shotgun for the cane and told him to hide the gun under his coat. Then the four followed in Behan's wake. Behan tried to intercept them on Fremont Street, but the party swept past him without pausing. The cowboys had withdrawn inside the alley next to Fly's. With them was Billy "the Kid" Claiborne, a twenty-year-old tough who fled when Virgil lifted Holliday's cane and called for them to throw down their arms. In fact, some of the cowboys were unarmed.

"You sons of bitches have been looking for a fight," Wyatt taunted them as Virgil gave the order to disarm.

Ike Clanton later claimed that at this point his brother told the Earps he didn't want to fight, and that Tom McLaury threw open his coat to show he was unarmed. It was probably an unwise move. The Earps opened up; several eyewitnesses testified that Holliday and Morgan Earp started the shooting. In any case, Billy Clanton immediately collected a bullet in the chest, and Frank McLaury caught one in the belly.

Tom McLaury tried to arm himself with a Winchester from a saddle scabbard on a horse belonging to one of the party, gave up, and allowed the horse to drag him out into Fremont Street. Wyatt fired, and his shot grazed the horse and sent it galloping off, exposing Tom to fire. Holliday swung the shotgun level and blew Tom almost in half, but Tom somehow kept running. Holliday threw the scattergun away and drew his nickel-plated revolver. By that time Tom had rounded the corner and collapsed out of sight.

Early in the exchange, the unarmed Ike Clanton grabbed Wyatt and attempted to turn him, but Wyatt flung him off and advised him to "get to fighting or get away." Ike chose the latter course and sprinted for cover inside Fly's photograph gallery. Sheriff Behan held the door for him.

The wounded Frank McLaury made Fremont Street, which was where Holliday had withdrawn to escape the blinding gunsmoke inside the lot. "I've got you this time!" Frank said, and he fired. Holliday returned fire almost simultaneously, and Morgan Earp, who had gone down with a bullet behind his shoulder, got up and shot at the same time. They hit Frank in the head and again in the belly, and he fell down dead. His bullet had grazed Holliday's hip. Meanwhile Virgil, who had fallen with a wound through one calf, exchanged fire with Billy Clanton.

Billy was also on the ground, his back propped up against the wall of Harwood's house. His first wound was mortal, but he'd taken another bullet through his right wrist as he fell, border-shifted his pistol, and continued firing with his left hand. More lead struck him as he sat on the ground. He was trying to recock his pistol when Camilius Fly stepped up from the passage between the two buildings and disarmed him.

"Give me more cartridges," said Billy Clanton. He died minutes later.

The bodies of Billy Clanton and Frank and Tom McLaury were put on display in silver-trimmed caskets in the window of a Tombstone hardware store under a sign that read MURDERED IN THE STREETS. Glass-sided hearses bore them to the hillside cemetery outside town, and fireworks and a brass band accompanied the procession. For the next month, Justice Wells Spicer heard testimony for and against Wyatt Earp and Doc Holliday—warrants weren't served against Virgil and Morgan, who were recovering from their wounds in Virgil's house on Fremont Street. At one point Will McLaury, an attorney from Fort Worth, Texas, and older brother of the late Frank and Tom, badgered Spicer into jailing Wyatt and Holliday, but by the last day of November the jurist ruled the killings justifiable and declined to hold the defendants for trial.

But it was far from over. Early in December an unsuccessful attempt was made on the life of John Clum, the pro-Earp mayor of Tombstone (and editor of the *Epitaph*), while he was riding in a stagecoach. Three days after Christmas, five ten-gauge shotguns opened up on Virgil Earp from across Allen Street and cut him down in front of the Eagle Brewery Saloon. Critically injured, he survived, but he spent months recovering and never regained the use of his left arm.

ON MARCH 18, 1882, AS MORGAN EARP WAS PLAYING BILLIARDS in the back of Hatch's Saloon, an assassin fired through a window. The shot took Morgan in the back, and he died that night. A second shot aimed at Wyatt missed. Among those believed responsible were Frank Stilwell, Pete Spence, and a half-breed called Indian Charlie. Wyatt, who had been appointed deputy U.S. marshal following Virgil's crippling, swore out a posse that included his brother Warren, Doc Holliday, and gunmen Sherman McMasters and Turkey Creek Jack Johnson.

They accompanied Virgil, his arm still in a sling, Virgil's wife, Allie, and Morgan's widow aboard the train to Tucson, from where Virgil and the women would see Morgan's body back to his parents' home in California. The posse alighted upon receiving a report that Frank Stilwell had been spotted hanging around the Tucson station.

Eyewitness accounts tell the rest. A man answering to Stilwell's description was observed running across the track in front of the westbound train. Four men from the posse, armed with Winchesters and shotguns, took off in that direction along the cinderbed. Moments later at least a half-dozen shots rang out. The next morning Stilwell's bullet-riddled body was found near the depot.

The posse hopped a freight back to Contention, where they reclaimed their mounts and set out after Stilwell's partners. In the Dragoon Mountains, at a stand of timber that belonged to Pete Spence, they cornered a Mexi-

FAMOUS FRONTIER FEATURES THAT NEVER EXISTED

BY LOREN D. ESTLEMAN

Wyatt Earp's Buntline Special

Dodge City's Deadline

Wild Bill Hickok's "Dead Man's Hand" of aces and eights

Calamity Jane's marriage to Wild Bill Hickok

The fast draw and the high-noon street duel

Davy Crockett's coonskin cap

can woodcutter named Florentino. Wyatt, convinced that the man was Indian Charlie, shot him to death. Spence had surrendered to Sheriff Behan in Tombstone, but Curly Bill Brocius, leader of the cowboys now that Old Man Clanton was dead, was reported near Mescal Springs in the Whetstone Mountains—where, ironically, he was said to be looking for Wyatt, having been deputized by Behan to arrest the Earps and their companions for Stilwell's murder. In a skirmish near the springs the Earp posse opened fire on a group of armed men, and Wyatt used a Wells Fargo shotgun to blow in half a man he claimed was Curly Bill. This started a century-long controversy over whether Brocius was even in the territory at the time.

Wyatt Earp and his posse were now wanted men. Rather than face lynching at the hands of Tombstone's aroused citizenry, they fled Arizona and didn't return until long after the last of their enemies had left. Wyatt's later claim to have sneaked back alone to kill Johnny Ringo in July 1882 is widely discounted.

Doc Holliday died of tuberculosis in Colorado in 1887 at the age of thirty-five. That same year Ike Clanton was killed while fleeing the law in Arizona. Warren Earp was shot to death during an argument in Wilcox, Arizona, in 1900, and pneumonia claimed Virgil in nearby Goldfield in 1905. Wyatt Earp went on to referee the 1896 Sharkey-Fitzsimmons fight in San Francisco and to keep a saloon in Alaska during the gold rush. In 1911 he was arrested in Los Angeles for running a confidence game, after which he raised racehorses and sold real estate in California until his death at age eighty in 1929. He was the last surviving participant in the most famous gunfight of the Old West, and what might truthfully be termed the first true gang war in American history. ∎

O.K., ALREADY!

BY LOREN D. ESTLEMAN

We're convinced that one of the reasons Hollywood has never told the complete story of what happened at the O.K. Corral is its reluctance to confuse audiences with the unwieldy size and diversity of the cast. In the interest of clarification, we will provide you with a scorecard so you can keep the list of participants straight.

Johnny Ringo, a peripheral figure in the events surrounding the gun-fight, should not be confused with Johnny Barnes, a fellow gang member, or with Johnny Behan, the local sheriff, who bore little resemblance to Tombstone *Epitaph* editor John Clum, and even less to John Henry Holliday, better known as Doc. Ringo must also be kept distinct from the Ringo Kid, who was a character played by John Wayne in John Ford's *Stagecoach*, and who should not be confused with Billy the Kid. Billy Clanton, a confederate of Ringo's, was on speaking terms with Billy Claiborne, who was sometimes called Billy the Kid but was not William H. Bonney, *the* Billy the Kid. Billy Claiborne never met Curly Bill Brocius, Ringo's boss, or Billy Breakenridge, deputy to Johnny Behan, who as you'll recall had nothing to do with either Johnny Barnes or Johnny Ringo.

Which brings us to Judge William H. Stillwell, another local representative of the law whom *nobody* called Billy and who was no relation to Frank Stilwell, another acquaintance of Ringo's, who was friendly with Frank McLaury, who died with his brother and Billy Clanton at the O.K. Corral in spite of his friendship with gunfighter Buckskin Frank Leslie, who later killed "Billy the Kid" Claiborne when Claiborne accused him of murdering Johnny Ringo, who may actually have been killed by somebody called Johnny-Behind-the-Deuce.

We hope this explanation has helped in some modest way to clear up the inexplicable confusion that usually accompanies this event.

LAWMEN

WILD BILL HICKOK

BY JOE G. ROSA

**Wild Bill Hickok
(courtesy of Joe Rosa)**

"HOW MANY MEN HAVE YOU KILLED, TO YOUR CERTAIN KNOWLEDGE?" Henry M. Stanley asked James Butler Hickok in April 1867. "Considerably over a hundred," Hickok replied, without batting an eyelid.

Stanley was but one of many journalists who fell victim to Hickok's sense of humor. In any case, most of the scriveners who sought him out concentrated on the sensational rather than the truth. In 1873 one editor remarked that Hickok's exploits would "furnish occupation for Western journalists yet unborn." His sister Lydia recalled in later years that "When we were children he was always telling such yarns to amuse the rest of us."

The exploits of the real and the legendary Wild Bill Hickok are firmly established in American folklore. How he got the name Wild Bill remains in doubt, but it was Hickok's role as a two-gun Galahad that inspired the myth and the legend of the gunfighter. Armed with a pair of Colt's cap-and-ball .36 caliber Navy revolvers, which he wore butts forward for the plainsman's underhand or "twist" draw, Hickok was said to draw and fire them "with a rapidity that was truly wonderful." His reflexes enabled him to do so "before the average man had time to think about it."

Wild Bill, however, dismissed speed in a gunfight. A gunman's survival depended upon his ability—or willingness—to shoot when being shot at. In 1871 he advised a friend: "I hope you never have to shoot any man, but if you do, shoot him in the guts near the navel. You may not make a fatal shot, but he will get a shock that will paralyze his brain and arm so much that the fight is all over."

Hickok's pistol skill has, of course, been grossly exaggerated. Although in frontier parlance he was a "dead shot," even he would have disbelieved some of the more lurid accounts. He could hit targets at up to 100 yards with *aimed* shots (hip-shooting was unknown in the Old West), but reports of long-range pistol shots at coins, playing cards, and corks in bottles were fiction.

Predictably, Hickok was fastidious with his pistols. He loaded each chamber carefully, checked each percussion cap and each nipple channel to ensure that the cap flash would reach the powder. "I ain't ready to go

**Wild Bill Hickok
(courtesy of Joe Rosa)**

yet," he once remarked, "and I am not taking any chances. When I draw and pull I must be sure."

Wild Bill was very much a lady's man and knew his share of cow town prostitutes. He also had several more serious affairs, and to one unknown lady he actually wrote a poem. But stories linking him to Calamity Jane are without foundation.

As for his personality, Hickok's friends claimed that he was generous to a fault, cool, and courageous, but of a quiet disposition unless he was aroused—all of which rather belied the "Wild Bill" sobriquet. His detractors alleged that he'd get the drop on an enemy with a disarming smile followed by a sudden shot. As to that, he said, "I never allowed a man to get the drop on me."

Hickok's appearance, at least, matched his legend. He was a little over six feet tall, well proportioned and muscular. His shoulder-length auburn hair was complemented by a straw-colored mustache. Despite years of exposure to plains weather, his skin was pallid, his forehead freckled. But his eyes were his dominant feature. Blue-gray in color, they were normally friendly, but they became coldly implacable when he got angry. Few could match his gaze.

Despite his man-killer reputation, Wild Bill was not a frontier bum or roustabout. He could trace his ancestry right back to Stratford-upon-Avon, Warwickshire, England, where his forebears were neighbors of William Shakespeare. He was born on May 27, 1837, at Homer (later renamed Troy Grove), Illinois, the fifth of seven children born to William Alonzo and Polly Butler Hickok. He enjoyed a normal childhood and at an early age showed a marked aptitude for firearms. He became a skilled hunter.

When the Kansas-Nebraska Act was passed in 1854, the Hickoks were interested in the newly available farming lands but were daunted by stories of the violence between pro-slavery Missourians and free-state Kansans. James, anxious to see Kansas, set off in 1856. By 1857 he had acquired sixty acres of land near the new township of Monticello, Johnson County, and in the following March was elected one of four magistrates' constables in the township. When his family interfered in his romance with Mary Jane Owen, the part-Indian daughter of his friend John Owen, he moved West to work for freighting outfits to Denver and Santa Fe.

On July 12, 1861, at Rock Creek, Nebraska Territory, he was involved in a shooting incident, the so-called McCanles Massacre. Russell, Majors & Waddell had purchased the Rock Creek station for use on the Pony Express route to California, but the new owners still owed money to the former owner, David C. McCanles. When they couldn't pay him (they were bankrupt), McCanles tried to regain the place, but he and two companions were killed in the attempt. James Hickok, who had been at the station only a short time, and two others were arrested and accused of murder. At a pre-liminary hearing they made a successful plea of self-defense in protection of company property. Recent research suggests that Hickok didn't kill McCanles, but when *Harper's New Monthly Magazine* published an account of the affair in 1867, it upped the tally to ten men killed by Hickok in single combat.

Serving during the Civil War as a wagonmaster, courier, detective, scout, and spy, Hickok had a good reputation among the officers and quartermas-ters who hired him. By the close of the war he was generally called Wild Bill, and had made his headquarters Springfield, Missouri, which had been his base for much of the war. It was there that he and a former companion named Dave Tutt shot it out on Public Square following a dispute over cards.

It seemed to Captain Albert Barnitz, the post commander at Springfield, who watched the fight, that they both "fired simultaneously," and Tutt was "shot directly through the heart." Barnitz ordered Hickok's arrest. The charge was later reduced to manslaughter, and the jury found Hickok not guilty.

In 1866 at Fort Riley, Kansas, Hickok served as a guide and as a special detective "hunting up government property" (stolen horses and mules). In 1867 and again in 1868-69 he was a scout for the U.S. Army in the field against hostile Indians. As a scout for the 7th Cavalry he won the admiration of General Custer, who described him as "the most prominent" of the white scouts and a "Plainsman in every sense of the word."

Between 1867 and 1870 Wild Bill also served intermittently as a deputy U.S. marshal, but it was his exploits as a peace officer in Hays City and Abilene that really established his name and reputation.

In the summer of 1869 Hays City was without law and order. Wild Bill was elected acting Ellis County sheriff pending the November election, and he made Hays City his headquarters. Within days of his election he shot and killed a man named Mulrey or Mulvey who had terrorized the town. On September 27, as Hickok broke up a disturbance in a saloon, Samuel Strawhun attempted to kill him. Hickok shot him dead. Later, when a number of men tried to lynch a teamster, Wild Bill stepped in and saved him, for which Hickok received the thanks of the post commander at Fort Hays. Despite this, Wild Bill (a Republican) lost the November election to his deputy, Peter Lanihan (a Democrat).

Hickok paid one last visit to Hays City in July, 1870. On the night of the 17th two drunken 7h Cavalry troopers named Lonergan and Kile attacked him in a saloon. Lonergan managed to keep Wild Bill from his pistols while Kile shoved a pistol into Hickok's ear. The cap failed to explode. Before the trooper could recock his pistol, Wild Bill had one of his own pistols in his hand. His first shot smashed Lonergan's knee, his second mortally wounded

Kile, who died the next day in the post hospital. Hickok spent the night on Boot Hill prepared to sell his life dearly, but the troopers' drunken friends didn't catch up with him. Once the fuss was over, he went to Junction City.

On April 15, 1871, Hickok was appointed marshal of Abilene in succession to Thomas James "Bear River" Smith, who had been murdered the previous November. Folks knew Hickok didn't bluff. He gave would-be troublemakers a choice: "Take the first east- or westbound train out, or go north in the morning." North was Boot Hill. His methods were unorthodox, but they got results. Aware as he was of the treacherous habits of some of the Texas cowboys, who delighted in shooting people through windows or from dark alleys, he was careful to avoid such places. The Texans, wary of his reputation and ability, usually gave him a wide berth.

Wild Bill's growing reputation as a "pistoleer" helped him keep the lid on during his period as Abilene's marshal. In the Texan part of town, where whiskey ran like water and was of a quality to make a "rabbit fight a bulldog," prostitutes and crooked gamblers gave him and his deputies a hard time. Finally the city council forced the roughs to move to a site outside the town limits so Hickok could isolate the violence.

Several top-notch gunfighters appeared in Abilene in 1871. Ben Thompson ran the Bull's Head saloon, and though he fell out with Hickok, they didn't shoot it out. John Wesley Hardin also incurred the marshal's wrath when he pursued the murderer of a fellow Texan to Sumner City and killed him in a restaurant, then came back to Abilene and shot another man for no reason. He skipped town when Hickok came looking for him. Later, he claimed to have worked the "road agent's spin" on the marshal, but no one, least of all Wes's friends, believed him.

On October 5 gambler Phil Coe and some fellow Texans went on a shooting spree. Coe told Wild Bill that he'd shot at a dog, but when he pointed his pistols at the marshal, Hickok drew. Both men opened fire. Coe missed, but Hickok shot him twice in the stomach. At that moment another man ran between them, brandishing a pistol. Again Hickok fired, thinking it was another Texan, but it was his friend Mike Williams. Tears streamed down Wild Bill's face as he carried Williams into the Alamo saloon and laid him out on a billiard table. Single-handedly, he then drove all the Texans from town. Coe lingered in great agony for two days, and the local newspaper decided he'd got what he deserved. Wild Bill paid for Williams' funeral at Kansas City. Ironically, Williams was the last man Hickok killed during a gunfight.

By December, Abilene had had enough of the cattle trade and advised the drovers to take it elsewhere. Wild Bill moved on to Kansas City. He was not unduly concerned. Threats had been made against his life for killing Coe. He foiled one attempt on a train to Topeka when he "circumvented the parties," disarmed them, and forced them to remain aboard when it reached Topeka. The press paid tribute to his policing, saying that "the safety of life and property within the city" had been secured "more through his daring, than any other agency."

Hickok moved on to Springfield, Missouri, where he became a familiar figure. He also appeared at Niagara Falls in August 1872, as master of ceremonies at a "Grand Buffalo Hunt"—it flopped, but his name alone did draw a large crowd. In September, at the Kansas City annual fair, Wild Bill risked death when, despite being faced by about fifty armed Texans, he stopped a band from playing "Dixie!"

In the spring of 1873 word flashed around the West that Wild Bill had been murdered, shot down by Texans at Fort Dodge. Hickok joked about

Wild Bill Hickok preferred Colt's Model 1851 Navy .36 caliber revolvers. This 4th Model revolver, produced from 1850–70, has a 7½" barrel, checkered ivory grips, an oversized trigger guard, and is presentation engraved. (photo by Tom Knowles, courtesy of Metzger Collection, Texas A&M University Sam Houston Sanders Corps of Cadets Center)

it, but later he wrote to several newspapers advising them that he was very much alive. To one he wrote: "I never have insulted man or woman in my life, but if you knew what a wholesome regard I have for damn liars and rascals they would be liable to keep out of my way." He also accused writer Ned Buntline of "trying to murder me with his pen for years; having failed he is now, so I am told, trying to have it done by some Texans, but he has signally failed so far."

In August 1873, Buffalo Bill Cody persuaded Wild Bill to join his theatrical "Wild West" then touring in the East. After five months with Cody's Wild West, Hickok quit. His constant practical jokes and unpredictable behavior finally convinced both men that he was no actor, so he returned West. He wore smoked-lens glasses for a time, which he blamed on stage lighting. Claims that he was really suffering from glaucoma or a form of opthalmia have been refuted by one expert who thinks his problem was trachoma, which was common on the plains.

In 1874 and 1875 Wild Bill spent much time in Cheyenne and Kansas City. It was in Kansas City that he met J. W. Buel, who would become his first biographer. When Buel originally asked if he could write about him, Hickok refused. He agreed that his life had been "a little interesting," but added:

"I never fought any man for notoriety, and I am sorry I've got the name I have." Buel claims that before parting from him, Hickok prophesied: "When I die it will be just as you see me now, and sickness will not be the cause. For more than ten years I have been constantly expecting to be killed, and it is certain to come before a great while longer."

On March 5, 1876, Wild Bill married former circus owner Agnes Lake Thatcher, with whom he'd corresponded regularly. They had a brief honeymoon in Cincinnati before Hickok returned West to lead an expedition to the Black Hills. He abandoned the venture and instead teamed up with Colorado Charlie Utter. The pair set off for Deadwood in June, arriving early in July.

On August 1, Wild Bill penned this prophetic letter to his wife: "Agnes Darling, if such should be we never meet again, while firing my last shot, I will gently breathe the name of my wife—Agnes—and with wishes even for my enemies I will make the plunge and try to swim to the other shore."

At about 4 P.M. on August 2, as Wild Bill sat in on a poker game in Saloon No. 10, Jack McCall, an insignificant cross-eyed character who bummed around under several aliases, came up behind Hickok and blew his brains out. McCall was tried by an illegal miners' court in Deadwood and found not guilty of murder. Many believed that he'd been bribed to kill Wild Bill. He was rearrested and placed on trial at Yankton, Dakota Territory, where he was found guilty of murder, sentenced to death and hanged on March 1, 1877.

Wild Bill's murder received nationwide publicity. Some detractors conducted character assassinations, but there were many who grieved for him. Old friends recalled his courage, his generosity and willingness to fight anyone—no matter the odds—in defense of a friend or if he believed it was the right thing to do. But the real impact of his death was felt by those closest to him. Three months afterward his wife wrote: "I can see him day and night before me. The longer he is dead the worse I feel." In Kansas, his grief-stricken sister Lydia wished that he had "died with Custer" rather than on a barroom floor. And back in Illinois, his mother suffered a lung hemorrhage when she was told of his death. She died two years later, still mourning him.

Even in death Wild Bill Hickok inspired legends: his preoccupation with death at the time; his reluctance to play that last game of poker because he had a door at his back; the fact that five out of the six cartridges in McCall's pistol were defective. It seemed that Fate had played a cruel hand. Indeed, the cards that supposedly spilled from his lifeless fingers—the Ace of spades, the Ace of clubs, the eight of clubs and the eight of spades, and either a Jack of diamonds or the Queen of diamonds, have since been immortalized as the "Deadman's Hand." ■

A COLOR ALBUM OF THE WEST THAT WAS

Indian Scout, 1897, Charles M. Russell
(courtesy of Texas A&M Development Foundation,
Bill & Irma Runyon Art Collections)

Corn Song—Taos, Joseph Henry Sharp
(courtesy of Texas A&M Development Foundation,
Bill & Irma Runyon Art Collections)

Target Practice, Tom Lovell (courtesy of
National Cowboy Hall of Fame and
Western Heritage Center)

Teton Range, Idaho, 1899, Thomas Moran (courtesy of Texas A&M Development Foundation, Bill & Irma Runyon Art Collections)

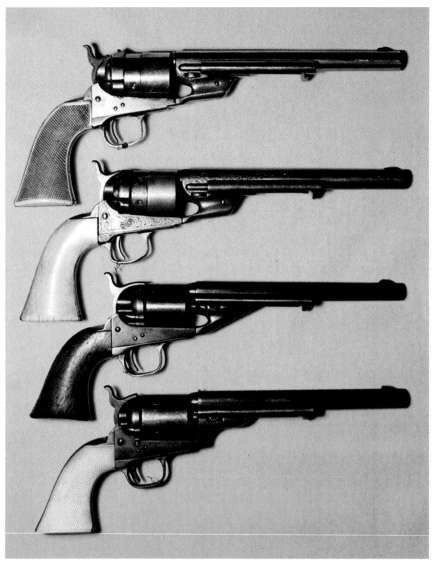

TOP:
These four Colt revolvers illustrate how weapons were converted to fire metal cartridge ammunition in place of the original percussion loads. Top to bottom: Two Colt Model 1860 Army revolvers with 8" barrels and ivory grips—first the Richards Conversion, second the Richards-Mason Conversion, both to .44 caliber centerfire. Colt Model 1861 Navy revolver with 7½" barrel and wood grips, the Civilian Conversion to .38 caliber rimfire. Colt Open Top revolver, circa 1872–73, with 7½" barrel, ivory grips, and integral rear sight, manufactured with a straight cylinder and without the conversion breechplate. This "transition model" was the design step between percussion-style revolvers and the Colt single-action revolver, better known as the "Peacemaker."

BOTTOM:
Two Colt Model 1877 double-action revolvers, the .41 caliber "Thunderer" (above) and the .38 caliber "Lightning," both produced from 1877 to 1909. Thunderer is presentation engraved, with ivory grips, a 4½" barrel, and a standard ejector. Lightning is presentation engraved, with pearl grips and no ejector.

(courtesy of Metzger Collection, Texas A&M University Sam Houston Sanders Corps of Cadets Center; photos by Tom Knowles)

OPPOSITE:
The Modern Comanche,
1890, Frederic Remington
(courtesy of Texas A&M Development Foundation, Bill & Irma Runyon Art Collections)

Ozark Autumn, **1944,**
Thomas Hart Benton
(courtesy of Texas A&M
Development Founda-
tion, Bill & Irma Runyon
Art Collections)

LAWMEN

BAT MASTERSON

BY BILL O'NEAL

WILLIAM BARTHOLOMEW MASTERSON CHANGED HIS MIDDLE NAME to Barclay, but he was better known as Bat—perhaps because he struck lawbreakers with his cane, or because he was something of a "battler." He acquired a reputation rather out of proportion to his actions as a gunfighter and a peace officer. He was rumored to have killed twenty-seven men, but in three decades on the frontier he was actually involved in only three gunfights and was responsible for only one fatality. His reputation alone was sufficient deterrent for most troublemakers.

Masterson was born in Canada in 1853; his farming family moved about before they settled in Wichita, Kansas, just prior to the Civil War. Bat and his brother Ed left the farm in 1872 and headed for Dodge City, where Bat joined up with hide hunters for buffalo-hunting expeditions into the Texas Panhandle. At Adobe Walls he helped fight off a large-scale Indian assault led by Quanah Parker, and he later joined up with the Army as a $75-a-month scout for General Nelson A. Miles.

In 1876 Bat began spending time with Molly Brennan in the Panhandle town of Mobeetie, just outside Fort Elliott. A 4th Cavalry sergeant named King jealously attacked them in a saloon, wounding Molly and Bat before Masterson gunned him down. Molly died on the spot. One newspaper reported that she'd been hit by one of Bat's slugs, possibly as she'd tried to intervene. King expired the next day. The wound Bat received in the shooting forced him to adopt the cane that later became his trademark along with his dapper bowler hat.

Bat returned to Dodge and opened a saloon. He got himself pistol-whipped by the marshal when he tried to help a prisoner. Shortly afterward he wangled an appointment as deputy sheriff of Ford County, in which Dodge City is located, and in November he won the county sheriff's post. He immediately distinguished himself by chasing down and arresting train robbers, rustlers, jail escapees, and con men. In January 1879 Bat was awarded additional authority—a commission as a deputy U.S. marshal.

Two months later, unconcerned by his responsibilities as a peace officer, Bat left Dodge temporarily to hire his gun to the Atchison, Topeka & Santa Fe Railroad. He led a large gang of gunmen to back the railroad in a dispute

Bat Masterson in his later years

A young Bat Masterson

with the Denver & Rio Grande line over right-of-way through Raton Pass in Colorado. A short time later Bat was defeated for the office of sheriff in a hotly contested campaign.

Bat next drifted into Colorado and New Mexico, then traveled to Nebraska to rescue a seriously wounded Billy Thompson, the younger brother of his close friend, Ben Thompson, a noted Texas gunslinger—the younger Thompson had angered the citizens of Ogallala. Masterson lived in Kansas City for a time, then joined several Dodge friends, including Wyatt Earp and Luke Short, at the Arizona boom town of Tombstone. Bat soon found himself pulled back to Dodge, where he participated in two minor gunfights before he moved on to Colorado.

Masterson began to dabble in newspaper writing but soon found himself in Fort Worth at the gambling tables. He also became increasingly active as a sportsman, especially as an official and promoter of horse races and prize fights. For the next several years he pursued the sporting life throughout the West, though his home base was in Denver.

In 1891 Bat married Emma Waters, and eleven years later he moved to

New York City. He spent the last two decades of his life frequenting the night spots of the Great White Way and skillfully writing sports news for the *Morning Telegraph.* President Theodore Roosevelt appointed Masterson a federal deputy marshal in 1905, but Bat resigned the post two years later when he found that it interfered increasingly with his newspaper duties. He died of a heart attack at his newspaper desk on October 25, 1921. He'd written his last words:

"These ginks say because the rich man gets his ice in the summer and the poor man gets it in the winter things are breaking even for both. Maybe so, but I can't see it that way." ■

LAWMEN

BILL TILGHMAN

BY BILL O'NEAL

Bill Tilghman, police chief

JUST LIKE HIS FATHER BEFORE HIM, WILLIAM MATTHEW TILGHMAN was born on the Fourth of July. He wasn't destined to lead a quiet life. By age sixteen he was hunting buffalo and was already well known among frontiersmen. On June 25, 1874, a local desperado named Blue Throat killed Tilghman's fellow buffalo hunter Pat Congers in Petrie, Oklahoma. That night Tilghman and a cohort named Hurricane Bill rode into town to retrieve the body from the saloon where the shooting had taken place. Blue Throat and several companions were still inside, and a fight broke out. As they exchanged shots a slug hit the lamp, and in the darkness the two buffalo hunters found Congers' body behind the bar. They carried it outside, rode out of town, and staged a decent burial the following day.

Tilghman scouted for the Army out of Fort Dodge, Kansas, until 1877, when he was appointed deputy sheriff of Ford County. Though he was twice arrested for theft, his reputation quickly improved when he married and settled down to raise livestock near Dodge City. Over the years he also operated two saloons in Dodge, and in 1884 he was appointed city marshal. Friends presented Tilghman with a unique badge made of a pair of twenty-dollar gold pieces.

He served Dodge well for two years. In the late 1880s he saw action in two of the Kansas county-seat wars; in both conflicts he was involved in killings.

The first clash occurred on Tilghman's thirty-fourth birthday. Farmer City was a hamlet between Leoti and Coronado, and as these two communities were keen rivals for the seat of Wichita County, there was a great deal of hard feeling among the citizens of all three towns. Ed Prether, an abrasive man who kept a saloon in Farmer City, went to Leoti on the Fourth in 1888 and began drinking and firing his gun. Citizens asked Tilghman to corral Prether; Tilghman braced Prether, who angrily returned to Farmer City, muttering threats.

About 7 P.M. Tilghman somewhat provocatively entered Prether's saloon. Tilghman, who may have been drinking, and Prether, who most certainly had been, began to argue. Prether placed his hand on his gun. Tilghman instantly whipped out his revolver and ordered Prether to remove his hand from his gun butt. A moment later Tilghman fired, and the slug entered the left side of Prether's chest and tore out his back. Stunned, the wounded man stood motionless while Tilghman again ordered him to move his hand. Tilghman then shot him in the head, and Prether collapsed and died on the spot.

When the county seat war broke out in Gray County the next year, Tilghman hired out his gun to the town of Ingalls. On Saturday morning,

Bill Tilghman

January 14, 1889, about a dozen Ingalls gunmen piled into a wagon and at 11:30 A.M. arrived at Cimarron with the intention of hijacking the county records. Tilghman and the others jumped out of the wagon and began looting the courthouse, but the local citizens soon discovered what was happening and opened fire on them.

The outnumbered Ingalls men fired back, then scrambled to escape. Shooting as he ran, Tilghman tumbled into a large irrigation canal and sprained an ankle. His compadres helped him into the wagon as the vehicle rattled away toward Ingalls. They'd abandoned three of their friends, who holed up in the courthouse for a time before they surrendered. The Cimarron folks later released them. Two of the Ingalls men were hit during the skirmish, and four Cimarron citizens were wounded, one fatally.

Tilghman was attracted to the spectacular Cherokee Strip land rush in 1889, and he managed to locate a claim near Guthrie, Oklahoma. He served as the city marshal of Perry, and then in 1892 he was appointed deputy U.S. marshal and moved his family to a stud farm near Chandler. He also served stints as sheriff of Lincoln County and as chief of police of Oklahoma City.

Over the next two decades Tilghman was instrumental in exterminating the outlaw gangs of Oklahoma. Along with fellow lawman Steve Burke, he brought in Jennie "Little Britches" Metcalf and Cattle Annie McDoulett, the teenaged consorts of the Doolin gang. On September 6, 1895, at a ranch eighteen miles south of Elgin, Kansas, Tilghman located Little Bill Raidler, a member of the Doolin gang. Armed with a rifle, Tilghman and two deputies, W. C. Smith and Cyrus Longbone, secluded themselves at the ranch about dusk. When Raidler rode in to eat supper, Tilghman ordered him to surrender, but the outlaw drew his sixgun. He snapped off a wild shot; Tilghman, standing just ten feet away, fired a bullet that broke Raidler's right wrist and sent his gun flying. Raidler turned to run, but Smith blasted him to the ground with a shotgun. Tilghman patched Raidler's wounds and later helped him obtain a parole. The outlaw reformed and married.

In 1910 Tilghman was elected to the Oklahoma state senate. In 1911 he resigned his legislative position to head the Oklahoma City police force. He supervised the production of a motion picture, *The Passing of the Oklahoma Outlaws*, which was released in 1915. Tilghman exhibited it for several years.

In August 1924 the citizens of Cromwell, a booming Oklahoma oil town, persuaded Tilghman to leave retirement and become city marshal. As marshal, he clashed with Wiley Lynn, a shady prohibition officer. On the night of November 1, 1924, Tilghman was seated in Murphy's Restaurant when he heard a shot fired outside. He rushed out to find Lynn drunkenly waving a pistol. A bystander seized the gun, and Tilghman led Lynn toward jail, but Lynn produced a small automatic and began firing. The old lawman crumpled to the ground and died in fifteen minutes. ■

Pat Garrett

PAT GARRETT: TALL SLAYER OF BILLY THE KID

BY LEON C. METZ

SHERIFF PAT GARRETT WAS THIRTY YEARS OLD WHEN HE PUT A BULLET through Billy the Kid's heart. That killing made him the most famous lawman in the West, a man respected by presidents, feared by politicians and hired gunmen. Garrett had it all together when he tracked down and shot Billy the Kid, but from that moment on the gods deserted him. Everything he touched seemed cursed. He dreamed big, struggled mightily, and fell hard. His own death at the age of fifty-three remains a controversial murder mystery.

He was born Patrick Floyd Jarvis Garrett on June 5, 1850, in Chambers County, Alabama. Three years later the family moved to Claiborne Parish, Louisiana, where John Garrett, Pat's father, owned a plantation. Shortly after the Civil War, John Garrett died, and his eight children bickered over his holdings.

Pat left it all behind and headed for the Texas buffalo range in 1869. Garrett was a tall man (six feet five) and stovepipe thin—the Mexicans called him Juan Largo, Long John. He was a strange combination of dreamer and hardheaded agnostic, and he had a sarcastic turn of wit that often brought him trouble. Garrett herded cattle and shot buffalo until the mid-1870s, when he teamed up with Willis Skelton Glenn, a Georgia-born hunter three years Garrett's senior. In the company of the itinerant skinners Grundy Burns and Joe Brisco, they worked the Double Mountain country north of Abilene, Texas.

On a cold and damp November morning in 1876, as the hunters sullenly sought comfort from a sputtering fire, Joe Brisco emerged from a nearby arroyo carrying wet clothes. Garrett sarcastically muttered that no one but a damned Irishman would be stupid enough to wash in that muddy water, and Brisco rose to the attack. Pat knocked him down several times before Brisco grabbed an axe. As Garrett raced around the wagons with Brisco in pursuit, Pat grabbed a buffalo gun, turned, and fired. The heavy slug knocked Brisco into the fire. By the time the others had pulled him out, he was dead.

Garrett went to Fort Griffin to turn himself in to civil authorities, but he was no-billed and released.

A few months later the Comanche struck the hunters' wagon group while Garrett was away. The Indians killed a few horses, wounded Glenn, and burned the equipment and supplies. Thus ended the buffalo-hunting enterprise. (More than a decade later, in 1892, Glenn filed suit for $15,000 damages from the government, holding Washington liable since it had a peace treaty with the Indians. Dozens of hunters testified, including Garrett, but Pat swore the entire outfit was worth only about $300. At that point the trial shifted from the subject of buffalo to the veracity and character of Pat Garrett.)

So Garrett left the buffalo range and headed for Fort Sumner, New Mexico. He found work as a cowboy for Pete Maxwell, scion of Lucien Maxwell, who had formerly owned one third of the Territory. Within months Garrett married Juanita Gutierrez, who later died during a miscarriage. On January 14, 1880, he married her sister, Apolinaria Gutierrez, an attractive, refined lady who eventually gave Pat nine children. Their daughter Elizabeth, who was blind and a disciple of Helen Keller, wrote the state anthem, "Oh Fair New Mexico."

Apolinaria stood by her husband in the turbulent times that followed. Theirs was a loving if formal relationship; Garrett was unfaithful on occasion, yet she remained trusting and apparently never considered divorce. Correspondence preserved by Jarvis Garrett, the surviving son, proves that Pat kept Apolinaria in his thoughts and confidence. Letters he wrote during his frequent absences were long and affectionate, although he addressed her as "Dear Wife" and closed with a stiff "Pat F. Garrett."

Garrett pretty much avoided the initial violence of the Lincoln County War. The main conflict had subsided by 1880, although the survivors occasionally and indiscriminately killed one another and kept Lincoln County, an area larger than several Eastern states, in anarchy. Garrett rallied the local Democratic Party and campaigned for sheriff on a promise to rid Lincoln County of Billy the Kid. The voters approved, and by Christmas Eve he had the Kid in custody. On April 15, 1881, a judge in Mesilla, New Mexico, sentenced the Kid to hang for the murder of Sheriff William Brady. Although Billy broke jail at Lincoln on April 28, Sheriff Pat Garrett relentlessly tracked him to Fort Sumner and sent him to his grave with a well-placed bullet on July 14.

Pat Garrett spent the next two months buying drinks for politicians, trying to win legislative approval for a $500 reward. He also started work on *The Authentic Life of Billy, the Kid, the Noted Desperado of the Southwest, Whose Deeds of Daring Have Made His Name a Terror in New Mexico, Arizona, and Northern Mexico.* Charles W. Greene, editor of the *Santa Fe New Mexican*, published the long-titled biography; Ashum Upson evidently ghostwrote the text for Garrett. Ash Upson, Garrett's best friend, was a garrulous, troublesome, heavy-drinking iconoclast, a journalist who lived hard and died early. While Garrett's name appeared on the 1882 book, Ash claimed to have written every word. The book flopped.

Garrett failed to win reelection, primarily because of his rancorous disposition, and for a while he operated as a Texas Ranger captain for the LS Ranch in the Texas Panhandle. In 1885 he disbanded the rangers and went to work as a cattle buyer and land speculator for Captain Brandon Kirby, who fronted for Scottish ranching interests, specifically the James Cree family, in the American Southwest. Although Garrett helped introduce Angus cattle to Lincoln County, droughts forced the Cree interests to withdraw.

By 1887 Pat Garrett and his family had moved to Roswell, New Mexico, where Garrett, always the visionary, conceived the idea of damming the Rio Hondo and irrigating the desert. To finance the project he approached wealthy New Mexicans such as Charles B. Eddy, cattleman and financier, and editor Charles Greene. They and others formed the Pecos valley Land and Ditch Company, but when expenses mounted and construction lagged, the corporation invited in Robert Weems Tansill, the Punch Cigar manufacturer, who in turn included James John Hagerman, a retired Colorado businessman who built railroads.

Hagerman bailed out the firm with $40,000 and reorganized—without Garrett. Pat had sunk his money and energy into these dreams, and his assets were now drier than the local canals. With no fanfare, with no return on his investment, with no acknowledgment of his contributions, he was dismissed.

For a while he lived in Uvalde, Texas, racing horses and playing poker with John Nance Garner, future vice president of the United States. Then word came that Colonel Albert Jennings Fountain and his nine-year-old son, Henry, had vanished. William T. "Poker Bill" Thornton, governor of New Mexico, wired Garrett to accept appointment as sheriff of Dona Ana County and investigate the apparent murder. Once again the Territory of New Mexico needed Pat Garrett.

Fountain, a former Texas state senator from El Paso, had moved to Mesilla, New Mexico, and established the *Mesilla Independent*, a Republican Party newspaper. His classic battles with Democratic powerhouse Albert Bacon Fall ended on February 1, 1896, when Fountain and his son disappeared somewhere on the eastern slopes of the San Andres Mountains. Garrett's investigation led him to suspect that they had been abducted and murdered by Oliver Lee, Jim Gililland, and Bill McNew, partisan cowboys allied with Fall.

Garrett located the wanted men at Wildy Well, a railroad stop and line shack forty miles northeast of El Paso, Texas. The posse arrived in the early morning hours of July 12, 1898, and after they tied their horses a quarter-mile from the house, they slipped quietly to the door. They heard loud snoring. Garrett shouldered his way inside, pointed his revolver at the bed, and shouted, "Hands up!" The woman sleeping on the bed, Mary Madison, screamed.

No one sleeping in the shack admitted to knowing the outlaws. Garrett commenced a search anyway. Kent Kearney, a school teacher who was with the posse, tried to examine the roof and was shot twice with a buffalo rifle. The desperados had camped out on the roof. From that position they pinned down the posse and forced Garrett's men to surrender, drop their weapons, and ride away. The wounded Kearney begged Mrs. Madison to remove the bullet that had lodged in him, and she did so with a butcher knife. Kearney died from loss of blood.

The three outlaws were on the loose, one lawman was dead, and Pat Garrett was publicly humiliated. Because the whole Southwest was in an uproar, the wanted men soon surrendered. With Albert B. Fall as their attorney, they went on trial in 1893 in Hillsboro, New Mexico, and the jury swiftly acquitted them. The Fountain case still remains officially unsolved.

Garrett took his family forty miles south to El Paso, where President Theodore Roosevelt made him collector of customs on December 16, 1901. A master of ceremonies at a local political gathering joked that Roosevelt hesitated to appoint Garrett because Pat played poker. "Hell," the speaker guffawed, "everybody in El Paso knows Pat Garrett isn't a poker player, he just *thinks* he's a poker player."

The old warrior enforced the collection of customs much more stringently than had his predecessors, but even so, his administration was poorly managed. Secretary of the Treasury Leslie M. Shaw repeatedly cautioned him to practice the virtue of politeness. Garrett was fifty-one and unable to get his life together. He whored around and gambled away his money. He brawled in the streets. The end came when President Roosevelt requested a meeting during a Rough Rider convention in 1905 in San Antonio, Texas.

Garrett's closest El Paso friend was Tom Powers, the disreputable owner of the Coney Island Saloon. Powers wanted to meet Roosevelt, so Garrett introduced him as a "West Texas cattleman." The three had photos taken together, and when President Roosevelt learned he'd been deceived, he refused to give Pat a new two-year appointment.

A disillusioned and depressed Pat Garrett climbed aboard a rickety Santa Fe Railroad coach in 1906 and rode back to Dona Ana County, his family, and his dilapidated ranch. He had no place else to go. The ranch was 160 acres of dry, mesquite-covered desert, rocks, and craggy ridges. Garrett had improved it with a $200 quitclaim deed to Sinking Springs in nearby Bear

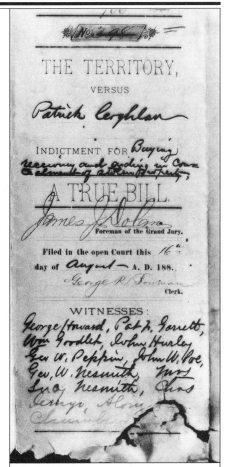

Front of a Lincoln County arrest warrant for a cattle thief; Pat Garrett signed it as a witness. (photo by Tom Knowles, courtesy of Moody Texas Ranger Library, Waco, Texas)

Wayne Brazel, slayer of Pat Garrett, is seated in the middle, holding a teddy bear. Standing are Elzy and Buster Brown and their wives. The photo was taken in Phoenix circa 1914.

Canyon, and since he controlled the water, he essentially owned the surrounding land.

But Garrett never prospered. His horses ran last, he rarely drew aces. He owed the banks, he owed his friends. He paid nobody.

Old debts came back to haunt Garrett. On July 12, 1890, the Albuquerque Bank of Commerce lent $1,000 to George Curry, who would become governor, John Eubank, and Pat Garrett. Pat was evidently a co-signer, the last name on the list of borrowers, but the bank foreclosed only against him. Garrett fought off that attempt, as well as county efforts to take his livestock for past-due taxes. In the process, however, Garrett mortgaged his land to businessman Martin Lohman for $3,567.50. In two years, after Garrett had not paid a cent, Lohman discounted the note to W. W. Cox for $2,000. Cox, a former Texas desperado, was one of Garrett's ranching neighbors.

Garrett's son Poe leased the Bear Ranch in March 1907 to Jesse Wayne Brazel, a local cowboy. Three months later Brazel borrowed nearly $600 from W. W. Cox and stocked the canyon with goats. Then Jim Miller, a gun for hire, offered to purchase the Garrett ranch for $3,000, saying he needed it to temporarily hold Mexican cattle. Garrett agreed to sell, probably figuring he could pay off Cox's mortgage and clear $1,000 for himself. But the goats presented a problem: Brazel's lease had four years to run.

Miller consented to purchase the 1,200 goats, and Brazel agreed to terminate the lease. Garrett and his family happily made plans to leave. Then Brazel said he had miscounted, that there were roughly 1,800 goats. Miller said he didn't think he could buy that many. As tempers soared, Garrett, Brazel, and Carl Adamson, a relative of Miller's, agreed to meet in Las Cruces and negotiate. Adamson picked up Pat in a buggy at the Garrett ranch on January 29, 1908. They left for town, winding through Organ and overtaking Brazel on the West side.

Brazel and Garrett quarreled until about four miles from Las Cruces, when Adamson and Garrett stopped the buggy to relieve themselves. Garrett removed his left glove, opened his pants, and began to urinate onto the sand. The old lawman's back was turned: he was vulnerable. A bullet slammed into the back of his head.

Historians generally perceive this as the successful conclusion to a twisted conspiracy to murder Pat Garrett. Most believe veteran hired gun Jim Miller pulled the trigger. Other suspects are Adamson, Cox, and Print Rhode, a Cox relative. However, when the facts are analyzed, logic points to Wayne Brazel, who feared and hated Garrett. He confessed to the killing, claimed self defense and was exonerated in court.

Today the old lawman lies in the Garrett family plot at Las Cruces. Few people visit the tombstone, and fewer still associate his name with those dramatic events in Southwestern history. ■

LAWMEN

MARTIN AGUIRRE, CHICANO LAWMAN AND HERO OF OLD CALIFORNIA

BY ABRAHAM HOFFMAN

MARTIN AGUIRRE, THE SON OF A SPANISH SEA CAPTAIN WHO TRAVeled to California in 1840 to become a rancher, was born in 1858 in San Diego. He grew up in Los Angeles; when he was two his father died, and at age nine he went to live on the ranch of his relatives, the Wolfskills.

A typical boy, Martin became a proficient swimmer and rider. His cousin accidentally shot him with an arrow, which left him blind in one eye, a disability that would disqualify him for law enforcement today. It apparently never troubled Martin's career.

When Martin was sixteen, the notorious bandit Tiburcio Vasquez was executed—an event calculated to persuade any young Chicano of Martin's time not to follow in Vasquez's footsteps. Martin soon developed an interest in politics, and around 1885 he joined the Republican Party and became a constable or a deputy sheriff. These political and professional allegiances remained his lifelong commitments.

Aguirre first gained fame in performing an act so heroic and selfless that the suspicions of modern cynics would understandably be aroused were not the circumstances so well documented. In January 1886 Los Angeles experienced one of those severe rainstorms which contrast so markedly with the region's semi-arid climate. Over seven inches of rain fell between January 12th and the 21st. The Los Angeles River, unrestrained at the time by its modern concrete straitjacket, eventually flooded and forced residents from their homes. The river, which resembled a "boiling yellow lake," according to one observer, swept away one bridge after another to leave Boyle Heights isolated from downtown.

On the morning of January 19, while rain still fell, a horse-drawn, open-air streetcar attempted to cross the river at Downey Avenue at the only remaining bridge despite obviously threatening conditions. As the river crested intermittently at fifteen feet (almost swamping the bridge), the streetcar crept slowly across. Suddenly the pilings at the east end of the bridge collapsed. Most of the frightened passengers immediately fled to safety, but the driver stayed with the streetcar and patiently urged his horse forward toward the still-standing west end of the bridge. Then that part of the bridge also collapsed and threw the streetcar into the raging current.

The horse in his panic managed to break his traces and swim to safety. The driver and one remaining passenger were trapped on the wooden streetcar, which lodged precariously between the bridge pilings and a soap factory at the river's edge. Meanwhile a crowd gathered, including Los Angeles mayor Edward Spence.

At this point Martin Aguirre arrived on horseback. People had unsuccessfully attempted to throw a rope to the stranded men, but Aguirre simply guided his horse, El Capitan, into the raging current. He rescued first one man and then the other. "The rescued men were thoroughly drained and chilled," the *Los Angeles Daily Times* reported, "but withal happy and thankful for their deliverance."

AGUIRRE'S HEROIC DAY DIDN'T END THERE. HE RODE ALONG THE flood plain, bringing one person after another to safety. The flood threatened to sweep away the home of a soap factory employee named Whitney. Without hesitation Aguirre rode through the swirling water to a window, and then he ferried each of the man's children to safety one by one. On his final trip he was just placing eight-year-old Theresa Whitney on his saddle when part of a nearby picket fence broke loose and toppled El Capitan. Aguirre managed to place the little girl on the part of the fence still standing (cutting his hands on some barbed wire in the process) before his horse stumbled again. His foot caught in the stirrup, Aguirre was carried some distance downstream. By the time he managed to free himself and get back, the flood had carried the little girl away. Even so, by the end of the day he had rescued at least nineteen people, many of them women and children.

Harris Newmark later mentioned the incident in his memoirs, calling it "an exhibition of great courage." The Newspaperman William A. Spalding lauded Aguirre as "the hero of the day." On January 23, after the young deputy had rested from his ordeal, the town honored him in a celebration at which the county prosecutor spoke in grand hyperbole: "Descendant of Spanish cavaliers, moved by his high sense of duty to his fellow man and in keeping with the conscience of the mandates of that highest of all courts, plunged into the seething waters and rescued from watery graves helpless women and children…"

Aguirre was given a valuable gold watch inscribed, "Presented by the Bar Association of Los Angeles to Martin Aguirre, for Bravery in the Flood of 1886." To this he humbly responded, "Gentlemen, I thank you. You have taken me by surprise. I am no speaker and therefore you will excuse me." Still, according to Harry Carr in his *Los Angeles, City of Dreams*, in spite of this acclaim, the memory of the one little girl he'd failed to rescue haunted Aguirre until his death.

In 1888 the Republican Party put forth its acknowledged hero, Martin Aguirre, as candidate for the office of sheriff of Los Angeles County. His Catholic and Hispanic background didn't hinder his campaign. As the historian Leonard Pitt has observed, a Californio candidate with the correct physical features, complexion, and old family ties could be elected to office up through the 1880s, so long as the Californio vote exercised some influence. Aguirre defeated his nearest rival, Thomas Rowan, 14,490 votes to 10,519.

As sheriff, Aguirre performed the necessary and routine tasks of collecting fines, serving subpoenas, and making arrests for crimes ranging from embezzlement to murder—a formidable task in a county that covered four thousand square miles of territory. Though Aguirre had only a dozen or so deputies, his office was noted for integrity and emphasis on fairness. Frustrated in his attempts to obtain confidential information, one reporter for the *Express* complained, "Sheriff Aguirre and his able deputies are about the hardest set of officials that the average reporter ever ran across for information. While they are very courteous to the newsgatherer, they have a happy faculty of keeping the secrets of the office to themselves, especially if they think that the ends of justice might perchance be thwarted."

Aguirre was remembered in his later years for not carrying a gun. According to his old friend Harry Carr, he preferred instead, "a razor-sharp bowie knife which hung from a scabbard under his armpit." Aguirre insisted, "The revolver is no good. I shoot at an escaped convict in a crowd, and I don't know where the bullets go." Carr claimed Aguirre could, "throw a knife fifty feet and pin the spot on the ace of spades."

Aguirre's refusal to carry a gun almost cost him his life on at least one occasion. Six months after Aguirre became sheriff, a French resident named Benoir Renault raped a woman named Mary Simmons. She filed charges,

Martin Geronimo Aguirre, 1858–1929. (courtesy of Mary Haggland)

and when Deputy Constable Dawes went to Renault's house with a warrant for his arrest, Renault fired several shots at Dawes and then barred the door. Dawes returned fire and then telephoned the sheriff's office for help. Three deputies responded, and more shots were fired; then Aguirre and two more deputies arrived on the scene with additional ammunition.

Aguirre decided against a frontal assault and entered the house from the rear. He found himself in a room adjacent to the one in which Renault had barricaded himself. Aguirre called through a connecting door that he had a warrant for Renault's arrest, but Renault didn't respond. He called again— still no answer. Finally Aguirre turned the doorknob. Renault fired through the door, wounding the sheriff in the left arm. By sheer luck, a half-dollar in Aguirre's vest pocket stopped a second shot. Aguirre retreated, and while the deputies bandaged his arm, Renault escaped. He was caught the next day while he was hiding in a Bunker Hill coal bin.

Aguirre's wound put him out of action for more than two weeks. When he returned to duty, he expected to see Renault tried and convicted for attempted murder. Renault engaged a prominent attorney, Horace Bell, to represent him at the trial. After Aguirre and his deputies gave their statement in superior court, Renault took the stand and insisted that the warrant hadn't been read to him and that Dawes had fired first. The trial took two days; in his closing argument Bell made the remarkable statement that Renault "ought to have killed" Aguirre, apparently on the justification of protecting his home from intruders. Prosecutor C. C. Stephens lambasted Bell for his remark. "It would be bad enough coming from a criminal," he said, "but from a lawyer and citizen it is outrageous."

One man held out for acquittal and hung the jury. In the new trial the case went quickly to the jury; they found Renault guilty not of attempted murder but of simple assault, a verdict that aroused considerable criticism and anger. The *Express* commented, "It is a sad state of affairs when an officer is not protected by the law. Sheriff Aguirre's record as a peace officer is well established. He has often exposed his life and spent his own money to bring criminals to justice, and it is not surprising that the verdict in question has excited comment."

Renault's sentence was a $350 fine or 350 days in jail. Aguirre responded with a display of mordant humor. When the grand jury ordered him to bring in a man of bad reputation to testify as a witness in another case, Aguirre took off his star and carried a white flag to the saloon where the man was drinking. He bought the man several beers before he asked him, as politely as possible, if he'd accompany him to the grand jury rooms. The man replied that he'd go when he "got damned good and ready." After Aguirre reported the details to the grand jury, it approved his use of more conventional methods.

Despite the popularity that had won him his office, Aguirre wasn't free from criticism while he served as sheriff. The press reacted unfavorably when he arrested *Los Angeles Tribune* editor H. H. Boyce on a blackmail charge, but as Aguirre pointed out, he was only doing his job. He was also criticized because some of the inmates at the county jail were suffering from serious illnesses, including one opium addict and one Chinese man who had a "loathsome disease" and was a "horrible sight to behold." Aguirre insisted that he could do nothing about the situation as long as the county hospital refused to accept diseased prisoners.

OVERALL OPINION OF HIS CONDUCT WAS GENERALLY FAVORABLE, and as the election neared, Aguirre announced his intent to run for reelection. Unfortunately, a month before the election he committed an error in judgment that allowed the Democrats to crack his support. Early in October of 1890, Sheriff O. A. Bexley of Lee County, Texas, contacted Aguirre with a warrant for the arrest of Nathan Willett on a charge of murder. Willett had lived in Norwalk, California, since 1872; he was known in his community as a family man and law-abiding citizen. Aguirre saw it as his duty to allow Bexley to make the arrest and remove Willett from his jurisdiction, but later information emerged which cast grave doubts on the validity of the charges. Outraged Norwalk residents held a mass meeting to protest Aguirre's role in what they believed to be the underhanded and unfair treatment of one of the community's citizens.

His political opponents made the most of Aguirre's perceived blunder, even though the grand jury's report found that he'd conducted the affairs of his office in a proper manner. Aguirre campaigned as best he could, but it was an uphill struggle. On November 5, he met defeat at the polls. But he didn't take that defeat with bitterness. At the time the sheriff's office was a partisan one; the Democrats and Republicans regularly changed places in the county positions. Although Aguirre never ran for sheriff again, he continued his law enforcement career as a deputy for many years under subsequent sheriffs. He eventually went on to serve a long and controversial term as the warden of San Quentin State Prison.

When he died on February 25, 1929, the eulogies recalled Aguirre's deeds of valor and made little reference to his San Quentin years. His career spanned a half-century of California history. He served as sheriff of Los Angeles County in the region's last days as a frontier town, and he lived to see the growth of major metropolitan areas replete with airplanes and traffic jams. In both the successes and the failures of his career, he earned respect for his bravery and his dedication to law enforcement, and he remained very much his own man. The one-eyed, knife-toting Californio sheriff who braved the flood of 1888 was remembered with admiration. ■

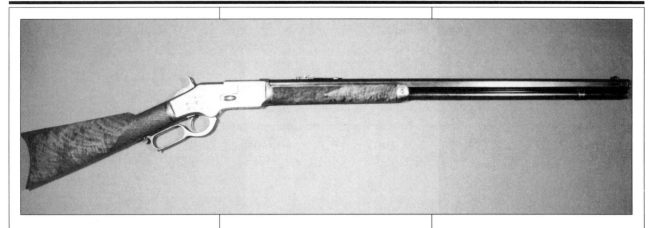

WINCHESTER, THE GUN THAT WON THE WEST

BY THOMAS W. KNOWLES

The name "Winchester" immediately brings to mind the lever-action repeating rifle we've seen in countless Western movies, the gun that won the West for those celluloid cowboys and lawmen. Without Tyler B. Henry, there would have been no Winchester Repeating Arms Company to manufacture it.

After a stint as shop foreman for Robbins & Lawrence beginning in 1849, Henry had the assistance of Horace Smith and Daniel Wesson in improving on Hunt's patent to produce the Jennings Repeating Rifle. Together they took the repeating arms design through further evolutions, including the Smith & Wesson and Volcanic pistols and rifles. These early model repeating firearms used caseless ammunition, a conical bullet with the powder charge sealed in the rear concavity.

Oliver F. Winchester wasn't a designer but a successful clothing manufacturer who had the investment capital Henry needed. When he bought into the gun manufacturing enterprise in 1855, Smith and Wesson dropped out, leaving Henry in sole charge of

development. Winchester and Henry formed the New Haven Arms Company in 1857 and continued to manufacture the Volcanic models.

It was in 1860 that Henry unveiled his two stellar advances in weapons design—the durable .44 caliber lever-action Henry repeating rifle and the practical, self-contained rimfire metallic cartridge it fired. He manufactured only about 13,000 of these revolutionary new rifles between 1860 and 1866, but many of them saw service in the Civil War and in the West after the war. The front-loaded tubular magazine held fifteen rounds, but it was the rifle's major weak point; a sharp blow could bend the tube and render it useless.

Henry improved on his original design, added a side-loading port, a more durable magazine tube, and a wooden forestock to provide a better grip and more protection for the magazine. This Model 1866, the first to bear the Winchester name, became known as "the gun that won the West." The Plains Indians called it "Yellow Boy" because of its brass frame. Between 1866 and 1898 the Winchester Repeating Arms Company manufactured more than 170,000 of the Model 1866 rifles, carbines and muskets. It was a tough, reliable weapon that put more game on the table, defended more homesteads, and rode out more miles in saddle scabbards than

any other. The State of Texas provided each of her Rangers with a Winchester rifle as his primary arm, then deducted the cost of the weapon from his pay.

The most famous Winchester, perhaps because of the motion picture Winchester '73, is the steel-framed Model 1873 repeating rifle. Winchester produced more of them (over 720,000) over a longer period (almost fifty years, 1873–1919) than of any other model. Despite the overall large numbers manufactured, this design produced the "rarest of the rare," supposedly the finest rifles Winchester ever made—the "One of One Thousand" and "One of One Hundred" 1873 models. These are deceptive titles since only 136 of the 1,000 were produced, and only 8 of the 100. They are the most sought-after collector's items from the Old West.

For the rancher and the cowboy, the lawman and the homesteader, the Winchester was much more than a collector's item—it was an important tool in the winning of the West. Winchester's president Oliver F. Winchester best summed up the effect of Tyler B. Henry's brainchild when he wrote: "It has become a household word, and a household necessity on our Western plains and mountains. The pioneer, the hunter and trapper, believe in the Winchester, and its possession is a passion with every Indian."

Above: The "One of One Thousand" Winchester Model 1873, the "gun that won the West" .44–.40 caliber, with adjustable trigger and checkered stock, "1 of 1000" inscribed on barrel behind the sight—the rarest of the rare. (courtesy of Metzger Collection, Texas A&M University Sam Houston Sanders Corps of Cadets Center)

LAWMEN

THEY RODE FOR THE LONE STAR

BY THOMAS W. KNOWLES

THEY COULD RIDE LIKE MEXICANS, TRACK LIKE INDIANS, SHOOT LIKE Tennesseans and fight like the very devil. Their uniform was whatever rough clothes they chose to wear in the field. Until late in the 19th century, they carried no badges of office except for the Colt's revolvers they wore. To the Mexicans, they were El Rinche or Los Diablos Tejanos. To the Comanche, they were death on horseback. To the Yankee military in the Mexican War, they were "those frontier ruffians." To the outlaws, they were the most feared of all lawmen.

They were the Texas Rangers, and in the truest sense, the were the first real Texans.

As the first Americans settled in Texas in the 1820s, they ran into the same barrier that had stopped Spanish expansion—the wild raiders of the plains, the fierce Comanche and Kiowa. To the emigrant Anglo with his eastern sensibilities, the convoluted Mexican code of honor and the relentless Comanche wanderlust were as foreign as something from an alien world. Concepts of morality didn't easily translate across cultures, especially between three peoples that met in competition for the same country. The inevitable conflict of this triangle grew into implacable hatred, often identified in racial terms, and led to a century of bitter border wars.

The Anglo found himself at a disadvantage. The Mexican and the Comanche knew the land and fought from horseback and according to their own rules. When confronted with a mounted enemy, the Anglo dismounted and took a defensive position that favored his single-shot rifle. In the time it took him to reload, a Comanche could fire 12 arrows, from horseback, with deadly accuracy. The Indians would charge to draw fire, and ill befell the Anglos that fired all their loads at once—they'd not have a chance to reload before Comanche arrows and lances finished them. For a generation, this disadvantage confined major Anglo settlement to the eastern woodlands.

But it was in the early settlement period that an evolution of character and nature began. During Stephen F. Austin's time, the settlements formed "ranging companies," irregular mounted militia forces designed to combat Indian raiders and other lawless elements. They provided their own mounts

John Coffee (Jack) Hays, Texas Ranger (courtesy of Library of Congress, Prints and Photo Division, Washington, D.C.)

and equipment, and often rode without receiving the promised government support. Men joined ranging companies for the time they could afford to be away from their farms and families, then others joined to replace them. Most of them, even their captains, were young men who could stand the rigors of the wild lands beyond the frontier.

Under their captains, these Rangers operated far beyond the boundaries of civilization, and so became almost self-contained in their traditions and methods of operation. Over time, they evolved into as deadly and efficient a mobile paramilitary force as has ever existed. They studied their opponents, the Mexicans to the south and the Indians to the West, learned from them and eventually surpassed them in technique and ferocity. By the time of the Texas Revolution and the Republic, the new nation had formally chartered the corps of Texas Rangers as an established force of three companies.

The Ranger was the new Texan, a fighting horseman capable of dealing with the frontier on its own terms. Only one element remained to make him superior—a weapon fitted to his needs. It came to him about 1839 in the form of Samuel Colt's Paterson revolving pistol. Suddenly, the Ranger had

Watercolor painting of Texas Rangers and a Mexican volunteer force attacking a Mexican garrison at Laredo, Texas, 1841. On horseback (left) is John Coffee (Jack) Hays and with him (right) is Captain Antonio Perez. (courtesy of Institute of Texan Cultures, San Antonio, Texas)

an accurate repeating firearm that he could use from horseback to match the Comanche's deadly arrows. The Ranger and the Colt's revolver became almost synonymous, for no one could think of one without the other.

Armed with these new revolvers in 1840, Captain Jack (John Coffee) Hays and his company of 14 Texas Rangers took on a party of 70 Comanches on the Pedernales River. He led his men on a desperate charge straight into the Indians, and though the company suffered some losses, they killed 30 Comanches and drove off the rest. In a later engagement against even greater odds, his company hit the Comanches and were in among them, dealing death at close range before the Indians could react. The Comanches had expected the Rangers to go into the typical defensive position, not to attack with weapons that fired again and again without pause. The Comanche war chief later sent a message that he was moving farther West. He said, "I will never again fight Jack Hays, who has a shot for every finger on the hand."

If the Rangers were the true Texans, Jack Hays was the epitome of the Texas Ranger. His Tennessee family was of the same stock as the Houstons and the Jacksons, frontiersmen, farmers, and Indian fighters. He came to Texas as a surveyor, but by age 23 he was appointed a Captain of Rangers. He was a slender man with a mild, reserved manner, but any who saw his ferocity in battle knew that he was a man without fear. By sheer force of will and personality he moved others to his command. He personally trained many of the great Ranger captains that followed him, men like Ben McCulloch, Samuel H. Walker, and Big Foot Wallace, and he influenced the others.

Flacco, the Lippan chief that served Hays as scout on his forays against the Plains Indians, said it best: "Me and Red Wing not afraid to go to hell together. Captain Jack heap brave; not afraid to go to hell by himself."

Under the Lone Star Flag of the Republic of Texas, Hays fought Indians, and he fought the Mexican Army during the skirmishes that followed the Revolution. He was instrumental in sending Captain Sam Walker to find Sam Colt so he could improve the Ranger's vital tool into the "Walker" Colt revolver. When Texas joined the Union in 1845, he found himself fighting for his new State under the Stars and Stripes instead of the Lone Star.

Some historians insisted that cavalry played no important role during the Mexican War of 1846–48. While it's true that there was no regular Union cavalry involved, the Texas Rangers were. Several companies of Rangers, most of them West Texas horsemen, acted as the Union's mounted scouts and shock troops against the Mexicans. Led by Hays, McCulloch and Gillespie, they time and again pulled the Union Army out of tight spots.

General Zachary Taylor didn't really want the Rangers in on the fight— he considered them to be an unruly, undisciplined mob of dangerous

This is the earliest type of Texas Ranger badge, made in the nineteenth century from a silver Mexican coin. (photo by Tom Knowles, courtesy of Texas Ranger Hall of Fame Museum, Waco, Texas)

wildmen. The eastern press often shared his opinion and presented the Rangers as caricatures in cartoons and drawings—mistakenly so, since many of the Rangers were educated men, doctors, attorneys, surveyors and writers in their civilian careers. Taylor agreed to use the Rangers as a politic way to make the Texans feel involved in the war. He got more than he bargained for. The Rangers, men born to excel at frontier combat, lived off the land, literally "rustled" up mules and supplies for the Army, terrorized and defeated the Mexicans at every turn, and generally outshined Taylor's troops.

As General Ethan Allen Hitchcock described them from the Union military's perspective: "Hay's Rangers have come, their appearance never to be forgotten. Not any sort of uniforms, but well mounted and doubly well armed: each man has one or two Colt's revolvers besides ordinary pistols, a sword, and every man a rifle…" Hitchcock added, "The Mexicans are terribly afraid of them."

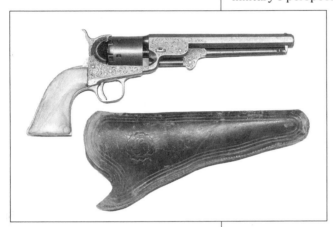

Samuel Colt presented this ivory-handled Colt 1851 Navy .36 caliber revolver (with holster) to Texas Ranger Captain Jack Hays; the inscription reads, "To John C. Hays with the compliments of Col. Colt." Hays' profile is engraved into the scroll-work pattern on the left-hand barrel lug. (photo by Tom Knowles courtesy of Texas Ranger Hall of Fame Museum, Waco, Texas)

And indeed the Mexicans had reason to fear and hate the Rangers, even and perhaps most especially those few "Devil Texans" of Hispanic heritage. Old hatreds and feuds that had festered on the border exploded during the war. The Rangers had evolved their own code of honor, which was to never brook insult or injury to one of their own. They always exacted a price for any slight, and they never gave a man a second chance. It was brutal and cruel by eastern mores, but it was the way things were done on the frontier.

Every time the Texas Rangers withdrew, the Union Army suffered. Ranger Captain Sam Walker died leading his men and the Union troops of Lane's Brigade in the taking of Huamantla in 1847. Even so, Taylor, hampered by his eastern sensibilities, once demanded that he be sent no more Rangers. "The mounted men from Texas," he wrote, "have scarcely made one expedition without unwarrantably killing a Mexican." His men didn't always agree; many of were sorry to see the Rangers leave a camp, and all of them wanted to get their hands on one of those Colt's revolvers.

When Hays and his company took over for the fallen Walker, they showed no mercy in pursuing and destroying the Mexican guerrillas and rancheros. They extracted an eye for an eye, and sometimes more; they burned much of Matamoros. When a Ranger named Adam Allsens was found murdered in one of occupied Mexico City's red-light districts, Robert's Ranger Company rode in that very night. The next morning, more than eighty bodies were collected from that street, where they'd been shot down and left.

When General Winfield Scott called in Jack Hays to protest, the mild-mannered Ranger Captain simply replied that no one could "impose" on the Rangers. He faced the General down, and in so doing he once again set the standard for the Ranger legend.

In later years, as the Rangers turned their attention to pursuing the last free Indian raiders, then to running down outlaws and badmen, they never backed down and they never gave up. Hays and the Rangers that followed him defined the image of the Westerner in the American mind—the tough, deadly, competent horseman who, when armed with his Colt's revolving pistols and his unshakable resolve, feared no man on Earth. ∎

JUDGES AND EXECUTIONERS

CHARLES ISAAC PARKER, THE HANGING JUDGE OF FORT SMITH

BY BILL CRIDER

AFTER THE CIVIL WAR, INDIAN TERRITORY (PRESENT-DAY OKLAHOMA) was known as a "Robber's Roost," a haven for assorted bandits, cutthroats, killers, and ne'er-do-wells who gloried in its freedom from the restraints of law. In this area bounded by Texas, Kansas, and Arkansas, there were only Indian towns, Indian police, and Indian courts. The Indian courts had no jurisdiction over white men, or even over an Indian who served as a white man's accomplice. Instead, jurisdiction belonged to the Court of the United States for the Western District of Arkansas, presided over in the early 1870s by an incompetent, corrupt weakling with a penchant for accepting bribes, in whose brief tenure more than one hundred murders occurred in the Territory.

In dealing with this outrageous situation, President Ulysses S. Grant, a man not generally known for his good judgment or his wise appointments, for once came up with exactly the right man for the job. He named Charles Isaac (Ike) Parker to the federal bench at Fort Smith, on the very border of Arkansas and Indian Territory. Parker, only thirty-six years old at the time, had already enjoyed a distinguished career as a prosecuting attorney, a circuit court judge, and a Congressman. In his private life, he was a cheerful, outgoing man, loved by children and devoted to civic duties such as ser-

Judge Isaac C. Parker

vice on the school board. In his public life, he proved to be more than equal to the difficult task assigned to him.

In his twenty-one years at Fort Smith, Parker tried more than 13,000 people in his court, often working six days a week from eight o'clock in the morning until nightfall. Of these 13,000 people, nearly three-fourths were convicted, and of this group 344 were convicted of crimes that carried the death penalty. Of these unfortunate 344, Parker sentenced 172 to hang; 88 eventually died on the gallows.

Parker held court in the first floor of a two-story brick building that had once served as a barracks and was located inside the military post. In the basement below the courtroom was the filthy, stinking, rat-infested jail, which soon became so crowded that he had a new jail constructed. Thanks to Parker's zealous enforcement policies, the new jail was quickly filled to overflowing as well.

To keep the jails full, Parker employed a small army of officers to wander around in the more than seventy thousand acres of Indian Territory and to locate, arrest, and bring in the criminals they found. More than two hundred deputy marshals worked for Parker, and it was dangerous work indeed. Over the years, sixty-five of the deputies died in the performance of their

GEORGE MALEDON: HE OPENED THE GATES OF HELL

BY BILL CRIDER

The Court of the United States for the Western District of Arkansas, otherwise known as Indian Territory, in the latter two-thirds of the nineteenth century required an exceptionally efficient hangman, thanks to the hard-nosed sentencing practices of Judge Charles Isaac Parker. In his twenty-one-year career on the federal bench at Fort Smith, Judge Parker, widely known as the Hanging Judge, sentenced 172 men to death by hanging. The executions were carried out in 88 of those cases, most of them performed by George Maledon, a Bavarian immi-

grant. It was said that Maledon never had a customer complain.

Maledon, who stood just five feet five inches tall, was not a man to trifle with. In addition to his unquestioned artistry on the scaffold, he also shot and killed two prisoners who attempted to escape from the Fort Smith jail. He was a man who took pride in a job well done, and he preferred to use well-oiled, hand woven Kentucky hemp ropes. He always took care to place the traditional hangman's knot behind the doomed man's left ear, since he believed this location to be the most effective as well as the most merciful. When Maledon dropped the trap, referred to by certain hardcases as "the gates of Hell," the careful placement of the knot caused the hanged man's neck to snap at the instant his fall ended, thus sparing the victim a slow and painful death by strangulation.

The scaffold itself was designed with efficiency and economy in mind. On two occasions Maledon pulled the trap with six condemned men standing on the scaffold; at times he dealt with groups of five, four, or three. Deuces were commonplace. Maledon, a thrifty

man, used the same ropes again and again.

Photographs of Maledon show us a dour man with a receding hairline and an unprepossessing beard, standing rigidly and staring glumly at the camera. But he did have a sense of humor, of sorts. He once told a woman that he was never troubled by the spirits of the men he'd hanged, since the ghosts didn't "hang around" the old gibbet. He could also be sentimental in his own peculiar way. When the man responsible for killing his daughter was arrested, Maledon asked for the honor of hanging him personally. When the city of Fort Smith decided to destroy the gallows and put the memory of its gruesome business firmly out of mind, Maledon begged to be allowed to keep it. The city refused, and though the greater part of the gallows was burned, Maledon was able to retrieve several of his cherished ropes, pieces of the scaffold, and parts of its mechanism. He took his prizes on tour and charged the curious public admission to view the last, grim relics from the "gates of Hell."

duties. They worked on a fee-based system that paid them ten cents a mile (one way) for serving papers or bringing in a prisoner. For serving a warrant, they were paid two dollars and fifty cents. Guardsmen who accompanied the deputies were paid a flat rate of two dollars a day. Deputies were allowed to supplement their incomes by collecting fines for small offenses, and some, little better than the criminals they were sent to apprehend, exploited this source of funds.

This habit was not the sort to create a climate of good will among even the law-abiding citizens of the territory, such as there were. Many of Parker's deputies traveled in groups of four or five for their own protection and took with them a wagon that served as shelter, arsenal, and portable jail for wounded prisoners. Healthy prisoners were forced to walk. The deputies liked to keep the prisoners healthy and rarely shot to kill unless absolutely necessary. This was not the result of kindness; deputies were paid an arrest fee for living prisoners but nothing for a corpse—unless the victim happened to be wanted "Dead or Alive." Quite often the deputies would even force the witnesses to a crime to travel to Fort Smith with them to await the trial, knowing that it would be difficult, if not impossible, to locate them later. This was another practice not calculated to endear the deputies to the respectable residents of Indian Territory.

Parker earned his reputation as the Hanging Judge almost as soon as he began his work in Fort Smith. Had the eighty-eight hangings for which he was responsible been spread out over his entire judgeship, they might not have caused too much comment. After all, the average was only a little more than four a year. Unfortunately, the hangings sometimes came in batches. In the first session of Parker's court, ninety-one defendants appeared before him. Fifteen were convicted of murder, and eight were sentenced to hang. One of the eight had his sentence commuted to life imprisonment (and was later pardoned), and another was shot in his attempt to escape. The remaining six went to the gallows together.

And what a gallows it was! At twenty feet long, with a crossbeam of twelve-inch timber, it was roomy and strong enough to accommodate twelve men, though six were the most ever to swing there at one time. Newspapers estimated that as many as 5,000 people crowded the streets of Fort Smith (population 2,500), arriving in wagonloads from forty and fifty miles away to view the grisly spectacle. At precisely 9:30 in the morning the six men were marched onto the scaffold. After a brief ceremony, which included the singing of hymns and the last words of the condemned men, the trap was sprung by George Maledon, Parker's small but efficient hangman, and the six black-hooded figures dropped to their deaths.

From this time on, Parker was branded as a heartless hardliner despite the fact that he had wept in open court as he pronounced his first death sentence. It is certainly true that Parker had little sympathy with theories of "rehabilitation," that he believed in quick and irrevocable punishment as the surest deterrent to crime, and that he was often heard to remark that the criminal, when born, had doubtless come into the world with the mark of Cain stamped on his brow. And it is true that Parker came to resent the appeals process. For the first fourteen years of his judgeship, Parker enjoyed the remarkable position of being the final arbiter of justice. From his court there was no appeal, not even to the Supreme Court of the United States. In effect, Parker's word *was* the law.

Later, as the federal government continued to shrink the area of his jurisdiction and opened his court to the appeals process, Parker spoke out bitterly, especially on one occasion when a jail guard was murdered by a notorious outlaw who had remained in jail long after his established execution date thanks to an appeal. In his last seven years on the bench, Parker saw fifty of his seventy-eight death sentences reversed on appeal. Justice was becoming modern and civilized; Parker was a remnant of the dying frontier, an embarrassment to the forward-looking legal establishment.

A DEATH SENTENCE

BY R.C. HOUSE

For sheer effulgence of words and vitriol, listen to this sentence in an Old West murder case. It is attributed both to Judge Roy Bean, the infamous "Law West of the Pecos," and to the judge who in 1881 heard the case of the United States vs. Gonzales, U.S. District Court, New Mexico (Taos):

"Jose Manuel Miguel Xavier Gonzales, in a few short weeks, it will be spring. The snows of winter will flee away. The ice will vanish, and the air will become soft and balmy. In short, Jose Manuel Miguel Xavier Gonzales, the annual miracle of the year's awakening will come to pass, but you won't be here.

"The rivulet will run its purring course to the sea, the timid desert flowers will put forth their tender shoots, the glorious valleys of this Imperial Domain will blossom as the rose, still you won't be here to see.

"From every tree-top some wild woods songster will carol his mating song, butterflies will sport in the sunshine, the busy bee will hum happily as it pursues its accustomed vocation, the gentle breeze will tease the tassels of the wild grasses, and all nature, Jose Manuel Miguel Xavier Gonzales, will be glad but you. You won't be here to enjoy it because I command the sheriff or some other officers of the county to lead you out to some remote spot, swing you by the neck from a nodding bough of some sturdy oak, and let you hang until you are dead.

"And then, Jose Manuel Miguel Xavier Gonzales, I further command that such officer or officers retire quickly from your dangling corpse, that the vultures may descend from the heavens upon your filthy body until nothing shall remain but bare, blazoned bones of a cold-blooded, copper-colored, blood-thirsty, throat-cutting, chili-eating, sheep-herding, murdering son of a bitch!"

A victim of diabetes and exhaustion, Charles Isaac Parker went home to bed after twenty-one years as a federal judge, just two months before Indian Territory was to be removed entirely from his jurisdiction. He remained ill at home on September 1, 1896, when the Court of the United States for the Western District of Arkansas was officially adjourned forever.

Two months later, Ike Parker died. ■

JUDGES AND EXECUTIONERS

HANGINGS, GRAVEYARDS AND BURYINGS

BY LEE SOMERVILLE

IN THE DAYS OF HANGING JUDGE CHARLES ISAAC PARKER, DEPUTY U.S. Marshal D. E. Booker trailed three outlaws across the Red River from Texas into Indian Territory and past what is now Idabel, Oklahoma. Finding that the men had left their horses and were riding in a surrey with women friends, Booker cut through the woods and waited beside the narrow dirt road.

Booker didn't do it the way fictional lawmen do it in the movies or on television. He got behind a solid tree and waited with his rifle ready. As the surrey neared, he saw he had a problem. A boy drove the team, and the three men were snuggled up dangerously close to their ladies.

Booker shouted to get their attention. The men stood up, clawing for their guns and looking wildly about. All they could see was woods. Booker fired three shots, then commandeered the surrey, drove it to Clarksville, Texas, and left the bodies at the courthouse. He'd not missed—the women and the boy were unhurt; the three outlaws were dead.

The good people of Clarksville had a holiday, a couple of hours to view the bodies, then a festive funeral. No one there knew the outlaws, but preachers and would-be preachers orated about Sin and Hell Fire and Judgment and Mercy. People pitched in and dug three graves outside the cemetery. You didn't bury outlaws and sinners and lost souls inside the cemetery with decent people, not in God-fearing Red River County. You didn't want them to be lonesome throughout eternity, though, so you buried them

A cowboy funeral, 1892 (courtesy of Kansas State Historical Society, Topeka, Kansas)

just outside the graveyard. That was mercy.

The good people added compassion to mercy and buried the outlaws with their feet to the west and their heads to the east. In most Southern and Southwestern graveyards, especially in Texas, bodies are buried with heads to the west and feet to the east so that redeemed souls may rise facing the Resurrection, "which cometh from the East on Judgment Morn." In the 1800s, most outlaws in Texas were buried in reverse so that when Gabriel blew his horn and Resurrection set in, their doomed souls would rise facing away from Judgment—this way they could get a running start from the Devil. Even in the early 1900s, the last man to be publicly hanged in Delta County, Texas, was taken to Klondike Graveyard and buried thus.

Many cowboys, ranchers, and travelers were buried in lonely graves on the lone prairie, buried without markers and buried hastily, since bodies were hard to tote and they didn't keep, especially in Texas in July. Others, especially those who died in the presence of friends and kin, were buried in more sociable places. When I lived in West Texas more than sixty years ago, I saw crude graves now and then alongside dirt roads we traveled. Sometimes my father would stop our Model-T Ford, get out, take his hat off, and read crude inscriptions scratched on rock markers or on wood stakes. "Somebody traveling through didn't make it, years ago," he would say. "Somebody buried beside the trail where folks will see the grave and the poor soul won't feel lonesome."

In the 1990s we have good roads in West Texas, and I whiz along at 55 or better. I don't see any trailside graves except those in cemeteries. Apparently, most of the wooden stakes and crude crosses have decayed or burned, and stones have been scattered.

My own great-grandparents lost a child on the way to Texas in the 1840s. They were fortunate enough to be near a settled area where the child could be buried properly. I've also heard stories like this: "My family was going lots farther West, but Grandpa's little sister died on the trail, and Great-Grandma said, 'This is it. My child is buried here, and here we will build our home and stay.' So they bought land and built a house close to the little grave, and here my family still lives."

GRAVEYARDS AND ISOLATED GRAVES WERE HONORED PLACES IN THE Old West. No matter how depraved a man might be he didn't vandalize a grave. When a person died in a settled area, neighbors came to dig the grave and help make the wood coffin, to do what they could.

Many families, especially those with a great deal of land, had their own family burying places near the house, sometimes in the yard. One family I know selected a spot on the hillside because the child had loved to play there before his death. A tree he loved, then about four inches in diameter, is now more than two feet thick, and the family graveyard has become a community "burying place," well-kept and well-fenced.

Some mothers who had children buried nearby would sit under shade trees on summer evenings among family graves, comforting and receiving comfort from the dead. It was custom.

It was custom also, in the 1800s, to "lay out" the dead at home if no undertaker was readily available. A family member combed the hair and tried to make the deceased more presentable. If an undertaker took care of the body in town, it was brought back to the home parlor or the best room. Neighbors and family would sit up with the body all night long—this was a social occasion, and it's still done in funeral parlors in many small towns in Texas. Neighbors come and go, but several people will remain even in the small hours before dawn. Leaving the body alone would be disrespectful.

In East Texas and Central Texas the finest, smoothest bit of dirt was placed on top of the grave and gently mounded. In West Texas, where winds blew hard, stones were placed atop graves to protect them from wind and coyotes.

Now and then the normal burying procedures would vary. One unusually large, rough old man who lived near Daingerfield, Texas, ordered his family to bury him standing up, a shotgun in each hand, so he could "go through hell a-popping." My mother, who knew the family, used to mention this in a horrified whisper. I think the old man had a great sense of humor and wanted to get the last laugh on his sanctimonious neighbors.

In Clarksville, Texas, the Hanging Tree still stands inside the Old Baptist or Clark Cemetery. The tree, an oak more than 260 years old, was just outside the cemetery in the heyday of the vigilantes of the 1830s and 1840s. It was only when the growing cemetery enclosed the tree that people stopped using it to hang thieves. That same cemetery contains the graves of a father and son who served in two revolutions. Benjamin Clark, the father, was a sergeant in the North Carolina Militia of the American Revolution. Captain Jim Clark, his son, served as a lieutenant in the Texas Revolution.

The fictional Western generally ignores the period after 1890, but some frontier violence continued even into the 1920s. When three men who lived near the Red River went on a drinking and gambling spree, one shot his buddy in an argument over a turn of the cards. The two survivors decided to throw their murdered companion's body in the river, but they first put a silver dollar in his pocket.

The body got tangled up in a floating tree and washed ashore on the Oklahoma side. The two men were tried for murder and got five years in the Texas penitentiary. The members of the jury laughed about the silver dollar—but perhaps that's why they passed so light a sentence.

Putting a coin with the corpse dates back to an ancient Greek belief that one must have a coin to pay Charon, the boatman on the River Styx, or else wander the shore, unable to gain entrance to hell. The word "cemetery" comes from the Greek *koimeterion*, sleeping place, and most of our funeral customs come from the ancient Romans—dressing in black, walking in procession, raising a mound on the grave (called *tumulus*, whence *tomb*), bringing flowers, and so on.

So if some people in rural sections of Texas and Oklahoma and other parts of the West still put a coin in the casket with a loved one or a friend, who's to say they are peculiar? After all, you've gotta have something to give to the ferryman. ■

OH, BURY ME NOT ON THE LONE PRAIRIE

FROM A POEM BY EDWIN H. CHAPIN, ORIGINALLY USED AS AN ELEGY FOR BURIALS AT SEA, ADAPTED FOR COWBOY BURIALS ON THE "SEA OF GRASS"

"Oh, bury me not on the Lone Prairie;"
These words came sad and mournfully
From the palid lips of a youth who lay
On his dying bed at the close of day.

"It matters not, so I've been told
Where the body lies when the heart grows cold,
But grant, oh grant, this wish to me;
Bury me not on the Lone Prairie."

"Bury me not on the Lone Prairie.
Where coyotes howl and the wind blows free,
In a narrow grave, six by three;
Oh, Bury me not on the Lone Prairie."

"Oh, Bury me not..." His voice failed there;
We took no heed of his dying prayer.
In a narrow grave, six by three,
We buried him there on the Lone Prairie.

And the Cowboys now, as they roam the Plains,
They mark the spot where his bones were lain;
Fling a handful of roses o'er his grave
With a prayer to God his soul to save.

VII. LIFE AND DEATH IN THE WILD WEST

TINHORNS, SHARPERS AND KINGS

BY BARBARA BEMAN-PUECHNER

GAMBLING WAS THE FEVER THAT MADE—AND BROKE—MORE MEN of the West than gold strikes or cattle booms. It scalped some worse than Indians on the warpath and made others wealthy beyond their wildest dreams. A man who didn't gamble was about as suspect as a man who didn't drink or tote a gun. Millions were won and lost on a throw of the dice, the luck of the draw, the spin of a keno ball, or the turn of a card. A sharper's ace or an ace in the hole—up the sleeve—could also get a man killed.

A man could choose his poison—from chuck-a-luck, a game of the lowly tinhorn grifter which relied on sleight of hand, dice, and a tin cup, to the aristocratic king of games, faro, which made "bucking the tiger" a common phrase and drew dealers whose name are legend. There was the wheel of fortune, and that sleeper, draw poker, that finally caught on in the 1870s, Spanish monte, hop-and-toss, blackjack, and over-and-under-seven. In the unlikely event that a man couldn't find a game of faro, keno, two-card monte, *vingt-et-un*, poker, or craps to bet his money on, some clever fellow would be sure to come up with another kind of wager. Some of them were downright inventive. If there weren't any fast racers, fast draws, or flying fists to bet on, a wager on a camel and a horse, a bicycle and a horse, or even a louse and an ant would do.

Some men—the professionals—made gambling into a high art. Wyatt Earp and Bat Masterson were sporting men first, though they are better remembered for their sidelines as lawmen. Doc Holliday, the occasional den-

Long Branch Saloon, Dodge City, Kansas (courtesy of Kansas State Historical Society, Topeka, Kansas)

PREVIOUS PAGE:
Bucking the Tiger, *Frank Leslie's Illustrated Newspaper*

tist and mean-tempered gun notcher, never made any claims to being a lawman, although he was a friend of Earp's. They traveled the same circuit, belonged to the same brotherhood of professional gamblers.

Brotherhood—some of them took it seriously. One of Bat Masterson's partners in a Denver venture called the Palace Theater was a gambling man named Bill Cates. Cates made most of his money—reckoned to be around the quarter-million mark at the time of his death—from the Cates Club, which he owned along with Ed Chase. When he cashed in his final chips, Cates asked Chase to give all his money to down-and-out gamblers and saloon bums. "There are plenty of folks to help women and children," he said, "but nobody cares for broken-down old men." Chase continued his partner's philanthropic work long after Cates's money ran out.

Other gamblers were the scum and dregs of society. They'd cheat their fellow man out of every penny or every speck of gold dust he had. "You'd cheat your own mother" was more than an idle expression. As the uneasy hand of civilization closed down on the East, gambling men followed the path of prosperity from the booming cattle towns to the suddenly rich mining camps in the West.

The circuit ran from San Antonio and Fort Griffin up through Abilene, Newton, Hays City, and Dodge City, onward to Tombstone, Virginia City, Deadwood, Leadville, Creede, and Cripple Creek, to as far north as Nome. Some gamblers hit every hot spot before moving on. The names of the saloons and gambling halls read like a Western litany—the Alamo, Alhambra, Arcade, Bee Hive, Bella Union, Bonanza, Bull's Head, and Boozer Brown's… the Coliseum, Combination, Criterion, and Crystal…the El Dorado, Esmerelda, and Elephant Corral…the Northern, Occidental, Oriental, Old Fruit, and Pearl…and the prosaic No. 10 Saloon, one of Deadwood's finest.

From Applejack to Zeke's, honky-tonks were often as fanciful as their names. Shlotz's Palm Garden was indeed the gambler's mecca in San Antonio. Each honky-tonk tried to outdo the other, with wall-to-wall gaming tables greening the interiors, Renaissance-like nudes on the walls, stringed orchestras playing day and night, shifts of bartenders, dealers, lookouts, and casekeepers. From the Mississippi River to the Pacific shore, gambling was a Western pastime and passion, a way of life. ■

BUCKING THE TIGER

BY BARBARA BEMAN-PUECHNER

Splashed across lurid posters on almost every saloon and tavern wall was the invitation, BUCK THE TIGER! The customers understood the challenge presented by the ferocious Bengali tiger the posters pictured—it was the call to play faro, the most popular betting game of the era.

From "soda" to "hock"—the first card to the last—it was a fast-paced game that suited the temperament of the times. The layout was simple, thirteen squares with numbers and face cards represented by spades, although suits were irrelevant. A player placed his bet on the board to see how it stacked up against the cards drawn from the dealing box.

The odds of finding an honest dealer were probably as bad as the odds of finding an honest dealing box—and those were roughly one in six. In the 1870s, only three out of nineteen dealing boxes manufactured by Will & Finck were straight.

Different dealers played—and cheated—differently.

A player bet on how the cards would emerge from the dealing box, with the first card dealt in every two-card turn, the one laid over the soda card, losing. "Coppering the bet" meant betting on a card to lose the turn. There was no set system by which one could beat the house, but when a player was hot on a game, he could almost feel the cards calling to him before he laid down his money.

The dealer might slide the soda card out and lay it face up. It wouldn't count for the bet. The next card would be placed face up over it, perhaps a deuce revealing another deuce face up in the dealing box. A pair. Impasse. Pairs meant the house got half the bet. A crooked dealer stacked the deck with pairs, not that it was the only way to cheat at the game.

The game moved quickly, twenty-five turns to a deck.

As the hand was dealt, the dealer used a device similar to an abacus to keep track of the cards that had been played. It held four small, mobile beads on a spindle for every number and face card. In larger establishments, where as many as twenty faro players might gather around one layout, a second dealer might be employed as the casekeeper. Some places also hired lookouts to keep an eye on the dealers. There was big money in faro.

When the deck was down to three cards, patrons had a chance to "call the turn" for a payoff of four to one. That meant a player would have to name the order in which the last three cards would be drawn, rather like a parlay. No doubt, many players went into hock calling the hock.

Faro made a lot of wily dealers and saloon keepers rich, but it broke others. Some gamblers were just too fond of their own game. There was a sporting man named Goldie Golden who operated out of Nome, Alaska. He lost everything he owned bucking the tiger in his own saloon. One night when it was too cold to go down the street for recreation, he started playing in his own gaming parlor.

Seventy-two hours and $180,000 later he hurled the faro box to the floor. "What the hell kind of faro bank is this," he said, "when not even the owner of the joint can make money bucking it?"

LIFE AND DEATH IN THE WILD WEST: A NECROLOGY

BY SCOTT A. CUPP

The acts of living and dying in the Old West were far from simple. The Western era was filled with more action and adventure than Hollywood could ever hope to depict. The West has captured the American imagination and taken roots there. We are fascinated by the way the Westerners lived—and by the ways they died.

The variety of rough characters who inhabited the Western territories found death in an equally varied manner. For some the release was due to natural causes, but many others met their fates at the hands of lawmen or outlaws, and the Indians played their part. There was murder and suicide. Some may not have died as was reported; sightings of many Old West characters continued until fairly modern times.

And the stories that accompanied their deaths are truly bizarre. Take, for example, Mike Fink, who was killed in 1823 following a boasting match in which he stated that he could shoot a cup off a man's head. Fink fired and missed, killing the man. His friends avenged themselves by killing Fink. And there was William Quantrill, whose mother had his bones disinterred for removal to a family plot. She was later found selling the bones as souvenirs.

Here we have in one place a brief description, listed in chronological order, of the deaths of 44 colorful folks who helped to make the Wild West the spectacle that it was.

NAME	DATE OF DEATH	PLACE	CAUSE	AGE
Jedediah Strong Smith	May 7, 1831	Cimarron River	Comanche arrow	32
Henry Plummer	Jan. 10, 1864	Bannock, Montana	Killed by vigilantes	26
William Quantrill	June 6, 1865	Louisville, Kentucky	Shot in a raid led by Capt. E. Terrill	27
Kit Carson	May 23, 1868	Ft. Lyon, Colorado	Illness	58
Lt. Col. George Armstrong Custer	June 5, 1876	Little Big Horn River, Dakota Black Hills	Killed in battle with Sioux and Cheyenne	36
James Butler "Wild Bill" Hickok	Aug. 2, 1876	Deadwood, Dakota Territory	Shot in the back by Jack McCall	39
Sam Bass	July 21, 1878	Round Rock, Texas	Shot by Texas Rangers during bank holdup	27
Wild Bill Longley	Oct. 11, 1878	Giddings, Texas	Hanged	26
Billy the Kid, a.k.a. Henry McCarty, a.k.a. William Bonney	July 14, 1881	Ft. Sumner, New Mexico	Shot by Pat Garrett	21
Jim Bridger	July 17, 1881	Kansas City, Missouri	Natural causes	77
William Clanton	Oct. 26, 1881	Tombstone, Arizona	Shot by the Earps in the O.K. Corral fight	19
Morgan Earp	March 18, 1882	Tombstone, Arizona	Murdered	30
Jesse James	April 3, 1882	St. Joseph, Missouri	Shot from behind by Robert Ford	34
Johnny Ringo	July 14, 1882	Turkey Creek Canyon, Arizona	Possible suicide	?
Dallas Stoudenmire	Sept. 18, 1882	El Paso, Texas	Killed by Doc Manning	36
Ben Thompson	March 11, 1884	San Antonio, Texas	Ambushed and murdered in a theater	41
King Fisher	March 11, 1884	San Antonio, Texas	Ambushed and murdered in a theater	29

NAME	DATE OF DEATH	PLACE	CAUSE	AGE
John Wesley Hardin	Aug. 19, 1885	El Paso, Texas	Shot from behind by John Selman	42
Longhaired Jim Courtwright	Feb. 8, 1887	El Paso, Texas	Killed by Luke Short	38
Clay Allison	July 1, 1887	Pecos, Texas	Fractured skull in wagon accident	47
John H. "Doc" Holliday	Nov. 8, 1887	Glenwood Springs, Colorado	Tuberculosis	35
Belle Starr	Feb. 3, 1889	Younger's Bend, Colorado	Ambushed and murdered	42
John C. Frémont	July 13, 1890	New York, New York	Peritonitis	77
Bob Dalton	Oct. 5, 1892	Coffeyville, Kansas	Killed during bank holdup	24
Gratton Dalton	Oct. 5, 1892	Coffeyville, Kansas	Killed during bank holdup	27
Luke Short	Sept. 8, 1893	Geuda Springs, Kansas	Dropsy	49
Bill Dalton	Sept. 25, 1895	Ardmore, Oklahoma	Killed by posse	29
John Selman	April 6, 1896	El Paso, Texas	Killed in a fight	56
Bill Doolin	Aug. 25, 1896	Lawton, Oklahoma	Killed by posse	38
Black Jack Ketchum	April 25, 1901	Clayton, New Mexico	Hanged	35
Harry Tracy	Aug. 5, 1902	Davenport, Washington	Suicide in the face of capture	27
Tom Horn	Nov. 20, 1903	Cheyenne, Wyoming	Hanged for murder	42
Harvey Logan, a.k.a. Kid Curry	June 8, 1904	Glenwood Springs, Colorado	Killed during a train robbery	39
Pat Garrett	Jan. 29, 1908	Las Cruces, New Mexico	Shot by Wayne Brazel	57
Harry Longbaugh, a.k.a. the Sundance Kid	1911?	San Vicente, Bolivia	Reportedly killed in a shootout with Bolivian troops	42?
Bill Miner	Sept. 2, 1913	Milledgeville, Georgia	Died in his sleep	66
Cole Younger	March 21, 1916	Lee's Summit, Missouri	Natural causes	72
Henry Starr	Feb. 22, 1921	Harrison, Arkansas	Killed in a holdup	47
William "Bat" Masterson	Oct. 25, 1921	New York, New York	Heart attack while at his desk	67
Texas John Slaughter	Feb. 15, 1922	Douglas, Arizona	Died in his sleep	80
Bill Tilghman	Nov. 1, 1924	Cromwell, Oklahoma	Shot by a drunken prohibition officer	70
Wyatt Earp	Jan. 13, 1929	Los Angeles, California	Natural causes	80
Emmett Dalton	July 13, 1937	Los Angeles, California	Natural causes	56
George LeRoy Parker, a.k.a. Butch Cassidy	July 20, 1937	Spangle, Washington	Cancer	71

Samuel Colt's Great Equalizer

BY THOMAS W. KNOWLES

"GOD MADE SOME MEN BIG AND SOME MEN SMALL, BUT COLONEL Sam Colt made them equal all" was a common saying in Texas, and with good reason. Colt's inventions, the first practical revolving firearms, were intimately connected with Texas and the rugged individuals who settled the Wild West. Even as a new breed of men came of age and readied themselves to conquer the frontier, so did Colt's vision come to fruition to provide them with the vital tool. The revolver was so important to the winning of the West that it has remained a symbol of power and individuality more than a century later.

It all started with the quick mind and clever hands of a young boy back East. Born in July 1814, in Hartford, Connecticut, Samuel Colt was the fourth of five children born to Sarah and Christopher Colt. When Sarah died in 1821, the Colt children were sent to live with various relatives and farmers in the area; Samuel went to a farm in Glastonbury, Connecticut.

America's active participation in the industrial revolution sparked young Sam's interest in machinery, and he began to tinker. Legend has it that in his early years he dismantled his father's old horse pistol and reassembled it. For three years he worked in a silk mill, watching newly designed machines do what was once strictly a housewife's job. He paid particular attention to the division of labor as each person performed a specific task. He also began experimenting with gunpowder with the factory's chemical specialist. In 1828 or 1829 he enrolled at Amherst Academy but soon got into trouble for discharging his horse pistol.

Colt's first experiment of note as an inventor came about on the Fourth of July 1829 when he passed out a handbill advertising that he'd "blow a raft sky-high on Ware Pond." His idea was to illustrate the effectiveness of submarine explosives—he'd used tarred cloth to wrap the wire carrying the electrical charge to the explosives. The raft didn't blow quite "sky-high," but the explosion sent a geyser of mud and water into the air, covering nearly all of the spectators who'd gathered to see the experiment. A young engineer named Elisha Root saved Colt from the angry crowd.

On August 2, 1830, young Sam set sail on the *Corvo* as a crew member, intent on becoming a navigator and ship's officer. During that voyage Colt

AN ORDER FROM BAT MASTERSON TO "COLT'S MFG. CO." FOR A SINGLE-ACTION ARMY REVOLVER, CIRCA 1885:

"You will please Make and send here to my address C.O.D. one of your short 45 Calibre pistols Nickel plated. Make it very Easy on trigger and Make front sight rather high and thick. Send as soon as possible."

whittled away at a wooden model of a pistol with a revolving, six-cylindered chamber. Legend has it that he was inspired by watching the captain steering his course with the ship's wheel, but the revolving cylinder had been used before, notably for the Collier flintlock revolver patented in England in 1813.

What made Colt's model unique was that he transposed the ship's pawl and ratchet to his revolving pistol, each serving the same purpose on a miniature scale—the pawl rotated the cylinder while the hammer was being cocked, and the ratchet held the cylinder in place while the weapon fired. On returning to Ware, Colt had full-scale models of both a pistol and rifle crafted. With his newly designed weapons and a letter of introduction from his father, he approached the U.S. commissioner of patents in Washington. But the commissioner thought the guns too crude and recommended that they be locked up secretly in the Patent Office until their design was perfected.

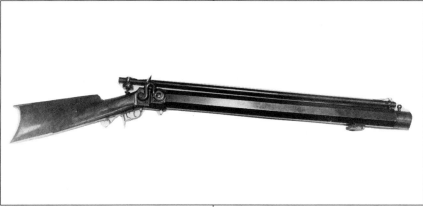

Colt spent the next two years going through a succession of three different gunsmiths as he attempted to improve his designs. To pay for gunsmithing fees, he toured the Eastern seaboard with a "laughing gas" show he'd put together. The show was popular with the public and profitable for Colt. Finally, in the summer of 1835, Colt applied for a patent on his much-improved pistol design. Confident that he would receive the American patent, he set sail for England and France, where he applied for and received patents. On February 25, 1836, Colt received the American patent on his revolver, and shortly afterward he opened the Patent Arms Manufacturing Company at Paterson, New Jersey.

This Colt's percussion .50 caliber single-shot sniper's rifle with telescopic sight, 28" barrel, and false muzzle is the only known complete version in existence. (courtesy of Metzger Collection, Texas A&M University Sam Houston Sanders Corps of Cadets Center)

Colt's first model, a five-shot .34 caliber revolver with a trigger that disappeared when not in use, he appropriately named the Paterson. It didn't sell well, and the U.S. Army Ordnance Department turned it down, considering it too fragile for military use. However, in 1837 Colt received an order for one hundred of his repeating rifles to be used by the Army in Florida fighting the Seminole War. By this time samples of Colt's work had filtered into Texas, which had just won its independence from Mexico. The Paterson soon became the favorite weapon of the Texas Rangers and the Texas Navy.

Controversy still exists over whether Captain Samuel H. Walker of the Texas Rangers actually did visit Colt in New York as early as 1839 to suggest improvements on the Paterson, but Colt filed a patent on August 29, 1839, for a loading lever for the newly modified Paterson. He issued a weapon in 1840 officially called the Model 5 but known on the frontier as either the Texas Paterson or the Walker Paterson.

While the frontiersman was enthralled with this new weapon, manufacturers and industrialists in the East were more interested in how it was produced. Colt's Paterson factory was the first to mass-produce interchangeable parts using an assembly-line procedure in which trained personnel made the final inspection of the product. Manufacturers and inventors were heartened by Colt's accomplishments, for his system could be used to manufacture other products as well. Yet Colt's line of firearms seemed

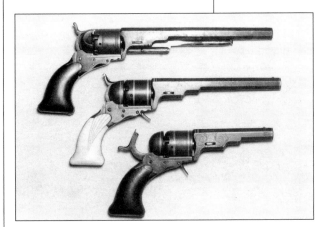

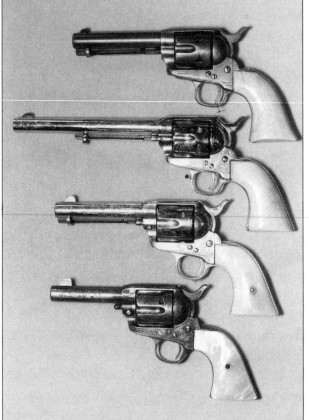

doomed to failure as sales dwindled and forced him into bankruptcy in 1842.

For the next four years Colt experimented on a number of inventions, which never quite reached the success of his pistols. Among these were a waterproof tinfoil cartridge, an underwater mine system for harbor defense, and underwater batteries. It was at this time that Colt became acquainted with Samuel F. B. Morse; Colt's underwater battery system was invaluable in Morse's development of the telegraph cable. But it took the Mexican War and the Texas Rangers to put Colt back in the field he loved so dearly, firearms manufacturing.

The Colt's pistols used by the Texas Rangers attached to General Zachary Taylor's unit were so effective that Captain Jack Hays got the general to order more of them. They sent Captain Samuel Walker to Colt with the order, but Colt was unable to find even a model to use (he advertised in newspapers for one), so he redesigned the revolver with some suggestions from Walker. The result was a huge, five-pound, fifteen-inch .44 caliber weapon that, according to Texas Rangers who used it, was capable of killing the enemy at a quarter-mile distance over flat ground. Called the Walker Colt in honor of the Ranger who assisted in its design, it was the first pistol to be called a "six-shooter."

It was also the gun that started Colt on a long line of government contracts for his firearms, which continued on even past his death. Since Colt had no factory of his own at the time, he persuaded Eli Whitney, Jr., manufacturer of cotton gin machinery and firearms, to produce the weapons at his plant in Whitneyville, Connecticut. Each pistol was stamped with the hallmark, *Address Samuel Colt, New York.*

Colt lost money on the deal, but the thousand Walker Colts he sent to the Rangers (along with the one hundred additional presentation models) made his reputation. With them, the Rangers conquered the West. When Captain Walker was killed in combat at Huamantla, Mexico, in October 1847, he died with his presentation Walker (No. 1020) in his hand.

In the meantime, Colt began construction of his own factory in Hartford, Connecticut. In one of the most important moves of his career, he hired Elisha Root as head superintendent to design and construct the new armory and its equipment. This gave Colt more time to design his future weapons and to play the role of master showman as he continued to sell his guns personally.

While the Walker Colt proved an effective weapon, it was too bulky to carry. Colt received requests for a lighter belt model, and by trimming down the frame in early 1848 Colt produced what he called the Improved Holster Model. Still .44 caliber, it became known as the Dragoon Colt. With only minor changes in design, it remained the standard sidearm of the U.S. Army until the Civil War. Colt sold 200,000 units over a twenty-year period.

FACING PAGE:

Top left: Three .36 caliber Colt "Texas" Patterson revolvers circa 1838–40. This model was manufactured prior to Colt's addition of a loading lever. (*top*) Holster model with a 7½" barrel (*center*) Ivory handles, 8¾" barrel with "Peter Dow" engraved on the frame (*bottom*) 4½" barrel with German silver trim and a stagecoach scene engraved on the cylinder; presentation engraved "to Gen. P. Briscoe"

Top right: This .44 caliber Walker Colt 1847 military model is stamped "B Co. #41." It is one of 100 surviving examples of the original 1000 sent by Colt to the Texas Rangers for the Mexican War.

Center left: This Colt's Dragoon 3rd Model 1851–61 .44 caliber revolver, with its 3½" barrel, is a rare example of the "Avenger." Designed to be concealed under a coat or jacket, its conversion and ownership are attributed to John Moses Browning.

Center right: A progression of "Peacemakers," the gun that became the legendary "six-shooter" of the frontier. Top to bottom: 1875–80 .44 caliber Henry rimfire with 4¾" barrel and ivory grips; 1872–1940 .44/40 caliber centerfire, factory engraved with 7½" barrel and ivory grips; 1872–1940 .38/40 caliber centerfire, factory engraved with 4¾" barrel and ivory grips; Sheriff/Shopkeeper's Model 1872–1940 .45 caliber centerfire ("long Colt" ammunition) with 4" barrel and pearl grips

Bottom left: Two Colt's Model 1851 Navy .36 caliber revolvers, produced 1850–73 (7½" barrels). (*top*) This 2nd Model is engraved, and has the Navy engraved cylinder and a squareback trigger guard. (*bottom*) First Model

(photos by Tom Knowles, courtesy of Metzger Collection, Texas A&M University Sam Houston Sanders Corps of Cadets Center)

The only other popular revolver Colt produced before the Civil War was the 1851 .36 caliber Navy Model, which enjoyed moderate success and became the standard sidearm for sailors and the wiry young riders of the Pony Express. Although business in America may not have been as brisk as he would have liked, Colt still managed to sell a quarter of a million of his revolvers in the four models available during the 1850s. He'd opened a plant in London, and many of his sidearms were bought by both sides during the Crimean War (1853–56).

The decade from 1846 to 1856 made Samuel Colt a millionaire and a noted industrialist in America. His employees were the best-paid factory workers in the country, and his weapons had gained a reputation for being aaccurate, reliable, sturdy, and well-crafted. But Colt's patent ran out in 1857, and by 1858, with the introduction of the metallic cartridge (which was viewed as a fad at the time), the gunmaker faced his first hard competition as Smith & Wesson, Sharps, and Henry entered the firearms field.

The other gunfighter's favorite, from Remington instead of Colt—E. Remington & Sons 1859 Rider's Patent Model .36 caliber double-action percussion revolver with a full-fluted cylinder and 6½" barrel (photo by Tom Knowles, courtesy of Metzger Collection, Texas A&M University Sam Houston Sanders Corps of Cadets Center)

By 1860, war between North and South seemed unavoidable. Colt and Root began designing a new Colt pistol. Although each new revolver was greeted with enthusiasm, all Colt really did was pare down the original cumbersome Walker design into a weapon that caught the fancy and need of the times. In the case of the 1860 Army revolver, Colt foresaw the need for a cavalry weapon. With knowledge that the War Department was preparing to equip five regiments of cavalry with his Dragoon pistol, Colt made it known that he had a weapon available with new and important changes. The Army contracted for the 1860 Army Model and the weapon became the most popular cavalry sidearm of the Civil War. Colt manufactured over 200,000 of them.

Patriotism ran high, but Sam Colt was a businessman first and foremost. He filled orders for both sides right up to the formal declaration of war. Although he thought slavery an inefficient economic system (but not a moral wrong), he had no love for John Brown and opposed Lincoln's election, fearing the Union would be destroyed. He hastily filled an order for what he sardonically called "my latest work on Moral Reform," his last shipment of 500 guns to Richmond, which left three days after Confederates fired on Fort Sumter. He had the guns packed in boxes marked HARDWARE. Thereafter, he supplied the Union Army with not only pistols but muskets, leaving a half-dozen smaller companies who put out various copies of his pistols to supply the Confederate forces.

If Colt's public life was marked by his showmanship, his private life was marked with controversy and estrangement. He'd met Caroline Henshaw in 1835 while obtaining his patents in England and married her; but by 1841 she mysteriously faded from Colt's life and became the mistress of his brother, John. He married Elizabeth Jarvis in 1856; apparently she was much better suited to Colt than his first wife. It was she who inherited the bulk of his estate upon his death.

Elizabeth may have been the only good thing to happen in Colt's private life. Problems mounted over the years. As manager of a Colt plant, his brother was lackadaisical if not incompetent. There was a suicide as well as a murder in the family, and the question of an illegitimate son plagued Colt. Perhaps these incidents in Colt's life led to his adopting *Vincit qui patitur* ("He conquers who suffers") as his motto. But the best key to his character comes from a letter to his half-brother William in which he stated, "If I can't be first I won't be second in anything."

Colt had been a workaholic all of his life, constantly greeting dignitaries from all nations with custom-made presentation models of his weapons in hopes of obtaining new orders. But in 1861 he suffered bouts with gout and rheumatic fever; as exhaustion set in, he turned the day-to-day management of business over to Root. By Christmas the gunmaker was bedrid-

ACE IN THE HOLE: THE DERRINGER

BY LEE SULLENGER

The derringer is an enduring part of the folklore of the West. It has appeared in countless Western novels and movies, a tiny single-shot pistol with a burnished hardwood or ivory grip inlaid with silver. In myth and fact it has found its place in the saloon girl's garter and in the fine lady's muff, in the card sharp's vest pocket and in the gunslinger's boot top. It was the boon companion of

those whose lot it was to live on the raw edges of passion and violence. Though small, sometimes with a barrel less than an inch long, it was a deadly weapon. It fired a large bullet, up to .51 caliber, and carried a heavy load of powder.

It was an ace in the hole, a lethal surprise package made to be used at very close range. Deliberate and polished and perfect, it was meant to kill.

The pocket pistol got its name from the Philadelphia gunsmith who first made it, Henry Deringer, Jr. His early efforts were percussion cap muzzle-loaders. First appearing in 1849, just in time for the hectic California gold rush, the derringer gained immediate popularity. Deringer usually sold his pistols in pairs to provide his customers with a second shot.

He was soon plagued by imitators who got rich copying his product; some even stamped Deringer's name on the barrels of their spurious weapons. Because the imitators often used an extra "r" in the name, nearly all similar pistols, regardless of the manufacturer, came to be known as "derringers." Deringer's lawsuits became landmarks in patent law.

President Abraham Lincoln became the most famous victim of the derringer when he was assassinated by John

Wilkes Booth. Shootist and gambler Wild Bill Hickok was known to secrete a pair of derringers on his person as backups for his six-gun. A fictional example of this kind of well-armed Westerner is the hero of *Yancy Derringer*, a 1950s television series starring Jock Mahoney as a professional gambler who put the small weapons to deadly use.

Deringer's single-shot muzzle-loader was made obsolete by the two-barreled cartridge weapon that's more familiar to TV and movie audiences. Though it wasn't as effective a deterrent as a six-shooter, Deringer's ace in the hole has earned him a permanent place in the pantheon of Western history and myth. As distinguished from the copycat models of his competitors, his deadly little works of art command high prices in today's antique market.

Above: A Deringer copy of J. Derringer—.50 caliber percussion 1837 model single-shot derringer with 5½" barrel. A double "r" in the name denotes a copy. (photo by Tom Knowles, courtesy of Metzger Collection, Texas A&M University Sam Houston Sanders Corps of Cadets Center)

den, though he regained enough strength in the early days of January 1862 to do some business from his bedside. But on January 10, 1862, he lapsed into delirium.

And so did Samuel Colt die at the age of forty-seven. His funeral was one of the most celebrated in the nation's history. His estate was valued at $15 million, quite a sum for the time, and he left his wife and family well provided for. He didn't live to see the invention of the six-gun that would become synonymous with his name—the Colt .45 "Peacemaker," which was first brought out for public sale in 1873.

A proud, stubborn, farsighted man, Samuel Colt was one of the most important inventors and manufacturers to come on the scene of nineteenth century America. His accomplishments in the field of mass production set the country on a course that would make it an industrial giant in the world by the end of the 19th Century. But it was Colt's development of the modern-day revolver that made him a legend in the American West. ∎

GUNMEN AND SHOOTISTS

DOC HOLLIDAY, THE DEADLY DENTIST

BY JORY SHERMAN

THE GAUNT MAN ROUSED HIMSELF FROM THE BED. HIS EYES CLEARED and he said firmly, "A glass of whiskey, please." The nurse brought it. He looked at it almost tenderly, tossed it off neatly, and lay back on the pillow.

"This is funny..." he said. And those were the last words of the deadliest killer the West ever saw—Doc Holliday.

His final words make sense if you know the story of his life. A onetime dentist, John Holliday had come West to die of consumption (tuberculosis). But as the wracking, blood-flecked coughs tore at his emaciated body, Doc Holliday decided he wasn't going to die in bed, "coughing my guts out," as he put it. He deliberately set out to meet a quicker, more merciful death via a bullet, a knife, or a blast of buckshot. Gambler, gunman, sometime lawman, in that hospital bed Doc Holliday played out one of his few losing hands—his bet was that he'd die with his boots on.

He'd often wagered that he'd die of "lead-poisoning" or at the end of a rope or with a bowie knife in his ribs, or even that he might drink himself to death—and drink he did, like a sailor on a twelve-hour shore leave.

Whichever way death came, Doc knew it would be accompanied by the sight and sound of violence. That's what he meant when he said, "This is funny."

His fatalistic attitude and his quest for a quick death no doubt colored his courage. He deliberately chose the one career where a man stood alone. The gambler couldn't rely on the law or his friends. If he got in a spot, he had three choices: a refund, fast talk, or a fast gun—and in Doc's case, it was usually the last.

But Doc Holliday had nothing to lose; the Fates had already measured him for a shroud, and he might as well spare himself a slow, torturous death. Doc didn't need Earp for his place in history—sixteen men died under his guns, although E. D. Cowan, noted historian of Western gunmen, says the records authenticate thirty deaths to the Georgia dentist's credit.

Doctors at the sanatorium where Holliday died reported that his body bore a number of scars from knife and bullet wounds. Doc Holliday walked with death every day of his adult life—by choice, just as he determined deliberately what he became. He was neither a leader nor a follower, but a classic example of the lone wolf. He was not egotistical like many gunslingers, nor was he ever ashamed. Colonel DeWeese, an attorney who often defended Holliday, once asked him if his conscience ever bothered him about all the men he'd killed. "No, I coughed up my conscience a long time back, along with most of my guts," Doc replied.

Born in Valdosta, Georgia, in 1852 of pure Southern "aristocracy," Holliday studied dentistry in Baltimore, and in 1872 he opened an office in Atlanta. But though he was rated a good dentist, fate took a hand. Doctors told him he had consumption—that he'd had it a long time, and had only a few months to live. Doc never dodged a problem, and when told he might prolong his life by a few months in a dry climate, the five-foot ten-inch, blond, blue-eyed doctor with the walrus mustache headed West, into history.

Dallas, Texas, was his first stop. From the day he hit town, Doc never drank less than three quarts of whiskey a day. Men who knew him intimately said he was seldom sober, usually well plastered. Some wonder how much more deadly he might have been had the sharp edges of his nervous reactions not been constantly dulled by liquor. Once when he was thoroughly inebriated, he was jumped by two men but drew and shot both of them dead before they could fire.

He once rode eight hundred miles through seething Apache country to avoid a rope party, and he helped men like Bat Masterson and Wyatt Earp in their deadliest battles. It's a matter of record that he single-handedly backed down twenty armed men who had set out to get Earp. During the Earp-Clanton ruckus, he was the victim of five armed assaults and four hanging attempts.

Doc never really said if he'd lost his practice through too much drink-

AN EPITAPH:

Here lies the body of Jeems Humbrick
who was accidentally shot
on the banks of the pacus river
by a young man
He was accidentally shot with
one of the large colt's
revolvers with no stopper for the
cock to rest on
it was one of the old fashion kind
brass mounted and of
such is the kingdom of heaven.

ing, too much card playing, or because his patients didn't want a consumptive pawing in their mouths. Doc studied gambling just as carefully as he'd studied dentistry. He knew all the tricks, and doubtless he used some of them. He had the important ingredients—a cool head, dexterous, strong hands, and a reckless scorn for death.

For fifteen years he marathoned through life at a hectic drinking pace. He often spent thirty hours at a stretch at the card table, substituting whiskey for food or coffee or sleep. He started and ended each day with a pint of whiskey drunk quick and straight, and kept adding shots about every twenty minutes. Wyatt Earp often said he was always amazed at the quantity of whiskey Doc drank without ever seeming actually drunk.

A weakling in a world where virility and physical strength were at a premium, Doc knew he had one equalizer—the Colt .45. Doc maintained that there was no such thing as a natural-born gunslinger. He practiced religiously; Masterson, Earp, and other experienced gunmen rated Doc as being better than most men with a gun. He went well armed with a shoulder gun, a revolver in a holster on his hip, and a knife on his belt. Despite the circumstances that forced him to use one at the O.K. Corral fight, Doc hated shotguns, thought of them as crude weapons. A frail man would have problems with the kick of a 12-gauge shotgun.

BAT MASTERSON SAID THAT DOC CONSTANTLY LOOKED FOR trouble, goading others with his deliberately nasty manner. Earp maintained that Doc was just a cold machine, always ready to die, but never pushing anyone. Colonel DeWeese described Doc's deceptive killing move: Holliday would appear meek, even seem to back off, and then suddenly his hand would flash to the draw. His victim would be dead with a look of infinite surprise on his face. Yet there is no record of Doc ever taking an unfair advantage or firing on an unarmed man.

Doc killed a man in Dallas, lit out for Jacks County, and dealt faro in a rough cowtown, Jacksboro, two miles from an Army camp. Then he killed a man in Jacksboro, and another, an Army private this time. So Doc headed out, followed by U.S. marshals, the Army, and Texas Rangers—plus local sheriffs armed with reward posters. He rode for Denver, eight hundred miles away, but stopped at Pueblo, Leadville, Georgetown, Central City, Denver, and rode into the Wyoming Territory. On the way, three more men fell under his guns.

Authorities in Cheyenne politely invited him to drift on. Back in Denver, he dealt faro at Babbitt's House under the assumed name Tom McKey. But when he killed Budd Ryan, a local gambler, everyone knew this was the famous Doc Holliday. Running hard now, Doc hit Fort Griffith, Texas, and met the one woman he ever tangled with. She saved his life, then almost got him hanged, and generally made things exciting, even if not very romantic, for four years. Her name was Big Nose Kate, and she was a dancehall girl—a Western euphemism for prostitute. She worked where Doc was dealing, and they worked together, slept together, and often fought like cat and dog. Kate was tough, fearless, rowdy, and hot-headed. She always carried a gun. She was a whore by choice and operated as a lone wolf.

Wyatt Earp was tracking Dave Rudabaugh, the one man Billy the Kid said made him nervous. Earp rode into the Flat, as the civilian settlement a mile from the fort was called. He was a gambler but also a lawman, and he wasn't sure how he'd be received in the hangout of the scum of the West. He'd not yet killed a man, but he delighted in gun-whipping them, so he was respected but not liked in the Flat.

Doc worked in Shansey's joint, and Shansey told Doc to cooperate with Earp. Doc did so because he owed Shansey a lot of money. In Earp's autobiography he tells of their first meeting. Earp was twenty-nine, Doc was twenty-five. Earp thought Doc was handsome and sharp but dangerous looking. They had distinctly different personalities. Earp drank only beer, and that seldom, for he preferred to be cold sober for gunplay and gambling. He gambled conservatively, played the percentages, went for the "sure thing" kill.

Doc got into a game with a man named Bailey, and when Bailey went for a gun, Doc swept out his knife—believing it quicker at that point than his Colt—and almost cut Bailey's stomach out. He knew it was self-defense and surrendered to the town marshal, but Bailey's friends, bolstered by generous slugs of whiskey, decided on lynch law.

But they'd forgotten about Big Nose Kate. She started a fire in a shed behind the hotel, and when everyone went to fight the fire, Kate easily got the drop on the one man they'd left to guard Doc. She sprang Doc, and they lit a shuck for Dodge City. Doc was a loyal man, and Kate's brave act of kindness went deep with him. In Dodge they lived together as man and wife, but Kate couldn't stand the domestic life and told Doc she was going back to her trade. This put Doc in a spot, for he had to take a stand and either fight for her or repudiate her and be known as a heel.

Bat Masterson, then the town marshal of Dodge, disliked Holliday intensely. Earp was a deputy, and in one case he was in charge when some cowhands began to shoot up the town. Earp headed for the Long Branch Saloon for his scattergun but ran into two men he'd once pistol-whipped. They got the drop on him, gleefully taunting him as about twenty of their cowhand friends joined them to surrounded Earp.

"Pray, you sonofabitch," one of them sneered, cocking his gun.

Just then the saloon door burst open; Doc Holliday stood there with his two guns leveled. "Up in the air, you dirty bastards," he commanded.

THEY NEVER SAW 40

BY LOREN D. ESTLEMAN

Wild Bill Hickok
Doc Holliday
Jesse James
George Armstrong Custer
Crazy Horse

Earp drew his guns, and for two solid minutes Doc cussed the crowd foully. Despite their superior numbers, the men in the mob knew the odds, and they stood still as Earp pistol-whipped the two instigators. After Doc put a bullet in one foolish would-be hero, the rest scattered. Earp always said he would have cashed in his chips that night had it not been for Holliday.

Doc's problem with Big Nose Kate was growing. He was drunk and mean almost all the time. Kate openly plied her trade, even bringing her customers to their house. Doc set out for Santa Fe. He left there after a killing, and after another in Trinidad, he opened a dental office in Las Vegas. It was the last time he worked as a dentist. A lucky streak let him abandon it and open a saloon on Center Street. But in August 1879 he killed a man on the street, and once again, like a desperado on the run, he headed for Dodge. There he learned that Earp had gone to Tombstone, so he decided to follow his friend. There was only one drawback—Big Nose Kate was already in Tombstone.

Doc faced the problem head-on. He decided he was still deeply obligated to Kate, so they simply went back together again while she openly operated as a prostitute.

During the Clanton-Earp fracas the Benson stage was held up and the driver killed. Tombstone seethed. Big Nose Kate was on one of her drunken, mean kicks and had fallen out with Doc. Sheriff Behan's men got her drunk as a skunk and convinced her to sign a statement naming Doc as one of the men in the stage holdup. The anti-Earp faction wanted to force a showdown through Earp's friendship with Doc. Doc had many witnesses who confirmed he'd been playing cards at the time, but he felt freed of his obligation to Kate. The slate was wiped clean by her betrayal, even though she later confessed to the shabby trick. But Doc still couldn't be completely disloyal to the big-nosed prostitute. He gave her a thousand dollars, and she left town. Their paths never crossed again.

When the showdown between the factions eventually came, Doc Holliday again proved loyal to his friend Wyatt Earp, standing beside him in the most famous gunfight in the history of the Wild West. After the O.K. Corral fight, Doc drifted, a wanted man. He couldn't make the transition, as some did, to a quiet citizenship. He lived and gambled in the red-light districts, even had one gunfight because he couldn't pay a five-dollar debt.

In May 1883 he went back to Silverton, Colorado, then on to Leadville, where he continued gambling and had two gunfights. But he'd grown even more scrawny, living on whiskey and nerves. Without the balance of his outdoor life in the saddle, he was a walking dead man. He headed for Glenwood Springs, a health resort famed for its mineral baths.

On Tuesday, November 8, 1887, Doc called for his last drink, spoke his ironic last words, and died. Wyatt Earp probably provided his best epitaph when he wrote: "Doc was a dentist whom necessity made a gambler; a gentleman whom disease made a frontier vagabond; a philosopher whom life had made a caustic wit; a long, lean, ash-blond fellow, half-dead of consumption, and all the while, the most skillful gambler and the nerviest, speediest, deadliest man with a six-gun I ever knew." ∎

GUNMEN AND SHOOTISTS

John Wesley Hardin, World Champion Desperado

by Bill Crider

John Wesley Hardin

THE REVEREND AND MRS. J. G. HARDIN CHRISTENED THEIR SECOND son John Wesley after the founder of Great Britain's Methodist movement. If they hoped the boy would grow up to develop the qualities of mildness and forbearance exemplified by that godly Englishman, they were disappointed. The Texas Rangers had their own name for John Wesley Hardin—to the Rangers, he was the World Champion Desperado, the meanest killer ever to pack a pistol.

And how mean was he?

He was so mean that he faced down Wild Bill Hickok on the streets of Abilene.

He was so mean that he killed a man for snoring too loud, shooting him through the wall that separated their hotel rooms.

He was so mean that by his own account he had killed thirty-nine men before he was twenty-one, and he killed the fortieth on the night of his twenty-first birthday.

Some may doubt Hardin's accounts of his exploits. We have only his own word for what happened in many instances, recorded in the autobiography he composed in the last year of his life. Still, Hardin's killings that are substantiated by independent witnesses number well over twenty. He got an early start by killing four men before he reached age sixteen.

By his own account, Hardin was a perfect wonder with a pistol, usually a Colt's .44 cap-and-ball revolver. He fooled Wild Bill in Abilene, getting the

Captain John Armstrong (courtesy of Moody Texas Ranger Library)

drop on him with the "border roll," a trick he is sometimes said to have originated. He presented his guns to Wild Bill butts first, then flipped them around so that Hickok found himself staring into their muzzles. Hardin is also credited with inventing a holster vest made of soft leather and containing two slanting pockets from which the high-riding pistols could be whipped in a fast cross draw. Others who tried the rig found it clumsy, but it apparently worked for Hardin. He was so proficient in the art of drawing, spinning, and twirling his guns that once when he was in jail the Texas Rangers gave him two unloaded pistols and asked him to perform. He obliged and amazed them with his skill.

The total number of Hardin's victims might have been far greater had he not spent sixteen years in prison for the murder of a Brown County, Texas, deputy sheriff named Charles Webb. Hardin celebrated his twenty-first birthday at a race in Comanche, Texas, where his three horses won him more than three thousand dollars in cash and a large number of cattle and horses. Webb had apparently come to town from the adjacent county not to enjoy the race but to kill Hardin. The two men met outside a saloon, and when Webb stated that he had no papers for Hardin's arrest, the desperado invited the deputy to step inside for a drink. Webb accepted, and Hardin led the way. Then Hardin heard a friend yell, "Look out!" Whirling around and drawing his pistols in the same motion, Hardin shot Webb in the face, killing him instantly. Webb, clearly not the fastest gun in the West, had managed to get off only one shot, which grazed Hardin's side.

The Webb shooting may have looked like self-defense, but such was Hardin's reputation that he had to run. He escaped, but vengeance fell on his older brother, Joe, who was lynched a few days later, as were his good friends Bud and Tom Dixon. Two more of his friends were eventually caught and shot, but no one could find Hardin—he had fled to Florida.

Pinkerton detectives located Hardin in Florida two years later, but he escaped again, this time to Alabama, where he lived for nearly another year. The Texas Rangers learned of his whereabouts and trapped him in the smoking car of a train in Pensacola, Florida. In his autobiography, Hardin depicts a scene in which he is overpowered by a dozen Rangers, but the truth is more dramatic, and far more comic. Ranger Lieutenant John B. Armstrong boarded the car with his Colt Peacemaker in his hand. Hardin immediately recognized the weapon as the one favored by the Rangers and stood up to go for his own handgun. The great pistolero must have been considerably flustered, or perhaps he had forgotten his vest—his weapon caught in his suspenders.

One of Hardin's traveling companions, evidently not wearing suspenders, drew and fired at Armstrong, but his bullet only punctured the Ranger's hat. Though Armstrong's return fire struck the man through the heart, Hardin's

LIFE AND DEATH IN THE WILD WEST

friend still had the strength to jump through the train window and run a few steps toward freedom before he fell dead.

Meanwhile, Hardin was still struggling to free his pistol from his entangling braces, looking like a man trying to jerk his pants off over his head. Armstrong kicked Hardin's legs out from under him, grabbed the elusive pistol, and clubbed Hardin over the head with the Peacemaker. Hardin was out cold for two hours.

After some technical delays, Hardin was returned to Texas to stand trial for the murder of Charles Webb. The courtroom was packed. The jury, probably influenced by the fact that Webb had apparently tried to shoot Hardin in the back, as well as by Hardin's eloquent plea in his own defense, returned a lesser verdict of second-degree murder. The judge sentenced Hardin to twenty-five years in prison and sent him to the penitentiary at Huntsville, Texas. He served sixteen years before he received a full pardon.

Most of Hardin's prison years were not peaceful. In the first ten years he attempted escape repeatedly, led rebellions, and once threw a boot at a guard who took some food from him. Once, he was beaten and put into solitary confinement without food or water. He eventually began to take it easier and devoted all his energies to the study of law.

On his release from prison, Hardin actually tried to reform. He opened a law practice in El Paso, Texas, where he was occasionally praised for his good citizenship. But something in Hardin wouldn't change. Soon enough he took up gambling and drinking again, and he was more than once found drunk in an El Paso gutter. In his later years he was a far cry from the young dandy who had once sported hundred-dollar boots, spurs the size of silver dollars, and a plush sash about his waist.

He came to a particularly ignominious end. John Selman, Jr., arrested Hardin's lady friend for carrying a pistol, and Hardin publicly berated him. Selman's father, one of Hardin's old enemies, heard about the fracas. Some days later, the elder Selman spotted Hardin shooting dice at the bar of the Acme Saloon, slipped up behind him, and shot him in the back of the head. Hardin dropped dead on the spot as the fatal bullet exited just above his left eye. Selman was so excited that he fired three more shots at Hardin's prone body. He managed to hit it twice.

At his trial, Selman was defended by Albert Fall, who later as a Secretary of the Interior was convicted of accepting bribes in connection with the Teapot Dome Scandal. In the case of Hardin's murder, both Fall and his client were luckier. They argued that Hardin obviously had a fair chance to see Selman sneaking up behind him with a drawn revolver. All Hardin had to do was look up into the mirror over the bar.

Selman was acquitted. After all, was it not a clear-cut case of self-defense? ■

POOR SPORTS

BY LOREN D. ESTLEMAN

It's a fact of human nature that the farther one is from authority, the less inclined one is to adhere to the rules of civilized behavior. Here are five Westerners whose enforcement of their own codes of conduct is legendary.

Johnny Ringo, possibly the West's most cultured and certainly its most enigmatic gunfighter, lost his manners while drunk during a losing game of poker near Tombstone, Arizona, and held up his fellow players for their winnings. He did, however, apologize and return their money upon sobering up.

Texas desperado *John Wesley Hardin* fired several shots through the wall of his room at the American House Hotel in Abilene, Kansas, when the man in the adjoining room disturbed him by snoring. One of Hardin's shots killed the man, and he was forced to flee in his nightshirt to escape arrest or death at the hands of his friend Wild Bill Hickok.

Cattle baron *Shanghai Pierce*, it's said, punished rustlers for their crimes by sewing them up in the hides of the cattle they'd butchered and leaving them in the hot sun to suffocate.

"Captain Jack" Slade, superintendent of the Sweetwater stage route, recovered from gunshot wounds given him by a larcenous station keeper and returned with some of his friends. They tied the offending party to a fencepost, where Slade target-practiced on him throughout the night before he shot him to death. He then sliced off the man's ears for souvenirs.

But it is mining-camp desperado *Sam Brown* who holds the record for refusing to lighten up. When he was accidentally jostled by a stranger in a saloon in Virginia City, Nevada, Brown cut out the stranger's heart with a bowie knife, spread a blanket on top of the warm corpse, and went to sleep stretched out on it in the middle of the saloon floor.

BILLY, THE KID

BY LEON C. METZ

I'll tell a true tale of Billy the Kid,
Of some of the wild and bad things
that he did,
Out in New Mexico long, long ago,
When a man's only friend was his
old forty-four...

THE BILLY THE KID WE KNOW IS A LEGEND, HIS NAME A SIGN TO conjure with and to sing songs about when one thinks of the badmen of the West. But who was the man buried under the legend built of half truths, folklore, and the outright lies told by dime novelists? Did he actually die at twenty-one, having killed a man for every year of his life? Did he die under Sheriff Pat Garrett's reluctant gun, or did he survive to live the remainder of his life in relative obscurity? We may never know the answers.

We do know that the Kid was born Henry McCarty in New York City on November 20, 1859, and that his older brother, Joseph M., was born there on August 25, 1854. Their mother was Catherine McCarty, a single woman who'd emigrated from Ireland in 1846, at age seventeen. While she worked as a house servant in New York she took up with a married fruit peddler, Edward "Dad" McCarty, who was no relation. Edward probably fathered her two boys.

The New York Children's Aid Society in 1873 bound young Henry out to the stern, humorless William E. Antrim, a farmer, miner, and developer. Antrim had gained some notoriety for his trial on charges of draft evasion during the Civil War and afterward drifted West to Kansas and Santa Fe, New Mexico. Antrim later "adopted" not only Henry but also his brother and mother. To avoid the hint of immorality, he married the tubercular Catherine in Santa Fe in March 1873. Two months later the family moved to Silver City, New Mexico, where she died. Young Henry, always a delinquent, got into serious trouble on the first anniversary of his mother's death. He and "Sombrero Jack" stole clothes from two Chinese as a prank. Henry went to jail, but within a week he slithered up the chimney and disappeared. He and Joe reappeared in New York City shortly afterward.

Henry took preliminary steps toward training as a tinsmith, but trouble was more in his line. On the night of September 9, 1876, he, Joe, a twenty-year-old Irish companion named Thomas Moore, and two unidentified girls were drinking on Pearl Street. The youths argued; during a drunken brawl Henry stabbed Moore in the neck with a cheese knife. Moore died within an hour, and Henry fled back toward New Mexico.

Henry paused in Silver City, then moved to Camp Grant, Arizona, a few miles north of Tucson. The itinerant eighteen-year-old called himself "Mr. Antrim" even though he looked like a kid. He stood about five foot eight and weighed 140 pounds. His intelligence and his fun-loving nature, even his leadership qualities, concealed a dark and wild streak. His physical liabilities were his protruding front teeth and shoulders so rounded that he must have had trouble keeping up his suspenders. He learned Spanish easily and spoke it fluently, though it's likely his English was colored with an Irish accent.

It was on August 17, 1877, that young Henry and thirty-two-year-old Frank P. Cahill collided. Cahill called Henry a pimp and Henry called Cahill a son-of-a-bitch. The two struggled, Henry pulled a revolver, Cahill tried to wrest it from him and took a bullet through the stomach. He died the following day, and Henry scampered on to New Mexico.

Henry Antrim now adopted the name "William Bonney," the William likely in deference to his stepfather. The origins of the name Bonney are obscure. From here it was a short jump to "Billy, the Kid" (with a comma in the middle), although he always signed his name "Wm. H. Bonney" or "Henry Antrim." Whatever he called himself, Billy the Kid came to the place of his destiny, Lincoln County in southeastern New Mexico, in October 1877.

Billy hired on with John Tunstall, a naive Britisher who believed his wealth and influence could overcome the House of Murphy, which controlled local military contracts and operated the general store and trading post in Lincoln. Lawrence G. Murphy, a retired major, started the subsequent Lincoln County war but drank himself to death before it ended. With him were Emil Fritz and Jimmy Dolan, the latter a short, scheming Irishman who survived longer than just about everybody else and did his best to protract the struggle.

The House of Murphy controlled Sheriff William Brady, who was paid in scrip that the House redeemed for full value. It also retained Jesse Evans, a rustler and gunman whose "boys" operated at Seven Rivers in the eastern part of the county.

Tunstall's supporters and allies were cattleman John Chisum (who remained on his ranch and avoided the fighting) and Alexander McSween, an outwardly pious but corrupt lawyer. Tunstall also had his stable of hired guns, one of whom was slope-shouldered Billy the Kid, a scrawny lad whom no one but Tunstall considered to be of significance. A farmer named Dick Brewer provided the real leadership for the riders.

Tunstall opened a store and a bank in Lincoln as a way to force the Murphy House to the wall. When the House retained McSween to collect a $10,000 life insurance policy on Fritz, who had died intestate in Germany, McSween obtained the money but neglected to turn it over. The House suspected fraud. Sheriff Brady tried to foreclose on Tunstall cattle, claiming

Billy the Kid. Nobody calls him Henry.

that a partnership existed between the Englishman and the attorney.

Tunstall agreed to meet Brady in town, and on February 18, 1878, Tunstall left the ranch with several riders, including Billy the Kid. As they neared Ruidoso, the majority of Tunstall's outriders chased off through the brush after a flock of wild turkeys. Only the Kid and John Middleton noticed a mob of Brady's deputies, led by Jesse Evans, storming over the hill. The Kid and Middleton headed for cover and advised Tunstall to do likewise. The law-abiding Englishman believed he had nothing to fear, so he didn't heed the Kid's advice. Evans and the posse murdered him.

The Tunstall riders organized themselves into a vigilante group known as the Regulators. In early March the Regulators caught Frank Baker and William "Buck" Morton, two of the Evans posse members, near a cow camp on the Pecos. A couple of days later, the Regulators shot them while they were "trying to escape."

Bob Olinger, slain by Billy the Kid during the Kid's Lincoln County jailbreak (courtesy of Fulton collection, University of Arizona Archives)

On April 1 the Regulators entered Lincoln for an audacious attempt at additional revenge. Billy and six other men waited in ambush behind a gate near the Tunstall store, and when Sheriff William Brady and deputies George Hindman, Billy Mathews, John Long, and George "Dad" Peppin strolled down the wide, dusty street, the Regulators opened fire. The subsequent silence was broken only by the sound of dogs lapping up the blood. Brady and Hindman lay dead. The other Brady officers took cover. When the Kid jumped over the fence, one of the deputies fired, inflicting a painful wound on the inside of the Kid's leg.

The blatant killings created a sensation, but the Regulators were far from finished. On April 4 they paused at Blazer's Mill on the southern pine-covered slopes of the Sacramento Mountains. While they ate, Andrew L. "Buckshot" Roberts rode down the hill on a mule. When he saw them, it was too late to run. He had been a posse member also, and he knew his long trail had ended. One of the West's classic gunfights followed, and when it finished an hour later, Dick Brewer lay with his brains oozing from his head. Buckshot would die within twenty-four hours of a stomach wound. George Coe nursed a shot-off trigger finger, and Billy the Kid complained about an arm wound.

Meanwhile, Governor Samuel B. Axtell appointed George "Dad" Peppin as the next Lincoln County sheriff, an act that gave the Murphy House, now controlled by Jimmy Dolan, renewed firepower as well as the legal and moral high ground. Alexander McSween, a man particularly unsuited for leadership, assumed control of the Regulators. Since he didn't know what else to do, the attorney returned to Lincoln and barricaded himself in his house. He and several others, including Billy the Kid, decided to make their stand in a showdown the Regulators had absolutely no chance of winning.

Peppin's deputies had been out in the hills searching for the Regulators, and it took time to reassemble in town. The sheriff asked for McSween's surrender, didn't get it, and the fight was on. After five days of battle and siege the Regulators were finally defeated when the Army sent troops from Fort Stanton and stationed them in the McSween faction's line of fire. A slow blaze set by a Peppin deputy gradually consumed the rafters and flooring of the house, forcing the Regulators from one room to another as they awaited darkness. When night came on July 19, the nineteen-year-old Kid came into his own. He assumed leadership and mapped out a plan to flee the inferno. Those who could make the hundred yards to the Bonito River would likely escape.

The Kid was the second man out, and he made it. Alexander McSween came out last, and he did not. He was shot to death in the street.

The Lincoln County war had ended with dramatic suddenness. The House had won but wouldn't survive its victory. There were too many

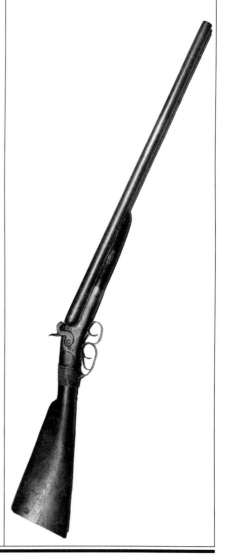

The Kid used this Whitney 12-guage shotgun to kill his last victim, deputy Bob Olinger, during his escape from the Lincoln County courthouse on April 28, 1881. Billy then broke the gunstock (note wiring at trigger guard) over a bannister and threw the weapon onto Olinger's body. (photo by Tom Knowles, courtesy of Texas Ranger Hall of Fame Museum, Waco, Texas)

Washington investigations, too many charges of corruption. Even Governor Axtell, a long-time supporter of the House, was replaced by Lew Wallace.

In February 1879 the Kid and Jesse Evans met in Lincoln to resolve their differences, but they encountered Huston Chapman, a one-armed attorney hired by Susan McSween to prosecute her husband's murderers. An argu-

BANDITRY WITH PANACHE

BY L.K. FEASTER

A stagecoach rumbles through a narrow, twisting rock draw in the Russian River country of California. Suddenly a masked man steps from behind a huge bolder and levels his rifle at the driver. The driver pulls up short on the reins as the bandit bellows, "Throw down the box!" The man riding shotgun starts to aim his own gun, then hesitates as he sees the rifle barrels aimed at him from advantageous positions along the draw. He hastens to comply and tosses the strong box at the outlaw's feet. The bandit waves his rifle to indicate the holdup is over. The coach moves on.

Later, when the authorities ride out to the scene of the crime, they find the painted broomsticks where the bandit positioned them to masquerade as rifle barrels. In the brush they find the empty strong box—empty, that is, except for a note from the holdup man:

I've labored long and hard for bread,
for honor and for riches,
But on my corns too long you've tread,
you fine-haired sons of bitches.
—Black Bart, the Poet

That was the modus operandi of Black Bart, a lone bandit who exasperated and frustrated peace officers, Wells Fargo agents, and Pinkerton detectives from his first robbery in 1877 to his apprehension in 1883.

Ironically, the man who used his pen to taunt his victims was done in by writing of another kind. James B. Hume, a

Wells Fargo operative, finally tracked him down on the strength of a laundry mark he'd dropped during one of his holdups. Hume took the handkerchief from laundry to laundry until he finally found the right one. The laundry owners identified it as belonging to one of their favorite customers. The larcenous poet, Black Bart, was in reality Charles E. Bolton, a gentle, elderly fellow who was known as something of a character in California. He had good taste in clothes, liked to show them off as he strolled about town with his walking stick, and favored a rather expensive lifestyle, living in a series of fancy hotel rooms.

When the detectives braced Bolton with their evidence, he surrendered peaceably and amicably. He was, after all, not a thug but a gentleman bandit. Bolton, rather a ne'er-do-well earlier in life, had found himself entering his declining years in a penniless state. He'd decided he was entitled to a measure of comfort and luxury in his old age, and he'd resorted to robbing stages in order to provide it.

While his purpose may have been criminal, his motive was understandable, and his methods were humane. Not once in the course of his daring career did Black Bart fire even a single shot at his victims. Even those lawmen who pursued and captured him admired the imagination he put into planning his holdups, as well as his flair for poetry.

Two relics of the Wells Fargo Company. The Remington .41 caliber over-and-under derringer is presentation engraved to Wells Fargo president, "Jas. C. Fargo, No. 56 Park Ave., New York, from C.G.S, Jany. 1st 1875." The magneso-calcite fireproof strongbox belonged to Charles Fargo, the Wells Fargo Western manager (California) in the 1870s. (photo by Tom Knowles, courtesy of Texas Ranger Hall of Fame Museum, Waco, Texas)

ment ensued, and as the Kid slipped away, Evans and James Dolan shot Chapman dead, poured whiskey on his clothes, and set the body afire.

The vicious murder aroused Lew Wallace from the governor's chair, where he had been writing *Ben Hur*, and on the night of March 17, 1879, he and Billy the Kid met in the Lincoln home of Justice of the Peace John B. Wilson. Wallace needed someone to testify against the House, the Seven Rivers boys, certain corrupt Army officers at Fort Stanton, and territorial politicians. If Billy would do this and submit to unchained and unlocked confinement, the governor promised amnesty in return. On April 14 the Kid testified before the grand jury. Evans and Dolan were indicted for Chapman's murder.

But Billy the Kid was also asked embarrassing questions in reference to the slayings that had occurred in the war. Without reassuring words from the governor, the young gunman suspected a double-cross. He walked out of the jail, an outlaw.

Meanwhile, George Kimball had become sheriff but was soon defeated at the polls by a tall, thin, former buffalo hunter, Pat Garrett. Garrett, who had been elected on a platform to capture or kill the Kid, grimly tracked the Kid and his friends to Fort Sumner, New Mexico, where Garrett's posse occupied an abandoned hospital building.

At eight o'clock on the evening of December 19, 1880, the outlaws filtered down from the hills in single file, their horses crunching through frozen snow. As they approached the hospital, Billy the Kid peeled off and asked the last man in line for a chaw of tobacco. He was still there when the lead horse stuck its head under the porch roof. The posse fired, mortally wounding Tom O'Folliard. The gang scattered. O'Folliard died five hours later.

Garrett followed the outlaws to a rock house at Stinking Springs and surrounded the building. At dawn a heavily bundled figure walked outside with an oat bag. Garrett thought it was Billy, and the posse pumped lead into Charles Bowdre. Bowdre stumbled back into the house; the Kid shoved a revolver into his hand and said, "They have killed you, Charlie, but you can get a few before you die." He pushed Bowdre back out the door. Charlie stumbled through the snow, his life's blood gushing out, saying, "I wish. I wish." Then he collapsed and died. The gang surrendered.

Garrett hauled the desperados off to Santa Fe, where from jail the Kid reminded Governor Wallace of the outlaw's previous commitment to testify in exchange for a pardon. He wrote to Wallace, saying he would like to see him if the governor could spare the time. Wallace apparently had no time to spare for the Kid. On March 3, 1881, the Kid wrote to Wallace again:

Dear Sir:

I wish you would come down and see me. It will be in your interest to come and see me. I have some letters which date back two years, and there are parties very anxious to get them; but I will not dispose of them until I see you. That is, if you will come immediately.

Yours respectfully,
William H. Bonney

Governor Wallace ignored the Kid's continued entreaties and threats, and on March 28 the Kid left Santa Fe for trial in Mesilla, New Mexico. On April 6, the jury found the Kid guilty of the assassination of Sheriff William Brady. Judge Bristol ordered the prisoner delivered to Lincoln where, on Friday, May 13, Billy was to "be hanged by the neck until his body be dead."

In the ugly two-story Lincoln courthouse, formerly the Murphy-Dolan store, the Kid was housed on the second floor along with a sprinkling of other prisoners. There were no jail bars—prisoners were clapped into leg irons fastened to the wooden floor. John Bell and Robert Olinger performed guard duty while Garrett collected taxes in White Oaks.

During Garrett's absence on April 28, as Olinger escorted other prisoners across the street for lunch at the Wortley Hotel, the Kid visited the outside privy. There he hid a concealed revolver inside his shirt, and at the top of the stairs he confronted Bell, who was coming along behind. The deputy turned and fled. Billy fired twice. Bell reached the bottom of the stairs, then stumbled into the yard and died. The Kid then snatched Olinger's shotgun from the gun cabinet and hobbled to an open window.

From across the street big Bob Olinger came running. When he reached the northeast corner of the courthouse beneath the second-story window, he paused to look up. Olinger probably never heard the two shotgun blasts that killed him.

The Kid freed one leg iron before he "borrowed" a horse and vanished. Within the next month Garrett received reports of the Kid's presence in Fort Sumner. The information probably came from Pete Maxwell, the village *jefe.* Indeed, Billy often visited Fort Sumner to dally with the local ladies, specifically Paulita Maxwell (Pete's sister) and Celsa Gutierrez, one of Maxwell's servants.

On the full-moon night of July 14, 1881, the Kid was with Celsa. He was stretched out in her bed reading a newspaper when he complained of hunger pangs. Celsa suggested he cut a slice of beef from a freshly butchered slab hanging on Pete Maxwell's porch, so the Kid rolled out of bed, picked up a knife, and started for the hacienda, all the while adjusting his trousers.

The Kid had no sooner reached the Maxwell porch than two figures loomed out of the night, deputies John Poe and Thomas L. "Tip" McKinney. Neither man recognized the Kid and figured him for a friend of Maxwell's. The three of them exchanged a few cautious comments before the Kid entered Maxwell's room. Worried by what he'd just run into, he asked, "Pete,

There's many a man with face fine and fair,

Who starts out in life with a chance to be square,

But just like poor Billy, he wanders astray,

And loses his life in the very same way.

who are those guys outside?" Then he noticed a shadowy figure awaiting him. He didn't recognize the man who stood in the dark, but the man knew him. His voice hoarse, Billy the Kid asked, *"Quién es?"* (Who is it?) He whispered again, *"Quién es?"*

His answer was the reverberating thunder of Sheriff Pat Garrett's pistol. ■

OUTLAWS AND BADMEN

The Betrayal of Sam Bass

BY JAMES M. REASONER

Sam Bass was born in Indiana, it was his native home;
And at the age of seventeen young Sam began to roam;
Sam first came to Texas, a cowboy for to be—
A kinder-hearted fellow you seldom ever see…

SUCH WAS THE SONG WHICH TEXAS COWBOYS SUNG SHORTLY AFTER the death of Sam Bass, the noted outlaw. This somewhat distorted story of Sam Bass's life and death soothed many an unsettled herd during the long nights. And it's evidence of the regard in which Sam Bass was held. While he was never quite a folk hero like Jesse James, Sam was generally regarded as not a bad sort, for an outlaw.

He was born July 21, 1851, in Mitchell, Indiana. His parents moved soon after to Marion Township, where they were respected citizens until their early deaths a few years later. Along with his two brothers and four sisters, Sam was raised by his uncle, David L. Sheeks. Sam and his uncle didn't get along well at all, and it came as no surprise when Sam left home to go out and see the world. He loved horses and was a fine hand with them, and he soon found himself in Denton, Texas, where he matched his mare against the local horses in races. His successful betting on the mare gave him a taste of money, after which he was never the same.

Though he had little schooling, Sam could read enough to get through newspaper accounts of a train robbery perpetrated by the Reno Brothers in Minnesota. He left Texas and traveled north, heading for the Black Hills. Along the way he acquired the gang that would accompany him for most of his career outside the law. They were young men much like Sam, out for adventure and excitement as much as for loot.

The gang began by holding up the stagecoaches that ran through the Black Hills. The hold-ups were frequent enough that the stage drivers came to know Sam and his gang. Law enforcement was almost nonexistent in the area, so Sam and his gang were able to strike at will and elude capture. They didn't prosper, however, because the take from the stages was always small; hardly worth the trouble most of the time, they had to hit frequently. Sam Bass eventually turned his attention to the railroads instead.

And from that decision was born the legend of Sam Bass.

Like other desperados who preyed on the powerful and sometimes despotic railroads, Sam found that many of the common people looked upon him as a hero. He and his gang committed a string of lucrative train robberies, including one haul of $60,000 from a train in Big Spring, Nebraska. A thirty-dollar-a-month cowhand couldn't make that kind of money in a hundred and fifty *years*.

It didn't hurt Sam's image that he was a fairly handsome man. He was quiet by nature but had a sense of humor that emerged in the company of his fellow bandits. He didn't drink heavily and wasn't a cold-blooded killer, though he could be ruthless if he was cornered. He also had a compassionate streak; in one instance he refused to rob a one-armed train passenger, claiming that the man had enough troubles already.

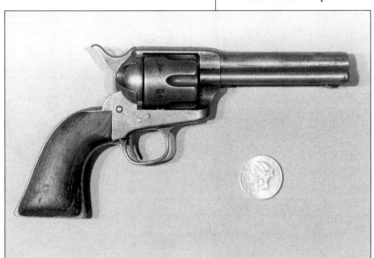

Lead and gold were unlucky for Sam Bass. He bought a round of drinks at the Ranch Saloon in Waco, Texas, with this 1877 twenty-dollar gold piece (San Francisco mint); he'd taken it in his Union Pacific train robbery. He tossed it onto the bar and said, "There's the last of that '77 gold, and it hasn't done me a damned bit of good." Shortly afterward, Texas Ranger George Herold used this Colt .45 single-action revolver to put an end to the outlaw's career. (photo by Tom Knowles, courtesy of Texas Ranger Hall of Fame Museum, Waco, Texas)

Bass and his gang ranged through the Midwest and down into Oklahoma and North Central Texas. One of his favorite hideouts was at Pilot Knob, near Denton, Texas, from which vantage point Sam had a good view of the surrounding territory. He seldom roamed any farther south than this robbers' roost. Maybe some instinct told Sam that he should stay away from Central Texas. His decision to go to Round Rock was the beginning of the end for Sam Bass.

Sam suspected that one of the members of his gang, a man named Jim Murphy, was not to be trusted. Many outlaws betrayed their companions and sold information to the authorities. Thinking that Murphy might have been in touch with lawmen, Sam threatened to kill him and might well have done it if Frank Jackson, one of the other bandits, hadn't stepped in and talked him out of it.

It would have been better for the gang if Jackson had kept his mouth shut. Secretly, Jim Murphy sent a telegram to Ranger headquarters in Austin, telling them that Sam Bass and his gang were on their way to Round Rock, thirty miles north of the capital city. "For God's sake," the telegram urged, "meet us at Round Rock."

The Rangers did just that. Three of them were on their way into town when Sam, Frank Jackson, and Seaborne Barnes arrived. When they stopped at a store to buy some tobacco, the local sheriff spotted them carrying guns and went up to them to arrest them for that minor crime, unaware that he was confronting one of the nation's most famous badmen. Bass, Barnes, and Jackson lost their heads and blazed away at the sheriff, killing him. Another local lawman heard the shooting and joined in the fight, shooting off two of Sam Bass's fingers. As the outlaws tried to make a run for it, the three Rangers arrived and shot and killed Seaborne Barnes. Sam Bass was mortally wounded by the gunfire, but with Jackson's aid he got on his horse, and the two of them made it out of town.

Sam didn't make it far. He slipped from the saddle and waited to die under a live oak tree. Frank Jackson went on, perhaps at Sam's urging, and escaped from the Rangers. Sam Bass was found by a deputy sheriff and lived long enough to turn over his gun and surrender. He died before he could be taken back into Round Rock.

Jim Murphy, the traitor who had set up his companions, was in the vicinity but had slipped away from the gang before the shooting started. Later, he died from an accidental poisoning, an agonizing death which many people regarded as justice for the man who betrayed Sam Bass.

Sam Bass was an outlaw, true enough, but he was also a happy-go-lucky young man who must have regarded his career of lawlessness as a sort of daring adventure. The words engraved on his tombstone perhaps say it all:

A brave man reposes in death here.

Why was he not true?

■

How Alan Pinkerton Bit Himself to Death and Other Ignominious Ends

BY LOREN D. ESTLEMAN

Pat Garrett, slayer of Billy the Kid, was shot in the back while urinating beside a road in New Mexico.

Outlaw Black Jack Ketchum was decapitated in Clayton, New Mexico, through a miscalculation on the part of his hangman.

Former Overland stage superintendent Captain Jack Slade was lynched by indignant spectators in Virginia City, Nevada, for calling upon an actress to strip onstage.

Apache war chief Geronimo got drunk, fell out of his buggy on the way back to the Fort Sill Indian reservation, and froze to death beside the road.

Texas badman Clay Allison also got drunk, fell out of his wagon and died when the wheel broke his neck.

Alan Pinkerton, former secret service agent and founder of the West's most famous detective agency, tripped and bit his tongue during his daily constitutional; he died of gangrene in Chicago.

THE LEGENDS OF JOAQUIN MURIETTA

BY MICHAEL MADONNA

In outlaw country, a man got only one chance to mind his own business.

NO ONE WAS SAFE FROM JOAQUIN MURIETTA'S GANG OF MEXICAN bandits during the early 1850s in San Francisco. Anyone with a dollar in his pocket was fair game, which kept stagecoach passengers, ranch owners, and storekeepers—among many others—nervous.

Joaquin's gang was constantly on the move; one or two quick holdups and they were on their way again. By 1853 Governor John Bigler had offered a reward for Joaquin's capture, dead or alive. The search for Murietta, who was also known as the Ghost of Sonora because he struck fast and disappeared even quicker, became so massive and frenzied that honest men who happened to be named Joaquin changed their names so as not to be mistaken for Murietta himself.

After all, Joaquin was a very common name in that territory. In fact, there was more than one outlaw named Joaquin, including Joaquin Bottilier, Joaquin Ocomorena, Joaquin Valenzuela and Joaquin Carrillo. Conflicting legends had it that the real Joaquin Murietta's best compadre was Manuel Garcia, known as Three-Fingered Jack because he was missing a couple of his fingers, or that Garcia was himself really Murietta.

A company of California State Rangers led by Captain Harry Love, himself a former Texas Ranger, was hired to resolve the problem of the five Joaquins. The incentive: one thousand dollars for every outlaw named Joaquin dead or in captivity. A couple of months later, on July 24, 1853, at a saloon called the Arroyo Cantina somewhere in the Panache Pass, Captain Love's men stopped for drinks and something to eat. Some newspaper articles later reported that Captain Love was not present at the time, that the Rangers were temporarily under the command of one Captain Burns. There the company of Rangers met a gang of six or so outlaws, among them Three-Fingered Jack, who had also stopped to drink and dine.

The surprised Rangers and the even more surprised bandits reached for their guns. When the shooting was over, Manuel "Three-Fingered Jack" Garcia lay dead. There are two versions of what happened next. In the first, the Rangers, incorrectly assuming Garcia to be the famous outlaw, removed his hand and decapitated him as well. In the second, they took another, unidentified outlaw's head from his body and declared it to be the bona fide head of Joaquin Murietta. They wanted the reward and figured that no one would be the wiser as to the real identity of the unfortunate Mexican.

The Rangers placed the head and Three-Fingered Jack's hand in separate jars of alcohol for preservation, and collected the initial thousand dollars plus a bonus of a few thousand more. The grisly displays almost immediately began showing up at public exhibitions as "The Head of the Renowned Bandit, Joaquin," and "The Hand of the Notorious Robber and Murderer, Three-Fingered Jack," in cities like Sacramento and places like the Stockton House. The crowds came out in record numbers to view them.

Meanwhile, various stories and newspaper editorials created a controversy by questioning the authenticity of the head. Those who claimed to have known or to have seen the *real* Joaquin Murietta denied that it was

Poster reads: "JOAQUIN and THREE-FINGERED JACK were captured by the State Rangers under the command of Captain Harry Love at the Arroya Cantina, July 24th. No reasonable doubt can be entertained in regard to the identification of the head now on exhibition as being that of the notorious robber, Joaquin Murietta, for it is recognized by hundreds of persons who have formerly seen him and described him as illustrated in the splendid etching that accompanies this happy announcement. As further proof, the hand of Joaquin's evil accomplice, Three-Fingered Jack Garcia, has been removed from its more ordinary position and is preserved in a jar of alcohol for display at the public exhibition."

THEY NEVER SAW 30

BY LOREN D. ESTLEMAN

Billy the Kid
Sam Bass
Billy Comstock
Bob Dalton
William Clarke Quantrill

the bandit leader's head in that jar. And there were those who believed that the members of the California "Get Joaquin" committee were incompetent, that the whole idea was a joke.

Or perhaps the legend of Joaquin Murietta was a myth nurtured in bunkhouses or over campfires and kept alive by hopes, fears, and the Southwest's romantic storytelling tradition. If so, it may have started quite innocently with a letter from a gold camp physician's wife, Louise Clappe, to the editor of *Pioneer Magazine*. She mentioned a "Spanish man" who was convicted for rioting in the camp. Severely whipped for this offense, he swore to seek revenge by killing as many gringos as he could. Mrs. Clappe said she believed the young man meant exactly what he'd said.

A journalist named John Rollin Ridge, who sometimes wrote under his proper Cherokee name, Yellow Bird, read of Murietta's "demise" sometime shortly after the shootout at the Arroyo Cantina. This, along with Mrs. Clappe's *Pioneer Magazine* letters gave him an idea which he turned into a book, *The Life and Adventures of Joaquin Murietta, Celebrated California Bandit*. Ridge completed his work circa April 1854, and it was highly successful—not deservedly so, since it portrayed Murietta as somewhat of a saint and Three-Fingered Jack as a carefree charmer who loved Joaquin like a brother. It was just about as far from fact as a writer could get.

The Mexican population of California embraced this new hero to the people's cause. He was the very spirit of Hispanic rebellion and revolution, a man who stood up to the gringos who were destroying their lands in their ever-growing, frenzied search for gold.

During the fall of 1859 a police magazine ran a rewritten version of Ridge's book with few of the original "facts" changed. It ran through ten installments. Many more stories and poems followed in the penny dreadfuls and dime novels, all of them different in many ways, none of them containing much truth. Even though "Joaquin's" head and Three-Fingered Jack's hand still circulated at fairs and sideshows twenty-five years after the killings, there were some who claimed to have seen him alive. Some said he settled down as a wealthy rancher in Mexico. Whatever the case, after Joaquin Murietta's "death" in 1853, the raids and robberies ceased—all the more reason to believe that Captain Love's Rangers had beheaded the actual Joaquin.

The head and the hand continued to attract curiosity seekers in droves for many years afterward. The exhibits finally wound up in a place called Jordan's Museum, a building full of medical oddities owned and operated by one Dr. Louis J. Jordan. The head and the hand were labeled exhibits 563 and 564, and both wound up on a shelf, lost among the various pickled heads, skulls, and other parts of infamous outlaws. Joaquin's head and Three-Fingered Jack's hand were displayed with other exhibitions, never again as main attractions. ∎

THE JAMES-YOUNGER GANG

BY BILL O'NEAL

"WE ARE ROUGH MEN AND USED TO ROUGH WAYS."

The badly wounded Bob Younger, bedridden after the abortive raid on Northfield, Minnesota, uttered this unrepentant declaration. It's a descriptive motto for the entire James-Younger gang.

Frank and Jesse James, born in 1843 and 1847 in Clay County, Missouri, were the sons of a Baptist preacher and his strong-willed wife. But the Reverend James caught gold fever and journeyed to California, where he fell ill and died. The widowed Zerelda entered her third marriage in 1855 with the docile, prosperous Dr. Reuben Samuel. The growing family remained on the old James farm and began to acquire slaves. When the Civil War broke out, they were naturally sympathetic to the Confederacy.

During the war Frank joined William Quantrill's infamous Missouri guerrillas, and Jesse followed him. Also riding with Quantrill were Cole and Jim Younger, who were out for revenge after Kansas jayhawkers raided the Younger property and killed their father.

In the years following Appomattox, Jesse, Frank, and other former guerrillas turned to outright thievery. On February 13, 1866, the James brothers and Cole Younger led several other hardcases on the first daylight robbery of a bank in the United States, the Clay County Savings Bank in Liberty, Missouri. The other Younger brothers, Jim, John, and Bob. soon joined up. For a decade the James-Younger gang committed robberies throughout Missouri and surrounding states while they maintained their home base in Missouri. In time, people blamed just about every such robbery—and the many shootings connected with the robberies—on the gang, even though Jesse regularly published newspaper letters proclaiming his innocence. Exactly which robberies were pulled by the James and Younger boys is unknown.

The James-Younger gang began robbing trains in 1873, and by the next year Pinkerton detectives were carefully scrutinizing the activities of the James and Younger brothers. Jesse and Frank were widely suspected of murdering the Pinkerton agent John Whicher near their mother's farm in 1874. That same year John Younger was killed in a bloody shootout with

Jesse James (*top*) and Frank James

HANGING AROUND

BY MARYLOIS DUNN

The preferred method of attending to outlaws was hanging. As they did for everything else, Westerners had colorful names for it:

California collar

cottonwood blossom

decorate a cottonwood

die in a horse's nightcap

dressed in a hemp
four-in-hand

exalted guest of honor at a
string party

gurgling on a rope

hemp committee, hemp fever

string up

telegraph him home

human fruit

Texas cakewalk

hung out to dry

trimmin' a tree

lookin' up a limb

viewing the sky through
cottonwood leaves

lynching bee

mid-air dance

necktie party, necktie social

playing cat's cradle with
his neck

riding under a low limb

rope croup, rope meat

stiff rope and a short drop

strangulation jig

detectives at Monegaw Springs, Missouri.

In 1874 Jesse married his lifelong sweetheart, Zee Mimms, and within the next few years they became parents of a son and a daughter. Jesse had been baptized into the Baptist church in 1868; aside from committing numerous robberies and a few murders, he remained a devout Christian throughout his life. In 1876 Frank eloped with a Kansas girl, Annie Ralston, who bore him a son two years later. Using various aliases, the James and Younger brothers often split up and hid out in different states between jobs.

Some saw the James brothers and their companions as Robin Hoods because they robbed the powerful banks and railroads that often ran roughshod over the common man. Ironically, it was a controversial and violent action by agents of the law that won the brutal outlaws the sympathy of many otherwise law-abiding citizens. On January 26, 1875, Pinkerton agents and other lawmen surrounded the James family's farmhouse near Kearny, Missouri. They were looking for the gang, but the boys weren't at home. Mrs. Samuel and her eight-year-old son were.

According to the original story, the Pinkerton agent tossed "flares" into the house to illuminate it so his men could be certain no gang members were holed up inside. One of the flares rolled into the fireplace and exploded. The child was killed. Mrs. Samuel's right arm was so damaged by the blast that she lost it below the elbow.

The Pinkerton agency, in preparation for the raid, had secured permission from General Philip Sheridan for its agent R. J. Linden to draw ordnance from the U.S. Arsenal at Rock Island, Illinois. According to Sheridan's letter, Linden was to use the ordnance to "aid him in arresting certain railroad robbers." Historical evidence suggests that Linden drew explosives, not flares, from the arsenal. Whether it was a flare or a bomb, the attack on his family further hardened Jesse James's heart against the "Yankee government" and the "Pinks."

On September 7, 1876, Jesse, Frank, Cole, Jim, and Bob, accompanied by Charlie Pitts, William Stiles, and Clell Miller, rode into Northfield, Minnesota, to rob the First National Bank. But the citizens of the northern town proved tougher than the gang had expected. Before the Missouri boys could shoot their way out of town, Miller and Stiles lay dead in the streets, along with three townspeople. Once clear of Northfield, Jesse wanted Cole to kill the severely wounded Bob. Cole refused, and Jesse and Frank abandoned the Youngers and eventually made their way back to Missouri.

Cole, Jim, Bob, and Charlie Pitts struggled on for two weeks, skirmishing several times with manhunters as they blundered through unfamiliar territory. Cole was wounded eleven times, Jim five times, and Bob four times. On September 21 a seven-man posse caught them and killed Pitts; the three Younger brothers surrendered. They were thrown into a wagon and transported to the nearest town, where Cole somehow stood up and made a sweeping bow to the astonished ladies who were present.

The Youngers pled guilty to escape hanging and were sentenced to life imprisonment. Bob was a model prisoner and devoted several years to studying medicine, but he contracted tuberculosis and died behind bars in 1889. For three years Jim suffered from a bullet that had shattered his jaw and lodged just below his brain. He was able to take only liquid nourishment; the constant pain was so intense that he finally prevailed upon a prison hospital intern to operate. Working at intervals over two days, the intern managed to remove the slug.

Jim gained parole in 1901. He fell in love with a newspaper writer, but the courts forbade him to marry. His health started a steady decline, and when he turned to selling insurance he discovered that as a former convict he couldn't write valid policies. Despondent, he committed suicide in St. Paul in 1902.

Cole also was paroled in 1901, and he received a pardon two years later. He worked briefly and ineffectually selling tombstones and insurance, even though as an ex-convict he was prohibited from drawing up legal contracts. He then teamed up with Frank James in a Wild West show venture, which failed because of criminal accountants. He later traveled widely, lecturing on his adventures and the evils of crime. He retired to Lee's Summit, Missouri, and died there in 1916 at the age of seventy-two.

Following the Northfield disaster, Jesse and Frank employed various aliases and moved from place to place, occasionally pulling off a robbery. Under the name Thomas Howard, Jesse moved his family to St. Joseph, Missouri, late in 1881. He planned new depredations, but greater rewards were posted for him. Bob Ford, a new gang member, decided to collect the reward, and on April 3, 1882, he murdered Jesse in James's own home. Some doubted Jesse's death, and for decades impostors claimed to be the outlaw.

Jesse James was only thirty-five at the time of his death. Mrs. Samuel buried him in the front yard of her farm and allowed visitors—for two bits apiece—to tour Jesse's home place and his grave. She also sold pebbles from her son's grave; she regularly replenished her supply from a nearby creek. Somewhat melodramatically, she wept for the persecution of her sons, cursed the detectives, and wished damnation upon Bob Ford. She got her wish—in 1892 Ed O. Kelly caught up with Ford in a saloon in Creede, Colorado, and killed him with a shotgun blast.

A few months after Jesse's death, Frank emerged from hiding to surrender. A long series of trials and legal maneuvers resulted in his acquittal. After he was released from custody in 1885, Frank lived a quiet, honest existence for thirty years. He died at the family farm in 1915; his ashes were kept in a bank vault until his wife's death in 1944, when their ashes were interred together in a Kansas City cemetery.

The outlaw James and Younger brothers captured the imagination of the public. They achieved (fictional) mythic proportions in dime novels and motion pictures. Controversy continues to surround them. Were they persecuted Robin Hoods or vicious badmen? Did the Pinkertons bomb the James brothers' mother and brother, or was it a tragic accident? Did Jesse James fall to Bob Ford's backshooting, or did he live on in obscurity?

One thing can be said with certainty—they were rough men and used to rough ways.

THE DALTONS: APPOINTMENT IN COFFEYVILLE

BY THOMAS W. KNOWLES

WHEN THE DALTON BOYS RODE INTO THEIR HOMETOWN OF COFFEYville, Kansas, on the morning of October 5, 1892, they meant to pay their respects by robbing two banks at once. Emmett Dalton was obsessed by the legends of Jesse James and Cole Younger and was determined to surpass them. Bob Dalton just wanted to show the people of Coffeyville that the ragtag Dalton boys had come up in the world. What they rode into wasn't a reunion or a payback but an appointment with destiny.

The Daltons grew up in turbulent post-Civil War Kansas and Indian Territory, an area steeped in the bloody legacy of the border wars and the influence of the James-Younger gang. A highly tenuous kin connection to the Youngers convinced young Emmett that he was the rightful successor to Jesse James. He was only eleven years old in 1882 when the report came of Jesse's death.

Lewis and Adeline Dalton had ten sons and three daughters, and most of their children never caused any trouble of note. The third son, Franklin Dalton, was killed in the line of duty as a federal marshal in Indian Territory. But four of the oldest boys—Grattan, Bill, Bob, and Emmett—made the Dalton name infamous. After Frank's death, deputies Grat and Bob didn't avenge him, as a pulp Western plot might have it, but took the opportunity to turn their badges into tickets for graft. With their two younger brothers, they drifted from rustling and extortion to more overt crimes. Eventually, along with other outlaws like Bill Doolin, Charlie Pierce, and Bitter Creek Newcomb, they turned to robbing trains, express offices, and banks.

Bill Dalton stayed in the background, acting the responsible family man and businessman as his three brothers and their confederates, led by Bob Dalton, rode the outlaw trail. They survived many murderous battles with agents of the law, and they successfully pulled off robberies in Arkansas, Texas, Oklahoma, Kansas, and even California. In their July 1892 robbery of the MK&T Railroad at Adair, Oklahoma, they wounded four officers; unfortunately, their stray bullets also wounded the town's two physicians, one of whom died of his wounds.

It was their last train robbery. The death of the innocent physician put on the pressure, and law officers broke through the Daltons' support among the country people. Deputy U.S. Marshal Christian Madsen concentrated his attention on the Daltons, gathered information, sent out undercover agents, and finally found reliable informants. Almost as soon as Bob and Emmett had conceived their grandiose plan for the simultaneous robbery of Coffeyville's First National Bank on Union Street and the C. M. Condon & Co. Bank, Madsen knew of it. So did the Daltons' old neighbors and friends. They were ready to make it a party the Daltons would never forget.

On that October morning, Bob, Emmett, and Grat rode into Coffeyville with Dick Broadwell and Bill Powers, and they tied their horses in an alley a few hundred yards from the two banks. They were decked out in their Sunday best, like businessmen come to town, but they carried brand-new Colt's revolvers they'd bought for the occasion. They even wore false beards as disguises, but no doubt the rifles they cradled under their arms were something of a giveaway.

The beards didn't fool storekeeper Alex McKenna or iceman Cyrus Lee. As Bob and Emmett entered the First National and Grat, Powers, and Broadwell entered the Condon Bank on the opposite side of the street, the cry went out—the Daltons had come to Coffeyville. The citizens armed themselves.

In the First National, Bob and Emmett held the customers and staff at bay with their rifles. Cashier Tom Ayers played for time, delayed as much as he could to give the citizens time to rally, and even deceived the outlaws as to the extent of the bank's assets. When Bob and Emmett had filled their sacks with $20,000 in loot, they marched the bankers and customers out the door in front of them.

They were too late. George Cubine, armed with a Winchester, fired at them from the drugstore. C. S. Cox backed him up with a handgun. They

GTT:
Gone To Texas, usually posted on the door of a cabin or a house in Missouri after the erstwhile occupant had a final disagreement with Kansas redlegs or federal troops.

missed, and the Daltons pulled their hostages back into the bank. Tom Ayers escaped and ran to Isham's hardware store for a rifle.

As Emmett repacked the loot, Bob fired back through the window and struck the shotgun from Charles Gump's grasp, wounding him in the process. The brothers pushed a teller out the back door in front of them into the alley. There Bob shot and killed Lucius Baldwin, who was waiting for them with a pistol in his hand. They ran on to Union Street, where they fired at random to clear their way to their horses. They killed George Cubine, who was watching the entrance to the First National and didn't notice them until it was too late. When Civil War veteran Charles Brown rushed to Cubine's aid, they gunned him down as well.

AS THEY NEARED THEIR DESTINATION, BOB DALTON SPOTTED TOM Ayers standing near Isham's store, a rifle in his hands. From a distance of seventy-five yards, Bob shot the banker through the head. After that, they made it unopposed to the alley, but Grat and the others weren't waiting for them.

Grattan Dalton's greed and his temper had gotten the better of him. When Grat demanded that the vault be opened, Condon Bank partner Charles Ball pretended that the time release lock wouldn't open until 9:30 A.M.—actually, it had opened at 8:00 A.M. Grat decided to wait, and even though he soon began to suspect he'd been fooled, he was too late. A volley of shots shattered the windows from the outside, and the fight was on.

Broadwell took a pistol round in the shoulder. Grat tried driving the customers and bankers out ahead of him, but the concerted fire from outside pushed them back. Faced with either surrendering to a rope or shooting their way out, Grat and his two comrades chose the latter. They dived out of the bank, directly into the townsmen's fire.

All three took hit after hit but, amazingly, managed to flee to cover. Even as the mortally wounded Grat's vision failed, he killed city marshal Charles Connelly, who had attempted to flank him and flush him from cover.

As Connelly fell, Bob and Emmett caught up with their brother and began trading shots with the townsmen in Isham's store. Bill Powers reached the alley, but a bullet took him down as he tried to mount his horse. Dick Broadwell crawled to his horse and pulled himself up, but he also took another hit; he died on the road out of town.

Bob Dalton was hit as he unwisely stepped back from cover to get a better angle for a shot. John Kloer stalked him and fired again, hitting him in the chest and sending him to the ground. Kloer followed Grat as the outlaw stumbled toward the horses. Kloer's next shot broke Grat's neck, and the outlaw dropped dead across the fallen Connelly.

The still unwounded Emmett got to his horse with the money from the

EMMETT

TIM EVANS BOB DALTON GROT DALTON DICK BROAD

First National. As he mounted, bullets struck him in his right arm and his left hip, but he held to the saddle. Then, though he could have made it if he'd ridden away, he turned his horse directly into the hail of bullets to rescue the dying Bob Dalton. As he paused to reach down to his brother, he fell to a shotgun blast fired by the town barber, Carey Seaman.

Bob and Grattan Dalton, Dick Broadwell, and Bill Powers were dead, as were four of Coffeyville's citizens. Tom Ayers miraculously survived his head wound. Emmett Dalton missed a lynch rope only because no one believed he could live with sixteen bullet wounds in his body—but live he did.

The last Dalton survivor of the Coffeyville raid eventually achieved a certain respectability (after he served 14 years in prison). Emmett married his sweetheart, Julia, became involved in (usually bad) Western films, and moved to Hollywood, California. He made his new fortune in Los Angeles real estate, and when he entered a bank it was as an honored customer. Before he died in 1937, Emmett Dalton was even accepted as an honored son of Coffeyville by the very citizens who had once traded shots with him. ▪

Dalton gang after the Coffeyville raid, 1892 (courtesy of Kansas State Historical Society, Topeka, Kansas)

Butch Cassidy, taken from original plate photo at prison

BUTCH AND THE WILD BUNCH

BY JAMES L. COLLINS

WHO'D HAVE THOUGHT THAT A NICE MORMON BOY LIKE ROBERT Leroy Parker would become Butch Cassidy, the most successful robber of banks and trains in the history of the American West? He was born in 1866 near Circleville, Utah, where his faithful parents kept him out of trouble until he met a shady character named Mike Cassidy.

Cassidy became the boy's hero, and he soon taught the teenaged Parker the fine art of cattle rustling. A brief brush with the law convinced Parker that it was in his best interest to leave Utah, and in 1884 he went to Telluride, Colorado, and took an honest job for a mining company. Parker soon started keeping bad company again, this time with a group of outlaws known as the McCarty gang. He took part in the robbery of Denver's First National Bank, as well as Telluride's own San Miguel Bank.

During a lull in his life of crime Parker worked briefly as a butcher in Rock Springs, Wyoming, and so picked up the nickname Butch. He combined it with the name of his boyhood hero, Mike Cassidy, and so did Robert Leroy Parker become Butch Cassidy. The alias followed him for the rest of his career as an outlaw. According to his family, Parker had a certain sense of honor. He wanted to keep the family name clean.

His expertise as a cattle rustler hadn't improved since he'd first turned to crime as a youth, so in 1894 he was caught and sent to prison in Wyoming. In 1896 he was released; he'd supposedly made a deal with the governor to "never worry Wyoming again." Considering that Cassidy never again rustled cattle in Wyoming, it's probably a true story.

Upon leaving prison, Cassidy drifted into Brown's Hole, an area which borders Colorado, Utah, and Wyoming; it was a haven for outlaws and unsavory characters. In Brown's Hole and the hideout along the northern Wyoming border known as the Hole-in-the-Wall, Butch Cassidy became acquainted with many of the outlaws who formed the infamous Wild Bunch. Harry Longabaugh, best known as the Sundance Kid, became Cassidy's closest associate. There were many others, including Kid Curry, Ben Kilpatrick (also known as the Tall Texan), Harvey Logan, Black Jack Ketchum, Harry Tracy, and Elza Lay.

This formidable group of outlaws soon became known far and wide for their activities from South Dakota to New Mexico. In many cases they were credited with—or accused of, take your pick—many a train and bank holdup that would have been physically impossible for them to have pulled. One outrageous story claimed that Cassidy and his Wild Bunch robbed a bank in Alaska during the time Cassidy and Longabaugh were actually in South America. Butch and his compadres certainly lived well with the proceeds from the robberies they did pull—they were able to afford their own lawyer on a permanent basis.

They pulled their first robbery in 1897 at the Castle Gate, Utah's Pleasant Valley Coal Company. From that point on, Butch Cassidy was the undisputed leader of the Wild Bunch. They spent the next few years specializing in bank and train robberies in the region near Hole-in-the-Wall. The gang was also quite successful at eluding pursuers and defending their strongholds against those who tried to penetrate them. The regular lawmen eventually combined forces with the Pinkerton detective agency, which had been hired by the railroads to discourage the Wild Bunch, and together these forces began to close in on the outlaws.

It was at that point that Cassidy and the Sundance Kid left the United States for South America. Their traveling companion was a young woman

Butch Cassidy and some of the Wild Bunch (courtesy of Union Pacific Railroad Museum Collection)

Harry Tracy, close associate of Butch Cassidy

known as Etta Place; depending on which account one believes, she was either a schoolteacher or a prostitute. From 1901 to 1906 the trio lived near the borders of Chile and Brazil. Their activities during that time are uncertain; in the many accounts of their actions it's hard to tell where history leaves off and legend begins. Some biographers and historians record that they lived quietly in the backcountry; others insist that they carried on their life of crime from the start. In all likelihood it was a combination of both, since neither Cassidy nor the Kid had ever done much manual labor in order to make a living.

According to reliable sources, in 1906 Etta Place became ill. The Sundance Kid accompanied her back to the United States, and thereafter she seems to have faded into obscurity. Sundance returned to South America and, according to most stories, aided Cassidy in a series of bank robberies. Their spree came to an end in 1911, in the village of San Vicente, when they tangled with Bolivian troops. The legends say both desperados died in the battle.

This is perhaps the most controversial point in the life and the legend of Butch Cassidy. Did both Butch and Sundance die in that Bolivian village, or did Cassidy survive to return to the United States, as his family claims? The Parker family states that a positive identification was never made. One of Cassidy's sisters claims that the outlaw stopped to see the family in 1929 and that he died in 1937 after living under an alias in Spokane, Washington. One of the more imaginative stories claims Cassidy had plastic surgery performed to alter his features when he returned to the United States. This is highly unlikely—plastic surgery was still in its infancy when it was first used during World War I.

Cassidy was of average build, quite a bit less handsome than Paul Newman, who played him in the movie *Butch Cassidy and the Sundance Kid.* And yet his exploits are the stuff of which legends are made. By all accounts, he was a personable man who would rather solve disputes with his brain or his fists than with a gun.

As with other famous outlaws like Jesse James and Billy the Kid, most biographies of Butch Cassidy make honorable mention of the story of the widow thrown out into the cold because she couldn't make her mortgage payment. Butch loaned the widow the money and then stole it back from the hardhearted banker. The story is as old as tales of Robin Hood, but if there's an ounce of truth to it, it's easier to believe it of Butch Cassidy than of Jesse James or Billy the Kid. James and the Kid, although as legendary in their own time as Cassidy in his, were vicious killers. It speaks well of Cassidy that although he spent most of his life as a bank and train robber, it's not once recorded that he ever shot, killed, or maimed anyone. And that, perhaps, is what has made him as much a folk hero as an outlaw. ▪

VIII. COWBOYS AND CATTLE KINGS

THE LONGHORNS

BY LEE SULLENGER

LIKE THE COWBOY WHO HARRIED HIM ALONG THE TRAIL, THE LONG-horn embodies the rugged, individualistic spirit of the Wild West. The cowboy and the longhorn were similar phenomena—immigrants from the Old World that adapted so well to the New World as to be considered a new breed. Cattle came to the Americas with the Spanish shortly before the end of the fifteenth century. Brought to the island of Hispaniola (now Haiti and the Dominican Republic), they did well and spread along with Spanish colonization. From the Caribbean herds came all the longhorns that ranged Central and South America, as well as the West in North America, by the beginning of the nineteenth century.

As the longhorns spread out and adapted to their various regions, they evolved to produce the *criollo*, a new breed that reflected their Spanish origins but was native to America. *Criollos* were rugged—they required little care and prospered wherever they could find grass and water. Though they carried a dreaded disease (later called Texas fever) that was devastating to less hardy breeds, they were not themselves affected, and they were resistant to a wide range of other cattle diseases.

It was in Texas—especially in the Gulf Coast area, where they ran wild—that the *criollos* came to be called longhorns. There were an estimated five million of these open-range cattle by the early nineteenth century, and they belonged to anyone who could rope and brand them. Not just anyone could. The longhorn was wild, a fighter with sharp horns that commonly reached a span of five feet from tip to tip; he tended to stay in deep brush by day and came out at night to feed and water. He was tall and lanky in appearance even when in his usual good health and condition, weighing in at an average of less than eight hundred pounds at maturity. His bad disposition was legendary, and he was said to be even more dangerous than a buffalo to a man on foot. Despite his character flaws, or perhaps because of them, it was the longhorn that first populated the cattle ranges of the Midwestern and Western states. It was certainly the longhorn's looks and nature that raised him to center stage in the mythology of the open range and the great Western trail drives, the subject of so many Western novels and movies.

The longhorn is synonymous with the trail drive and the Wild West; by the 1890s an estimated ten million head of longhorns had been driven north and West out of Texas to meet the nation's need for breeding stock, tallow, and beef. The cowboy and the longhorn actually opened new country and broke trail for the new immigrants of the Westward expansion to follow. Although most people think of the Kansas railheads as the single goal of the Texas trail herds, drives were actually made to points all over the West. Some of the most famous trails went from the southern tip of Texas into Wyoming, Oregon, Washington, Montana, the Dakotas, and up into Canada. A Westward trail took the longhorns into California.

Two technological developments, the Western expansion of the railroad and the use of barbed wire, put an end to the era of the longhorn and the open range. Because the longhorn was physically suited to the rigors of range life and the trail drive, its body was all horn, bone, and tough muscle—it was never noted for the quality of its beef. As the railroad established new lines, it was no longer necessary for cattle to be driven long distances to market. The appearance of barbed wire in 1873 gave the rancher a cheap and easily installed way to control cattle. Fenced ranges greatly reduced the cost of producing beef by reducing the number of cowboys required to work the cattle, as well as by improving the efficiency with which cattle could be dispersed to available grazing and water.

With these more efficient methods available, the rancher could concentrate less on the range survivability of his cattle and more on actual beef production. European breeds, called American cattle to distinguish them from the Spanish *criollo*, had already been raised successfully in the East. When the more beef-heavy American breeds were introduced into the Western cattle industry, it was only a matter of time until all the Western ranchers eliminated the pure longhorn as a commercial breed. They were sometimes interbred with American cattle, but many longhorns were accused of transmitting diseases or stealing valuable grazing and so were destroyed outright. The longhorn's era was a memory before the end of the

nineteenth century, and the distinctive breed exists today in only a few herds kept to preserve it from extinction.

Today's cattle operations are scientifically managed, and the vastly increased production of superior beef vindicates the changes made in the industry. But those of us who think of the West in terms of the cowboy and the trail drive look to the mythmakers—the painter, the writer, and the moviemaker—to recreate the past for us. It is there, in that past of the imagination, that we still smell the branding fires and feel the cool breeze at a spring roundup, and we still see the endless herds of longhorns strung out along the trail north to Abilene. ■

THE CATTLE BARONS

SHANGHAI PIERCE

BY LEE SULLENGER

EVEN AS A BOY SHANGHAI PIERCE DREAMED OF SEEKING ADVENTURE and his fortune in the West. He found both, and in the process he built one of the West's greatest cattle empires.

Able Head "Shanghai" Pierce was born in 1834 in Rhode Island, the son of hardworking puritanical parents from whom he learned at an early age the value of a dollar. His family was related to a number of prominent Americans, including President Franklin Pierce, the railroad magnate Thomas Wentworth Pierce, and the poet Henry Wadsworth Longfellow, but his parents lived a hardscrabble existence on their farm.

Pierce grew to be an impressive youth: six foot five inches tall and over 200 pounds. He was argumentative and strong-willed, and he had a deep, powerful voice. He used that voice often and emphatically to express his dissatisfaction with his parents' puritanical habits. From an early age he longed to escape to where, to borrow a phrase from Kipling, "there ain't no Ten Commandments and a man can raise a thirst."

His teen years were marked by heated arguments with his father, mostly over money. When he left home, he swore not to return until he was a millionaire. Despite his aversion to his heritage, he had the puritan tendency to carry a grudge—to his dying day he resented his father's treatment of him. In this respect his life reflected the classic American experience, the rite of passage that required a break with the past.

MAVERICK:
a calf without a brand

ESTANCIA:
a large ranch or expanse of range land

RIATA:
a lariat or lasso

Pierce went to work in his uncle's store in Petersburg, Virginia, but he found that the combination of puritanism and penny-pinching he'd left home to escape were doubly present in Virginia. The same conflicts he'd had with his father redoubled with his uncle as an employer. To Thomas Wolfe's lament, "You can't go home again," Pierce might have added, "You can't leave it, either."

Pierce didn't last long as a storekeeper. He stowed away on a freighter that sailed to Indianola, Texas, and when he was discovered, he was put to work as a deckhand. His great strength and his willingness to work made him welcome. That trip is most probably the source of his nickname, Shanghai, from the term used to describe sailors recruited by force. Five months later he landed in Texas, work-hardened and anxious to make his fortune.

TEXAS—IT WAS A WILD NEW COUNTRY WHERE SPANISH CATTLE ran free, where there was land for the taking, where the attitude toward life was anything but puritan. Pierce and Texas were made for each other. The young adventurer must have thought he'd stepped off the ship at his own version of heaven.

He first went to work for a man named Bradford Grimes, another Northerner. The work ethic, the one puritan trait he admired, was branded into Pierce's brain. And he worked hard for Grimes, became accomplished in managing horses, cattle, and cowboys, thereby developing the foundation for his financial success and his place in history. Typically, though, Pierce grew to dislike his boss. It seems fair to say that Pierce was destined to be his own boss and so naturally resented anyone who had authority over him—a typical characteristic of the classic American empire builder.

During the Civil War Shanghai and his brother Jonathan, who had joined Shanghai in Texas, served in the Confederate Army. The two transplanted Yankees saw little action but served honorably, and when the war ended they returned to Texas. When Grimes refused to pay $500 Shanghai felt was owed him, Pierce again held a grudge. That enmity would ultimately force Grimes to leave Texas.

Shanghai and his brother established a ranch in central Wharton County, near the Gulf Coast. Their Rancho Grande was the beginning of one of the fabled Texas financial empires. Jonathan ran the operation while Shanghai did what he called the "outside work," which consisted primarily of "mavericking"—capturing and branding as many as possible of the vast numbers of cattle that ran wild on the prairie. Shanghai understood that his fortune lay in capturing the wild cattle and getting them to market. It was dangerous and hard work, but Shanghai excelled at it, laboring prodigiously and building his herd rapidly. He also developed a very good business sense, a solid understanding of the marketing of cattle.

Dehorning bulls on a ranch near Englewood (courtesy of Kansas State Historical Society, Topeka, Kansas)

Shanghai's accomplishments began to take on mythic qualities. He was doing what any number of other people were doing, but he was much more successful at it. He became expert at keeping his cattle in good condition and finding a market for them. It wasn't long before the ranch started turning a huge profit. Later, as the wild cattle were all taken, Pierce developed a line of credit with bankers so he could become a cattle buyer. Because he knew where he could sell at the best profit, he could pay top dollar at the moment of purchase—which made him a popular man. One of the enduring images in Texas folklore is of the bearded and bull-voiced Shanghai riding into a cattle camp to buy the entire herd; he was invariably followed by his black servant, Neptune Holmes, who rode on the mule that carried saddlebags loaded with gold coin. After he assembled the herds, Pierce drove them to New Orleans or Denver or Cheyenne or to the railheads in Kansas, where he sold them at a hefty profit. He also bought a ship and traded cattle internationally, thus setting the pace for future Texas wheeler-dealers. He diversified into a variety of partnerships and businesses, railroads, banks, and shipping, but the cattle business remained the focus of his personal interest.

Pierce was an effective self-promoter, very comfortable in groups, talkative and confident. He made up stories about himself and repeated tales

Broken Arrow

Curry Comb

Flying V

Rocking Chair

Cattle brands (courtesy of Lois S. Knight)

others had invented. His favorite way of explaining his nickname, probably not the actual truth, was that someone had once seen him stepping about smartly to make a new pair of spurs jingle and had compared him to the Chinese Shanghai rooster, a long-necked, long-legged, rangy bird known for its strut and ferocity. The description fit him, at least in his early years, and most Texans never heard his given name, Able.

Shanghai considered himself the top expert on cattle. According to one Pierce biographer, Chris Emmett, Pierce once introduced himself in Kansas City as "Shanghai Pierce, Webster on cattle, by God, Sir!"

By the early 1870s, mavericking practice was losing its original respectability. The vast herds of unbranded longhorns had all but disappeared, which meant that small-time cattle raisers and maverickers were having to look hard for cattle to add to their herds. Some of them had always had a tendency to play fast and loose with other people's cattle, and as is usual when resources grow scarce, there were frequent conflicts. Shanghai, by now an established rancher with his own large herds, naturally began to share other large ranchers' views about the small ranchers and to translate "mavericker" as "rustler."

Shanghai was never a person to keep his frustrations to himself, and before long he got crosswise with a certain John N. "All Jaw" Smith, thought to be the leader of a gang of cattle thieves. Smith swore he'd shoot Pierce on sight, and Shanghai started riding with his carbine across his lap. A group of about eighty vigilantes caught All Jaw and his gang literally red-handed as they butchered stolen cattle. The vigilantes hanged the thieves, and tempers flared between the small and large outfits as a result of the hangings. Threats flew. Shanghai decided to leave until the trouble simmered down, sold his herd, and moved to Kansas for almost two years.

The trouble hadn't completely died down by the time he came back, but Shanghai was able to get back in business. He entered into partnership with a rancher named Daniel Sullivan to begin a ranching business that eventually took in 250,000 acres and thousands of cattle.

Shanghai's last significant act as a cattleman was to identify a breed of cattle—the Brahman breed from India—that could resist the devastating Texas fever. Shanghai did a lot of research and traveled widely before he decided to import the Brahman breed, but he died before he could carry out his plan. His nephew, Abel Pierce Borden, did import the breed, using it to establish improved, fever-resistant cattle in Texas and throughout the United States.

By the time of his death in 1900, Shanghai Pierce had made his dreams a reality. He'd seen the wild country, had found a place to grow beyond the narrow restrictions of the East, and had far more than the million dollars he'd sworn to his father he'd earn.

BRANDS AND BRANDING

BY LEE SULLENGER

THE BRANDING OF CATTLE, THE BURNING OF AN OWNERSHIP MARK into the hide of the animal, is also burned into the lore of the American West. It has been written into many books and has found its way into movies, radio, and television.

It's widely assumed that branding is a unique part of Western American history, something started by Mexican vaqueros and continued by the North American cowboys who succeeded them. Not so. Cattle branding was an invention of the ancients. The earliest record dates back to almost 3000 B.C.—paintings on the walls of the tombs of the Egyptian pharaohs depict branding much the same way as it's done today. A hot iron was applied to the hide of the animal after the animal was roped, thrown, and tied down. Thus the practice of branding is at least five thousand years old, and probably older than that.

Branding worked its way through the Arab world to Europe. Horses were branded in England and Germany as early as A.D. 700. Branding horses and cattle had become a common practice in Europe during the latter part of the Middle Ages.

The earliest branding in the Western Hemisphere dates from the time of the Spanish conquest of Mexico. Three Latin crosses ($\dagger \dagger \dagger$) formed the brand of Hernán Cortez, the conquistador who took up ranching in Mexico. The first recorded brand in Texas was that of Richard H. Chisholm, who used the brand HC as early as 1832. Another famous early brand was the Old Spanish Cross ($\ddagger$) of Stephen F. Austin, the colonizer who is today called the Father of Texas.

Letters and numbers were the most frequently used signs in branding, and their position on the hide was varied in every conceivable way—leaning, backward, and upside down, among others. If a letter was applied in the ordinary vertical position, it was likely to have an additional symbol placed beside it, under it, over it, or around it, which gave rise to the brand names that the reader of Western novels will find familiar—the Bar A (-A), the Rocking A (⟨A⟩), the Rafter A (⟨A⟩), the Circle A (⟨A⟩), and so on.

In addition to letters and numbers, branders used a wide variety of other

Anvil

Laurel Leaf

Hog Eye

6666

Four Sixes

Cattle brands (courtesy of Lois S. Knight)

symbols, including birds, bells, spurs, snakes, hats, and knives.

Brands drew out the artistic impulse in some of the most unlikely individuals. The Deathshead brand of the Mexican bandit Pancho Villa may well be the most elaborate of all time. It looked like this:

BRANDING WAS, OF COURSE, USED TO ASSERT OWNERSHIP OF THE animal. Once owned cattle became numerous on the open range, the opportunity for one of mankind's oldest occupations, thievery, was ripe. Ancient cattlemen were probably as concerned with the problem as their brethren in the American West, although there is little written record of their concern. But the American cattlemen went all out to control it. Brands came to be carefully registered, typically in the rancher's home county, and cattlemen hired brand inspectors to monitor sales of cattle. Inspectors had to have an encyclopedic knowledge of the brands of their area, as well as an understanding of the ways in which a brand could be altered. During the time of open-range ranching, when half a dozen or more ranchers would gather for the monumental task of branding calves, the inspector's ability was crucial to the success of the spring roundup. He carried a brand book in his pocket, but with a bawling calf being dragged to the branding fires every few seconds, he had to make rapid decisions as to the proper ownership of each animal.

Cattlemen's associations formed all over the West, their main objective to protect the cattlemen from rustlers. An unregistered brand was highly suspect, widely assumed to be used in rustling. While rustling could be a very lucrative activity, it was a dangerous one; justice was traditionally harsh and swift. Unregistered brands thus rapidly came to be rare. The stage was set for the second phase of the battle between cattleman and rustler.

The rustler would register a brand that was similar to the brand of a large rancher in the area so that he could quickly and convincingly alter the rancher's brand to his own. If it was carefully done, the brand alteration could be detected after the brand healed only by killing the animal, skinning it, and examining the underside of the brand. This revealed the different time periods in which the brandings had occurred and made clear the evidence of alteration.

In the nineteenth century, the dispensation of justice for cattle rustling was frequently handled by the aggrieved owner of the rustled cattle. In his book *Hot Irons*, Oren Arnold tells of a cattleman who noted that his herd was not increasing as rapidly as expected, while that of his new neighbor was growing amazingly fast. He killed one of his neighbor's yearlings, skinned it, and examined the underside of the brand. Then he went to the neighbor's cabin, hung the neighbor from a cabin rafter, and rode away, confident that his herd would again begin to increase according to expectations. It did. Problem solved.

When law and order was strengthened so that accusations of rustling ceased to be a problem of interpersonal relations between cattlemen and became instead a problem for the courts, then, as Arnold notes, brand alteration turned into a battle of wits. The rancher tried to devise an unalterable brand; the rustler tried to alter it. Arnold notes the case of a rancher in California whose brand was a series of wavy lines depicting the low hills of his ranch. The brand looked like this: (⌒⌒⌒)

The rustlers made an imaginative alteration, which looked like this: (☺)

The rustlers were executed by a firing squad.

There is no record of Pancho Villa's Deathshead brand being successfully altered. ∎

THE STREETS OF LAREDO

A COWBOY'S DIRGE BASED ON AN OLD IRISH BALLAD
(ALSO "THE COWBOY'S LAMENT")

As I walked out on the streets of Laredo,
As I walked out in Laredo one day,
I spied a young cowboy wrapped up in white linen,
Wrapped up in white linen, as cold as the clay.

"I see by your outfit that you are a cowboy,"
These words he did say as I boldly walked by,
"Come sit down beside me and hear my sad story;
I'm shot in the breast and I know I must die."

"Oh beat the drum slowly, and play the fife lowly,
Play the dead march as you carry me along;
Take me to the green valley and lay the sod o'er me,
For I'm a young cowboy and I know I've done wrong."

"It was once in the saddle I used to go dashing,
It was once in the saddle I used to go gay;
First to the dram house, and then to the card house;
Got shot in the breast, and I'm dying today."

"Go gather around you a group of cowboys,
Tell them the story of this, my sad fate;
Tell one and the other, before they go further
To stop their wild roving before it's too late."

We beat the drum slowly and played the fife lowly,
And bitterly wept as we bore him along,
For we all loved our comrade, so brave, young
and handsome;
We all loved our comrade although he'd done wrong.

Charles Goodnight, 1836-1929

CHARLES GOODNIGHT, MONARCH OF THE STAKED PLAINS

BY L.K. FEASTER

LLANO ESTACADO, THE STAKED PLAINS—A VAST, SEMI-ARID OCEAN of grass that covered what is now eastern New Mexico and the Texas Panhandle. It was a forbidding place, the stronghold of the Comanche. Early ranchers were careful to build their herds in more hospitable climes—that is, until things got tight for Charles Goodnight up near Pueblo, Colorado, in 1876.

Goodnight knew well the reputation of the Staked Plains. He'd also heard of the traditional Comanche rendezvous and winter camp in Palo Duro Canyon. The canyon contained enough water and sweet grass to sustain huge herds; in their heyday, the Comanche grazed from ten to twelve thousand horses there. Then the last Comanche finally came in to the reservation and left Palo Duro waiting for Charlie Goodnight.

By the time Goodnight made his decision to drive his stock from Colorado into the heart of the Texas Panhandle, he was already a veteran rancher. He grew up around the fledgling Texas cattle industry during the decade that preceded the Civil War. He started as a cowboy but soon ventured into partnership with his stepbrother. In 1856 they contracted to tend cattle for the CV Ranch, their payment being every fourth calf born to the herd.

When war broke out between North and South in 1861, most of the ranchers and their hired hands went off to join the Confederate Army, leaving their cattle to shift for themselves. Charles Goodnight enlisted in the Texas Rangers instead, scouting for them as they struggled to maintain order on the depleted frontier.

He left the Rangers in 1864 to rejoin his stepbrother on the Brazos River. There they intended to gather their share from the CV herd and start ranching for themselves. By that time the CV herd numbered around five thousand head. Instead of cutting out their portion of the CV stock, the brothers managed to buy the entire herd on credit.

In 1866 most Texas cattle were being driven east and north to Kansas or Missouri. Charlie knew that the Indian reservations and Army posts in Colorado needed beef. He tried to persuade his neighbors to join him, to drive their stock due west and then north through New Mexico, skirting the Staked Plains, to deliver the needed beef to Colorado. Only an old-time rancher named Oliver Loving was willing to join him.

Loving and Goodnight combined their herds, driving them over the route Charlie proposed. Much of the land they crossed was as dry as the Staked

"BOB WAR" COMES TO TEXAS

BY MARYLOIS DUNN

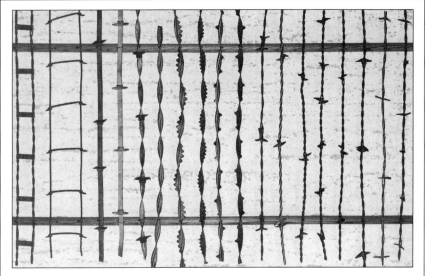

Just eighteen examples of hundreds of different types of barbed wire used on the frontier (photo by Tom Knowles, courtesy of Texas Ranger Hall of Fame Museum, Waco, Texas)

He was called "Bet-a-Million" Gates, but that was many years later after he'd proved he was willing to take a chance. The young John Gates came to Texas from Illinois in the early 1870s with samples of a new product, barbed wire for fences. He dismounted from the train several times along the way to Texas, the heart of cattle country, but cattlemen were not interested in the fragile-seeming strands of wire he laid out for them. They knew what a determined longhorn could do, and it didn't seem to them that narrow strands of wire, even wickedly-barbed wire, would stop those critters once they decided to move. Gates reassured them that it would make the best fences in the world, but his words meant little to men who were hardened to the brush country and the cattle trail.

Gates took his wire to San Antonio, Texas, in 1876, determined to sell those hardheaded cattlemen on his idea. He began to earn his nickname on a win-or-lose proposition he made to city officials. If they'd allow him to build a corral downtown in the Military Plaza, he'd show them and the cattlemen something they'd never expected to see.

On the day the corral was completed, John Gates took himself down to the Buckhorn Saloon and dared the cattlemen there to bring on their longhorns. "The cow hasn't been born that can run through my fence!" he bragged.

Like a shot the cattlemen were out the swinging doors and back with their meanest, toughest steers. Word of the contest spread through town, and a crowd gathered to see the Yankee trader lose his bet. The cattlemen drove their longhorns into the pen.

But what was this? At the fence the longhorns stopped and turned, then charged another side of the corral. Each time they charged, the barbs pricked them and they turned again. Before long the small herd was milling around in the center of the corral, kicking dirt and bellowing in rage and frustration. The Buckhorn did a booming business that night as the cattle-men waited in line at Gates's table to buy his "bob war."

Before the advent of barbed wire, Texas and the other plains states ran chronically short of fencing material, and timber and stone had to be shipped in at great cost. Cattle ran free; rounding them up and separating them out every year was a tiresome and expensive process for the ranchers. The barbed wire that Gates brought gave the cattlemen a way to keep their cattle on their own land and to protect and preserve their grass and precious water for their own cattle. Within four years barbed wire was coming into Texas not by the carload but by the trainload. In 1880, 80 million pounds of wire was sold in Texas alone. The coming of the "bob war" marked the end of the open range in the West.

LOOKING BAD:
"That ol' cowpoke looks as if he was rode hard and put away wet."

A BLUE NORTHER:
"There's nothin' between that wind and the North Pole but a two-strand bobwar fence, and it's down."

LEAVIN' CHEYENNE:
to a cowboy, getting bucked off, retiring, or dying.

Plains. They lost three hundred head to thirst and stampede, but they reached their destination. They sold the surviving cattle in two bunches for a total of $12,000 in gold. Their course became known as the Goodnight-Loving Trail. During the brief life of the cattle drive in the West, Charlie and others used that trail to move thousands of Texas steers to market.

By 1870 Goodnight was a wealthy man, a cattle baron, firmly established on a ranch that he'd built at the end of his cattle trail near Pueblo. The baron was temporarily deposed when the bank he started with other ranchers, the Stock Growers Bank of Pueblo, fell victim to the great financial crash of 1873, taking Goodnight's fortunes with it. He compounded his problems by making one of his few mistakes in raising cattle: He added to his herd in an effort to recoup his losses. Instead, the cattle overgrazed his range and wrecked it.

He turned his attention to the Staked Plains and the lush grazing land in Palo Duro Canyon. He rounded up what was left of his herd, pointed it southeast, and made the arduous drive across the dry plains to the canyon. There Goodnight found that what he'd heard about the Palo Duro was true. The canyon would indeed sustain thousands of cattle.

Goodnight realized he could also run his stock on the plains that abutted both rims of the canyon. The headwaters of the Red River, which meandered through the Palo Duro, provided the basic water source, and the few watering holes on the plains provided supplementary moisture. But he needed extensive credit to finance the operation, and in view of his 1873 debacle, he knew the banks weren't likely to give it to him.

On a visit to Denver in 1877 Goodnight met a wealthy Irish couple named John and Cornelia Adair. John Adair expressed an interest in livestock investments, and the canny Texan was quick to play it up. Charlie invited the Adairs to summer with him at his newly established ranch in the Staked Plains. They accepted his invitation and were so impressed by what they saw on the Palo Duro that they offered to provide Goodnight with a stake to rebuild his cattle empire.

Goodnight used their backing to purchase land within the canyon and beyond the canyon rims. He bought only select parcels with water rights, good grazing, and building sites so he could exclude other potential ranchers from the area. The Adairs saw a handsome return on their investment as Charlie built the JA Ranch into one of the largest in the West. And so the once-deposed cattle baron secured his place as the Monarch of the Staked Plains. ▪

A ROPE FOR TOM HORN

BY BILL O'NEAL

Tom Horn

TOM HORN WAS BY TURNS A STAGECOACH DRIVER, A CIVILIAN SCOUT during campaigns against the Apache, a genuine cowboy and horseman, a lawman, a soldier, a detective, and a hired gun for the cattle barons in their wars with the sheepherders. He was as expert with a rope as he was with his assassin's rifle, and his favorite pastime was braiding intricate bridles and lariats. A tall, muscular man with a quiet and reserved demeanor, the very picture of the classic fictional cowboy, Horn would periodically travel to Denver or Cheyenne to blow off steam in a drunken spree. His life epitomized the rough-and-tumble story of the Wild West, and he died as hard as the West itself did, just as the twentieth century turned the final page on that story.

Born in 1860 to a farm family near Memphis, Missouri, young Tom became a habitual truant from school. A whipping by his father prompted the rebellious fourteen-year-old to run away to the West. He worked for the railroad in Newton, Kansas, was hired to drive a wagon to Santa Fe, and tried his hand at driving a stagecoach. He signed on with the Army as a scout in 1876 and soon succeeded the famed Al Sieber as chief of the civilian scouts. He was involved in the campaign that resulted in the final capture of Geronimo, though he didn't play as significant a role as he later claimed. He first hired out his gun in the Arizona Pleasant Valley war in 1887, then secured an appointment as a deputy sheriff in Yavapai County. While in Arizona he occasionally worked a gold claim near Tombstone.

In 1890 Horn joined the Pinkerton detective agency in Denver, and in 1892 he enlisted with the Wyoming Cattle Grower's Association as a "range detective." The term was a euphemism for the hired gunmen who rid the cattle ranges of rustlers, sheepherders, and squatters. He helped recruit gunmen for the association, but he apparently missed out on the Johnson County war.

The Swan Land and Cattle Company hired Horn as a horsebreaker in 1894, but his true job was to remove rustlers and bothersome homesteaders. Once a member of the company turned in the name of a troublemaker, Horn supposedly tracked his target and methodically learned his habits. He arranged an ambush and killed the offender with a high-powered rifle. He then carefully collected his shell casings and any other evidence, set two stones under his victim's head as a sort of trademark, and left the scene to collect his $600 fee. Horn's observation on killing was typically pragmatic: "I looked on it as a business, and I believe I had a corner on the market."

Horn rejoined the Army when the Spanish-American War broke out and went to Cuba as the master of a pack train. At war's end he returned to Wyoming and to his trade as a hired killer. Matt Rash and Isom Dart, slain in separate incidents in 1900, were victims of long-range shootings typical of Horn's style.

Horn signed on in 1901 with John Coble, the owner of a large ranch north of Laramie near Iron Mountain, and he became friendly with the local schoolmarm, Glendoline Kimmel. Miss Kimmel's family was conducting a feud with a neighboring homesteader named Kels P. Nickell. Coble also found Nickell to be a nuisance, and Horn apparently decided to kill the man. Unfortunately, Nickell's fourteen-year-old son was shot to death either by mistake or by someone who wanted to frame Horn. The subsequent furor over the child's murder put lawman Joe LeFors on Horn's trail.

After tracking Horn to Denver, LeFors got Horn drunk and extracted what amounted to a confession. This controversial statement, taken down by eavesdropping deputies, resulted in Horn's arrest and conviction for the murder. While awaiting execution in a Cheyenne jail, Horn broke out on the morning of August 3, 1903. Horn and fellow inmate Jim McCloud jumped Deputy Sheriff Richard Proctor, and though Proctor fired four shots and managed to wound McCloud slightly, the two escapees overpowered him. Once outside, McCloud galloped off on the only horse in the jail corral. He was caught and subdued after a brief chase.

A citizen named O. M. Eldrich charged after Horn, who was fleeing on foot. Eldrich fired several shots from his revolver, one of which grazed Horn's head. Horn, unfamiliar with his pistol, was unable to release the safety catch. A swarm of officers beat him into submission and dragged him back to the jail.

Horn spent his months of confinement braiding tack and writing an understandably one-sided autobiography. Despite the tearful pleas of Miss Kimmel and the legal efforts of some of the big cattlemen, Horn was hanged at high noon on November 20, 1903. There were rumors of a planned breakout, perhaps by the Wild Bunch, and a machine gun was mounted atop the county jail as a precaution, but the hanging proceeded without com-

Tom Horn's Colt model 1878 double-action .45 caliber revolver (with holster), taken from him when the cowboy assassin was arrested for murder (photo by Tom Knowles, courtesy of Texas Ranger Hall of Fame Museum, Waco, Texas)

plications. Horn met his end with his typical fatalistic calm. His last words were to one of the deputies with whom he had become friends; he said, "I hear you're just married?" "Yep," said the deputy. "Well," Horn said, "treat her right."

Tom Horn died at age forty-two, and as the evening's twilight fell over the West he had known, some of his former employers held a party to celebrate their relief that he'd taken certain potentially embarrassing facts to his grave. For reasons known only to himself, John Coble committed suicide a few years later. ■

BULLDOGGIN' BILL PICKETT

BY BILL O'NEAL

THOUGH HE WAS A WORLD-FAMOUS CHAMPION COWBOY FROM TEXAS, Bulldoggin' Bill Pickett didn't exactly set the stereotype for the celluloid heroes who would later portray cowboys. Like many of the cowboys who helped to settle the West, he was black, a mixture of African, Cherokee, and Caucasian heritages. Though he was one of the earliest rodeo stars and single-handedly created a major rodeo event, he was accepted as a performer only because the divided society of his time chose to make an exception for an exceptional man.

Willie M. Pickett was born in 1871 in Travis County, Texas. He grew up in the country near Austin, and as a boy he observed working cowboys with rapt fascination. Many cattlemen used bulldogs to work their livestock; the dogs controlled the steers by biting their upper lips. When Pickett was ten he saw a bulldog handle a steer in that fashion, and a few days later he decided to try it on his own. He seized a calf by the ears, sank his teeth into the animal's upper lip, and, to the astonishment of the veteran cowboys, threw it with ease.

Pickett had little trouble securing work as a cowboy even after his family moved to Taylor in 1888. When he was in thick mesquite and brush that frustrated his attempt to build a loop, Pickett would lean from his horse, grip the steer's long horns, and "bulldog" it. Pickett always approached the steer from the left side, the side from which his horses were accustomed to being mounted and dismounted. By the time he was sixteen he began

Bill Pickett, famous black cowboy credited with the invention of bull-dogging, seen here at the height of his career. He was billed for his rodeo appearances as the Dusky Demon.

A LOAD OF BULL

BY MICHAEL MADONNA

Bull Durham, sold in small cloth bags with a handy sheath of rolling papers, was the most poular brand of tobacco in the West, the favorite of cowpunchers, trailsmen, and dudes alike. It could also be smoked in pipes, and if no chaw was on hand for those who indulged, it could be chewed in lieu of the real thing.

On the trail it was legal tender for slight fines, gambling debts, and trades. The packaging made it easy to carry on the long trail, and the careful cowboy could ration himself. Cigars and cheroots didn't travel well and were too expensive; they were luxuries to be savored at the end of a drive.

Because of the demand, storekeepers in cattle towns ordered and stocked it in great quantities, especially when the great herds were due to arrive. It didn't take long for the cowboys to deplete their stock.

That Bull Durham is still sold in certain parts of the country in more or less its original packaging is a tribute to the tastes and traditions of the American cowboy.

to show up at fairs and other minor occasions to demonstrate his unique method of wrestling steers.

Pickett married in 1890, and he and his wife, Maggie, eventually produced nine children. His seven daughters lived to adulthood, but both of his sons died in infancy. He supported his young family by picking cotton, working cattle, hunting, and fishing. He also served as a deacon at a Baptist church. Bat Lee Moore, a Taylor-area rancher who regularly employed Pickett, booked his top hand at fairs and similar events all over Texas. Delighted by the applause of appreciative crowds, Pickett began to travel extensively for exhibitions. By the turn of the century he was demonstrating his expertise in Colorado, Arizona, and North Dakota.

In 1903 Pickett became affiliated with Dave McClure, a gifted promoter who booked him for appearances all across the West. McClure billed Pickett as the "Dusky Demon"—a mild subterfuge, since blacks were barred from entering most competitions. Pickett—the only professional "bulldogger" in the world—proved to be a great attraction. By 1905 he was employed by the Miller Brothers' 101 Ranch in Oklahoma; he made that ranch his home for most of the rest of his life.

The Miller brothers organized a spectacular Wild West show, and for years Pickett was their only headliner and in fact the only performer specifically listed in the billing. At different times Pickett worked with a young Tom Mix, Geronimo, Charles Gebhard (later famous among Western movie fans as Buck Jones), Lucille Mulhall ("America's First Cowgirl"), and the inimitable Will Rogers. During his prime the five foot seven inch Pickett weighed 145 pounds, and he had strong teeth, but over the years he lost several in the line of duty. The Miller brothers paid him eight dollars per week, plus room and board, and during the off-season he worked stock on the ranch. They gave him a raise to twelve dollars a week in 1912.

His favorite horse was Spradley, a nine-hundred-pound bay. On occasion Pickett didn't use his horse but threw steers with his hands tied behind his back; after he sank his teeth into the steer's lip, he'd have his hands secured, then dash the beast to the ground with a toss of his head. In a Mexico City arena, amid a great ballyhoo, Pickett once grappled with a bull before a crowd of twenty-five thousand spectators. In 1912 and 1913 Pickett and the Miller Brothers Show toured South America and England. In England and Arizona he ran into trouble with puritanical souls who forced his event to be curtailed on humane grounds, but most people remained eager to see him in action. Pickett continued to enter rodeo competitions even into his fifties, and he estimated he'd dogged more than five thousand critters during his career.

At the age of sixty, still a working cowboy, Pickett was working horses on the 101 Ranch when a freak accident with a rope toppled him from his

COWBOYS AND CATTLE KINGS

mount. As he went down, an outlaw bronc kicked him in the head. He lingered in a coma for fourteen days before he died on April 2, 1932. It was forty years later that the Dusky Demon, the only individual performer known to have originated a rodeo event, became the first black man elected to the National Rodeo Cowboy Hall of Fame. ■

THE COWBOYS

JOHN B. STETSON'S "BOSS OF THE PLAINS"

BY L. K. FEASTER

John B. Stetson (courtesy of the Stetson Company)

IT WAS THE LAST THING A COWBOY TOOK OFF WHEN HE TURNED IN for the night, if he took it off at all. It was the first thing he put on when he arose in the morning. It protected him from rain and hail. It shaded his eyes from the glare of the sun. He used it for a pillow when he slept on the ground. He fanned dwindling campfires with it to rekindle the flames. He used it as a matador uses a cape to wave aside a charging steer or a spooked horse.

When he rode into the brush looking for strays, it kept low-hanging branches from scraping his face. In a pinch, he could even use it as a bucket to water his horse. It was an extension of his personality, so he'd carefully clean and crease it when he headed for town to impress a girl or to strut around on a Saturday night like a "Kansas City swell." It was, of course, his hat. More often than not, it was manufactured by the John B. Stetson Company.

The original Western hat was a poor copy of the Spanish sombrero with a flat, low crown and an equally flat, round brim. It was a poor copy because it often was made of coarse wool, which quickly lost its shape when exposed to the elements. The wearer had to fasten its front edge to the crown if he wanted to keep it from drooping over his eyes. John B. Stetson noticed the inferior quality of those hats and did something about it.

Stetson came from a family of hatmakers in Orange, New Jersey. Quite naturally, he learned the family trade, but his older brothers assumed control of much of their father's business. Although he had knowledge and

THE ORIGINAL HOT PANTS

BY DALE L. WALKER

Levi Strauss probably didn't do a lot of hunkering, so how was he to know what his rivets wrought? He came to New York from Bavaria in 1847 and found work as an itinerant peddler of clothing and household goods. In 1850, lured by tales of argonauts and boomtowns, he landed in San Francisco and opened a drygoods business. His mainstay was canvas for tents and wagon covers. When he detected a need for sturdy trousers for the rough-and-tumble work of prospecting, he made a few pairs out of canvas. He switched to a tough cotton fabric woven in France— *serge de Nimes*, a name soon shortened and Anglicized to "denims." He dyed the fabric indigo blue and reinforced certain stress points in the garment with copper rivets.

Certain very stressful points. Like the crotch.

Cowboys and other outdoorsmen had certain problems with the rivets— the hip pocket rivet scratched saddles, for example—and Levi Strauss always came up with a solution. The crotch rivet was a problem, too, but maybe the outdoorsmen were too genteel or too macho to get specific about their nether parts and the effects of copper as a heat conductor.

The Levi company sold a lot of the 501 jeans between 1870 and 1939. But in 1939 Walter A. Haas, Sr., then president of Levi Strauss, had a personal experience with the crotch rivet. He was on a fly-fishing trip and hunkered down in front of the campfire to listen to his guide spin a tale or two. When Haas stood up, he discovered exactly what the cowboys hadn't complained enough about. He promptly issued a oral edict that the crotch rivet be banished forever.

This riveting story remained known only to company insiders until 1972, when Bud Johns, an executive with Levi Strauss, told it to a *Life* magazine writer. When the story appeared in print, Walter Haas, at that time in his eighties and retired from the company, stormed into Johns's office and roared, "Who in the hell told them that damn story?" Before Johns could confess, Haas added, "It is a *good* one on me, isn't it?"

After that, and until his death in 1979, Haas delighted in recounting the tale himself.

Above: Men on bunkhouse porch, C.E. Doyle ranch, near Englewood, Clark County Kansas. (courtesy of Kansas State Historical Society, Topeka, Kansas)

ability, his future in hatmaking looked limited. His lungs were ailing, and his doctors advised him that he hadn't long to live.

He decided to do what many others did—move to the West for his health. Missouri was the frontier in the 1850s, so Stetson moved to St. Joseph, where he worked in a brickyard for several years. He eventually became part owner of the business but lost everything when the Missouri River flooded, virtually washing the brick yard away. In an effort to recoup his loss, Stetson joined a gold prospecting party headed for Pike's Peak. His luck in the gold fields wasn't much better than it had been in the brick business, but at least the drier climate in Colorado healed his diseased lungs.

In 1865, with $100 in his pocket—all he'd managed to save from his prospecting—he returned East. There he opened a small hatmaking shop in Philadelphia. He did tolerably well, manufacturing and selling hats that were in style in the larger cities, but John Stetson felt stifled. The prevailing men's hat styles in the East were influenced by European styles, but Stetson wanted to make and sell hats that were original.

In his frustration he considered other possible markets. Then he recalled the need he'd noticed for a sturdy, serviceable hat during his years West. He dubbed his new design the "Boss of the Plains." He obtained a list of hat and clothing dealers in the frontier territories, sent each of them a sample as well as an order blank, then waited to see what would happen. He was swamped with orders. He sold his cowboy hats as fast as he could make them. By the middle 1870s John Stetson was the leading hat supplier for the Western market.

THE BOSS OF THE PLAINS BECAME THE BASIC WORKING COWHAND'S hat, Stetson's mainstay, even though his company sold many hats of different Western styles in the years that followed. Stetson's hats generally had a dome-shaped crown instead of the disc-shaped crown of earlier days. It came new without dents or creases—the wearer shaped the crown to his personal taste.

The brim was wide and flat like that of the original sombrero. Depending upon the model, the crown could vary in height from 5½ to 7½ inches, while the brim could be as narrow as 2½ inches or as wide as 4½ inches.

The hats came in two colors, black and white, although the white was closer to being a pearl gray. Texas cowboys generally favored the black, wide-brimmed hats, while Wyoming and Montana cattlemen leaned more toward the narrower-brimmed white hats. The Texans wanted the wider brims to protect them from the sun. The northerners preferred the narrow-brimmed hats because they were less likely to blow off in the wind.

The names of the various styles were as colorful as the names of many

A proper cowboy never stands when he can sit, never sits when he can lie down.

of the men who wore them. There were the Laloo, the Dakota, the Big Four, the Carp, the Kalispell, the Jolan, the Campie, and, of course, Stetson's best seller, the Boss of the Plains. Most of those names have receded into history, but the name of the man who created the cowboy hat lives on. "Stetson," along with "Levi Strauss" and "Winchester," became part of our Western heritage. Those names appear on the hats, jeans, and firearms of the working men who hunker down at campfires even to this day. ■

THE GALLOPING GOURMET

OR WHAT THOSE LONG-RIDERS ATE WHILE ON THE TRAIL

BY BARBARA BLACKBURN

BEING ON THE TRAIL WITHOUT THE OLD CHUCK WAGON LIMITED THE lone cowboy, outlaw, lawman, trapper, or trader. The long-rider, like the modern backpacker, was forced to carry compact items and do a little foraging along the way.

The term "long-rider" usually means a lawman or outlaw of the Old West who sometimes rode a hundred miles a day or more. By expanding the term to include other men who spent a l-o-n-g time on a horse, we can get a better idea of what the long-riding outlaws and lawmen ate. Personal accounts often mention eating meals, but some riders-turned-writers went into more detail about what they ate.

Will James, in his *Lone Cowboy*, wrote about the joys of eating as well as the work involved. He described the grub pile as made up of flour, soda, a side of salt pork to season with, dried potatoes and apples, and salt and pepper. The potatoes were a good source of Vitamin C, which prevented scurvy. When James cooked he was careful to use only the necessary amount of potatoes — one a day for himself. He said, "I liked to watch 'em swell up when I'd put 'em in boiling water."

As a youth Will James accompanied a trapper whom he called Bopey. The trapper sometimes left him alone for a few days at a stretch, which forced young Will to prepare many of his own meals, although Bopey often left him some stew. As with the dried potatoes, he learned to conserve heavy items like flour, recording that "they were not to play with."

Without benefit of a Dutch oven in which to bake, the lone rider got to missing the good sourdough, also "huck dummy [a quick raisin bread] and such like." Everything was cooked in a pan; nothing was ever baked, "as there was no way to do that."

The long and the lone riders often missed coffee as well, for it was too heavy to pack. A pound of it didn't go as far as a pound of tea and wasn't as warming. But they sometimes took coffee along anyway. In *Lone Cowboy* James says, "That supper of fried beef and fried potatoes, biscuits and coffee, sure tasted good, even if there was not butter." There was always something missing, but they still enjoyed the food.

In summer the lucky long-rider could make ends meet with small game, and once in a while a hunk of beef, deer, elk, or bear meat might supplement the basics. Among the good parts of bear meat, the hump was reported to be the tastiest.

The long-rider sometimes stumbled upon a temporarily abandoned miner's cabin where he could find other supplies. These often included salt and sugar in cans, pepper, seasonings, flour, rice, raisins, and potatoes, and occasionally a can of milk. Canned milk became available after the Civil War,

Irwin Brothers chuck wagon near Ashland, Clark County Kansas 1898 (courtesy of Kansas State Historical Society, Topeka, Kansas)

Chuckwagon Coffee

Take two pounds ground Arbuckle's beans.

Dump out the pot.

Pour fresh ground beans in pot.

Add enough water to bring to hard boil.

Boil thirty minutes to an hour.

Wipe off horseshoe.

Toss shoe in pot.

If shoe sinks, boil another hour.

Chuckwagon Pie

Lay 2 halves of a cold sourdough biscuit on a plate.

Pour cooked, well-sugared, dried fruit (any kind) over biscuit halves.

Eat while still warm.

and if he had the space, the traveler could add it to his staples.

The rider might have started his journey with a supply of jerky or pemmican, but when it ran out he was happy to kill some game for his fresh meat. Trappers like Will James and his friends were seldom short of that. Perishable or heavy supplies like butter, sugar, and eggs, on the other hand, were out of the question. "But somehow I never missed them last things much," said James.

The lone rider learned how to cook without much in the line of tools and grub. Although it was simple fare, what there was filled the space, "and when the tin plate was pushed away I felt just as satisfied as if I'd got around one of them seven course dinners." The fur trapper traveled light. On one expedition Bopey and James set out with some cooked rabbit and duck, salt, tea, and half a dozen pan-size bannocks, cakes of coarse meal usually made on a grill. On that trip they killed a moose; they fried the meat in bear grease.

The line rider's job was to cover a fifteen-mile area to see that none of his outfit's cattle strayed and that the neighbors' cattle didn't get onto his own outfit's land. It was tough, monotonous work. Because the line rider seldom packed a lunch and sometimes not even a canteen, he had only two meals a day, breakfast and supper, which he cooked by himself at his base camp or the line shack. Supper might have been rabbits and rice. Rice was a good compact food for anyone to have on hand.

When the long-rider was between jobs, he often hunted up a place where he could get a good meal. He might have found a restaurant near the supply store and treated himself to a plate of ham and eggs, some beer, or maybe a "creekful of coffee." A song about a hotel where some cowboys had stopped went like this:

> Sure it's one cent for coffee and two cents for bread,
> Three for steak and five for a bed.
> Sea breezes from the gutter waft a salt water smell,
> To the festive cowboy in the Southwestern Hotel.

Meeting buffalo on the trail was a tasty diversion, especially for someone who'd had no fresh meat in a while. Buffalo calf was a delicious substitute for veal. Sometimes the lone cowboy took his meat "carne fresco," a trifle rare, garnished with some herbs like wild sorrel to add a lemony zest. Even the horses grazed on the wild sorrel and other species of sour plants, according to one source. The riders often foraged for wild berries and fruits to add interest to their menu. Along the San Antonio River Will James enjoyed some mustang grapes. He said it was a land of milk and honey, even without the fig tree.

Charles Siringo, a cowboy detective who spent two decades on horseback, some of it chasing rustlers and fugitives for the Pinkerton detective agency, was a long-rider who later wrote just as hard as he rode. His *Riata and Spurs* and *A Texas Cowboy* make only brief mention of food. His meals depended on the locale and his job at the time. Once when he worked unloading bananas from a ship, he made his breakfast on bananas. When he fought a prairie fire he had nothing to eat except broiled beef without salt. At other times he dined on raccoon or wild turkey. He also mentioned eating cantaloupes and watermelon, which was undoubtedly a treat for him. One noteworthy meal was young mustang prepared in the same way as buffalo meat. He spoke of "flapjacks being left on the stove to burn up." Flapjacks weren't the only breakfast fare—sometimes it was a well-roasted side of ribs or a nice yearling venison. Along with canteens of water to wash it down, there was mescal or plenty of wine, according to Siringo.

Andy Adams told of his travels as a cowboy along the old Western trails in *The Log of a Cowboy*, but he made few references to eating meals and didn't detail the menu. As for the outlaws, they didn't leave many records of their meals, but rustled cattle was probably the main course. Those who didn't want to risk the telltale smoke from campfires were often forced to eat cold food, like hardtack, jerky, and biscuits.

And of course the record from Alfred Packer's trial in Colorado tells us what *he* ate: four of his companions.

DISTRICT ATTORNEY STEW

A.K.A. SON-OF-A-BITCH STEW

BY MARYLOIS DUNN

It was at branding time that the cook produced that prized chuck wagon delicacy, district attorney stew. In the midst of the dust and heat, the cook moved with an iron kettle in his hand among the bawling calves and cursing cowboys. As each little bull was turned into a steer, he caught the "prairie oysters" in his kettle. When he had enough, he cleaned them and put them on to boil.

The next step in his preparations was to slaughter a dogie staked out for him by the cowboys, usually an orphan calf of uncertain health and ability to endure range life, or even a fat calf from someone else's herd. The cook butchered the carcass and hung it up to drain and cool, then took the tongue, heart, liver, kidneys, stomach, sweetbreads, some of the smaller intestines, the brain, and sometimes the eyes back to the fire to be cleaned, chopped, and tossed into the pot with the boiling prairie oysters. He seasoned the stew with peppers, onion, garlic, and a dollop of whiskey, and cooked it at least eight hours. For a truly superb district attorney stew, he allowed it to simmer over the fire overnight.

Sourdough biscuits and district attorney stew were a welcome reward for the hungry, weary cowboys at the end of the day. What may sound terrible to modern folks was, to those like myself who have dipped into that kettle, the finest of fare.

SASSPARILLY

BY CAROL J. SCAMMAN

REAL MEN DON'T DRINK SARSAPARILLA, AT LEAST NOT IN WESTERN movies—and not without a fight. But the legendary "sassparilly" has a long and sassy history. The earliest versions were probably home brewed with yeast or sold as noncarbonated elixirs. Carbonated mead was patented in 1819, sarsaparilla mead in 1824. The soda that caused all the commotion out West originated back East around 1840. The Ayer Company of South Groton, Massachusetts, was producing sarsaparilla in the 1870s. Ayer's product was so popular that the town's name was changed to Ayer.

The sarsaparilla (or sassparilla) plant is a tropical vine native to Central America. It grows in swampy forests from the coastal regions of southern and western Mexico to Peru. The name "sarsaparilla" comes from the Spanish *zarza*, meaning bramble, and *parrilla*, meaning little vine. Sarsaparilla belongs to the genus *Smilax* of the lily family and it has shiny net-veined leaves, prickly stems, small flowers, thick root stalks, and thin roots several feet long. The main commercial species are the Mexican, Honduran and Ecuadorian varieties; after harvesting and drying, the roots are exported. Slippery *Norte Americanos* often substitute roots of the wild sassafras, the American spikenard, and the false or bristly sassafras for true sarsaparilla.

Sarsaparilla has long held a false reputation as an "alterative," something that improves the body's metabolism. The root of the sarsaparilla plant was first brought to Seville from New Spain sometime between 1536 and 1545 and was used in European medicine beginning in the mid 1500s.

What really went into this much-maligned drink of yesteryear? Although it was called sarsaparilla, the principal ingredient of a sarsaparilla soda was oil of sassafras, along with sugar and carbonated water. Sass, as it's known in the beverage trade, would have included some alcohol, oil of sweet birch, root derivatives, possibly some cinnamon, anise if a licorice flavor was desired, and of course sarsaparilla root. Flavors were produced by a percolation method or by steeping the sarsaparilla root in a hot solution. As with all early soft drinks, the flavor varied from batch to batch.

It took a real man to swallow some of the medical preparations labeled as sarsaparilla in the early 1900s. One medication contained sarsaparilla,

COWBOYS AND CATTLE KINGS

yellow dock, stillingia, burdock, licorice, sassafras, mandrake, buckthorn, senna, black cohosh, pokeroot, wintergreen, cascara sagrada, cinchona bark, prickly ash, alcohol, glycerin, and iodides of potassium and iron. Very few of the concoctions contained more than a trace of sarsaparillia, but they typically listed an alcohol content of from 7 to 12 percent. One which listed *no* alcohol was 45 proof — no sissy drink, that! The label of another sarsaparilla medication urged patients to avoid the use of alcohol in any quantity whatsoever. It contained 5.1% alcohol. These sarsaparilla potions were supposed to cure everything from gout to syphilis to impotence, but the eleventh edition of the *Encyclopedia Britannica*, published in 1911, confidently declared sarsaparilla to be "pharmacologically inert and therapeutically useless."

Just the right drink for your typical medicine show—without the snake oil. ■

Cowboys bathing in a stream (courtesy ofKansas State Historical Society, Topeka, Kansas)

THE CHUCK WAGON VOCABULARY

BY MARYLOIS DUNN

airtights: canned goods, usually limited to corn, peaches, tomatoes, and milk

Arbuckle's axle grease: the coffee most often used on the range—many cowmen didn't know any other brand; also called jamoka, brown gargle

bait: food

belly-wash: weak coffee

biscuit roller: waitress in a restaurant

blackstrap: molasses, the thick, black kind

blue meat: veal, meat from an unweaned calf

boggy-top pie: pie with only a bottom crust

calf slobbers: meringue on pie

canned cow: canned milk

Charlie Taylor: mixture of syrup or molasses and bacon grease, a substitute for butter

chili: the famous Mexican-Texican meat stew, named for the major ingredient, the red-hot chile pepper

chuck: food; also called grub

chuck wagon chicken: fried bacon

cook, cooky: He ran the chuck wagon. Also known as the bean master, belly cheater, biscuit roller, biscuit shooter, *cocinero*, coosie, dinero, dough belly, dough puncher, dough wrangler, grease robber, old woman, pothook, pot rustler, Sallie, sheffi, sop n' taters, sourdough, swamper

cow grease: butter; also known as skid grease

cut straw and molasses: poor food

dip: pudding sauce

district attorney stew: another name for son-of-a-bitch stew, also known as son-of-a-gun when ladies were present—a stew made of the visceral parts of a butchered animal, best when cooked twenty-four hours or more

doughgoods: biscuits; also called hot rock, sourdough bullet (but not in earshot of the cook)

dry camp: a camp without water, tough on the cook

dulce: candy (Spanish)

Dutch oven: thick, three-footed iron skillet with a heavy lid

fancy fluff-duffs: fancy food, doughnuts, frosted cakes, fancy pies of the kind served at dances, fandangos, and "dinners on the grounds"

fried chicken: a contemptuous name for bacon rolled in flour and fried

frijoles: (pronounced *free-hole-lays*) Mexican dried beans, usually pintos; also called Mexican strawberries, prairie strawberries, whistle berries

greasy sack outfit: small ranch that can't afford a chuck wagon and packs its grub in sacks on mules

"Grub Pile!": call to eat

gun-wadding bread: light bread; also called wasp nest

hen fruit: eggs

hen fruit stir: pancakes

horse-thief's special: pudding made of raisins and boiled rice

huckydummy: (also huck dummy) baking-powder bread with raisins

immigrant butter: gravy made by mixing bacon grease, flour, and water

jerky: dried beef

John Chinaman: boiled rice

Kansas City fish: fried pork

larrup: molasses; also called lick and long sweetnin'

larrupin' truck: great food

lining his flue: a cowboy eating

machinery belt: tough beef

"Man-at-the-pot!": yelled at any man who gets up to refill his coffee cup; he's obliged to go around with the pot to fill all the cups held out to him

moonshine: homemade whiskey

moonshining: rounding up cattle in country so rough the chuck wagon can't come up with the outfit, so the chuck is brought in on pack mules

muck-a-muck: derived from an Indian term for cooked food

music roots: sweet potatoes

padding out his belly: describes someone who eats anything, anytime

pie box: a wistful name for a chuck wagon

pig's vest with buttons: salt pork or sowbelly; also known as sow bosom

pooch: a sweet dish made of canned tomatoes, sugar, and bread—as good as chicken soup for sick folks

poor doe: lean venison

pot luck: food contributed by a guest, or a meal taken where the menu isn't known in advance

prairie oysters: calf's testicles; also known as mountain oysters

sea plum: oyster

slow elk: someone else's steer slaughtered for food; also known as big antelope

soft grub: hotel or restaurant food

son-of-a-bitch in a sack: pudding made of dried fruit rolled in dough, put in a sack, hung over a bucket, and steamed—so named because it requires a liberal cussing to acquire the proper flavor

sop: gravy

sourdough keg: clay crock or wooden keg where the cook kept his sourdough starter

splatter dabs: hotcakes

spotted pup: rice and raisins boiled together

staked to a fill: treated to a satisfying meal

swamp seed: rice

Texas butter: gravy made from steak grease and flour, and milk if available

throat-tickling grub: food of the kind never served from a chuck wagon

trapper's butter: bone marrow boiled from bones or made into a stew

whiskey: base burner, brave maker, bug juice, coffin varnish, conversation juice, dynamite, fire water, gut warmer, neck oil, nose paint, redeye, red ink, scamper juice, snake head, snake poison, tarantula juice, tonsil varnish, tornado juice, wild mare's milk

wool with the handle on: mutton chop